Mysteries of Jesus' Life
Revealed

Mysteries of Jesus' Life Revealed

His Birth, Death, Resurrection, and Ascensions

(When and Where Did They Really Happen?)

How Could the Church
Have Gotten It So Wrong?

Joseph Lenard

Co-author of *The Last Shofar!–
What the Fall Feasts of the Lord
Are Telling the Church* (2014)

www.truthinscripture.net

Copyright © 2018 by Joseph Lenard

Mysteries of Jesus' Life Revealed
–His Birth, Death, Resurrection, and Ascensions
by Joseph Lenard

Printed in the United States of America

ISBN: 978-1-78324-091-3 (hardback)
ISBN: 978-1-78324-092-0 (paperback)
ISBN: 978-1-78324-093-7 (ebook)

All rights reserved solely by the author. No part of this book may be reproduced, stored in a retrieval system, or transmitted, in any form or by any means—electronic, mechanical, photocopying, recording, or otherwise—without the prior written permission of the author. The views expressed in this book are not necessarily those of the publisher.

Unless otherwise indicated, Bible quotations are taken from The Holy Bible, conformable to the Edition of 1611, commonly known as the Authorized or King James Version; The Holy Bible, New International Version (NIV) ©1973, 1978, 1984 by International Bible Society—used by permission of Zondervan, all rights reserved worldwide; The Interlinear Hebrew-English Old Testament with Greek Lexicon, Third Edition Copyright © 2005 by Authors for Christ, Inc., Lafayette, Indiana 47903

Because of the dynamic nature of the Internet, any web addresses or links contained in this book may have changed since publication and may no longer be valid.

Book cover art design by Bob Brown.
Photograph of four-pane stained glass image from Dreamstime, copyright Denis Kelly, ID 21974393. Right to use acquired.

Published by Wordzworth
www.wordzworth.com

Table of Contents

List of Diagrams and Tables	ix
Dedication	xi
Acknowledgements	xiii
Foreword by Nelson Walters	xv
Preface	xvii
A Beginning Word	xix

Part I   Mysteries of Jesus' *Birth* Revealed   **1**

Introduction to Part I	2

Section A   *When* Was Jesus Born?   **3**

Introduction to Section A		4
Chapter 1	*Traditional* Date vs. *Actual* Date of Jesus' Birth	7
Chapter 2	Eight *Puzzle Pieces* Determine *When* Jesus Was Born	13
Chapter 3	*Puzzle Piece #1*–Birth of John the Baptist	15
Chapter 4	*Puzzle Piece #2*–Astronomical/Zodiacal References	19
Chapter 5	*Puzzle Piece #3*–Born on the Feast of Trumpets?	29
Chapter 6	*Puzzle Piece #4*–The Wise Men (Magi)	35
Chapter 7	*Puzzle Piece #5*–Star of Bethlehem and Magi's Visit	43
Chapter 8	*Puzzle Piece #6*–Roman History	57
Chapter 9	*Puzzle Piece #7*–Death of King Herod	63
Chapter 10	*Puzzle Piece #8*–*Sabbatical* and *Jubilee* Years	71
Chapter 11	Summary Sequence of Historical Events	87
Chapter 12	Conclusion of *When* Was Jesus Born?	91

Section B   *Where* Was Jesus Born?   **95**

Introduction to Section B		96
Chapter 13	*Traditional* Site vs. *Actual* Site	97
Chapter 14	Case for *Migdal Edar*	99
Chapter 15	Significance of *Migdal Edar*	111
Chapter 16	Conclusion of *Where* Was Jesus Born?	113

Part II	Mysteries of Jesus' *Death, Resurrection & Ascensions* Revealed	115
Introduction to Part II		116
Section A	***When* Were Jesus' Death, Resurrection & Ascensions?**	**117**
Introduction to Section A		118
Chapter 17	Traditional Dates vs. Actual Dates	123
Chapter 18	Eleven *Puzzle Pieces* Determine the *Days*	129
Chapter 19	*Puzzle Piece #1*–Which Jewish Passover?	131
Chapter 20	*Puzzle Piece #2*–Hebrew Timing Issues re Passover	137
Chapter 21	*Puzzle Piece #3*–Timing of the Spring Feasts	141
Chapter 22	*Puzzle Piece #4*–Passover Lamb Inspected 4 Days	147
Chapter 23	*Puzzle Piece #5*–Two Sabbaths in Crucifixion Week	151
Chapter 24	*Puzzle Piece #6*–The Sign of Jesus Being Messiah	153
Chapter 25	*Puzzle Piece #7*–Events Right After Jesus' Death	157
Chapter 26	*Puzzle Piece #8*–Chronology of the Women	161
Chapter 27	*Puzzle Piece #9*–Tradition for Visiting Burial Site	171
Chapter 28	*Puzzle Piece #10*–Astronomical Considerations	173
Chapter 29	*Puzzle Piece #11*–Traditions (Christian & Jewish)	175
Chapter 30	Summary Table–Days of Crucifixion Week	177
Chapter 31	Reference to Hard Scriptures	179
Chapter 32	How Did the Church Err?	183
Chapter 33	*When* Were Jesus' *Two* Ascensions?	185
Chapter 34	*Year* of Death & Resurrection: *AD 30*	191
Chapter 35	Conclusion of *When* Were Jesus' Death, Resurrection, & Ascensions?	201
Section B	***Where* Were Jesus' Death, Resurrection & Ascensions?**	**205**
Introduction to Section B		206
Chapter 36	Traditional Sites vs. Actual Site	209
Chapter 37	Eight *Puzzle Pieces* Determine Sites	213
Chapter 38	*Puzzle Piece #1*–Crucifixion Accounts in the Gospels	215
Chapter 39	*Puzzle Piece #2*–Plausibility of Mount of Olives?	217
Chapter 40	*Puzzle Piece #3*–Red Heifer Sacrifice	225
Chapter 41	*Puzzle Piece #4*–Area Designated for Executions	233
Chapter 42	*Puzzle Piece #5*–Executions Outside the Camp	235
Chapter 43	*Puzzle Piece #6*–Firstfruits' Barley Sheaf: Represents Resurrection of Jesus	239

Chapter 44	*Puzzle Piece #7*–Pattern of West-to-East Movement	243
Chapter 45	*Puzzle Piece #8*–True Temple Location Is Key Factor for Location of Crucifixion	247
Chapter 46	Conclusion of *Where* Were Jesus' Death, Resurrection, & Ascensions?	249

Section C ***How* Did Jesus *Really* Die? *(Not Just Crucifixion!)*** **257**

Introduction to Section C		258
Chapter 47	Traditional Cause vs. Actual Cause	261
Chapter 48	Four *Puzzle Pieces* Determine Cause of Death	263
Chapter 49	*Puzzle Piece #1*–The *Stoning* of Stephen, Paul, and James	265
Chapter 50	*Puzzle Piece #2*–Jewish Law vs. Roman Law	269
Chapter 51	*Puzzle Piece #3*–Suffering-Servant Considerations	287
Chapter 52	*Puzzle Piece #4*–Place of Stoning Matches Crucifixion Site	297
Chapter 53	Conclusion of *How* Did Jesus *Really* Die?	299

Part III ***New Insights – Where* Was Herod's Temple?** **303**

Introduction to Part III		305
Chapter 54	Nine *Puzzle-Pieces* Determine Validity	311
Chapter 55	*Puzzle Piece #1*–Jesus' Prophecy	313
Chapter 56	*Puzzle Piece #2*–Eye-Witness Accounts	317
Chapter 57	*Puzzle Piece #3*–City of David/ Gihon Spring/Temple	321
Chapter 58	*Puzzle Piece #4*–Can Spring Push Water Up to Temple?	331
Chapter 59	*Puzzle Piece #5*–Fort Antonia on "Temple Mount"?	333
Chapter 60	*Puzzle Piece #6*–What About the Rock on "Temple Mount"?	339
Chapter 61	*Puzzle Piece #7*–Martin's Graphic	343
Chapter 62	*Puzzle Piece #8*–Critiques by Ritmeyer and Franz & Rebuttals by Martin and Sielaff	355
Chapter 63	*Puzzle Piece #9*–Nancy L. Kuehl's "Temple"	369
Chapter 64	Final Movements of Jesus–With Martin's Temple Location	375
Chapter 65	How Could the Rabbis Forget?	381
Chapter 66	Conclusion of *Where* Was Herod's Temple? –Martin's Proposed Location	393
Epilogue		395
Afterword: The Profound Mystery–*Why* Did Jesus Come to Die?		399
Appendix: Longer Dedication Featuring *Handel's Messiah*		405
Endnotes		411

Other Information	**443**
Section Images and Attributions	444
About the Author	449
Website for *Mysteries of Jesus' Life Revealed* and *The Last Shofar!*	451

List of Diagrams and Tables

Figure 4.1.	Symbols depicted in Rev. 12:1–6	24
Figure 4.2.	Diagram of Virgo, Sun and Moon (Rev. 12:1-6) on September 11, 3 BC	25
Figure 7.1.	Illustration of Retrograde Motion of a Planet Compared to Another Planet	50
Figure 8.1.	Governors of Syria for 7 BC to AD 1	60
Figure 19.1.	Month of Nisan (Aviv), AD 30—Crucifixion Week and Days Before and After	133
Figure 19.2.	Mosaic and Pharisaic Passovers of Crucifixion Week	134
Figure 22.1.	Passover Week, Month of Nisan, AD 30	149
Figure 22.2.	Timing of Various Jewish Sects' Passover Sacrifice	149
Figure 26.1.	Chronology for Women to Purchase, Prepare, and Anoint Jesus' Body	166
Figure 30.1.	Crucifixion Week—How This Puzzle Looks When Put Together for Jewish month of Nisan of AD 30 (See also Figure 35.1 in Conclusion of Section A of Part II)	178
Figure 35.1.	On What Day Did Christ Really Die?[241] (See also Fig. 19.1, 19.2, and 26.1)	204
Figure 36.1.	The Two Traditional Sites of Calvary in Jerusalem (Church of the Holy Sepulchre and the Garden Tomb)	211
Figure 46.1.	(Copyright with enhancements) Ancient Jerusalem and Mount of Olives with Martin's location of the Temple at Gihon Spring, located to the west of the Bethany Jericho Road crossing of the southern spur of the Olivet Ridge —possible location of crucifixion and burial of Jesus	254
Figure 50.1.	Temple at the Time of Christ Showing "Chamber of Hewn Stone" where Jesus was tried by the Sanhedrin	275
Figure 57.1.	Photograph with ancient City of David located south of the traditional Temple Mount (Fort Antonia) with labels for locations of historical structures	323
Figure 57.2.	Topographical Map of Jerusalem at Time of Jesus with City of David to the South, within the crescent of the ridge south of the traditional Temple Mount; Mount of Olives is to the East	324

Figure 57.3.	City of David, Traditional Temple Mount, Traditional Fort Antonia at NW corner	325
Figure 59.1.	*Traditional* Depiction of Jerusalem During Second Temple Period; note *traditional* location of Fort Antonia at NW corner of *traditional* Temple Mount	336
Figure 61.1.	Ernest L. Martin's Diagram of Herod's Temple & Fort Antonia, looking from south-east from temple. [From internet search "Temple and Fort Antonia graphics;" credit to Ernest L. Martin]	344
Figure 61.2.	Model of Herod's Temple, on *traditional* "Temple Mount," and Fort Antonia in upper right (NW) corner	345
Figure 61.3.	(Copyright; with enhancements) Ancient Jerusalem and Mount of Olives with Martin's location of the temple at Gihon Spring, located to the west of the Bethany Jericho Road crossing of the *southern spur* of the Olivet Ridge —possible location of crucifixion and burial of Jesus	352
Figure 61.4.	Photograph with ancient City of David located south of the *traditional* Temple Mount (Fort Antonia) with labels for locations of historical structures	353
Figure 64.1.	"The Final Movements of Christ" Used with permission of H. Dye and T. Parrott and ASK (see text)	376
Figure 64.2.	"Final Movements of Christ–Jerusalem Area" Used with permission of H. Dye and T. Parrott and ASK (see text)	377

Dedication

This book is dedicated to Jesus. It begins and ends with dedications to Him.

It is all about Jesus, looking at the mysteries of His life—His birth, death, burial, resurrection, and ascensions.

He is God's beloved Son ("God's only begotten Son"), our Savior and Lord, the one and only Messiah spoken of in the Hebrew Scriptures and the New Testament.

Praise God the Father for sending His son, Jesus, to earth to be born as a baby by a righteous virgin, Mary, and grow up and then die as an acceptable sacrifice for the sins of the world—offering eternal life for all those who trust in Him for the salvation only He provides (John 3:16).

Acknowledgements

Many people contributed to the formation of *Mysteries of Jesus' Life Revealed–His Birth, Death, Resurrection, and Ascensions*. I want to mention a few who contributed significantly to this book.

Of course, I credit the **Holy Spirit** for giving me the hunger for the truth of His Word. I thank Him for helping me in the researching and writing this book. I have felt His hand in these efforts, from bringing important research information to my attention to help me with researching and writing. Any mistakes are, of course, mine alone.

I want to thank my dear wife, **Judy**, for her patience with me in spending the great number of hours invested in this book. I could not have completed this book without her support and understanding. She carried much of the load of "normal things" in life to allow me to complete this work. I am so grateful for her—she is the love of my life and God's gift to me.

I want to thank my "writer friends" for their encouragement and help in so many ways—Nelson Walters, Bob Brown, and Donald Zoller.

Nelson Walters is my good friend in the Lord and kindred spirit in many ways; our minds think much alike, and God has led each of us into new insights. He has been an encouragement and model for me, helping with my writing and editing. Nelson is the author of five landmark books—*Are We Ready for Jesus?* (2015); *Revelation Deciphered* (2016); *Rapture: Case Closed?* (2017); *70 Times 7: Daniel's Mysterious Countdown and the Church's Heroic Future* (2018); and *Simplifying the Rapture* (2018). He has given me the opportunity to be involved in each of his books in different capacities.

Bob Brown, my friend in the Lord, has been with me through the last several years of this writing project, providing key encouragement; designing and administering our website; editing, writing, and posting edited chapters of this book to the website; general editing of the manuscript; and helping to keep me focused and engaged to complete this book in a reasonable timeframe.

Donald Zoller is my co-author of *The Last Shofar!* (2014) and a truly dear friend in my life. He has given me his advice related to many areas of this book. I treasure his friendship.

I want to also acknowledge all my **Critical Readers** who have offered helpful suggestions and advice. Often, they are "under-appreciated," but I can't thank them enough for their help.

This is to also acknowledge **Dr. Ernest L. Martin**, a remarkably insightful biblical researcher, historian, archeologist, and author. His books are referenced in every Section of this book. Indeed, this book would largely not have been possible without the voluminous research and writings of Dr. Martin. He was bold in his quest for truth related to the life of Jesus—His birth, death, resurrection, ascensions, as well as the location of the temples in Jerusalem. He is now deceased, but his remarkable insights live on in the books he authored. He was willing to buck established *traditions* and present viable alternatives which better align with Scripture and history. A special thanks to David Sielaff, Director of Associates of Scriptural Knowledge (ASK) for permission to use information and graphics from all of Dr. Martin's books and materials.

Information from Nancy L. Kuehl's book, *A Book of Evidence–The Trials and Execution of Jesus* (2013), which is highlighted in Part II Section C of this book, is gratefully used by permission of Wipf and Stock Publishers (*www.wipfandstock.com*). Other permissions have been duly requested and received.

Most important, I acknowledge what **Jesus Christ** has done in my life, and I am eternally grateful. I commit this book to Him and pray that my efforts bring Him glory. I pray that the faith of believers in Him might be strengthened and that even some might come to trust in Him as their Savior and Lord from reading this book about Him.

Foreword
by Nelson Walters

Humans are "wired" to want to learn more about the things they love. For some that "love interest" is their favorite sports team. For others, it might be a hobby. Hopefully for all Christians, our greatest love is for our Lord and Savior, Jesus Christ. For that reason, most of us have an innate desire to learn more about Him.

Jesus's biographies (the four gospels) give us some information, but many rudimentary facts about his life are hidden. When was he born? Where was the manger? When did he die? Where exactly was Calvary? Historians and Bible scholars have attempted to answer these queries for generations. For most of my Christian life, I have assumed the answers were unknowable this side of heaven.

Dr. Joseph Lenard, however, seems to have solved many of these dilemmas. He has spent a lifetime researching them and has recorded his journey to discover the real-life facts about Jesus in this book, *Mysteries of Jesus' Life Revealed*. You will find it fascinating. Like clues in a great mystery novel, evidences have lain strewn about in the Bible waiting for us to search for and uncover and understand them.

Dr. Lenard didn't unearth all the clues himself. Rather, this book is the culmination of many generations of scholarship. Dr. Lenard has painstakingly investigated the historical records of Biblical scholars throughout the ages. Then with precision he assembled the clues like puzzle pieces to reveal the beauty of God's design for the life of his Son.

And God's beautiful design for the life of Jesus is the unexpected treasure within this book. As you read it, you will learn that the details of Jesus's life such as his birthdate and the location of the manger were not happenstance or accidental. Rather they were planned by the Father with meticulous care to reveal various aspects of Jesus's role as our Savior, Healer, Sanctifier, and King. Yet without this book, I would have never been able to fully appreciate this aspect of the richness of Jesus's life.

This is not a book about apologetics, yet it is an amazing testimony to the hand of an all-powerful God who designed the life events of Jesus in such a profound and symbolic way. I was left in awe at the majesty of our Creator. This unmistakable signature of God is made all the more amazing when one considers that these details of Jesus's life are just now being more widely presented. I encourage you to read this book with that thought in mind. That the truth and depth of the Word of God is more unfathomable and richer than any of us could imagine.

You are probably also wondering why this information is just now coming to our attention. If the clues have existed in the Bible and in reliable historical documents all along, why are we just now discovering the answers? There are several reasons. First, clues have been uncovered one-at-a-time for generations. But it took Dr. Lenard to assemble and interpret them into a beautiful tapestry that is this book.

Second, unfortunately, sometimes tradition seems stronger than truth. A hundred years of Holy Land tours promoting *traditional* sites are sometimes hard to overcome. But we need to remember that the dispersion of the Jews in AD 70 left Israel with amnesia. At that time, the accurate oral traditions about sites and dates were violently expelled along with the land's inhabitants. The traditions we currently consider are hundreds or even thousands of years removed from reality.

So, I invite you on a journey; a journey of discovery about the life of the God who created you and the world you live in. His is the most important life ever lived. You will not only learn more about Jesus, but your faith will be deepened and strengthened in the process.

Nelson Walters
Founder of The Gospel in the End Times Ministry
(*http://www.thegospelintheendtimes.com*)
Author of: *Are We Ready for Jesus?* (2015);
Revelation Deciphered (2016);
Rapture: Case Closed? (2017);
70 Times 7: Daniel's Mysterious Countdown and the Church's Heroic Future (2018);
Simplifying the Rapture (2018)

Preface

Mysteries of Jesus' Life Revealed–His Birth, Death, Resurrection, and Ascensions touches on many mysteries about Jesus which have become mumbled and jumbled in history.

You will find that the information in the cases presented for the *dates* and *sites* of Jesus' birth, death, burial, resurrection, and ascensions is clearly arranged and formatted for you to evaluate. References for the sources of the information are given.

These presentations are arranged as "case studies." Based on the evidence for the cases made, you are invited to arrive at your own conclusions as to their credibility. Do I "make the case"? You can decide—much like a jury.

My recommendation for our readers is exemplified by the believers at Berea, as expressed by the Apostle Paul, "*… they received the word with all eagerness, examining the Scriptures daily to see if these things were so*" (Acts 17:11). I encourage the same.

I have assembled the evidence for these cases realizing that "new" ideas which differ from *traditional* beliefs are often uncomfortable and difficult to accept. Yes, some readers will cast dispersion on the cases presented in this book. I expect that. As a biblical researcher, I can state that the truth of Scripture is my ultimate guide.

As with most books of this type, very little of the content being presented is original insight. Beyond the Scriptures, I have leaned heavily upon historical documents revealed in the works of other researchers I have deemed to be reliable. These sources are carefully referenced for further study and investigation.

It is recognized that some knowledge has been lost in history, but cases can be assembled from bits and pieces of what is known, to arrive at the most-probable cases of historical events. I do not claim infallibility. I am only a messenger and analyst of this case material which has been handed down from others. I believe the information contained in these cases to be accurate and true.

I believe you will find this to be a mind-changing study about various aspects of the life of Jesus.

A Beginning Word

There are many mysteries in Jesus' life about His birth, death, burial, resurrection, and ascensions. Indeed, exactly *when* and *where* did they *really* happen?

Many of us are familiar with the navigational aids on our smart phones, iPads and in our cars. The quality of these electronic aids is seen in how reliable they are to bring us to our desired destination. Most of us have been surprised and annoyed when we arrive in a *farmer's field* instead of at the desired address.

For over two thousand years, the church has been misdirected to incorrect places and times of Jesus' birth, death, and resurrection. This has largely resulted from a poor navigational aid provided by Helena, Roman Emperor Constantine's mother (as well as Constantine himself). Neither an archeologist or Bible scholar, Helena set out to identify the places of Jesus' birth, death and resurrection during one of her trips to the Holy Land in the fourth century.

Unfortunately, the sites Helena and Constantine identified were erroneous, and yet the *traditions* have persisted. Since this was the unquestioned navigational aid available for most of church history, the church mistakenly has been taken to the *"farmer's field"* instead of to the *actual places* of Jesus' birth, death and resurrection as recorded in both Scripture and accurate historical documents.

Similarly, for various reasons, the church has gotten it wrong on the *dates* of these important events of Jesus' life.

Basically, the church has gotten it wrong from *not* following clues given in *Scripture*—as well as reliable historical references—rather than listening to Helena and Constantine and others in church history (even today) who have not adequately searched the Scriptures for clues.

To determine truth, *all* the statements in Scripture related to the subject must be in alignment. For example, we can't take one statement given in Scripture and run with it to draw a conclusion, without also considering *all* the other statements given in both the Old Testament and New Testament which touch on that subject. Sometimes, the clues are big and easy to understand, but, other times, they might seem small and insignificant. However, all the clues must be in alignment to determine truth. These clues are *our navigational aids* to use our analogy. They, like the Star of Bethlehem to the Magi, lead us to where we want to go in determining the correct information on the birth, death, and resurrection of Jesus.

We, of course, also pray for the Holy Spirit to guide and lead us to truth. Historical documents which are deemed reliable and which align with the clues given in Scripture can also be helpful guides in our search. However, continually, the starting point and focus is on what Scripture teaches, and any historical documents consulted must be judged in light of what is stated in Scripture. Scripture, in the original autographs, is true, and every word is true.

This book is an attempt to relook at the *dates* and *places* in Jesus' birth, death, burial, resurrection, and ascensions—and determine what is true. Part I relates to His birth; Part II relates to His death; and Part III relates to the location of the temple—because this directly affects the locations of Jesus' death, burial, and resurrection.

We can use the term "biblical sleuthing" for the process of searching Scripture for relevant clues; as such, we need to become "Sherlock Holmes" as we search for those clues. The clues might be thought of as *puzzle pieces* which need to be fitted together to arrive at a complete picture of truth. And, hence, this book uses an analogy of assembling *puzzle pieces* of information contained in the chapters to come up with the conclusions of our cases.

So, am I saying that I have *absolute truth* about the conclusions of these cases? No, but I do believe that the evidence laid out related to these cases for the dates and places in Jesus' birth, death, and resurrection is strong and the cases are worthy of serious consideration. However, as in any historical consideration, it is impossible to *totally prove* a case. In summary, you need to evaluate the strength of the evidence provided.

Some may question why this is all that important. After all, aren't these holy *sites* of Jesus primarily symbolic anyway? And why do we need to know actual *dates*?

I would argue that to know Jesus as a real person, who was born and died in *real places* and *real times* in history, is of strategic importance in appreciating the *real Jesus* of the Bible. I believe these "latest navigational aids" presented in this book help point us in the right direction in looking at the real history of Jesus. In so doing, they help authenticate both the reality of Jesus and reliability of the Scriptures. For example, the *actual* place of the crucifixion makes the spiritual teachings in the Old Testament regarding the significance of the sacrificial temple offerings apply specifically to Jesus. It further highlights the substitutionary role that Jesus played in his crucifixion in redeeming Israel and the world to the Father. The *proper place* of the crucifixion makes these parallels become crystal clear. Hence, this is important, and I will explain further in Part II, Section B, "*Where Was Jesus' Death & Resurrection?*"

Of unique importance for the reader is to see that the events of the birth, death, burial, and resurrection of Jesus all occurred on the specific days of the *Feasts of the*

Lord (Leviticus 23) with their related significance. There are seven "Feasts" which God gave through Moses to His people Israel at Mount Sanai over 3,400 years ago. Although called "Feasts," they are not meals as such but specific days each year to come together to meet with God during these "appointed times." God uses the Feasts of the Lord to remind His people—in a manner they would not forget—of His plan to redeem them and the entire world, a plan that extends to the end of the age. Within each Feast is a veiled view of future fulfillment in His plan of redemption.

With the intrigue of a great mystery revealed, this book provides an insight as to how the Feasts are aligned to match perfectly with the *First Coming of Jesus* to earth, largely aligned with the four *Spring Feasts* on the Jewish Calendar (Passover, Unleavened Bread, First Fruits, and Pentecost). In our previous book, *The Last Shofar!* (2014), we make the case for the *Second Coming of Jesus* fulfilling the three *Fall Feasts* (Trumpets, Day of Atonement, and Tabernacles).

About 1,900 years ago, the church began to leave its Hebraic foundations, and much has been lost as far as correct biblical understanding. Messianic Rabbi Avi Ben Mordechai states the following in the Introduction to his insightful book, *Messiah Volume 2: Understanding His Life and Teachings in Hebraic Context* (1997):[1]

> Thus, as Hebraic thought was replaced with pagan ideas, the image of HaMashiach (the Messiah) also changed from that of a Torah-true Jewish Rabbi to that of a *goyishe* [Hebraic slang term that means lacking Jewishness or Jewish character] Christian. The result? HaMashiach was stripped of His Jewishness and was unfortunately reduced to something other than what He was prophesied to be in *D'varim* (Deuteronomy) 18:18 and *Yochanan* (John) 1:17:
>
> '(The L-rd speaking to Moshe [Moses]): *I will raise up a prophet from among their countrymen like you, and I will put My words in his mouth, and he shall speak to them all that I command him.*'
>
> '*For the Law was given through Moses; grace and truth were realized through Jesus Christ.*'

God's redemptive plan for mankind focuses on Jesus Christ. As found in the biblical record, God has fixed the times and places to reveal His plan in history. God uses the *Feasts of the Lord* (Leviticus 23) to announce to the people of Israel and to the world the unfolding of His plan of redemption—a plan that is anchored in time, place and history to a real Jesus—with His birth, death, resurrection, and His coming again in the future.

It is my hope and prayer that the teachings in this book will find a place in your heart as you consider once again the historical reality of God's magnificent Son. *"But when the fullness of time had come, God sent forth His Son, born of woman, born under the law, to redeem those who were under the law, so that that we might receive adoption as sons" (Galatians 4:4).*

The purpose of this book is to move Jesus from the *"farmer's field"* of symbolism into the light of reality and truth—being born and having died as a real person in real times and places in history.

Now, let's assemble the various *puzzle pieces* to come up with the *when* and *where* of His birth, death, resurrection, and ascension(s). See what you think.

PART I

Mysteries of Jesus' *Birth* Revealed

Introduction to Part I

"Oh, little town of Bethlehem …" is a tune all of us know. We have heard it sung each traditional Christmas season related to the birth of Jesus. It is a nice tune and is accurate for depicting the town of Bethlehem as the birthplace of Jesus—the hope for the entire world.

There are, however, mysteries to be revealed. Mysteries like: Was Jesus born on the traditional day of Christmas? If not, then what day? And exactly *where* in Bethlehem was He born?

This **Part I: Mysteries of Jesus'** *Birth* **Revealed** deals with the mysteries related to the *birth* of Jesus and is divided into two Sections:

- **Section A**: "*When* Was Jesus Born?" introduces the case for the *actual birth date* of Jesus.

- **Section B**: "*Where* Was Jesus Born?" presents the case for His *actual birthplace* at a particular place "in Bethlehem."

I present these cases based on clues from Scripture and from reliable historical documents for each of these two questions. Various *puzzle pieces* are assembled to arrive at these conclusions. You will see clearly that the cases presented do *not* agree with *traditional* dates and locations.

I believe the evidence is strong for the cases presented, but I ask you to evaluate the evidence yourself to make your own decision about the validity of the cases.

SECTION A

When Was Jesus Born?

Introduction to Section A

> The case presented is that Jesus was born on *Tishri 1*—on the Feast of Trumpets (Hebrew: *Yom Teruah;* also called *Rosh HaShannah*) on the Jewish calendar—in the year of 3 BC. This is equivalent to *Wednesday*, September 11, 3 BC on the Gregorian Calendar. Jesus was not born on December 25, AD 1, which has become church *tradition*. Overwhelming evidence is provided for this case.

Not even the Pope believes in the traditional Christmas as the birthdate of Jesus! Yes, it's true. Even Pope Benedict disputes Jesus' traditional date of birth, *December 25, AD 1*. Absolutely, that was *not* the birth date of Jesus.

The former Pope Benedict XVI in his book, *Jesus' Childhood* (2012)—Part III of his series, *Jesus of Nazareth: The Infancy Narratives*—admittedly, did not exactly put it that way, but he did reveal that Jesus may have been born *earlier* than previously thought. He explains in his book that Dionysius Exiguus (AD 470–AD 544), a sixth century monk who is considered the originator of the Christian calendar, "… made a mistake in his calculations by several years. The actual date of Jesus' birth was *several years before*" (emphasis mine).

So, even the former Pope admits that the *December 25, AD 1* date for "Christmas" is *not* the actual date![2] Of course, former Pope Benedict XVI is a bit late in joining the chorus of historians who have concluded that the present *traditional* date of *December 25, AD 1* for the birthdate of Jesus is not historically correct.

Related to the traditional Christian holiday of Christmas, Messianic Rabbi Avi Ben-Mordechai puts it bluntly in his book, *Messiah, Volume 2: Understanding His Life and Teachings in Hebraic Context* (1997):

> First-century believers in Mashiach [Messiah], most of whom were Jews, knew nothing about 'Christmas.' It is a pagan festival embellished by ancient anti-Semitic Gentiles and should be avoided by all those who truly love G-d and His Jewish Mashiach [Messiah].[3]

This Section A of Part I presents the background for the *traditional* date as well as many other *proposed* dates by historians. In addition, the case is carefully presented for the *actual* date of Jesus' birth being on **Wednesday, September 11, 3 BC, after sunset** (on the Gregorian calendar; **Tishri 1** on the Hebrew calendar—on the **Feast of Trumpets!**). So, how is this date derived? The evidence for the case presented is laid out for your review.

In fact, the *actual* date can be stated unequivocally! How can we say this? The actual date is derived from a careful analysis of Scripture, review of secular history records, and a review of the astronomy related to the period on each side of Jesus' birth as well as the astronomy on the very day! All this evidence is presented as I lay out the "case." Of course, many *other* dates have been proposed by historians, but, in my opinion, the strongest case is for *September 11, 3 BC*. I think you will find this case edifying. I will show you how we get to that date.

Why does it matter? A good question. We are to worship God *"in spirit and in truth"* (John 4:24). God puts great value on truth, and we should strive to obtain truth, especially biblical truth. This goes for the actual history of the birth and crucifixion of Jesus, especially when it can be based on biblical truth—and it can—as well as being based on other reliable contemporary historical accounts.

Another reason that the actual birthdate of Jesus is important is that it helps to further confirm the validity of Scripture in that various Scripture passages are shown to tie together to present historical truth about the birth of Jesus.

In addition, the actual birthday of Jesus links the *First Coming* and the *Second Coming* of Jesus (at the Rapture of the Church—the first event of His *Second Coming*; Greek *parousia*), as both occur on the same date on the Jewish calendar—*Tishri 1*: *Day of Trumpets!* This is astonishing and highly significant—the day of Jesus' birth is on the same day on the Hebrew calendar as His return at His Second-Coming-Rapture event (see Chapter 5 of this Section A: "Born on the *Feast of Trumpets?*"). Once again, the Feasts of the Lord come into play for important events involving God's plan of redemption, which is a theme of the first book by Lenard and Zoller, *The Last Shofar!–What the Fall Feasts Are Telling the Church* (2014).

Much of the material in this Section A of Part I is presented in the insightful book by Dr. Ernest L. Martin, *The Star That Astonished the World—The Star of Bethlehem* (1996).[4] This book by Martin gives much of the historical, biblical, and astronomical evidence that makes the identification of the star of Bethlehem as well as the birthdate of Jesus possible. Because of the historical and astronomical research in Martin's book, most of the planetariums around the world are now showing what was astronomically happening at the crucial time in history when Jesus of Nazareth was born.

In addition to the material from Martin's book, *other* material is presented, all duly cited and organized. Hence, this presentation is the compilation of insights from many references, uniquely condensed together and organized to help readability.

As you will see, the case for **September 11, 3 BC** is based on evidence from the following areas: 1) Scriptural clues; 2) Historical records related to Rome and King Herod; and 3) Astronomy [including the astronomical signs observed by the Magi, a specific lunar eclipse which occurred just after Herod's death, and the astronomical signs shown in Revelation 12]; and 4) Knowledge of the Jewish calendar---including the Feasts of the Lord, Sabbatical Years, and Jubilee Years.

Specifically, the case is laid out as *puzzle pieces* in Chapters 2–10 in this Part I, Section A, "*When* Was Jesus Born?"

CHAPTER 1

Traditional Date vs. *Actual* Date of Jesus' Birth

So, how did the *traditional* date of *December 25* come to be incorrectly associated with Jesus' birthday? It is widely recognized that *Christmas*—with its date and many of its popular customs and celebrations—is nowhere found in Scripture and, frankly, the customs come from pagan origins.

A. Traditional Date: December 25, AD 1

1. How Did the Traditional Date Come About?

In summary, the celebration of December 25 has roots in ancient Persia, as *Mithra*, the Persian god of light, was said to be born out of a rock on December 25. The Roman emperor Aurelian in the third century (AD 274) established the festival of *Dies Invicti Solis*, the Day of the Invincible Sun, on December 25. *Mithraism* became Rome's official religion with the patronage of Aurelian, and Emperor Constantine adhered to *Mithraism* up to the time of his purported conversion to Christianity in the fourth century AD.[5]

In addition, there are Greek roots for celebrating a festival at the end of December, in honor of *Dionysus* (also called *Bacchus*), the god of wine. The Latin name for his celebration was *Bacchanalia*. The Romans also celebrated another holiday, the *Saturnalia*, held in the honor of Saturn, the god of time. Both celebrations were observed around the winter solstice—the day of the year with the shortest daylight (December 21). When the Julian calendar was instigated in the first century (46 AD), the winter solstice was declared by law as December 25, to be an official Roman celebration.[6]

It is difficult to determine the first time anyone celebrated December 25 as *Christmas*, commemorating the birth of Jesus, but it is generally agreed by historians that it was sometime during the fourth century, about 300 years after Jesus' death.

So why would the Roman church choose to celebrate the birth of Jesus on December 25? It has been proposed that religious leaders wanted to give a pagan festival a name-change to make it easier to attract pagans to convert to Christianity.[7]

Eastern churches commemorate Jesus' birth, the visit of the Magi, and His baptism on January 6. However, most Christians worldwide today have adopted December 25.

It should be noted that not one of the biblical writers says anything about commemorating Christ's birth, nor did Jesus. Jesus did, however, give explicit instructions as to how His followers were to commemorate His *death* (1 Cor. 11:23-26), but nothing about formally commemorating His birth. Jesus' birth is, however, richly covered—especially in the Gospel of Matthew—and was announced by the angels, celebrated by the shepherds and by Simeon and Anna in the Temple, and, later, by the Magi.

2. History of the Celebration of Christmas (December 25)

It is good to understand the history of the church related to celebrating the birth of Jesus and the Christmas traditions. For the first three centuries of Christianity, "Christmas" was not part of the Christian calendar. Some church fathers, like Origin, were opposed to the celebration of the birth of Christ; he argued that "It would be wrong to honor Christ in the same way Pharaoh and Herod were honored. Birthdays were for pagan gods."[8]

The Reformed tradition has mixed positions concerning Christmas. It is widely acknowledged that the Reformers, and particularly the Puritans, were against the festivities related to the birth of Christ. They raised both historical and theological questions, largely centered around the point that for the first 300 years Christians did not celebrate the birth of Christ and that Christmas was associated with the Roman Catholic tradition. However, not all Reformers were against the celebration. John Calvin wrote a letter in 1551 to a Swiss pastor regarding his "moderate course of keeping Christ's birth-day as you are wont to do."[9]

The English Puritans in 1644 banned this "pagan" and "Roman Catholic" celebration in England as a step "to purify religious belief and remove everything that was not directly commanded or described in the Bible." King Charles in 1649 repealed the ban after he took office. In America, after the 1830s when Puritanism waned, Americans began to celebrate Christmas with a mix of Dutch and English traditions.

3. Should We Celebrate Christmas?

No, I'm not trying to take away anyone's Christmas (or Easter), but it should be understood that "December 25" was not the date of birth of Jesus.

Celebrating these *events* of Jesus' birth, death and resurrection, even though the *traditional* dates and places may be wrong, still has value in honoring Jesus. However, in this book, we are presenting other cases for the *actual dates and places*, which we believe to be more accurate from a scriptural and historical standpoint. As we have emphasized previously, every reader can evaluate the evidence for these cases and come to his or her own conclusions.

It is certainly proper to celebrate the incarnate birth of Jesus, the Son of the living God. Such celebration is found throughout Scripture. The biblical writers infallibly reported about the incarnate birth of the Lord Jesus, testifying:

> "… to this historical, timely, spatial, purposeful event, and to remind us every day (not just once a year) that *'for unto us a Child is born, unto us a Son is given; and the government will be upon His shoulder, and His name will be called Wonderful, Counselor, Mighty God, Everlasting Father, Prince of Peace.' (Isaiah 9:6, NKJ)*"[10]

We can celebrate the incarnation of God's Only Son, the Lord Jesus, with great joy. And we can celebrate and remember His birth (incarnation) and presence with us every day, not just once a year. Related to this celebration of the incarnation, Dr. Medeiros states the following:

> "It is biblical. It is proper. It is reasonable. Christ came. Christ was born. Christ died. Christ was buried. Christ rose from the dead. Christ ascended into the heavens. Christ is here with us And He will come back. Are we ready to celebrate His second appearance as well?"[11]

B. No Year "0"

You would think that with the year numbering system of BC ("Before Christ") and AD (Latin *Anno Domini*, "The Year of Our Lord") Jesus would have a birthdate of *Year Zero*, with years numbered from his birth. However, this is not the case as there is no *Year Zero* in either the Julian calendar (proposed by Julius Caesar in 46 BC) and the Gregorian calendar (promulgated in 1582 by Pope Gregory XIII, and used in most western countries today).

The sequence of years "Before Christ" ends at 1 BC and the AD series picks up the very next year with AD 1. This seems surprising to us as we are used to having a timeline with a zero separating the negative and positive numbers. However, this wasn't the case back when the Christian calendar was developed by *Dionysius Exiguus* ("Dennis the Short"), a 6th-century monk.

Dionysius renumbered the years starting with the incarnation (birth) of Jesus, beginning with the *year 1* (AD 1) as the Roman numbering system had no way at that time to indicate a zero. Therefore, in counting the number of years spanning from BC to AD, zero is not counted; for example, from 3 BC to AD 3 is *five years* rather than six years. Hence, 1 BC to AD 1 is counted as one year; and 1 BC can be considered 1 CE (Common Era) in counting years.

C. Commonly Accepted but Incorrect "Actual" Dates

Most modern theologians insist on a year before 4 BC and as early as 5, 6, or 7 BC—even as early as 12 BC—for the birth of Jesus. This is despite the early Christian writers who say that Jesus was born *after 4 BC*.

Why the confusion? The confusion is largely due to the scarcity of good historical records during the period which has been called the *Dark Decade* of history, from 6 BC to AD 4.[13] This is further covered in Chapter 8: "Roman History."

In addition, there is confusion over a particular *lunar eclipse*. Josephus mentions that an eclipse of the moon occurred not long after the death of Herod the Great. Indeed, there was a lunar eclipse on March 13, 4 BC, and this is the eclipse that most scholars, incorrectly, select as the one associated with the death of Herod.

There were, however, *other* eclipses near the same time, and a range of factors and information needs to be evaluated correctly to determine which lunar eclipse to select as being relevant to the death of Herod the Great. There is good evidence that the memorable lunar eclipse of *January 10, 1 BC* is the one to which Josephus was referring. This lunar eclipse and the related death of Herod occurring shortly before this eclipse (also in 1 BC), is a better fit with other historical events and records. This is further discussed in Chapter 9: "Death of King Herod."

D. The Actual Date: September 11, 3 BC

Who would guess that a specific date for the birth of Jesus could, indeed, be accurately determined among all the confusion? Actually, not just the month, day, and year, but also the exact time (within an hour or so)!

This Section A of Part I will lay out the case for just that—*Wednesday, September 11, 3 BC, between 6:18 p.m. (sunset) and 7:39 p.m. (moonset)*. This specificity is amazing, and you can evaluate the validity of the case presented; see particularly Chapter 4: "Astronomical/Zodiacal References" (Subsection B. 3.: "Interpretation of Signs in Revelation 12:1–6").

1. Date Understood by Early Christians

Related to the year of Jesus' birth, it is insightful to determine when the early church leaders—taught by the Apostles and the disciples of the Apostles—stated that Jesus was born. After all, they had many historical written sources not known to us today, as many of the ancient libraries were destroyed.

It should be noted that not even one of the Christian scholars who was able to do research at the ancient libraries (at Alexandria, Pergamum, Caesarea on the Mediterranean coast of Israel), as well as investigate the official records at Rome, stated that Jesus was born in the timeframe of 7 BC to 5 BC.[14] Most of the early writers focused on a birthdate between 3 BC to 2 BC. Every one of them disagrees with modern historical opinion on this subject, which holds to an earlier date of birth. Who were some of these early scholars? Irenaeus of Lyon, Clement of Alexandria, Tertullian, Julius Africanus, and Hippolytus of Rome all wrote in the late AD 100s or early 200s—and these and others supported a birthdate of 3 BC or 2 BC.[15]

2. Evidence for September 11, 3 BC Is Given Here in Part I

The evidence given for *September 11, 3 BC* being the birthdate of Jesus is laid out in this Section A of Part I. This includes evidence from multiple sources—the Bible; historical records relating to Herod; and astronomy, including astronomical signs at the time the Magi were in Persia as well as in Jerusalem, both before and at the time of the birth of Jesus. This is all presented with references cited. The number of ways to determine the birthdate of Jesus are surprising, and they all point to the same date.

CHAPTER 2

Eight *Puzzle Pieces* Determine *When* Jesus Was Born

The true birth date of Jesus is a mystery. We have established that the *traditional date* for the birth of Jesus—December 25, AD 1—is not true. What is the answer to the mystery of His true birthdate?

To solve this mystery, this Section A (of Part I) assembles eight *puzzle pieces* to build our case for the *actual* birthdate of Jesus. These eight *puzzle pieces* are presented in the various chapters of this Section A. They fall under the categories of biblical, historical, and astronomical evidence.

These eight *puzzle pieces* are as follows:

1 *Puzzle Piece #1*–**Birth of John the Baptist**

2 *Puzzle Piece #2*–**Astronomical/Zodiacal References**

3 *Puzzle Piece #3*–**Born on the *Feast of Trumpets*?**

4 *Puzzle Piece #4*–**The Wise Men (Magi)**

5 *Puzzle Piece #5*–**Star of Bethlehem and Magi's Visit**

6 *Puzzle Piece #6*–**Roman History**

7   *Puzzle Piece #7–*Death of King Herod

8   *Puzzle Piece #8–Sabbatical* **and** *Jubilee* **Years**

I believe you will find the investigation of the various pieces of evidence interesting and illuminating. As in determining truth in Scripture, all Scripture needs to align to determine truth—even small seemingly obscure passages. Similarly, all these *puzzle pieces* must be properly considered, and they must align to determine the true birthdate of Jesus.

Often, we find commentators who come up with a date for the birth of Jesus, yet have not considered a correct view of Roman history and/or a proper view of related astronomical happenings like the correct lunar eclipse in relationship to Herod's death, etc. They often go astray from not properly considering ***all*** the *puzzle pieces*.

In the following chapters, we will consider the evidence in each *puzzle piece*, starting with "*Puzzle Piece #1–*Birth of John the Baptist" to see how the birth of John the Baptist can provide evidence in solving the mystery of the birthdate of Jesus.

The graphic at the start of each upcoming chapter illustrates the *puzzle piece* being examined.

CHAPTER 3

Puzzle Piece #1 –
Birth of John the Baptist

It is easy to eliminate any proposed birthdate for Jesus that is not in the fall of the year. For example, some have speculated that Jesus was born in the springtime, including on Passover. However, in the spring is not a good possibility due to this biblical method for calculating the month of Jesus' birth—by calculating the birthdate of John the Baptist as described in this chapter.[16]

A. Zechariah—Priestly Order of Abijah

This biblical method to calculate the birthday of Jesus involves figuring the birthdate of John the Baptist and applying other information in Luke's Gospel about the time difference between their births. This clearly places Jesus' birthdate in the fall.

The Gospel of Luke covers the birth of John the Baptist before giving details on the birth of Jesus. There is a reason for this—because the two are inseparably linked in the chronology of their births as well as their ministry.

Determining the birth date of John the Baptist is *Puzzle Piece #1* for solving the mystery of Jesus' birthdate.

Luke provides clues related to John the Baptist's father, Zechariah the priest, which help us unlock the date for the birth of Jesus. This requires some biblical "sleuthing" to derive the months and days of the year for the births of John the Baptist and Jesus. Some important information from the Old Testament as well as from the Jewish *Mishnah* (the first legal law code of basic Jewish law governing all aspects of life, based on the interpretations of the Torah; the *Mishnah* contains the basic oral law as developed through the generations) is needed to calculate John's birthdate—the initial step in figuring Jesus' birthdate.

It is stated in Luke's Gospel: *"In the time of Herod king of Judea there was a priest named Zechariah, who belonged to the priestly division of* **Abijah** *..."* (Luke 1:5 NIV; emphasis mine). This is an important clue as the priestly division of *Abijah* was the *eighth* of the 24 divisions which King David, on God's instructions, had set up to service the Temple (1 Chronicles 24:1-19; 28:12-13). King David had divided the descendants of the sons of Eleazar and Ithamar, the two sons of Aaron, into 24 groups (courses) and set up a schedule for the priests (*Kohanim*) to service the Temple in an orderly manner all year long. Each course served for one week (2 Chr. 23:8, 1 Chr. 9:25) from Sabbath to Sabbath—twice a year; in addition to all the courses serving together during the three Pilgrim *Feasts of the Lord* (the three Feasts when all adult Jewish men were required to come to Jerusalem—Unleavened Bread, Pentecost, and Tabernacles). As previously stated, the seven *Feasts of the Lord* are given in Leviticus 23, and are not "feasts" as we think of as dinners but "appointed times" with the Lord.

The 8th priestly course served in late spring and again in late autumn. Jewish tradition stated that the first priestly course started its duty on the Sabbath before Nisan 1 (Nisan being the first month of the Jewish religious year; this is the month in which Passover falls). The Jewish *Mishnah* indicates that each course served a week during the first half of the year and a week during the second half of the year, as well as a week during each of the three annual festival weeks (the Pilgrim Feasts, when all adult males in Israel were to appear at the temple in Jerusalem—Unleavened Bread, Pentecost, and Tabernacles), for a total of five weeks during a normal year. A normal year on the present Hebrew calendar consists of 12-lunar months of 29 or 30 days, for a total of 354 days, which is about 11 days less than a solar year (365.24 days). During a regular Jewish year, which occurs 12 times in a 19-year cycle, a total of 51 weeks of coverage would be needed to provide Temple coverage throughout the year (24 courses x 2 times per year + 3 weeks of Pilgrim Feasts weeks = 51 weeks coverage).[17]

B. Calculated Dates of Births of John the Baptist and of Jesus

In 4 BC (Jesus' birth is assumed to be in 3 BC from other historical evidence as well as astronomic evidence, as given in Part I), Nisan 1 was the equivalent of our March 29, and the preceding Sabbath was March 24, making the week of the duties of the first priestly course from Sabbath noon, March 24, to Sabbath noon, March 31 (and the 2nd course from March 31 to April 7, etc.). The 3rd course (which started on our April 7) was interrupted by the Passover/Unleavened Bread week-long celebration, when all the priests officiated together, and this caused the 3rd course not to end its service until the Sabbath after Passover, which was April 21 in 4 BC.[18]

The period for the 8th course of *Abijah*, for which Zechariah belonged, was from May 19 to May 26. It was most likely that it was this late spring administration when Zechariah's service was interrupted by the angel's appearance to him, announcing his wife's imminent pregnancy. Because of his unbelief, he was struck dumb during his service in the Temple, which immediately disqualified him as of that moment from his priestly duties (Lev. 21:16-23). Therefore, he left for home, and, near May 26 to June 1, Elizabeth would have conceived and later given birth to John the Baptist *near March 10 in 3 BC* (after the gestation period of 9 months and 10 days; 280 days). This would place the birth of Jesus six months later (Luke 1:26-38) in the first half of September, in 3 BC.[19]

Of course, the other possibility is that the date that the angel struck Zechariah and caused him to lose his speech was during Zechariah's *second* service term in the second half of the year, rather than during the first term of service in the spring. However, this is not believed to be the case as this would have caused the birth of John the Baptist to be near mid-September, and Jesus' birth in March, during the rainy season. Ramsey demonstrates in his book, *Born in Bethlehem*, that the general time of year for the start of censuses was from August to October, to encourage higher participation, and not in the rainy season in mid-March.[20]

Due to the probable time of year for the Roman census being in the fall and not during the rainy season of the spring, we know that Jesus was most probably *not* born in the spring, since we know that Joseph was taking his family to Bethlehem for the census, at which time Jesus was born. From all this about the probable timing of the Roman census, we know that Zechariah's service in the temple when he was struck dumb was during the *first half* of the year rather than during the second half.

From this method of calculating the birthdate of Jesus from the information provided related to the birthdate of John the Baptist in Luke's Gospel, as well as the information on the timing of Roman censuses, we see that Jesus was born in the fall of the year—specifically, in September of that year. Admittedly, it is impossible to arrive at a *specific* date for either John the Baptist or Jesus based on the priestly courses and the information in Luke's Gospel, but it helps to approximate a likely range of dates.

Tishri 1 (the first day of the seventh month on the Jewish calendar, called *Yom Teruah*, the Feast of Trumpets) began at sundown of *September 11, 3 BC* (on the Julian [Roman] calendar), when the day changed from Elul 30 to Tishri 1. We will see shortly in Chapter 4, related to the astronomical/zodiacal reference in Rev. 12:1-6 (*Puzzle Piece #2*), that Jesus was, indeed, born precisely on *September 11, 3 BC*, when the astronomical signs given in Revelation line up precisely and uniquely with that specific date. Therefore, these two methods for figuring the birthdate of Jesus are supportive of each other—for Jesus' birthdate to be in the fall of the year.

CHAPTER 4

Puzzle Piece #2–
Astronomical/Zodiacal References

Even the evidence from astronomical/Zodiacal references in Scripture supports the date of the birth of Jesus, as this chapter will show. This is our *Puzzle Piece #2* in solving the mystery of the birthdate of Jesus.

A. Background of "Signs" and of the Biblical Zodiac

1. Signs in the Heavens Given by God

Who has not looked up into the sky on a clear night and marveled at the vastness of the universe with the lights scattered throughout and wondered about the God who created all things? What is it all about? In Genesis, God explains His purpose for creating all those lights in the universe. He said,

> *"Let there be lights in the firmament of the heavens to divide the day from the night; and let them be for **signs**, and for seasons, and for days, and years; And let them be for lights in the firmament of the heaven to give light upon the earth; and it was so."* (Genesis 1:14 KJV; emphasis mine)

It is interesting that God gave the stars, planets and other objects in the universe for "signs" among the other reasons stated. Certainly, the Magi who came to seek out the Jewish Messiah saw some kind of "sign" or "signs" in the heavens. The Bible calls our attention to starry objects, and the Psalmist gives us context in poetic style as the King James Version captures so well in its translation—

> *"The heavens declare the glory of God; and the firmament sheweth his handywork. Day unto day uttereth speech, and night unto night sheweth knowledge. There is no speech nor language, where their voice is not heard. Their line is gone out through all the earth, and their words to the end of the world. In them hath he set a tabernacle for the sun ..."* (Psalm 19:1-4 KJV)

The heavens are for His glory, and they show us knowledge. It is wonderful that there is a reason for all these things we see. God has said so. Remember that He named each star (Isaiah 40:26) despite their vast number.

2. Scriptural References to the Stars and the Biblical Zodiac

It is interesting the number of times that the stars and the constellations are mentioned in Scripture. The Book of Job is reported by some commentators to be the oldest book of the Bible, going back to approximately 2,150 BC, which is 650 years before Moses wrote the Pentateuch. Job has several listings in Chapters 9 and 38 related to the stars and constellations:

> *"[God] which alone spreadeth out the heavens, and treadeth upon the waves of the sea. Which maketh **Acturus**, **Orion**, and **Pleiades**, and the chambers of the south."* (Job 9:8-9 KJV; emphasis mine)

> *"Canst thou bind the sweet influences of **Pleiades**, or loose the bands of **Orion**? Canst thou bring forth **Mazzaroth** [Hebrew: "The Constellations of the Zodiac"] in his season? Or canst thou guide **Arcturus** with his sons? Knoweth thou the ordinances of heaven? Canst thou set the dominion thereof in the earth?"* (Job 38:31-33 KJV; clarification and emphasis mine)

Let's review the *zodiac*. Undoubtedly, the zodiac with the graphical depiction of the 12 starry constellations in the sky is used in the occult arts, astrology and fortune-telling. It is well known that this is forbidden in the Bible (Leviticus 20:27), largely because they can involve demonic spirits (Acts 16:16-19). Tim Warner, in his recent book, *The Mystery of the Mazzaroth* (2013), which has some wonderful insights, states, "Yet, the zodiac was not originally designed for such nefarious purposes. In His response to Job, God attributed the zodiac to Himself."[21]

In addition, the book of Amos mentions constellations of the ancient zodiac: *"Seek him that maketh the seven stars [**Pleiades**] and **Orion** ... "* (Amos 5:8a KJV; clarification and emphasis mine).

The original zodiac was given by God to man to display the Gospel story before the written word came through Moses. The *"Mazzaroth"* mentioned in Job literally means "the twelve signs [constellations] of the zodiac."[22] God brings out each of the twelve signs of the zodiac throughout the year in their proper months.

3.   Biblical Astronomy in Prophetic Themes

(a)   *The Gospel in the Stars*

Strangely, there are early writings of virtually all civilizations describing the major stars in the heavens contained in the twelve "Constellations of the Zodiac." The chart of the zodiac shows 12 major signs around the ecliptic which is the apparent path that the sun travels through the heavens, caused by the earth's path around the sun over a year's time.

Going back to Egypt, Persia, Assyria, or Babylonia, regardless of how far their records go, there is mention of this ancient zodiac. D. James Kennedy in his book, *The Real Meaning of the Zodiac* (1989), says, "Archaeologists, historians, and antiquarians have searched the dustiest libraries, uncovered the oldest tables, ciphered the most difficult hieroglyphics, and have failed to discover how it is that in so many nations all over the world the same signs [of the zodiac] exist."[23]

Where did these descriptions of these twelve constellations come from? As mentioned, the earliest book of the Bible, the book of Job, mentions several of these constellations as well as the *"Mazzaroth"* (Job 38:31-32), which is the zodiac. A good case can be made that they were originally established in the heavens by God, described by God to either Adam or a descendant, and, in fact, depict a picture story of God's plan of salvation for mankind through His Son, the Redeemer, Jesus. This case is made by several influential authors—D. James Kennedy in his book, *The Real Meaning of the Zodiac*[24]; by Joseph A. Seiss in his book, *The Gospel in the Stars*,[25] written in 1882; as well as by E. W. Bullinger in his book, *The Witness of the Stars*,[26] written in 1893. It is a fascinating account.

According to Arabic tradition, the signs of the zodiac came originally from Seth, the son of Adam, and Enosh, the son of Seth.[27] We know that the *protoevangelium* (the first evangel, the first Gospel) was given by God to Adam in the

Garden of Eden (Genesis 3:15); this is the story of the future Messiah, the Seed of the woman, crushing the head of the serpent, representing Satan.

Jesus Christ is the subject of the written Word of God from Genesis to Revelation. Likewise, He is also the subject of the Word of God written in the heavens from Virgo (the initial, lead constellation) to Leo (the last, 12th constellation). Jesus is the promised *Seed of the woman* (Virgo) and the coming King of Glory as *the Lion of the tribe of Judah* (Leo). He is also depicted in the heavens as *the sun*—the *righteous one*, the *bridegroom* (spoken of in Psalm 19:4-5) racing through the heavens to redeem and restore His bride to glory.[28]

David in Psalm 19 said a message was proclaimed by the sun's path through the constellations, *"Their sound has gone out to all the earth, and their words to the ends of the world"* (Psalm 19:18, NIV). Paul in Romans 10:18 quoted David's Psalm as proof that the ancient nations had already heard *the Gospel*. Indeed, the revelation of God to man was seen *"since the creation of the world."*[29]

Of course, Scripture condemns *astrology* (Isaiah 47:13). Satan corrupted the use and purpose of the ancient zodiac. Instead of being simply the story of the redemption through a future Redeemer, Jesus, the heavenly signs of the zodiac came to be taken as deities which have an influence on the lives of humans. This is not the original purpose. The word *zodiac* comes from the Hebrew *sodi*, and in Sanskrit means: "A Way," "A Path," "A Step." Kennedy states, "At a deeper level we see the zodiac picturing The Path, The Way of salvation revealed beautifully for us in the heavens."[30]

(b) Balaam's Prophecy (Numbers 22-24)

The prophecy of Balaam, recorded by Moses, spoke about a "star" which was to arise in Israel that would relate to ruler-ship or dominion: *"A **star** shall come out of Jacob and a **scepter** [ruling rod] shall rise out of Israel"* (Numbers 24:17; clarification and emphasis mine).

Balaam's reluctant, but divinely inspired, prophecy stated that a unique star associated with Israel would accompany a future King who, as we know from other Scripture, would eventually rule the world.

(c) The Woman in Revelation 12:1-6

Another usage of astronomical signs and the biblical zodiac in prophetic Scripture is found in Revelation 12:1-6. This involves the sign of the constellation of Virgo, and this is covered below in Section B.

So, we see that stars and the constellations of the zodiac are used in both the Old Testament *and the New Testament* in conveying prophetic messages.

B. Revelation 12:1-6 Conveys Exact Year, Day and Hour of Birth of Jesus!

1. Biblical Text of Revelation 12:1-6

The events of the birth of Jesus are recorded in only three places in the New Testament—Matthew's Gospel, Luke's Gospel, and in *Chapter 12 of the Book of Revelation* (Revelation 12:1-6). It is true that Revelation contains much figurative language which is highly symbolic. However, within this figurative language are contained clues needed to precisely date the birthdate of Jesus—the day and precise hour of His birth! This, in fact, absolutely "nails it."

An analysis of Revelation 12, including an analysis of the astronomy depicted, provides additional support for the birthdate of Jesus derived from Luke's Gospel—the birthdate of John the Baptist and the eighth priestly course of *Abijah*, covered in Chapter 2. Both point to the fall season, the Hebrew month of *Tishri* (September). However, an analysis of Revelation 12 gives us the precise day and hour.

The Apostle John wrote the following interesting account of the "Woman and the Dragon" in Revelation Chapter 12, which has a veiled reference to God's plan of redemption for mankind—the birth of Jesus:

> *"A great and wondrous sign appeared in heaven: a **woman** clothed with the **sun**, with the **moon** under her feet and a crown of **twelve stars** on her head. She was pregnant and cried out in pain as she was about to give birth. Then another sign appeared in heaven: an enormous **red dragon** with seven heads and ten horns and seven crowns on his heads. His tail swept a third of the stars out of the sky and flung them to the earth. The dragon stood in front of the woman who was about to give birth, so that he might devour her child the moment it was born. She gave birth to a **son, a male child**, who will rule all the nations with an iron scepter. And her child was snatched up to God and to his throne. The woman fled into the desert to a place prepared for her by God, where she might be taken care of for 1,260 days.*
>
> *And there was war in heaven. Michael and his angels fought against the dragon, and the dragon and his angels fought back. But he was not strong enough, and they lost their place in heaven. The great dragon was hurled down—that ancient serpent called the devil or **Satan**, who leads the whole world astray. He was hurled to the earth, and his angels with him."*
> (Revelation 12:1-9 NIV; emphasis mine)

A graphical depiction of the cosmic image described in Revelation 12 is helpful to grasp what is being communicated. The following subsection 2 presents two graphic depictions, and subsection 3 provides their interpretation.

2. Graphic Depictions of Revelation 12:1–6

The following Figures 4.1 and 4.2 show the symbols depicted in Revelation 12:1–6. These diagrams help with understanding the written explanation of this passage of Scripture.

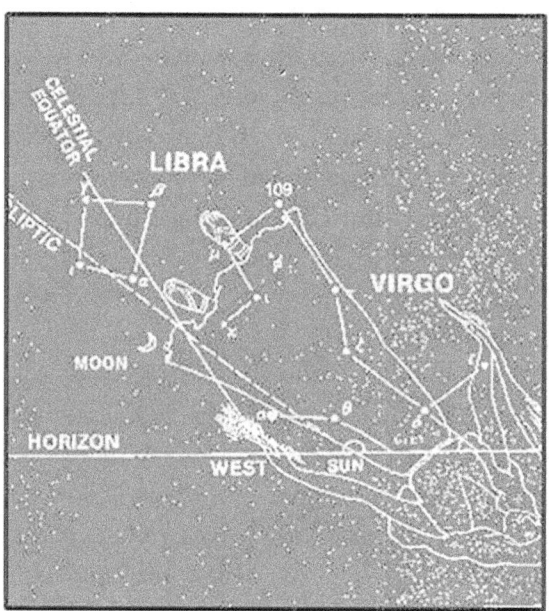

Figure 4.1. Symbols depicted in Rev. 12:1–6

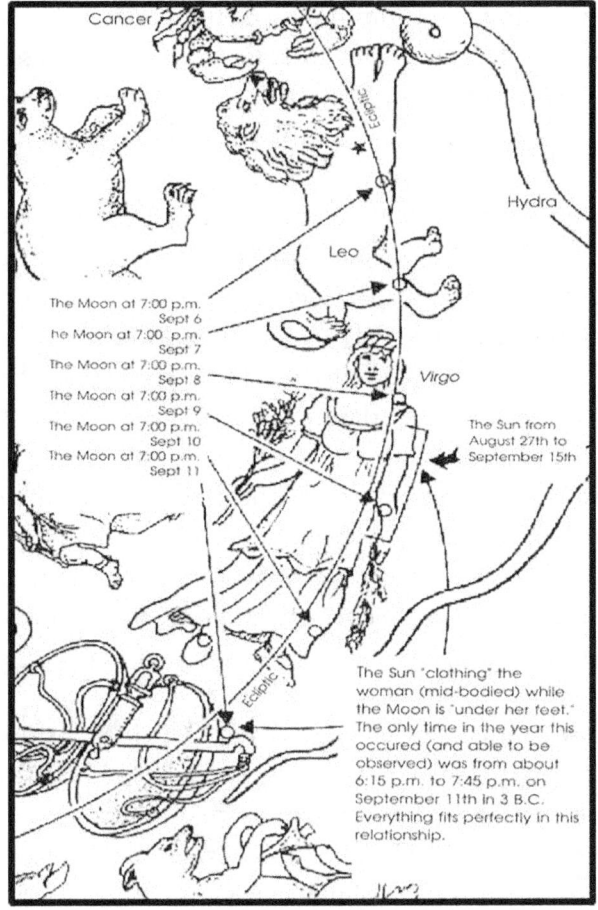

Figure 4.2. Diagram of Virgo, Sun and Moon (Rev. 12:1-6) on September 11, 3 BC

3. Interpretation of Signs in Revelation 12:1-6

For sure, the scene described in Revelation 12:1–6 is highly symbolic. Remember that Genesis tells us that one of the reasons that celestial bodies were made by God is to give *signs* (Genesis 1:14), which the above scene incorporates.

It should be recognized that this depiction in Revelation 12 could not be a literal description of the Virgin Mary, as this *"woman"* had the heavens associated with her—the sun, moon and the twelve stars. In addition, John stated that the display was a *wonder* (KJV; a great *sign*) and that it was *in heaven*. There are three "heavens"—where the birds fly; that of the sun, moon, planets and stars (Genesis 1:17); and where God lives (II Corinthians 12:2). The reasonable interpretation of the *"heaven"* as used in Revelation 12 is where the sun, moon and the twelve stars are located.

What is all this symbolism communicating to us and how exactly does it tell us the precise birthdate of Jesus? The key to understanding the passage in Revelation 12 is to analyze the *astronomy* depicted in conjunction with the biblical account in Scripture. This is a case of the written Word and the Word written in the stars coming together in parallel truths.

The sign given in verse 1 is that of a woman. The only sign of the zodiac which depicts a woman is the constellation of Virgo. The "birth" of the Messiah is associated with this heavenly spectacle (Revelation 12:2). The books by Seiss and Bullinger, mentioned previously, give wonderful details about the heavenly woman called Virgo—holding in her left hand a green branch and in her right hand a sprig of ripe grain; these depict Jesus, prophetically called *"the Branch"* (Zechariah 3:8, 6:12; Isaiah 4:2a).

The vision given to John associates specific positions of the sun and the moon in relationship to Virgo, located within the normal paths of the sun and moon across the heavens. The specific locations of the sun and moon in relationship to the woman give us clues to the specific day and time for the birth of the Messiah. As stated by Martin,

> "The only time in the year that the Sun could be in a position to 'clothe' the celestial woman called Virgo (that is, to be mid-bodied to her, in the region where a pregnant woman carries a child) is when the Sun is located between about 150 and 170 degrees along the ecliptic. This 'clothing' of the woman by the Sun occurs for a 20-day period each year. This 20 degree spread could indicate the general time when Jesus was born. In **3 B.C.**, the Sun would have entered this celestial region about **August 27** and exited from it about **September 15**. If John in the Book of Revelation is associating the birth of Jesus with the period when the Sun was mid-bodied to this woman called Virgo (and this is no doubt what he means), then Jesus would have to be born within that 20-day period. From the point of view of the Magi ... this would have been the only logical sign under which the Jewish Messiah might be born, especially if he were to be born of a virgin."[33]

The sign of the sun *"clothing"* the woman (Virgo) defines a period of 20-days (August 27 to September 15 for the year 3 BC). It is the additional sign of the moon being *"under her feet"* which actually pinpoints the nativity to within a day—to within a period of an hour and a half (within 90 minutes) on that day. In the year 3 BC, these two relationships of the sun and moon and Virgo came into alignment for only an 81-minute period, as observed from Palestine in the twilight period of *September 11th*. This relationship began at *6:18 p.m. (sunset) and lasted until 7:39 p.m. (moonset).*[34]

It should be noted that this is the only day (*September 11*) in the whole year (*3 BC*) that this astronomical phenomenon described in Revelation Chapter 12 could take place. That the birth of Jesus was after sunset is confirmed in Luke's description—*"And there were shepherds living out in the fields nearby, keeping watch over their flocks **at night**. An angel of the Lord appeared to them ... **Today** [the day started at sundown] in the town of David a Savior **has been born** to you . . ."* (Luke 2:8-9a NIV; clarification and emphasis mine).

The timeframe of the Luke account matches the timeframe of the interpretation of Revelation 12:1-6. This gives further credibility to the interpretation of Revelation 12:1-6 and the timeframe of Jesus' birth just after sundown, the start of a new Jewish day.

It should also be noted that the timing of the sun and moon relationship with Virgo was a *New Moon* day, with the small sliver of the moon setting after the setting of the sun, with Jesus born at that time in the early evening. This New Moon day was *Tishri 1* on the Jewish calendar (*September 11, 3 BC*), which is *Yom Teruah* (the Feast of Trumpets). Additional coverage about this significant timing of the birth of Jesus on the Feast of Trumpets is given in Chapter 5 of this Section A of Part I.

It should also be noted that the vision of Revelation 12 with Virgo giving birth has a "Near/Far" fulfillment, which is the case with much of biblical prophecy (see Chapter 2 of *The Last Shofar!*). Obviously, Jesus on *September 11, 3 BC* fulfilled this vision of the birth of Messiah. Satan later tried to kill the Messiah through the actions of Herod, after the Magi arrived and left. There is, in addition, a *future* fulfillment of this vision, in the end times. How do we know this? We know this due to the usage of future tense *"has"* not "had" in the original Greek language in Revelation 12:6—*"Then the woman fled into the wilderness where she **ha(s)** a place prepared by God, so that there she would be nourished for one thousand two hundred and sixty days"* (Revelation 12:6 NASB; emphasis mine). Credit goes to Nelson Walters for presenting these insights.[35] Nelson states the following:

> "The actual word in the Greek is present tense "has" but this confused the translators of the NASB. They translated it "had" and left a note that the actual word was "has" because they probably failed to see the near/far fulfillment. The time the woman is in the wilderness should catch prophecy students [sic] attention as well: 1260 days. This is the reign of the Antichrist. This is a picture of the flight of the righteous (Israel and

the Church) … Mary and Joseph's flight to Egypt then is a prophetic picture of the flight of the righteous out of Israel at the Midpoint of the Tribulation."[36]

The above *future* fulfillment of Revelation 12, related to the vision of the huge red dragon (represents Satan) confronting a woman who is about to give birth (Israel), is further discussed by Mark Davidson in his book, *Daniel Revisited—Discovering the Four Mideast Signs Leading to the Antichrist.*[37]

However, for the purpose of this chapter, the important thing for us to take away from Revelation 12:1-6 is that it supports the birth of Jesus being on *September 11, 3 BC*—just after sunset, at the start of *Tishri 1* on the Jewish calendar. Other researchers, including Ernest L. Martin,[38] agree on this date for the birth of Jesus. This date is also in conformity with all other evidence (the other *puzzle pieces*) for the date of the Jesus' birth, as is presented in the following chapters of Section A of Part I.

CHAPTER 5

Puzzle Piece #3– Born on the Feast of Trumpets?

From the proper astronomical interpretation of Revelation 12:1–6 (see Chapter 4, B. 3.), the only day in *3 BC* which meets these astronomical confluences is *September 11, 3 BC,* during the period of sunset to moonset, 6:18 pm to 7:39 pm. It turns out that this date is the date of the *Feast of Trumpets.*

A. Evidence for the Birthdate of Jesus Being on Feast of Trumpets

The disciple John in Revelation 12:1–6 is presenting something of high significance in a symbolic way. As mentioned previously, this date of *September 11, 3 BC* is *Tishri 1* on the Jewish calendar in 3 BC, which, of course, is the 1st day of the first Jewish month on the *civil* calendar. This date is also call *Yom Teruah*: The Day of Trumpets; also called the Feast of Trumpets; also called *Rosh Hashanah*: Head of the Year, or the Feast of the New Year. As background, on the Jewish *religious* calendar, *Tishri* is the seventh month. This Jewish religious calendar was given by God to Moses and begins with the month of *Nisan*, during which the first Feast of the Lord, Passover, occurs.

Jesus was, indeed, born on the *Feast of Trumpets,* and no other day of the year in 3 BC could astronomically fit Revelation 12:1-3. The close-proximity positions of the sun and the moon as described in these verses of Revelation indicate a *new moon* timeframe, exactly the case with the first day of a Jewish lunar month, as is the case on *Tishri 1*—the Feast of Trumpets.

Therefore, it can be noted that Jesus' birth was *not* on the *Feast of Tabernacles* or *Passover*, as others have postulated (further explained in Section C below). Neither on Tabernacles or Passover, which are both in the middle of lunar months, is there a new-moon occurrence as is depicted in Revelation 12:1–6. Conversely, a full moon is seen in the middle of lunar months, as on the *Feast of Tabernacles* and *Passover.* The Feast of Trumpets, occurring on Tishri 1, the first day of the lunar month, uniquely of all the Feasts has a new-moon occurrence. This conclusion of the alignment of the Feast of Trumpets is our *Puzzle Piece #3* in determining the true birthdate of Jesus.

B. Significance of Tishri 1 (Feast of Trumpets)

There is great significance of the Feast of Trumpets and Jesus being born on this date, which was evident to the Apostle John when he wrote Chapter 12 of the book of Revelation.

What is the significance of this date of the Feast of Trumpets? The early Jewish Christians looked on Jesus as the Messiah (Christ), and due to His birth on the Feast of Trumpets, also looked on Him as the *King of the Universe*, as the Feast symbolically shows this. The theological understanding of the Jews within their synagogue services for the Day of Trumpets was that God rules overall and that He is the King of kings. Zechariah 14:16 was commonly quoted, *"The king, the Lord of hosts."* Some have argued that the "enthronement psalms" (Psalms 47, 93, 96-99) in which *Yahweh* reigns were a part of the liturgy of the ancient synagogues on this date.[40] This was the very date on which Jesus was born.

The Feast of Trumpets, *Rosh Hashanah*, is the start of the Jewish civil year, and, before God told Moses that the month of the Exodus (*Nisan*) was to become the start of the religious year, *Tishri 1* in the fall was the start of all the years before the Exodus, hence, this was the case from Creation to the Exodus. There is an impressive accompaniment of biblical and prophetic scenes which align with this date. The Day of Trumpets was the memorial day that commemorated the creation of the world, the first day of Genesis 1:1-5. Moses gives that impression. We're talking the birthday of the world.[41] Very fitting that the Creator of the world (John 1:1-3, 14) would come into the world on this date!

Related to the patriarch Noah while on the ark, *"By the **first day of the first month*** *of Noah's six hundred and first year, the water had dried up from the earth. Noah then removed the covering from the ark and saw that the surface of the ground was dry"* (Genesis 8:13 NIV; emphasis added). This was not only the birthday of Noah but, in a sense, a new birth after the Flood for the earth as well—on *Tishri 1*. *Tishri 1* was the exact day that many of the ancient kings of Judah reckoned as their inauguration day of rule. This was certainly the case with **Solomon**.[42] The Day of Trumpets was also the time for counting the years of their kingly rule. Once again, it seems fitting that Jesus came into the world on this auspicious date. A theme of the Day of Trumpets is kingship. It is possible that the patriarch **Joseph** of Egypt, who is a type of Christ in the Old Testament, rose to "kingship" on this New Moon day which began the month of *Tishri*. He had been in captivity in a dungeon for "two full years" (Genesis 41:1). Martin gives us insight that this was not simply a two-year period which Moses was intending, but the passage *"of two full years."* The implication is that Joseph rose to "kingship" on a New Year's Day. Psalm 81 (vv. 3, 5) is a New Year's psalm referencing Joseph's royal enthronement (Genesis 41:40); the kingdoms of the world became Joseph's on the day intended for coronations—the day which later became the Feast of Trumpets. Pharaoh retained the top leadership, just as God the Father still maintains supreme rule over Jesus even when He is prophesied to rule the kingdoms of this world.[43] Joseph prefigured Jesus in many aspects of his life.

Other important events happened on *Rosh Hashanah*, on *Tishri 1*. **Joseph** was freed from an Egyptian prison after 12 years, on *Rosh Hashanah*. He became viceroy of Egypt, provider of food to "the world," and leader of Jacob's family. Joseph set in motion the years of exile and enslavement of Israel, which led eventually to Israel's *freedom*, nationhood, exodus, and entrance into the Promised Land. Hence, *Rosh Hashanah* is shown to be a *day of freedom*, and is illustrated by an entry in *The Machzor*. The book, *The Complete Artscroll Machzor*, provides a summary of accounts found in the *Jewish Talmud* (*Rosh Hashanah* 10b-11a). Here is a quotation from the *Machzor*: "On *Rosh Ha-Shanah*, the Jewish people in Egypt stopped their slave labor [they began their time of liberty and freedom], while they waited for the Ten Plagues to play themselves out so that Moses could lead them to *freedom*"[44]

The Day of Trumpets in the biblical and Jewish calendars is also New Year's Day for commercial and royal reckonings. This day signified a time of "new beginnings" to all those of Israel who accepted biblical teachings. The *Machzor* also and has some interesting quotes related to important biblical figures of the Old Testament. For example, "The Patriarchs **Abraham** and **Jacob** were born on *Rosh Hashanah*. Abraham was a new beginning for mankind after it [mankind's] failure to realize the promise of Adam and Noah; Jacob as a new beginning for the Jewish people, for it was with him that Jews advanced from the status of individuals to that of a united family on the threshold of nationhood." Additionally, other prominent men—**Isaac**, **Joseph**, and **Samuel**—were also born on *Rosh Hashanah*, the Day of Trumpets.[46]

Jesus was prophesized to be the King of the world, to lead all people into a time of freedom and peace. All these are characterized by The Day of Trumpets, *Rosh Hashanah*, and there could not have been a better day in the ecclesiastical calendar of the Jews to introduce the Messiah to the world from a Jewish point of view.

Lastly, it should be mentioned, per the case presented here as well as the case presented in my first book co-authored with Donald Zoller (*The Last Shofar!–What the fall Feasts Are Telling the Church*), both the birth of Jesus (His First Coming) and His Second Coming (at the Rapture/resurrection of the Church) are on the *Feast of Trumpets*—two bookends of the life and redemption ministry of Jesus; both at the appointed times on this significant date on the Jewish calendar.

C. Birth of Jesus Was *Not* on Feast of Tabernacles (Sukkot) or on Passover

Others have postulated that Jesus was born on the *Feast of Tabernacles (Sukkot)* or on *Passover*. Even some prominent Messianic rabbis have written articles on this correlation. For example, Avi Ben Mordechai, author of *Messiah–Volume 2: Understanding His Life and Teachings in Hebraic Context* (1997), has taken the position that Jesus, the Jewish Messiah, was born on the first day of the Feast of Tabernacles (*Sukkot*— an eight-day festival beginning on *Tishri 15*).[47] However, it should be noted that I agree with Avi Ben Mordechai on the Jewish *month* of Jesus' birth (*Tishri*), but I disagree on the day in Tishri which he proposes. In my humble opinion, the case for Jesus birth on the *Feast of Trumpets* (*Rosh Hashanah*; *Tishri 1*), is much stronger, and *Revelation Chapter 12* is the clincher (as has been covered in Chapter 4, subsection B). But there is even other substantiating evidence; many have never fully considered the totality of evidence summarized in Part I of this book.

True, the Apostle John said in his Gospel that Jesus "... *tabernacled among us*" (John 1:14 *Interlinear Hebrew-Greek-English Bible*). However, this does *not* mean that he was saying that Jesus was *born* on the Feast of Tabernacles, which will have its fulfillment in Jesus at His *Second* Coming; at that time, He, indeed, tabernacles with men—during the Millennium and for eternity, when all believers are with Him.

The Feast of Tabernacles, an eight-day Feast, in the year 3 BC was from September 26 to October 3 BC (*Tishri 15-22*), and Jesus' birth during that time is *impossible* for several reasons. There is obvious proof that Jesus' birth could *not* have been during any one of the three *Pilgrim Feasts*—Passover/Unleavened Bread, Pentecost, and Tabernacles. These were times when all Jewish men in Israel were required by the Law given by God to Moses to be *in Jerusalem* (Deuteronomy 16:6, 11, 16). However, Luke tells us that during Jesus' nativity *"everyone went to his own city"* (Luke 2:3). Joseph and Mary went to *Bethlehem*, not to Jerusalem at the time of His birth! This necessarily rules out both Passover/Unleavened Bread and Tabernacles for his birth. This is just another case of the importance of knowing our Hebrew roots to be able to properly interpret Scripture as well as history!

Joseph and Mary travelled specifically to *Bethlehem* for a census. The Romans would not have selected the three primary festival seasons for a census in Israel. No way. The Romans wanted full compliance, and not scheduling the census during these three festival seasons would have been of primary consideration by the Romans to increase compliance by the Jews. It is probable that Joseph indeed traveled to Jerusalem from Bethlehem for the Feast of Tabernacles, starting on *Tishri 15* (two weeks after the birth of Jesus on *Tishri 1*); it makes sense that Joseph would time his trip to register for the census in Bethlehem and then, shortly later, attend the Feast of Tabernacles in Jerusalem, located only 6 miles away, two weeks later.

But why was there *"no room in the inn"* for the family when Joseph and Mary arrived? Of course, this means that they must have arrived during a festival season when Jews from all over Israel flocked to Jerusalem. Not necessarily. Yes, it is true that high influx of Jews occurred during the festival seasons, but this does *not* necessarily mean that the family arrived at Passover/Unleavened Bread, Pentecost, or Tabernacles. Luke tells us that they were there to be registered for a Roman *census*, and *that* is what caused the numbers of Jews to increase in Bethlehem at *that* time.

Also, why does it make sense that Mary necessarily accompanied Joseph? Women were not required to attend the three Pilgrim Feasts in Jerusalem, as was required by Jewish men in Israel. The historical background related to the Roman census sheds light on this. A new understanding of history, as explained by Martin shows that the census and the oath of allegiance to Augustus (for the *Pater Patriae* award—as further explained in Chapter 8, B. 1.) were the *same census*. Since Mary was by biblical law able to bear a rightful king of the Jews because of her being of the linage of David, she would have been required along with Joseph—who was also of the line of David—to register and give an oath that she and her offspring would remain loyal to the existing government under Augustus.[48]

Also, traveling from Nazareth to arrive in Bethlehem exactly on the Feast of Tabernacles, if this was the case—when males were required to be at the Temple, the very day that Mary delivered Jesus—would not have been planned as such by Joseph, who was a Jewish man faithful to the Law.

All the *puzzle pieces*, as presented in this case, fit together to support the birth of Jesus on the *Feast of Trumpets* on *September 11, 3 BC*, in the evening, and, hence, *not* on the Feast of Tabernacles in the fall or Passover/Unleavened Bread in the spring. This is becoming clearer as we consider each of the *puzzle pieces* represented in the chapters of this Section A of Part I.

CHAPTER 6

Puzzle Piece #4 –
The Wise Men (Magi)

The account of the story of the birth of Jesus and the visit of the Magi is forever etched in the minds of most people. They see them in most manger scenes related to the traditional celebration of Christmas.

A. Who Were the Magi?

1. Biblical Description of Magi: Matthew 2:1-12

Let's look more closely at this visit of the Magi, including who they were and *when they actually came* to worship Jesus. The Magi are our *Puzzle Piece #4*.

The Gospel of Matthew is the only Gospel that tells us about the visit of the Magi who came from the east to visit Jesus in Bethlehem. As Brent Landau states in his Introduction to his recent translation of a forgotten ancient manuscript, *Revelation of the Magi—The Lost Tale of the Wise Men's Journey to Bethlehem* (2010), "The Magi—usually known as the 'Three Wise Men' or 'Three Kings'—are easily the most famous of the visitors who appear at Jesus' birth (sic) ... Whether or not one is a churchgoer, practically everyone has heard of them."[49] So true. Here is the account given in Matthew:

"**After Jesus was born** in Bethlehem in Judea, during the time of King Herod, **Magi from the east** came to Jerusalem and asked, 'Where is the one who has been born king of the Jews? **We saw his star in the east** and have **come to worship him**.'

When King Herod heard this he was disturbed, and all Jerusalem with him. When he had called together all the people's chief priests and teachers of the law, he asked them where the Christ was to be born. 'In Bethlehem in Judea,' they replied, 'for this is what the prophet has written: 'But you, Bethlehem, in the land of Judah, are by no means least among the rulers of Judah; for out of you will come a ruler who will be the shepherd of my people Israel.' [Micah 5:2]

Then Herod called the Magi secretly and found out from them **the exact time the star had appeared**. He sent them to Bethlehem and said, 'Go and make a careful search for the child. As soon as you find him, report to me, so that I too may go and worship him.'

After they had heard the king, they went on their way, and **the star they had seen in the east went ahead of them until it stopped over the place where the child was**. When **they saw the star, they were overjoyed**. On coming to the house, they saw the child with his mother Mary, and they bowed down and worshiped him. Then they opened their treasurers and **presented him with gifts** of gold and of incense and of myrrh. And having been warned in a dream not to go back to Herod, they **returned to their country** by another route.

When they had gone, an angel of the Lord appeared to Joseph in a dream. 'Get up,' he said, 'take the child and his mother and **escape to Egypt**. Stay there until I tell you, for Herod is going to search for the child to kill him.'

So he got up, took the child and his mother during the night and left for Egypt, where he stayed until the death of Herod. And so was fulfilled what the Lord had said through the prophet: 'Out of Egypt I called my son.'

When Herod realized that he had been outwitted by the Magi, he was furious, and he gave **orders to kill all the boys in Bethlehem** and its vicinity who were **two years old and under**, in accordance with the time he had learned from the Magi. Then what was said through the prophet Jeremiah [Jeremiah 31:15] was fulfilled." (Matthew 2:1-17 NIV; clarification and emphasis mine)

What do we know about the Magi from the *biblical* account? They came *"from the east"* to Jerusalem, spoke with Herod and then went to Bethlehem; they had seen *"his star in the east;"* and they came to worship the king of the Jews; they followed the star which *"went ahead of them until it stopped over the place where the child was,"* and they were overjoyed when they saw the star; they brought expensive gifts and worshipped Him; and they returned to their own country. Secular history can add some additional insights.

2. Secular History of the Magi

(a) *Background of Magi*

Church *traditions* give us most of what we associate with the Magi. Church tradition says that there were three of them, although the biblical account does not supply a number. Over the years, the traditions became increasingly embellished—with names given to each of the Magi; they were viewed as kings, etc. Supposed relics from the Magi emerged in the 4th century, transferred from Constantinople to Milan in the 5th century, and transferred to Cologne in 1162, where they are still enshrined. Most of these church traditions might be filed under *wild speculations*.

It is widely believed that the Magi were "a hereditary priesthood of the Medes (known today as the Kurds) credited with profound and extraordinary religious knowledge."[50] Darius the Great established the Magi over the state religion of Persia; they had proved themselves able in the interpretation of dreams. According to Dr. Missler, the Magi were not originally followers of Zoroaster, which came later. They "… became the supreme priestly caste of the Persian empire and continued to be prominent during the subsequent Seleucid, Parthian, and Sasanian periods."[51]

Victor Paul Wierwille is in agreement with Missler's position about the Magi and Zoroasterism. He states the following:

> "Ancient records indicate that the earliest Magi lived in Media and Persia as a religious caste before the time of **Zoroaster** (ca. 600 BC), the founder and prophet of the Zoroastrian religion. Prior to Zoroaster, the Magi religion is thought to have been a type of nature worship.
>
> When *Zoroastrianism* became prominent in Persia, many Magi adopted it as their own and became the priesthood of that religion. Following the death of Zoroaster, the Magi splintered into two major sects: (1) those who continued following the religion of Zoroaster [the "Eastern Magi"],

and (2) those who returned to the ancient forms of nature worship, especially emphasizing sun worship."[52]

What was the teachings of Zoroaster that the Magi from the east (Persia) adhered to at the time of Christ? It is interesting to note the significant parallels between Zoroaster's teachings and those of the Old Testament. Wierwille states the following related to Zoroastrians:

> "Zoroastrians believed in **one supreme God** who created the heavens and the earth, who authored all that is good. They also believed in a spiritual adversary who authored evil. They believed in **a coming redeemer**, a prophet who would be sent by God to save mankind. They strictly forbade the worship of idols. They believed in angels and in devil spirits and the eventual triumph of good over evil. They set forth a system of laws and ethics stressing a strict code of moral behavior."[53]

While the teachings of Zoroaster would have influenced the Magi at the time of Jesus, the influence of Daniel having served in both the Babylonian and Persian courts and being over the "wise men" would have also influenced the Magi's beliefs and would have made them receptive to an astronomic sign in the sky as a sign of a coming Redeemer; this is covered later in this chapter in section B.

(b)   *Magi—Astronomers or Astrologers?*

A question which is frequently asked is whether the Magi were astronomers or astrologers, as astrology is clearly condemned by God in Scripture (Deuteronomy 4:19).

Matthew 2:1 states that the Magi are said to be *"from the east."* They were men "reputed for their knowledge of religion, astronomy, and the spiritual significance of astronomical phenomena."[54] King Herod was interested in obtaining their astronomical observations related to *"the star"* as they were respected for their knowledge of these things. Henry M. Morris states—in his article "When They Saw the Star"— that the Persian Magi in particular "were very competent observational astronomers, not astrologists. If they were not Jews or Jewish proselytes (either of which is a good possibility), they were Zoroastrians, and the Zoroastrian religion was similar to Judaism in many respects, among which was an aversion to astrology."[55]

Even as Zoroastrians, the Magi would *not* have worshipped the stars, as they believed in one supreme God who created the heavens and the earth, so we can assume that they were not astrologers who worshipped the stars. They were, however, very competent astronomers who made careful observations of the starry heavens.

B. Daniel's Influence on the Magi (Timing)

1. Scriptures Available through Daniel to the Wise Men

A strong case can be made for the Magi being students of the Hebrew Scriptures. The knowledge of a future King of the Jews who was to be the Redeemer might have first come to the Magi *"in the east"* through the Scriptures available to them through Daniel and the other Hebrews who took their holy writings with them to Babylon—the Old Testament up to that point (Daniel 9:2a). Daniel was taken captive by the king of the Babylonians, Nebuchadnezzar, in his first attack on Jerusalem in 606-605 BC, when he brought many of the brightest young Jewish men to Babylon to be trained to serve in the Babylonian court.

Because of Daniel's God-given ability to interpret dreams and visions, he was appointed by Nebuchadnezzar (Daniel 4:9) and later by his grandson, Belshazzar, to be *"chief of the magicians [master of the 'Magi'], enchanters, astrologers, and diviners"* (Daniel 5:11 NIV; clarification mine). Daniel also later served in the courts of the Medes (King Darius; Daniel 9:1) and the Persians (King Cyrus; Daniel 10:1). Daniel had an amazingly long term of service in these eastern courts, obviously orchestrated by God.

Undoubtedly, Daniel would have introduced the Magi to the one true God and shared with them the Scriptures which told of the God to whom Daniel prayed daily. After all, Daniel shared with the kings of Babylon, Media and Persia—that his ability to interpret dreams and visions came from his God who is over all things. Surely, he also would have shared with the Magi all these things.

Daniel might very well have shared the prophecy given in the Book of Numbers, the fourth oracle of Balaam, foretelling the coming of a "Promised One" who would be coming in the future: *"A **star will come out of Jacob**; a scepter will rise out of **Israel**"* (Numbers 24:17 NIV; emphasis mine). Although this prophecy does not give a timeframe, it would have provided valuable information that this "star" would come out of Judah in Israel at a future date.

Apparently, Daniel also entrusted the Messianic vision he received to this group of Magi, of which he was over them. He would have told them, as recorded in Daniel 9:21-22, about his visit by the angel Gabriel and the message and vision of the 70 Weeks ("Week" here is a seven-year period) prophecy (Daniel 9:24-27). Contained within this prophecy is the teaching that after 69 Weeks (69 x 7 = 483 years) *"the Anointed One [the Redeemer, Jesus] will be cut off, but not for himself"* (Daniel 9:26 NIV). Hence, the Magi would have known from Daniel the precise timeframe for this Jewish Messiah, prophesized in the Scriptures, to come and later die in Jerusalem. It is not hard to imagine that Daniel entrusted the later generations of the Magi to welcome the Redeemer, when He came to be born in Bethlehem (Micah 5:2).

Over the next 500 years, these important prophecies would surely have been passed down among the Magi from generation to generation. When the Magi at the time of the birth of Jesus saw what was to them unmistakable cosmic signs, their observations of the heavens and their writings would have alerted them to the birth of this prophesized Jewish Messiah. Wild camels could not have held them back from going to see this King of the Jews and bring Him royal gifts. And so it was.

2. Gifts of the Magi—From Daniel?

So, how did the Magi know to bring the specific gifts of gold, frankincense and myrrh (Matthew 2:11) when they came to pay homage to the young child, Jesus? Perhaps, this too was instruction by Daniel and passed down from generation to generation of the Magi. The gold and frankincense were customary gifts brought to kings (Isaiah 60:6). Perhaps, Daniel instructed that they were to also bring myrrh, used to anoint a body before burial. Knowing that the *Anointed One* would be *"cut off"* indicated His physical death.

Matthew's Gospel tells us that these three specific gifts, perfect to represent Jesus' ministry, were brought by the Magi—gold speaks of His kingship (the true King of kings), frankincense was a spice used in priestly duties (the perfect High Priest), and myrrh was an embalming ointment anticipating His death (the supreme Savior of men who came to die for mankind's sins).

How did the Magi understand the aspects of Jesus' ministry when those in Jerusalem did not? Once again, Daniel seems to be the answer. Some Bible commentators have speculated that these very gifts brought by the Magi might even have been provided by Daniel himself and kept for the appointed time for the Magi to take to the Messiah. Nelson Walters presents this possibility with the following comments:

> "These were the gifts of a wealthy man. Was Daniel wealthy enough to leave these gifts as an inheritance? We have learned already that Nebuchadnezzar made Daniel Chief of the Magi. Later he was made chief administrator of two kingdoms, both Babylon and Persia under four different kings ... He was most likely a eunuch. Nebuchadnezzar entrusted all the young Hebrew captives to the *'Master of the Eunuchs'* in Daniel 1:3. Being wealthy and having no heir would make it completely likely that Daniel might leave his fortune as an inheritance to give to the messiah.

This is a tradition that [is] known throughout the Middle East. That Daniel did leave his vast fortune to provide for the study of astronomy among the Magi and for gifts for them to carry to the messiah upon his birth. The Bible does not collaborate this tradition. We will never truly know if it's true until we ask Daniel ourselves in the millennial kingdom. Personally, I hope it is true. I think it adds to the character of one of God's greatest saints that even in his death he provided all he had for his Messiah."[56]

Of course, the gift of the gold was indeed timely as it gave the earthly parents of Jesus, Joseph and Mary, the needed funds to travel to Egypt with the young child Jesus and stay there until after the death of King Herod (Matthew 2:13-15), then return to Nazareth and set up home there again (Matthew 19-23).

We know that Joseph and Mary were poor in earthly possessions before the Magi arrived with their gifts, as they were only able to bring *"a pair of doves or two young pigeons"* to the Temple presentation of Jesus (Luke 2:24b). This was following Mary's time of purification after Jesus' birth (after the 8 days before He was circumcised and an additional 33 days for Mary's time of purification). They brought two birds as they could not afford a customary lamb offering (Leviticus 12:8).

Obviously, the Magi made their visit and gave their gifts, including the gold, *after* this first Temple visit of Jesus. Hence, this is evidence that the Magi did *not* arrive and give their gifts on the day of Jesus' birth. Unfortunately, church tradition has it wrong again; the church manger scenes typically show the Magi standing around the newly born Jesus—the Magi did not arrive when Jesus was born or even when he was an infant; they arrived in Bethlehem when the family moved from Nazareth to Bethlehem, when Jesus was a "toddler," as is covered in the next chapter, Chapter 7. This timing of the arrival of the Magi is our *Puzzle Piece #4* and is further explained in Chapter 7: "*Puzzle Piece #5–Star of Bethlehem and Magi's Visit.*"

CHAPTER 7

Puzzle Piece #5– Star of Bethlehem and Magi's Visit

The Star of Bethlehem and the Magi's visit to Bethlehem are forever linked in the minds of believers in Jesus. The reason, of course, is that Scripture links them together.

A. What Did the Magi See in the Sky?

1. Biblical Description of the Star (Matthew 2:2b,9b)

There are two verses in the Gospel of Matthew which make mention of the Star of Bethlehem which the Magi observed and followed. They are as follows:

> "… *Magi from the east came to Jerusalem and asked, 'Where is the one who has been born king of the Jews? We saw **his star** in the east [or: when it rose] and have come to worship him.*" (Matthew 2:1b-2 NIV; clarification and emphasis mine)

*"After they had heard the king, they went on their way, and **the star** they had seen in the east [or: seen when it rose] went ahead of them until it stopped over the place where the child was. When they saw **the star**, they were overjoyed."*
(Matthew 2:9-10 NIV; clarification and emphasis mine)

From these couple of verses, we see that the star was defined by the Magi as *"his star"* and that it was seen when it rose in the east when they were in Persia. Later, the star seemingly moved in the sky, heading in a southern direction as the Magi travelled from Jerusalem to Bethlehem. The *"star"* then stopped any movement and was directly overhead when the Magi arrived at the place where Jesus was in Bethlehem. These are all wonderful clues to help identify the *"star."*

The details about this "Star of Bethlehem" is our *Puzzle Piece #5* in our case for determining the true birthdate of Jesus.

2. Unusual Astronomical Activity in the Years 3 to 2 BC

So, what cosmic events would have focused the Magi's attention and caused them to travel the long distance to Jerusalem and then to Bethlehem in search of the One born King of the Jews? This investigation is really interesting and leads to a pearl of great price, so to speak.

As it turns out, the night sky was literally ablaze with signs in the Zodiac written in the heavens, occurring in the years immediately before the birth of Jesus and a couple of years after. These signs in the heavens were discerned and interpreted by the Magi, but the Jews in Jerusalem seemingly had no clue and did not recognize the signs. Perhaps, they did not even see the signs in the heavens as they were not trained in the movements of the heavenly bodies and, sadly, were not even looking for a Messiah who had been prophesized to come per Daniel's prophecy (Daniel 9:26).

Certainly *"the heavens were declaring the glory of God"* (Psalm 19:1), and God was giving signs all over the heavens. However, these were not like the obvious sign which Moses saw of the burning bush, causing him to turn aside and investigate further (Exodus 3:1-6). The signs in the heavens which the Magi saw were much more subtle, and indications are that King Herod and the Jews did not even notice them.

Martin sums up the cosmic signs during the period 7 BC to 2 BC:

> "We are told in the New Testament that the main factor that brought the Magi to Jerusalem was 'his star.' What star or heavenly body could this have been? Though there was an interesting **conjunction [alignment of**

two or more planets or a planet and a star] of Jupiter and Saturn in **7 BC** with **Mars** forming a triangular aspect with those planets in early **6 BC**, the planets at that time were at least two diameters of the Moon away from one another and they could not in any way be considered as a single 'star.' ['The conjunctions of **Mars, Jupiter, and Saturn**, occurring in Pisces, are the ones some present-day historians feel were connected with the signs indicated by Matthew in his account of the birth of Christ']. As for the years of **5 and 4 BC**, there was nothing of astronomical importance that would have impressed anyone to journey to Jerusalem. But in **3 and 2 BC, the whole heavens burst forth with astronomical signs and wondrous displays**. It may well be, that the celestial occurrences in this latter period of time were the very ones that prompted the Magi to go to Jerusalem."[57]

Another writer states, "The year **3/2 BC** stood far above any near contenders for a period of exceptional signs in the heavens to herald Christ's birth (Genesis 1:14)."[58] What kind of signs? Beginning in August, 3 BC, and ending December, 2 BC, a number of conjunctions of planets occurred (involving Jupiter, Venus, Mercury, Mars, and Saturn); in addition, movements of planets in key constellations associated with the Messiah occurred [Leo the lion, Virgo the virgin, and Cancer the crab ("rest secured")]; and planetary conjunctions with key stars occurred [Jupiter with Regulus (the "King star"—in the constellation of Leo, the "Royal Constellation")].[59, 60] This was quite a show in the heavens for those trained to see it!

What caught the Magi's eyes? What might have been the *first* celestial event that caught the Magi's attention when they were in Persia---that heralded the upcoming birth of the Messiah, Jesus Christ? In the words of Wierwille, it probably "… began in August of 3 BC, when Jupiter the king planet became visible above the eastern horizon as a morning star, seen by the Magi 'in the rising.' On August 12, Jupiter came into conjunction with Venus, the bright and morning star, in the constellation of Leo, the sign of Judah."[61] This might be the *"first sighting"* which the Magi later communicated to King Herod when they were questioned by him after arriving in Jerusalem. Perhaps, the Magi started preparing for their long trip to Jerusalem to find the Jewish Messiah after this initial sighting. The Magi undoubtedly were in awe of Jupiter's multiple celestial displays in 3/2 BC and the significance of these, which they deciphered.

The conjunction of Jupiter, the "King planet," had a highly-unusual three conjunctions with Regulus, the "King star," occurring on September 14, 3 BC; February 17, 2 BC; and on May 8, 2 BC. Then on June 17, 2 BC, Jupiter again came into conjunction with Venus, when the two planets came into a rare close conjunction and formed a dramatic brilliant "star" in the western night sky. On August 27, 2 BC Jupiter came into conjunction with Mars in another dramatic astronomical configuration.[62]

Related to the constellations and their component stars, the planets, and the Magi's interpretation of everything, Joseph A. Seiss has proposed the following insight:

> "How, then did these Magi come to know so much about Christ as an adorable King and Saviour? How did they come to such full conviction that His birth had occurred in Judea? The true answer is: **By the signs and constellations of the primeval astronomy, and the legends connected with them, interpreted as we have been contemplating them in these Lectures** [his book] ... **It was to Jesus ... that the primeval astronomy conducted these remote Gentiles believers** [Magi]."[63]

B. What Was the Star of Bethlehem?

1. Was the "Star" a Real Star?

Martin states, "The language that Matthew employed to describe the Star of the Magi strongly suggests that it was an ordinary star **or planet**."[64] He further notes:

> "The word '**star**' in the first century could refer to a **planet** as well as a **fixed star**. Could the 'star' have been the planet **Jupiter**? The historical records recorded in the New Testament about the 'Star of the Messiah' chronologically occurred precisely at this time [May, 3 BC to December, 2 BC], and this is the period early Christian scholars [first few centuries after death of Apostles] said Jesus was born."[65]

The primary occupation of the Magi was the study of the motions of the heavenly bodies, and all indications from Matthew's Gospel are that this is what the Magi were basing their decisions on in going to Jerusalem and Bethlehem. After all, they were professional observers and expert interpreters of the heavenly signs involving the sun, moon, planets and stars. This certainly falls within the parameters of Genesis 1:14, and King Herod and the Jewish authorities would *not* have found such interpretations by the Magi as being strange or outside the bounds of Scripture—in fact, Herod asked the Magi for the exact time that they had seen *"the star"* appear.

2. Various Theories of the "Star"

Over the centuries, Bible commentators have proposed various theories for what the *"star"* was which guided the Magi to Bethlehem. Most of the theories can be eliminated easily by comparing them to the biblical description of the object and its movement in the heavens. Let's look at the options.

- Was it a ***comet***? Most probably not, as comets were almost always interpreted as being harbingers of evil, not of good—as the *"star"* of the Magi certainly suggests. Colin R. Nicholl in his recent book, *The Great Christ Comet---Revealing the True Star of Bethlehem*,[66] makes the case for a *long-period comet*, appearing in the heavens in 6 BC as being the "star." Although the amount of research on comets by Nicholl is impressive, I, however, am not convinced by his case, especially the 6 BC date assigned to the comet, which I judge to not be in alignment with the 3 BC date of Jesus' birth—supported by all the evidence presented in this book.

- Was it an ***actual star, Super Nova,*** or a ***new star***? Probably not an actual star, as stars do not move in relationship to other stars, nor do they stop in the heavens to remain over a particular location on earth.

  In addition, the position of a fixed star in the heavens varies at most one degree each day so a fixed star could not have moved before the Magi as to lead them to Bethlehem. A nova, which is a star which suddenly increases in brightness then gradually grows dimmer, is not a good possibility either as Matthew records two separate appearances of the "star" (Matthew 2:2 and 2:9), and a nova will seldom flare up more than once, and very rarely will it repeat its initial brilliance. Some have postulated Haley's Comet—there was an appearance of Haley's Comet in 12 BC, but that is too early to align with other historical records surrounding the birth of Christ.

- Was it ***God's Shekinah Glory***? Probably not from the description of a "star" rising in the east and other biblical descriptions.

- Was it, specifically, a ***"Shekinah Glory" orb of light***? Probably not. If so, it could have been observed as hovering over Bethlehem at an altitude of about 38+ miles—visible on the western horizon to the Magi in Persia—and later as hovering above the house of Jesus in Bethlehem to guide the Magi to the Christ child. This theory has been proposed in a paper by Andrew Webster. The theory, however, is most probably not realistic, as a bright orb of light present for a period of over 15 months (from the birth of Jesus to the Magi's appearance at Jesus' house in Bethlehem) would likely have been noticed by Herod and his court officials. In addition, it does not align with Scripture as *"when it rose"* [some translations *"in the east,"* which, admittedly, may not be the correct translation]; therefore, not being stationary in the sky. It is more likely that what the Magi observed was a cosmic sign that was "hidden in plain sight," moved in the heavens, and was uniquely deciphered by them.

- Was it an ***angel***? Probably not, from the biblical description. Angels are not spoken of as being "signs" in Scripture, although their appearance certainly brought information and help.

- Was it a ***miracle***? One could say that all the heavenly bodies and their precise movements are miracles, but it seems that the best explanation of the *"star"* is that it was within the natural realm of other stars and planets within the Magi's understanding and knowledge.

- Was it a ***planetary conjunction***? A planetary conjunction is the aligning of either two or more planets, or a planet and a star, as seen by an observer on earth. The problem with this theory is that a conjunction of two planets, even if they were seen to have merged one over the other, simply can't be referred to in the singular as a *"star."* Also, conjunctions of two or more planets do not move together for long periods of time. However, planetary conjunctions are notable and certainly would have caught the eye of the Magi, especially occurring in key constellations, and conjunctions very well might have been considered a sign to them of an impending event, including a birth of a great leader.

- Was it a ***planet*** of our solar system? Planets are also referred to as *"stars"* in the first century. This is the *best explanation* for what the Magi saw as the "Star of Bethlehem" and followed and which stopped directly overhead and remained stationary in the heavens over Bethlehem. This type movement is possible with a planet and is further discussed below.

3. Was the "Star" Indeed Most Probably a Planet (Jupiter)?

Planets are sometimes called *"wandering stars."* The main reason for believing that the "Star of Bethlehem" was a *planet* (and most probably ***Jupiter***) is that planets can exhibit strange behavior in the heavens as viewed from earth—*standing still* in the heavens and appearing stationary compared to the backdrop of the stars which, due to the rotation of the earth, appear as rotating as a group across our sky. This behavior of planets is exactly as described in Matthew, *"... the star they* *had seen in the east **went ahead of them** until it **stopped over the place** where the child was"* (Matthew 2:9b NIV; emphasis mine).

The ability of planets to stand still in the heavens is due to their rotation around our sun in relation to the earth's rotation about the sun. Because the rotations of planets and the earth around the sun are on different rotation paths and different speeds of rotation around the sun, this can cause "stationary" and even "retrograde motion" in the sky for an observer on earth.

This description of the star standing still has caused many to characterize the whole account in Matthew as either fictitious or a miraculous event. Most people have difficulty in imagining a normal heavenly body having the capability of stopping its movement over a small village in Judea. However, this is merely describing a celestial phenomenon in common language, of which an astronomer and those acquainted with basic planetary motions would have been fully aware. Martin explains it:

> "Planets do come to a 'stop' at prescribed times in their heavenly motions. This happens at the time for a planet's **retrogression** and **progression**. It may be that Matthew was simply showing that Jupiter had become *stationary* in its motions through the fixed stars at the time it reached its zenith over Bethlehem.
>
> The theologian F. Steinmetzer, back in 1912, wrote an article stating his belief that Matthew was referring to one of these normal 'stationary' positions of the **planets**.[67] Indeed, Steinmetzer suggested that the **planet** that suited Matthew's account the best was **Jupiter**. This is true."[68]

Figure 7.1 illustrates the occasional retrograde motion observed on earth of planets like Jupiter. This motion can also make the planet appear stationary in the sky for a period of time, as was the case of the "Star of Bethlehem" stopping overhead as the Magi observed it over Bethlehem when they arrived there.

A schematic of how retrograde motion works when Earth (T) passes an outer planet (P) as they both orbit the sun (S). The changing viewing angle from Earth makes the projection of the planet against the celestial sphere (A) move backwards (A2-A4) as we pass the slower planet.

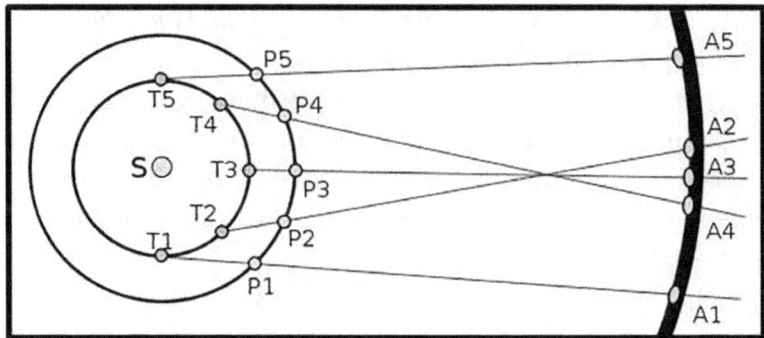

Figure 7.1. Illustration of Retrograde Motion of a Planet Compared to Another Planet

So, what is the best identification for the "Star of Bethlehem?" The planet *Jupiter*, due to its movements in the heavens is the best candidate. *Jupiter* is the "King planet" and the Magi would have observed its movements, including its conjunctions with other planets and conjunctions with the star Regulus, the "King star"—all this occurring in the timeframe stated by Daniel for the coming of the Messiah. Jupiter (Hebrew name *Tzedek*) is the same conclusion made by Dwight Hutchison in his recent book, *The Lion Led the Way* (Editions Signes Celestes, Third Edition, 2016, p. 333). Further description is provided in the next section related to the date of the visitation of the Magi in Bethlehem—*December 25, 2 BC*.

C. Visitation of Magi—Exact Date: December 25, 2 BC

What information can we bring together to help us determine the actual day that the Magi arrived in Bethlehem to see and worship the Christ child and present their gifts? First, we have to separate fact from fiction. The church tradition that the Magi arrived in Bethlehem just after the birth of Jesus makes for a nice photo-op—showing "baby" Jesus, Joseph and Mary, the animals, the shepherds, and the Magi all together in the "stable," following the birth of Jesus. This *traditional* picture is, however, purely fiction. The Magi did not arrive just after the birth of Jesus but came 15 months later.

The Magi would have undergone a journey of 1000–1200 miles by either horse (some suggest that the regal Magi traveled by horse) or by camels. Such a distance may have taken an estimated three to 12 months by camel, and besides the travel time, there were probably many weeks of preparation. Hence, it has been estimated that "The Magi could scarcely have reached Jerusalem till a year or more had elapsed from the time of the appearance of the star."[70]

WHEN WAS JESUS BORN?

In fact, the Magi did not arrive right after the birth of Jesus. It is implied in the Gospel message that when the Magi visited with King Herod in Jerusalem, they reported that they had first seen the star rising in the east (Matthew 2:1–2, 7), signaling to them that a great king had been born. They, however, arrived over a year later—after following the "star" on their journey from Persia. Matthew 2:11 states that the Magi saw Jesus as a *"young child"* (Greek: *paidion*; Aramaic: *talya*; a "toddler," not a baby/infant!) and found him in *"the house"* (not a stable!)—where the Magi bowed down and worshipped him. However, at the actual time of the birth of Jesus, the angel announced to the shepherds in the field that a Savior (Jesus) had been born, and that they would find the "baby" (Greek: *brephos*; Aramaic: *ula*) in a "manger" (Luke 2:11–12). Clearly, the Magi came at a later date, where they found a *child* in a house, not a *babe* in a stable.

Here is my summary of the complete story from Matthew's and Luke's Gospels of the events after Jesus' birth, showing when the visit of the Magi fits into the chronology.

> After the birth of Jesus on *September 11, 3 BC* (per the evidence presented in this Part I), Luke's account states that the baby Jesus was circumcised (at 8-days old) and then presented in the Temple (following the additional days allotted for the purification of "them," including Mary—an additional 33-day period for the birth of a male, per Leviticus 12:1–8). Still no Magi. Then Luke states that **the family returned to *Nazareth***, after Jesus was presented at the Temple (Luke 2:39)—this is often overlooked! A short time later, **the family moved back to *Bethlehem*** when Jesus was a year old or so. Matthew 2 picks up the story in Bethlehem with **the visit of the Magi** at *this* time (Matthew 2:9–12). Subsequently, per a warning in a dream, the family immediately escapes to Egypt (Matthew 2:13–15). Herod kills the children in Bethlehem, *"two years old and under"* (Matthew 2:16–18)—Herod picked this age range to insure himself of killing Jesus. In Egypt Joseph was informed by an angel that Herod was dead, and the family moved back to Israel and settled back in *Nazareth* (Matthew 2:19–23), where the young Jesus grew up. This is the summary of Jesus' life for the first few years.

So, what was the date that the Magi arrived at the house in Bethlehem to worship the Christ child and present their gifts? Once again, it gets back to astronomy to help us arrive at the date. Matthew described two distinct appearances of the same "star." The first appearance is described in Matthew 2:2 where this star was first observed by the Magi in their homeland; they saw it *"in the rising"* above the eastern horizon. The other appearance to the Magi is described in Matthew 2:9, when they left Jerusalem for Bethlehem and the star is described as going ahead of them and *stopping* over the place where Jesus was (Matthew 2:9b). As discussed previously, this *"star"* was most probably the planet *Jupiter*, the "King planet." We have seen previously that a planet can exhibit this strange behavior of appearing to stop in the heavens.

At the end of 2 BC, on the Gregorian Calendar, Jupiter arrived at its ordinary time for *retrogression*, and it became *stationary* among the stars. It was at this time in *December of 2 BC* that this something unusual happened, and Martin describes the details of this particular occurrence:

> "But this time something unusual happened. In 2 B.C. as viewed from Jerusalem, Jupiter came to its normal *stationary* position directly over Bethlehem on December 25th. That's right! Just before dawn (the regular time the Magi would have begun their normal observations of the heavens), Jupiter came to a 'stopped' position on December 25th directly over Bethlehem as witnessed from Jerusalem. Not only that, the planet assumed its *stationary* position while in the middle of the constellation of Virgo, *the Virgin*. What a remarkable circumstance this was.
>
> … We are told in the New Testament that Jesus was born of a virgin. And precisely on **December 25, 2 B.C.** Jupiter 'stopped' in the abdomen region of Virgo, *the Virgin* (in the middle of the constellation). This position was right where a woman carries a child in pregnancy. On that day the 'King planet' stopped its lateral motion through the stars and remained *stationary* for about six days. During those days it did not move longitudinally more than one fortieth of the Moon's diameter from its *December 25th* position. To an observer on earth it appeared completely *stationary* in the midst of Virgo.
>
> … How was it possible for Jupiter to be stationary over the *village* of Bethlehem at this time? There is not the slightest problem for it to do so … On **December 25, 2 B.C** … Jupiter would have been seen in meridian position (directly over Bethlehem) at an elevation of 68 degrees above the southern horizon. This position would show **the planet shining directly down on Bethlehem** while it was stationary among the stars."[71]

So, how could the Magi have noted that Jupiter was precisely stationary over the small village of Bethlehem? This is a remarkable statement. Remember that there was a well located near the gate of the entrance into Bethlehem, of which David, a thousand years previously, had longed for a drink of water during a military encounter: *"David longed for water and said, 'Oh, that someone would get me a drink of water from **the well near the gate of Bethlehem!**'"* (2 Samuel 23:15–16, NIV; emphasis mine).

I would speculate that the Magi, upon arriving at Bethlehem, stopped at the gate to have a drink of water from the well located *"near the gate of Bethlehem,"* and upon looking down at the still water in the well, saw the reflection of Jupiter, the "King planet" which they had been following in the night sky during their short journey from Jerusalem to Bethlehem. Seeing the reflection of Jupiter down in the well indicated that the planet was *directly overhead Bethlehem* that night, as stated in Matthew 2:9-10. This is too good to miss, and it surely was a confirmation to the Magi that they were in the right place of which Jesus, the Jewish Messiah, had been born and where they were to find Him. Granted, this is speculation that the Magi might have used this well at the gate to Bethlehem to determine that the "star" was directly overhead, but it may not be too far-fetched. Of course, this would only have worked at night when the Jupiter would have been visible, but this is possible after the Magi stopped to meet with Herod in Jerusalem earlier in the day that they arrived in Bethlehem. Yes, it is conjecture, but I like the idea that this well might have been used to help point the Gentiles (Magi) to Jesus! At night, the well would not be crowded, and the well was *"near the gate of Bethlehem."* I would think that the Magi would not have passed up the opportunity of giving themselves and their camels/horses a drink from the well. Perhaps, the Magi used this well before they sought the source of "Living Water."

Was *December 25, 2 BC* the date that the Magi arrived in Bethlehem to greet and worship the Savior and present their gifts? Certainly, the unusual astronomical signs of Jupiter being *stationary* directly over Bethlehem and while it was in the constellation of *Virgo*, would support this date for the Magi's visit. All other timeframes related to the actual birthdate of Jesus being *September 11, 3 BC*, including the timeframe for the Magi to arrive there after their long trip from Persia, would support the *December 25, 2 BC* date for the Magi's visit. This visit was exactly 15 months after the birth of Jesus, per the sign of His birth given in Revelation 12:1–6.

D. Magi's Visit and the Jewish Feast of Hanukkah

It is interesting to note that *December 23, 2 BC* corresponded on the Hebrew calendar to *Hanukkah* in that year. *Hanukkah* is an *eight-day* Feast which commemorated the time in 164 BC when the Temple had been cleansed of defilement, caused by Gentile idols placed there by Antiochus Epiphanes. In the 9th month of *Kislev* on the Jewish calendar (see Chapter 6 of *The Last Shofar!*)), on the 25th day of *Kislev*, the Temple services were begun again by the Maccabees, after the Temple had been desolate of its holiness for three years.

Hence, *Hanukkah* (Hebrew: means "dedication") was a festival of Dedication (actually, Re-dedication) of the Temple and of the Jewish people to the God of Abraham and Moses. The Jews viewed *Hanukkah* as a second Feast of Tabernacles, the prior Feast on the Jewish calendar. It was a time of festivity and celebration, and no fast or mourning was permitted during those eight days. Lamps and torches lighted the Temple, synagogues and all homes during this time. Josephus called the festival "the Feast of Lamps."[72]

December 25, 2 BC, the most probable date for the Magi visiting Jesus, occurred in that year on the *third day* of the *Hanukkah* celebration in Israel. This was a traditional time of giving gifts. It is interesting that in this unique calendar circumstance in 2 BC, the Magi would have also given their gifts to the Jewish child (Jesus) during the *Hanukkah* festivities ongoing at the time.

It is also interesting to note that from calculation of the birth of John the Baptist (near *March 10, 3 BC*—see Chapter 3, B.) and the birth of Jesus (*September 11, 3 BC*), being six months following that of John, this would place the *conception* of Jesus in *December of 4 BC* (assuming the normal 9-months-and-10-days gestation period). Hence, this timing of Jesus' conception was very probably during the eight-day period of *Hanukkah* in 4 BC. If so, this would align the actual conception of Jesus in 4 BC with the later visit of the Magi in 2 BC, both during the celebration of *Hanukkah* on the Jewish calendar. What a gift to the world from God the Father, at *Hanukkah*, that the conception of the Messiah was!

E. How Did the Magi Find Jesus' Specific House?

Once the Magi arrived in Bethlehem, having been "led" by the Star of Bethlehem, whatever that "star" was, the next question is how did the Magi know how to arrive specifically at the house where Jesus was located? This is another mystery and is often not addressed by commentators. Scripture states:

> ***"The star which they saw in the east went before them until it had come and stood over where the child was.*** *And seeing the star, they rejoiced exceedingly (with) a great joy. And having come into the house, they saw the child with his mother Mary. And falling down, they worshiped Him."*
> (Matthew 2:9–11a *Interlinear Bible*; emphasis mine.)

What is unclear from the literal translation of the *Interlinear Bible* is whether the "star" stood over the town of Bethlehem or somehow stood over the specific house where Jesus was located. If the "star" was Jupiter, the King's planet, as this case concludes, then the planet could have been both over Bethlehem as well as over the house. As mentioned previously, by looking down into a deep well and seeing the reflection of the planet in the center of the surface of the water below, the planet would be precisely overhead (Matthew 2:9–10), confirming to the Magi that the star had led them to the precise place they were seeking.

However, how did the Magi know which specific house they were to go to once they arrived at Bethlehem? Of course, the option of the Star of Bethlehem being an orb of Shekinah Glory hovering close over the house occupied by Jesus would have precisely pinpointed the specific house. However, in my opinion, there are numerous problems with this theory, one of which is that this would have also alerted Herod's soldiers in Bethlehem as to the location of Jesus.

If it was not due to the "star" hovering close over the house occupied by Jesus and Joseph/Mary, what are other possible ways that God might have used to communicate the location to the Magi? This is conjecture, but it might have been by the same means that God communicated to the shepherds in the field 15 months prior—**announcing by an angel** the birth of Jesus (Luke 2:9–12), giving them a cryptic description of the whereabouts of Jesus, which they understood (see our case for *Migdal Edar* in Section B of Part I). Another possible means could have been similar to **Simeon being drawn by the Spirit** to meet Jesus when He came to the temple to be presented to the Lord, and *"by the Spirit he [Simeon] came into the temple"* (Luke 2:27). Another possible method would have been for the Magi to **merely inquire** about the whereabouts of a young child of 15 months age being a descendant of the family of David. Being a tight-knit community, "everybody" would have known this and could have directed the regal Magi to the specific house.

No, we don't know all the details of how the Magi knew which house to find the child, Jesus. However, considering the two ways in which God used to notify key people—the shepherds in the field and Simeon in the temple—related to the birth of Jesus, are also possible ways which God might have used to point the Magi to the house in which Jesus was residing in Bethlehem. In my opinion, these possibilities help to bridge this unknown which is not covered in the gospel accounts.

Yes, God could have used a "Shekinah Glory" orb of light hovering above the house of Jesus to notify the Magi of the location of Jesus in Bethlehem. My point is that there are other means of communication which God could have used within the scope of our case for the planet Jupiter (the King planet) being the Star of Bethlehem, which better fit with the other puzzle pieces we have assembled. I think our case for Jupiter being the "Star of Bethlehem" is still the stronger case looking at all the evidence.

The study of the background of the Magi and when they came to visit Jesus are our *Puzzle Pieces #4* and *#5*. We can next look at what Roman history tells us—our *Puzzle Piece #6*.

CHAPTER 8

Puzzle Piece #6–Roman History

Chronological indicators as presented in this Section A of Part I point to 3 BC (*September 11, 3 BC*) as the nativity of Jesus. Are there *secular historical records* which have come down to us that confirm this as the proper birthdate of Jesus? Yes, and this is *Puzzle Piece #6*.

A. The "Dark Decade" in History—6 BC to AD 4

Yes, there are secular historical records which help confirm Jesus' birthdate, but it must be recognized that, unfortunately, secular records are very scanty for the Roman Empire for the years around the birth of Jesus---for the period from 6 BC to AD 4. Martin has stated, "It is a common lament among Roman historians that this ten-year period (one of the most important in the history of western civilization) bristles with many historical and chronological difficulties because of garbled or imperfect records that have come down to us."[73] This has been echoed by Sir Ronald Syme when he wrote about "… the hazards inherent in the **obscure decade** 6 B.C. – A.D. 4."[74]

It should also be recognized that even Josephus presents several difficulties during this particular period. Martin writes,

"One must exercise caution in reading of **Josephus**—especially in chronological affairs from about **9 B.C. to A.D. 6**. We do not know why Josephus in that period neglected to give cross-references to internationally recognized eras of time, but he was negligent! And this is precisely where our problem lies. Not only are the records from Roman historians very deficient at this period of time (it was when that **dark decade** was in effect), but Josephus himself fails us too when it comes to precise chronological indications. It is no wonder historians are confused regarding the time of Jesus' birth."[75]

In spite of deficiencies in secular historians' records for the period around Jesus' birth, the early Christian historians were remarkably consistent in showing that Jesus was certainly born *after* 4 BC, and *not* before 4 BC, which is, unfortunately, held so firmly by scholars today. However, in opposition to the scholars of today, the overwhelming majority of early Christian historians stated that Jesus was born between 3 BC – 2 BC.[76]

B. Roman History Preceding Jesus' Birth

Obviously, the purpose of this Section A of Part I is not to cover all history and all information related to the chronology of the birth of Jesus. Related to the area of Roman history preceding Jesus' birth, it is necessary to "go light" on coverage due to space limitations. However, a few particularly pertinent historical items related to the birth of Jesus are covered: 1) the period of glory of Rome and the award of the *Pater Patriae* to Caesar Augustus, and 2) the Census of Quirinius.

1. Significant Roman Events Happening—the Glory of Rome and Augustus

The period of 3 BC – 2 BC was especially important to Rome. This was a period of celebrating the glory of Rome. Throughout the Roman Empire, all the political areas of the imperial domains were in festival and celebration. In 2 BC, Caesar Augustus celebrated his 25th jubilee year of being emperor of the Romans, counted from the time he was proclaimed "Augustus" on January 16, 27 BC. This date of 2 BC also coincided with the 750th year of the founding of Rome.[77] This was a period focused on the glory of Rome.

Also occurring in 2 BC, Augustus was given his most prestigious title: *Pater Patriae* (Father of the Country). The Roman Senate bestowed the award on February

5, 2 BC (the Day of Concord). This award to Augustus is significant related to the chronology for the birth of Jesus because in the year prior to the award, in 3 BC, a decree went out from Augustus that required *"the entire Roman people"* throughout all the territories of the Empire to register their *oath of allegiance* to Augustus related to his receiving the *Pater Patriae* award.[78] This is the *census* spoken of by Luke:

> *"In those days Caesar Augustus issued a decree that **a census** should be taken of the entire Roman world. (This was the first census that took place while **Quirinius** was governor of Syria.) ... So Joseph went from the town of Nazareth in Galilee to Judea, to Bethlehem the town of David, because he belonged to the house and line of David. He went there **to register** with Mary ..."* (Luke 2:1-5a NIV; emphasis mine.)

It is important to note that this census/oath/registration mentioned in Luke took place in the summer to early fall of 3 BC, which aligns with the proposed date of *September 11, 3 BC* for the birth of Jesus. Ramsay stated that the normal time for Roman censuses was from August to October;[79] not in late autumn, winter, or early spring during the rainy season. The timing for this census in 3 BC (from August to October) is further supporting evidence for the birth of Jesus in September, 3 BC—as Luke's Gospel states about Joseph and Mary traveling to Bethlehem related to a census.

All the celestial signs observed by the Magi and interpreted by them as related to the King of kings, were also observed in Rome and interpreted as relating to *Augustus* and the dawn of a new and glorious day for Rome with their celebrations. The planet Jupiter was reckoned as the "guardian and ruler of the Empire and it was supposed to determine the course of all human affairs."[80] Obviously, the Magi were not impressed with the claims of Rome related to the celestial signs in the heavens, as the Magi went to *Bethlehem* rather than *Rome* to find the Christ child.

2. Census of Quirinius

Luke said that Jesus was born at a census/registration when *Quirinius* (KJV: *Cyrenius*) was *"governor of Syria."* This reference by Luke has caused a big problem for historians as they have reported that they could not find any record of a census of Quirinius which occurred from 7 BC to 1 BC.

There is undisputed evidence that Quirinius (Sulpicius Quirinius) was governor of Syria beginning in *AD 6/7* and that he conducted a census at *that* time, as mentioned also by Luke in Acts 5:37. Martin has stated:

"... up to now, no available information has been discovered to show that Quirinius was an *administrator* (and a census taker) in 3/2 B.C. or in previous years. This new historical research, however, can find that census of Quirinius in the historical records which took place at Jesus' nativity."[81]

At first, there appears to be a real problem with the historical records. The confusion involves three characters involved in the governance of Syria in various capacities in the general timeframe of the birth of Jesus—Quintilius Varus, Sentius Saturninus, and Sulpicius Quirinius. The names are enough to cause one's head to spin. From coins found and testimony of Josephus and other records, we find that Quintilius Varus was twice governor of Syria—from 7 or 6 BC to 4 BC; and a second time from 2 BC to AD 1.[82] In between those two governorships by Quintilius Varus, Sentius Saturninus was governor of Syria from 4 BC to 2 BC; this is per a statement made by Josephus.[83] Chart 8.1 shows all the data taken together, forming a reasonable picture of the governors of Syria for the period of 7 BC to AD 1.[84]

Governor of Syria	Dates
Quintilius Varus	7 or 6 BC to 4 BC
Sentius Saturninus	4 BC to 2 BC
Quintilius Varus (2nd time)	2 BC to AD 1

Figure 8.1. Governors of Syria for 7 BC to AD 1

Of course, the key question is what about *Quirinius* (Sulpicius Quirinius vs. Quintilius Varus), mentioned in Luke's Gospel as being *"governor of Syria"* in all this line-up of rulers of Syria previously mentioned? Some have said that Luke got his facts mixed-up with the census of Quirinius of AD 6/7, as there was a census at that time and there is undisputed evidence that Quirinius was governor of Syria in AD 6 to AD 7. So, what is going on with Luke's account? Where is Quirinius in the historical records in relationship to the Roman census taken at the time of Jesus birth, as Luke stated? There is an interesting answer which clears up the problem.

Thankfully, Josephus and Tertullian provide clues to straighten out the mystery. This gets a little complicated, but hang in here. The early Christian historian,

WHEN WAS JESUS BORN?

Tertullian, stated that Roman records supported the fact that *censuses* (he used the plural) were conducted at the time of Jesus' birth, in Palestine. Tertullian said they took place at the time when *Saturninus* was governor of Syria, and stated the time as 3/2 BC. This seemingly conflicts with Luke's account. However, this is where Josephus, thankfully, provides an answer to straighten out the mystery. Yes, this is a little complicated, but all this validates Luke's Gospel account. Josephus mentioned that there were "*governors*" (*plural!*) in Syria during the rule of Saturninus.[86] As it turns out, Quirinius indeed conducted the census in Judaea at the time that Saturninus was governor of Syria, but Quirinius had the title of "*procurator*" in Judaea, as stated by the Christian historian, Justin Martyr, and Justin furthermore dated this political role of Quirinius to the time when Jesus was born.[87] These *procurators* were appointed by the Emperor independently of the governor (*legatus*).

It certainly appears that Luke was well aware that Quirinius was in Palestine conducting a registration (census) when Saturninus was the actual official governor in Syria. So, why did Luke call Quirinius "*governor*," as many Bible translators have rendered it, when, in fact, his title was "*procurator*"? Actually, Luke did not use the Greek word *Legatus* ("governor"), but Luke used the Greek word *hegemoneuontos* (a present participle which simply means "ruling" or "administrating") referring to his handling of his duties from the region of Syria. Hence, translators incorrectly used the title "governor" rather than the term "administrating" in Syria or "procurator" for a more accurate description for Quirinius during this term in Syria at the time of Jesus' birth in September 3 BC, which led to this confusion.

But was the census mentioned by Luke involving *taxation*, and, hence, could it be that the "census" conducted by Rome during 3 BC have been mainly for taxation, and, hence, we can't assume that the census of Luke is the census/registration/oath conducted by Rome for the purpose of conferring the title of *Pater Patriae* on Caesar Augustus? Not so. The idea of taxation can be totally discounted. The official censuses involving taxation were in 28 BC and 8 BC, exactly 20 years apart. The next official census according to Augustus was in AD 14. No, the census of Luke was not for taxation purposes but was, indeed, related to Augustus' exaltation to the title of *Pater Patriae*.

All these proper understandings of Roman history summarized here give overwhelming support to the birthdate of Jesus on *September 11, 3 BC*. This date conforms to the "*census of Quirinius*" as stated by Luke and conforms to the well-established Roman census conducted also in 3 BC for Augustus' award.

No wonder that even skeptical historians, who investigate fully and accurately, call Luke a brilliant historian for his accurate historical accounts given. Roman history—our *puzzle piece #6*—and the biblical record are reconciled and support the proposed birth date for Jesus of *September 11, 3 BC*.

CHAPTER 9

Puzzle Piece #7–Death of King Herod

Following the account in Matthew of the visit of the Magi to see and worship the Christ child and the family's escape to Egypt, there is very little stated in the Bible related to the death of Herod and the early years of Jesus' life. Herod's death is, however, mentioned in three verses in the Gospel of Matthew.

A. Biblical Record of Death of Herod (Matthew 2:14–23)

Here is the biblical account of the death of Herod the Great as stated in the Gospel of Matthew:

> *"So he [Joseph] got up, took the child and his mother during the night and left for Egypt, where he stayed until the **death of Herod**. And so was fulfilled what the Lord had said through the prophet: 'Out of Egypt I called my son'*
>
> *When Herod realized that he had been outwitted by the Magi, he was furious, and he gave orders to kill all the boys in Bethlehem and its vicinity*

who were two years old and under, in accordance with the time he had learned from the Magi ...

*After **Herod died**, an angel of the Lord appeared in a dream to Joseph in Egypt and said, 'Get up, take the child and his mother and go to the land of Israel, for **those who were trying to take the child's life are dead.'***

So he got up, took the child and his mother and went to the land of Israel. But when he heard that Archelaus was reigning in Judea in place of his father Herod, he was afraid to go there. Having been warned in a dream, he withdrew to the district of Galilee, and he went and lived in a town called Nazareth. So was fulfilled what was said through the prophets: 'He will be called a Nazarene.'" (Matthew 2:14–16, 19-23 NIV; emphasis mine)

From the biblical account, we can see that Herod died certainly *after* the birth of Jesus and *after* the Magi's visit and *after* the family's sojourn to Egypt for a period.

Why is it important to establish the date of Herod's death? Simply because the birth of Jesus and the visit of the Magi must be prior to Herod's death. For example, if Herod died in 4 BC, then Jesus' birth would have to be *prior* to that date, per the biblical account. If the death of Herod is after *September 11, 3 BC* (birth of Jesus per our case) and after *December 25, 2 BC* (visit of Magi per our case), this would help to *validate* these proposed dates of our case.

The death of Herod is our *Puzzle Piece #7*.

B. Secular History of Death of Herod

The Bible gives very little information to determine the date of Herod's death. What about secular history? Can that provide verifiable information to help us establish the date of Herod's death? Unfortunately, as has been mentioned previously in Chapter 8, reliable secular historical records during the "Dark Decade" of history (6 BC to AD 4) are largely lacking.

Secular history is not much of a help during this period around the death of Herod, but, once again, *astronomy* provides us a very close approximation of the date of Herod's death. This time, rather than the Star of Bethlehem, the planet Jupiter, and constellations in the heavens, a specific **lunar eclipse** is key and is explained in the following subsections.

There are statements by Josephus which can be woven together to help give us a timeframe from a recognizable dated event in the Roman history of Judaea (the

Roman census/oath/registration in Judaea, covered previously), which provides an approximate period of a few months of Herod's death. Martin states, "Josephus mentioned that an *oath of allegiance* was demanded by Augustus ***about twelve or fifteen months*** (12 to 15 months) before the death of Herod. This event would fit nicely with a decree going out from Augustus in 3 B.C ... "[88] We have determined that this is the same census mentioned by Luke (Luke 2:1-5a). Hence, from our date determined for the birth of Jesus (*September 11, 3 BC*), adding 12 to 15 months would equate to September of 2 BC to December of 2 BC for the *approximate* death of Herod. This seems a reasonable approximation, and the pieces of the puzzle are fitting together.

1. Specific Lunar Eclipse After the Death of Herod (Josephus)

(a) *Several Lunar Eclipses Occurred in 7 BC – 1 BC*

Who would think that a lunar eclipse would be so important? But in Herod's death it definitely is! The majority of theologians, in spite of historical evidence against it, have placed the birth of Jesus before the spring of 4 BC. The reason for their insistence on this date is due to a well-known statement by Josephus that *King Herod died soon after a lunar eclipse and before a Passover Feast in the spring.*[89] This referenced lunar eclipse has become an important benchmark in determining the year of Herod's death. There is no arguing with a chronological marker of an eclipse; these dates are well known from astronomical calculations. However, the problem with this is that there were *several* lunar eclipses in the general period from which to choose the correct one.

Indeed, there were four total lunar eclipses which were visible in Judaea and are viable candidates—on March 23, 5 BC; September 15, 5 BC; March 13, 4BC; and January 10, 1 BC.[90] Fortunately, only one of these lunar eclipse dates stands up to scrutiny, to help us validate our presumed date of the birth of Jesus (*September 11, 3 BC*) and the visit of the Magi 15 months later (*December 25, 2 BC*). The proposed lunar eclipse of *January 10, 1 BC* is the best candidate and evidence is given in the following sections of (b.) and (c.) below.

(b) *Timeframe of Herod's Death and Funeral Eliminates Some Eclipses*

Part of the scrutiny for picking the correct lunar eclipse which Josephus made reference to is that the period of time from the lunar eclipse, prior to Herod's death, to his funeral has to be sufficient to fit in all the planning and activities related to his funeral. On the other hand, the timeframe can't be too long from the lunar eclipse to Passover to not be realistic for Josephus to have referenced Herod's death "before a Passover." For example, if Herod had died close after a Passover, he would not have stated that Herod had died "soon after a lunar eclipse and before Passover."

It is important to catalogue all the known activities which had to transpire from the day of the lunar eclipse until Herod died and, then, add on the time which elapsed for his elaborate funeral and burial, period of mourning, etc. and, then, count the period from Herod's burial to the Springtime Passover which found Herod's son (Archelaus) reigning in Jerusalem. Fortunately, these events are well recorded by Josephus. Although Josephus does not give the number of days from the lunar eclipse to the next Passover, this period can be estimated fairly well, with time estimates for each of the known activities related to Herod's death and funeral which happened during this period. A total time period of *10 – 12 weeks* is needed to fit in all the events.[91] Hence, almost *three-months* is needed from the time of the lunar eclipse to the following Passover to fit in all the events. Anything less would eliminate that lunar eclipse candidate.

All considered, the best date for Herod's death is ***January 28, 1 BC*** (***Schebat 2*** on the Jewish calendar).[92] This fits all the chronological parameters, including Josephus' statement about his death being soon after a lunar eclipse [*January 10, 1 BC*—explained in Section (c.) below] and before Passover. This date is one of the undesignated festival days of the Jews mentioned in the *Megillath Taanith*.[93] One of the dates mentioned in this Jewish document, which dates back to the destruction of Jerusalem in AD 70, is *Schebat 2* (which corresponds to *January 28, 1 BC*), and very well commemorates the joyful happening of Herod's death, as Herod was considered a usurper to the throne and was hated by the Jews. Josephus stated that just before Herod died he said, "I know that the Jews will celebrate my death by a festival."[94] Indeed, the date of Herod's death later became a festival in celebration of his death.

Many of the "inconsistencies" with Josephus' chronologies, which have been a consternation of historians, including the length of Herod's reign and the regnal years of his sons (Archelaus, Antipas, and Philip), can, indeed, be better correlated to the *January 28, 1 BC* death of Herod. Martin provides a good discussion of the confusing practice of "antedating" (overlapping of years), "*de jure* regnal years" (rewarded additional historical years to a king's reign), and "joint-rules" (co-rulerships), which were accepted practices in the Hellenistic east that were in existence in Herod's time.[95]

(c) *Important to Pick the Correct Lunar Eclipse*

Of course, of the possible lunar eclipse candidates for the period, it is important to pick the right one for being the lunar eclipse referenced by Josephus as occurring right before Herod's death and being before a Passover—and the Passover occurring after Herod's burial. Otherwise, an incorrect date for the death of Herod is assigned by this method. Fortunately, there are clues, along with other known historical and archaeological documentation (even in this "Dark Decade" of history), to eliminate the poor candidates and to pick the correct lunar eclipse—the *January 10, 1 BC* lunar eclipse. This is summarized below.

What about the eclipse on **March 23, 5 BC**? Although this is a spring eclipse and would align with an upcoming Passover, there are only 29 days between this eclipse and the next Passover. This is insufficient time for all the elaborate funeral arrangements to be made and carried out for a king of Judaea. Remember, we estimated a period of three months is needed. In addition, early 5 BC causes problems with the chronological markers and indications of Josephus and Roman records that we do have regarding the period of Herod's death.[96]

What about the eclipse of **September 15, 5 BC**? The elapsed time between the eclipse and Passover is seven months. Among other reasons, this eclipse does not work.[97] Besides, Josephus would not have referenced a Passover that far removed from the death of Herod.

What about the eclipse of **March 13, 4 BC**? This is the eclipse *incorrectly chosen* by most historians, as they do not properly consider all the events which can't be crammed into a 29-day period. This was only a *partial eclipse*, and the time between the eclipse and Passover is the same problem with the March 23, 5 BC eclipse—insufficient time to fit in all the recorded events associated with Herod's funeral procession, the period of his mourning and other events that occurred before that Passover.[98]

What about the eclipse of *January 10, 1 BC*? This lunar eclipse meets all the historical and chronological parameters[99]—including a period of *12 ½ weeks* from the eclipse to the Passover.

There are other modern historians in agreement on the *January 10, 1 BC* eclipse—W. E. Filmer, Ormund Edwards, and particularly Dr. Paul Keresztes in his two-volume work titled *Imperial Rome and the Christians* (1989). Still others in the past are similarly in agreement—Scaliger in the 16th century, the German historian Calvisius (recorded nearly 300 eclipses as benchmarks for reckoning historical events of the past), William Galloway, H. Bosanquet, C. R. Conder, as did Professors Caspari and Reiss of Germany in their chronological research.[100]

2. The "Missing" War—The War of Varus, After Herod's Death

See what happens when a wrong date in history is chosen? Yes, you lose a war. Not in a military sense, but in a historical sense! You lose a perfectly good war which should not be lost in history—as it is, it can't even be found. Indeed, we see that wrongly assumed dates have consequences. This is exactly the case with what Jewish scholars call *The War of Varus,* a major war that occurred within the "Dark Decade" of 6 BC to AD 4.

But who has ever heard of this war? Most people have not. It has been a mystery to historians as they could *not* find this war in contemporary Roman records. They could not find this war in Judea between the Jews and Romans because they have tried to place it three years *before* it actually happened. They got it wrong because they have gotten the death of Herod (and other events) wrong—they assumed the war to be in 4 BC, rather than early AD 1.

With a proper understanding of the actual dates of the birth of Jesus (*September 11, 3 BC*), the visit of the Magi (*December 25, 2 BC*), and the death of Herod (*January 28, 1 BC*), much historical evidence pops on the scene and takes away much of the confusion of this period. For example, it is now possible to correlate several Roman documents that mention not only this war but other historical events. This is further confirmation of the accuracy of the assumed dates presented in this Section A of Part I. *The War of Varus* is one example of this confirmation.[101]

Indeed, Jewish records make it clear that this war, indeed, occurred, but Roman records (literature, coins, or inscriptions) do not show such a war in 4 BC. Thankfully, in 1 BC, we find a number of Roman references to it. In fact, Rome fought no wars from 7 BC to 2 BC, which we know from Roman troop records which show that troops were being *discharged* during that period, definitely not a sign of being engaged in a major conflict. However, in 1 BC this was not the case. There were no troop discharges in 1 BC. Indeed, this is the time of *The War of Varus*. And Roman records confirm it.[102]

But who cares about a silly little war? Actually, this was a *significant* war—not a small skirmish. Rome brought in the regular Roman military forces from Syria, estimated at 20,000 troops in addition to support personnel. It has been described as one of the most serious military operations to occur in Palestine from the time of Pompey (63 BC) until the Roman /Jewish War of AD 66/73! It is amazing that few people know about this war.

What was this war all about? *The War of Varus* took place in Galilee, Judaea and Idumaea and started a little over two months *after* the death of Herod, which is now properly established *in January, 1 BC*. The war took place in the spring and summer of the year of Herod's death.[103]

Josephus stated that this war against the Jews was directed by *Quintilius Varus*, the Roman governor of Syria; and this is where *The War of Varus* derives its name. The final mopping-up of the war was in Idumaea, the southern part of Herod's kingdom, and was accomplished by *Gaius Caesar*, the grandson of Augustus, who was sent to the region to help Varus with the war effort; this occurred in the autumn of 1 BC.

The war was fought as a result of three things—Herod's death, the killing of two influential rabbis by Herod immediately before his death, and a Jewish rebellion and Passover massacre by government troops. It started with the brutal massacre of 3,000 Jewish worshippers in the Temple by the Romans at the Passover of 1 BC.

What brought this action about? In large measure, per the reports by Josephus, it all stemmed back to the actions of two important rabbis. Due to a false report of an early demise of Herod, on December 5, 2 BC (*Kislev* 7), a few days prior to the lunar eclipse (of *January 10, 1 BC*) before Herod's death (of *January 28, 1 BC*; *Schebat* 2), two prominent rabbis encouraged a number of young men to destroy a golden eagle which Herod had placed over the eastern gate of the Temple. The placement of the eagle was contrary to the Law of Moses. The young men and the two rabbis were rounded up, tried and sentenced by Herod in Jericho. The young men were given lighter sentences, but the two rabbis were ordered to be burnt alive on Friday, January 9, 1 BC, to correspond with the lunar eclipse which was predicted to occur that night of *January 10, 1 BC*. Delaying the executions a few nights to then align with the lunar eclipse would have allowed Herod to tell the people that even God was frowning on the actions of the two rabbis and that God would show his displeasure that night with an eclipse.[104] Knowledge of impending events, even astronomical events, is powerful, and can give the appearance of divine approval to rulers.

The two illustrious rabbis were admired and esteemed by the whole nation, and following their deaths, at the subsequent Passover, a riot of the Jewish people broke out and, on order of Archelaus (the successor to Herod), 3,000 Jewish worshippers were slaughtered in the temple precincts.[105] Obviously, this was not looked upon favorably by the people in Jerusalem and surrounding areas.

The riot and massacre resulted in the unusual cancellation of the whole Passover services (Numbers 9:6-14) due to the 3,000 dead bodies being within the Temple precincts. This was, indeed, a most extraordinary event and *had never happened before* in such a way in Jewish history.

The slaughter of the worshipers in the temple led directly to a major war between the Jews and Romans, during the summer and autumn of 1 BC. Josephus stated that this war was not a minor skirmish.[106] This was the *War of Varus*. Three Roman legions plus auxiliary forces in Syria were called in (about 20,000 armed men in all). In addition to those killed in the war, following the war, 2,000 Jews were crucified and 30,000 sold into slavery.[107]

That eclipse of *January 10, 1 BC* was long remembered by the Jewish people due to not only Herod's death which closely followed it but also due to the execution of the two rabbis, the massacre of the 3,000 Jews, and the ensuing *War of Varus*. All these events occurred in 1 BC, and the eclipse and Roman history, including the accounts of Josephus, all are in alignment with these events and dates.

Indeed, *The War of Varus* is no longer missing—it has been found in its proper place in history such that Jewish records and Roman records are in alignment. This gives further support for the lunar eclipse of *January 10, 1 BC* being the correct eclipse and the death of Herod on *January 28, 1 BC* being the correct date for his death.

The angel would have reported Herod's death to Joseph in Egypt at or after *January 28, 1 BC*, and Joseph and Mary and Jesus would have travelled back to Israel sometime after the *January 28, 1 BC* date.

The death of King Herod and related events, our *Puzzle Piece #7*, all fit together as to dates and bolster our case presented for the correct chronology of Jesus' birth and related events.

CHAPTER 10

Puzzle Piece #8– Sabbatical and Jubilee Years

Determining the correct dates for Jesus' birth and events in His life involves investigation into chronological evidences (sometimes just hints) to establish a correct chronological background to those historical events.

This Part I has looked at several means for determining a correct chronology of Jesus' birth—evaluating biblical, historical, and astronomical evidence.

However, in addition to what we have been presenting in the preceding chapters, there is another method in the Bible of obtaining chronological information—the study of the Jewish calendar, namely the *Sabbath Days, Sabbatical Years* and *Jubilee Years*. This constitutes our *Puzzle Piece #8* which can help us better understand the birth, life, and ministry of Jesus as well as other events in the Bible.

A. Jesus' Birth and Start of His Ministry Were During *Sabbatical Years*

Evidence has been uncovered which gives a different way to determine the proper chronology of the start of Jesus' ministry, the year of His crucifixion, and even the exact year in which Jesus was born. This new insight from the New Testament helps to make the other chronological indicators of the New Testament more understandable.

What is this key? It involves understanding the chronology of the *Feasts of the Lord* (Leviticus 23) during the ministry of Jesus as well as understanding the Jewish law related to the *Sabbatical* and *Jubilee Years and cycles* (Leviticus 25). Please note that **Sections B–F** of this Chapter 10 provide background details about the *Sabbatical* and *Jubilee* years and their cycles.

It is well known that the Gospel of John gives some prime chronological references for reckoning Jesus' years of ministry that the other three Gospels do not. John mentions specifically *three Passovers* which occurred during the ministry of Jesus (John 2:13; 6:4; 13:1). In addition, there was an *"unknown feast"* between the first two Passovers (John 5:1), and, additionally, the Feast of Tabernacles and Hanukkah are mentioned after the second Passover (John 7:1). These Feasts provide some chronological information about the proper sequence of the years of Jesus' ministry.

However, there is another piece of chronological information which has come to light, and is reported in Ernest Martin's book, *The Star That Astonished the World* (1996). It relates to a statement given by Jesus, positioned between his first two Passovers (John 2:13 and 6:4) and before his "unknown" feast (John 5:1). According to Martin, this piece of historical information has previously been overlooked and misunderstood. But once properly understood, it gives us a significant key for understanding the chronology of Jesus' life and ministry.

What is this statement made by Jesus? It has to do with the account of *Jesus at Jacob's well in Samaria*, after Jesus left Jerusalem on His journey with His disciples to Galilee (John 4:3), following the first Passover mentioned by John. Jesus talked with a Samaritan woman while his disciples went into the village to obtain food. Jesus' teaching to the disciples after they returned solves a major chronological problem with the timeframe and length of Jesus' ministry. Jesus said to the disciples:

> *"Say ye not, 'There are yet **four months and then cometh the harvest?**' behold, I say unto you, lift up your eyes and look on the fields; for **they are white [ripe] already for harvest**."* (John 4:35; clarification and emphasis mine.)

What is this description by Jesus of *"... four months and then cometh the harvest"* all about? There is no known proverb in Jewish literature which refers to a four-month season from sowing to harvest.[108] The period for wheat growing before harvest was more like six months. In addition, Jesus' statement acknowledges that the grain was ready for harvesting (it was late May or early June), but Jesus stated that there would be another *four months* before harvesting it; this would put the grain harvest in September to October. However, there was no grain harvest in Israel during that period of months—the barley and wheat harvest had been harvested much earlier in the year. This all fits together with the understanding that this applies to the agricultural laws which were given by Moses, applying to the Jews and Samaritans living in the Promised Land—Jesus made his statement to the disciples during a *Sabbatical Year*.

The *Sabbatical Year* allowed no sowing or reaping during that year, extending from autumn to autumn. This is the reason that Jesus stated that it was still *"four months"* to the period of harvest. In addition, during this year, Jesus used other terms only applicable to a *Sabbatical Year*, as well as His experience of visiting the Synagogue in Nazareth (Luke 4:17–21) with the Scripture reading He was handed to read (Isaiah 61:1–2) and Jesus' comments after reading that Scripture—all tying into a *Sabbatical-Year* theme.[109]

What does all this mean? It means that this year in Jesus' ministry, which was the *first year of his ministry*, occurred during a *Sabbatical Year*. During this year, the Jews were off from their normal farming jobs, as all farmland in Israel was not to be farmed every seventh year, during the Sabbatical Year. Hence, this explains why Jews could freely travel to hear John the Baptist preach down by the Jordan River, and how the disciples and others could so easily go to hear His teaching and follow Jesus when He called them. Now, that all makes sense—they were not working that year.

According to Martin, this particular *Sabbatical Year* of Jesus' first year of ministry is, hence, now known, and this particular year can be identified (*autumn AD 27 – autumn AD 28*).[110] This is key to determining the year that Jesus' ministry started, which heretofore has been uncertain. This and other Bible information—Luke 3:23 states, *"Jesus began [his ministry] about 30 years of age"*—allows us to link from this now known chronological date (autumn of AD 27) back to **Jesus' birthdate**, for another confirmation of the year of Jesus' birth—*autumn of 3 BC*.

We can see how this method of backing into Jesus' birthdate from this known Sabbatical Year (autumn AD 27 – autumn AD 28) and knowing that Jesus was 30 years old during that year gives the same indication of Jesus' birthdate as our other dating methods. In fact, this method of using *Sabbatical-Year* information is a further confirmation of the *Tishri 1 (September 11, 3 BC)* birthdate of Jesus derived from the other methods described in this Section A of Part I.

B. Biblical Background on *Sabbatical Years* and *Jubilee Years*

Sections B–F of this chapter provide good background information on *Sabbatical Years* and *Jubilee Years*, which are referred to in this chapter. This background information clarifies the discussion related to the Jewish calendar. Further discussion of the Jewish calendar is found in our book, *The Last Shofar!*, in Appendix II: "The Jewish Calendar—God's Time."

It is God who determines what is important. Specific days on the calendar are important to God, and it pays to understand what they are all about. Jesus, born a Jew and being an observant Jew during his life and ministry on earth, was careful to observe specific days on the Hebrew calendar as taught in Scripture.

Observances of *Sabbath, Sabbatical Years* and *Jubilee Years*, in addition to the *Feasts of the Lord*, are specified in Leviticus 23 and 25. Indeed, what are they all about? *And what does all this have to do with the birthdate of Jesus?*

From Chapter 5: "Born on the *Feast of Trumpets*?", we presented the strong case for Jesus having been born on *Yom Teruah* [the Feast of Trumpets, on Tishri 1 (*September 11, 3 BC*)]. In this Chapter 10, the case is presented for back calculating the birthdate of Jesus, knowing that the first year of Jesus' ministry was a Sabbatical Year. As stated previously, this allows for further confirmation of the birthdate being in *September, 3 BC*.

So, what are these *Sabbatical Years* in Scripture all about? It suddenly become much more interesting as to how they relate to the birth and ministry of Jesus! Unfortunately, commentators seldom mention the importance of understanding the *Sabbatical Years*. We first need to understand some background related to *Sabbatical Years* and *Jubilee Years*, covered in this Chapter.

The *Sabbath **days*** mentioned in Scripture include the 7th day of the week—the weekly *Sabbath*—as well as the special *Sabbath* days (*High Holy Days*) of some of the *Feasts of the Lord* (see Chapter 6 of *The Last Shofar!*). Their regulations are presented in Leviticus 23 and 25.

In addition, *specific **years*** are important to God—these are the *Sabbatical Years* and the *Jubilee Years*. The Old Testament law in Leviticus 25:1–7 commanded that the Israelites let their lands in the Promised Land lie dormant each 7th year—the **Sabbatical Year** (also called the *Shemitah* or *Shmita*). This word is most often translated as "the release" or "the remission."[111] Just as the weekly *Sabbath* was a day of rest instituted by God for man (Genesis 2:2-3), the *Sabbatical Year* was a year of rest for the land. In addition, debts of fellow Israelites were to be forgiven in *Shemitah* years (Deuteronomy 15:2).

Leviticus 25:1-7 seems to indicate a continuing cycle of every 7th year being a *Sabbatical Year* in perpetuity, forming a chain of continuous seven-year periods. That may sound obvious, but it is not, as explained below—there is a complication, and it is called the *Jubilee Year*.

The year *following* the 7th *Sabbatical Year* was the **Jubilee Year**. The *Jubilee Year* occurred every fiftieth year, the year after seven *Sabbatical Years* (after seven weeks of years) had passed (Leviticus 25:8-11). Commentaries frequently say that its timing is to years what *Shavuot* (Feast of Weeks; Pentecost) is to days. However, it is not that straightforward. As per the understanding used in this book, *Shavuot* occurs on the fiftieth day—the day after seven weeks following the *weekly* Sabbath [Saturday], which proceeds Firstfruits [Sunday] of the Passover week (Leviticus 23:15-16)—this formula places *Shavuot* always on the first day of the Hebrew week, on Sunday, as is the case with Firstfruits, being the day after the [*weekly*] Sabbath of the week of Passover (see the discussion on Firstfruits in Part II, Section A, Chapter 19). Actually, this is nothing like the determination of the *Jubilee Year*, which seems so much more straightforward, but I emphasize the word "seems." There is, for sure, a lot of controversy over how it is figured going forward in time.

The 7th *Sabbatical Year* and the *Jubilee Year* are separate back-to-back years. Everyone agrees about this because this is clearly stated in Scripture (Leviticus 25:8-10). The name "*Jubilee*" is the Latin term (means 50), which is from the Hebrew word *yovel* (means "ram's horn")—the year being so called because the ram's horn was sounded when the year was proclaimed (Leviticus 25:9). In the *Jubilee Year*, the land also rested for that year, but, in addition, slaves and prisoners were released and all lands were returned to the proper tribal owners of that land—per the original land assigned by God to each of the 12 tribes of Israel.

So, the *Jubilee Year* was celebrated consistently in Israel after the 7th *Sabbatical Year*. Right? Well, no. The Talmudic view is that the *Jubilee Year* was not observed during the whole Second Temple period because the majority of Jews no longer lived in the land of Israel. Howard and Rosenthal have stated the following:

> "The observance of the **Jubilee Year**, like that of the **Sabbatical Year**, was also neglected during Israel's early history. In fact, *there is no historical record, biblical or extrabiblical, that Israel ever once observed the Jubilee Year.* Josephus often cited *Sabbatical Year* observance, but never that of the *Jubilee Year*.
>
> The ancient rabbis generally believed that **the Jubilee** was no longer in effect after the exile of the northern ten tribes (722 B.C.) since the biblical command for observance was for *'all the inhabitants thereof'* (Lev.

25:10). They believed that the ***Jubilee Year*** applied only when all the Jewish people were in the land, with each tribe in its own territory. Perhaps this is the reason that only the ***Sabbatical Year*** (not the *Jubilee Year*) was mentioned in the people's solemn oath in the time of Nehemiah (Neh. 10:31) ... Since the timing is not known today [for the *Jubilee Year*], the shofar (ram's horn) is blown in the synagogue as a memorial of the *Jubilee Year* at the close of **Yom Kippur** each year."[112]

According to Howard and Rosenthal, the *Jubilee Year* cycle has been lost and is unknown. However, God has not lost count. He is still interested in the *Sabbatical Year* and *Jubilee Year* cycles. Others say that the *Sabbatical Years* and *Jubilee Years* can be known, and are known—this is covered in **Sections C–F** which follow below.

C. Controversies About *Sabbatical Years* and *Jubilee Years*

There are several controversies involving the *Sabbatical Year* and the *Jubilee Year*. The purpose of this section is to present some background on these controversies to help you understand why this information on these years and their cycles are not "clear cut" to everyone.

Indeed, some have expressed frustration about the lack of present clarity over how to figure *Sabbatical Years* and *Jubilee Years*. An example are the comments made by Dr. David R. Reagan, the Founder/Director and Senior Evangelist of *Lamb and Lion Ministries* (founded in 1980), in an interview with Messianic Rabbi Jonathan Cahn (February 2015):

> "One of the problems I have with your [Jonathan Cahn's] theory [Jonathan's book, *The Mystery of the Shemitah* (2014)] is that **the Jewish calendar is a mess. It's a mess!** It's lacking about 250 years that should be in there, because the sages short-termed the Persian rule. They put it down for about 52 years when it lasted over 200 years [see Appendix II of *The Last Shofar!* for a thorough description of the Jewish calendar, including this problem]. So, **the whole calendar is off.** Since they don't know when the Jubilee years are, **how can they know when the Shemitahs are?**"[113] (Clarification and emphasis added)

Yes, in a lot of ways, the Jewish calendar is presently "a mess." Below is a presentation of the controversies related to the correct determination of *Sabbatical Years* and

Jubilee Years, which can lead to frustration for Bible students and commentators, as exhibited with the above comments by David Reagan.

1. First Controversy

The **first controversy** involves the determination of the exact start of the *next Sabbatical Year* following the *Jubilee Year*. Jonathan Cahn, Joseph Dumond, Yves Peloquin, Ernest L. Martin and many others hold to the position that the *Jubilee Year* (the 50th year) is also the first year of the next seven-year *Sabbatical-Year* cycle—hence, a repeating **49-year cycle**.[114, 115, 116, 117]

In addition, the two heavy-weight scholars—with slightly opposing views as to which years are *Sabbatical Years* (two sets of dates, being off by one year from each other in their determination of *Sabbatical Years*)—**also hold to the view of a 49-year cycle**, with the *Jubilee Year* also being the first year of the next *Sabbatical Year* cycle.

The first of these two scholars is **Benedict Zuckerman** (with his theory proposed in 1857).[118] It should be mentioned that Zuckerman's chronology is consistent with the *geonim* (medieval Jewish scholars) and the calendar of *Sabbatical Years* used in present-day Israel.

The second scholar is **Ben Zion Wacholder** (with his theory proposed in 1973).[119] Wacholder's proposed set of *Sabbatical Years* are offset by one year, being *one year later* than Zuckerman's set of years.[120]

Conversely, Howard and Rosenthal, Tim Warner, Todd D. Bennett,[121] and others have stated that the first year of the next *Sabbatical-Year* cycle starts *after* the completion of the *Jubilee Year*—hence, a repeating **50-year cycle**. This understanding is a significant variation from an assumption of a continuous 49-year cycle of *Sabbatical Years* through history. Howard and Rosenthal state emphatically:

> "Others have postulated that the **Jubilee Year** was the *fiftieth year and also the first year in the counting of the next sabbatical cycle*. This, too, finds no biblical support. In addition, the overwhelming majority of ancient Jewish sages clearly taught that the Jubilee Year was ***the fiftieth Year ... and distinct from the first year in the next sabbatical cycle*** (Nedarim 61a; Talmud Yerushalmi, Kiddushin 1:2, 59a). Seven complete sabbatical cycles preceded each Jubilee Year, and seven complete cycles followed it."[122]

Tim Warner takes the same position as Howard and Rosenthal related to the *Jubilee Year* not being counted as the first year of the following seven-year Sabbatical-Year cycle:

> "In Leviticus 25, we learn of God's Jubilee calendar of **50-year cycles** which God commanded Israel to observe ... Some claim that these cycles are actually 49 years. However, the Sedar Olam Rabbah, the ancient 2nd century Jewish chronology and the oldest word on the subject, states plainly that ***the cycles were 50 years***. (Sedar Olam Rabbah, ch. 11, translated by Ken Johnson, PhD., p. 61). There is an example in Scripture of a *Sabbatical year* being followed by a *Jubilee Year* (15th and 16th years of Hezekiah), which requires a **50-year cycle** (sic) (Isaiah 37:30)."[123]

So, now you can better understand this first controversy, but which is the correct interpretation of how the cycles are calculated? Indeed, a good question. I believe the better case is that the Jubilee-Year cycle is **49 years** rather than 50 years, **with the Jubilee Year following the 7th Sabbatical Year and also being the first year of the next seven-year Sabbatical-Year cycle**. This allows the seven-year cycle to continue un-erupted throughout time, as is the case for the weekly Sabbath being the seventh day and the next day, Sunday, starting the first day of the next week.

2. Second Controversy

The **second controversy** involves the *calendar date* for the start of the *Sabbatical Year*. Leviticus 25:9-10 clearly states that the biblical *Jubilee Year* starts on the Day of Atonement (*Tishri 10*), and it might be inferred that the *Jubilee Year* would end one-year later at sundown of the previous day (*Tishri 9*). It might also be inferred from this Scripture that the biblical *Sabbatical Years* would also start on *Tishri 10*; this is the assumption of Martin.[124] However, some, including Jonathan Cahn, have stated that the *Sabbatical Years* start on *Tishri 1* and end at sundown on *Elul 29*, the last day of the civil year on the Jewish civil calendar.[125] Admittedly, the modern State of Israel also starts their official *Shemitah Year* (*Sabbatical* Year) on the Jewish New Year (*Tishri 1*); with the most recent beginning on October 2, 2016, corresponding to the Hebrew calendar year 5777.[126]

To add to the confusion, Joseph Dumond states that the start of a *Sabbatical Year* is **Abib 1** (*Nisan 1;* March/April), in the first month of the Jewish religious calendar given by God through Moses, rather than beginning in the seventh month of *Tishri* (September/October).[127] However, there does not seem to be much additional support for this understanding of the start of the *Sabbatical Year* being in *Nisan* (*Abib*).

Although there is confusion about the starting date of the *Sabbatical Year*, the most accepted seems to be that ***Sabbatical Years* start on *Tishri 1* and the *Jubilee Years* start on *Tishri 10*.**[128] It should be noted that, according to this counting with the different starting dates, the last *Sabbatical Year* before the *Jubilee Year* is *one-year-and-ten-days* long. This is actually an important insight as Nelson Walters has uncovered related to eschatology—the last year of the future 70th Week of Daniel (Daniel 9) appears to be a *Sabbatical Year*, with duration of *one-year-and-ten days*. This is very possibly the exact count of days that the Church will be in heaven after the Rapture, before the Church physically returns to earth with Jesus. This *one-year-and-ten-day* period equates to the same number of days Noah was protected in the Ark; this is calculated from Genesis 7 and 8—from the day Noah entered the Ark on 17th day of the second month (Gen. 7:11-13) until he came out on the 27th day of the second month (Gen. 8:14-16), exactly *one-year-and-ten days*. Coincidence? Probably not! If interested, I recommend referring to the interesting discussion in Nelson Walters' landmark book, *Rapture: Case Closed?–Stunning New Biblical Evidence* (2017), specifically, Chapter Ten: "The Favorable Year of the Lord (The Enhanced Prewrath Rapture)."

Why is all this important? These special years (*Sabbatical Years* and *Jubilee Years*) provide chronological markers and, if they can be determined, can help determine proper dates of many events in the Bible, including events in Jesus life and ministry.[129]

Obedience was not a small thing in God's eyes. All the laws which God gave to Moses were to be obeyed, and in Leviticus 26 God listed the blessings He would give Israel for obedience as well as the curses for lack of obedience. Take, for instance, the *Sabbatical Years*. The destruction of Jerusalem and first exile of Judah to Babylon was a direct result of their lack of keeping the law, including not keeping the *Sabbatical Years* in Israel. How do we know that? Jeremiah 9:11–16 clearly lays out this punishment. God told them what their punishment would be if they did not obey Him—exile from the Land (Leviticus 26:31–35). Indeed, this is what they experienced.

Seventy years were decreed for Judah's exile to Babylonia (Jeremiah 25:11; 2 Chronicles 36:20–21; Daniel 9:1–2). The reason for the 70-year exile was to fulfill (make-up for) the *Sabbath Years* (for the land to rest and not be tilled) over the previous period of 490 years (70 *Sabbatical Years* which had been missed). One general thing to take away from this God-decreed exile is that God keeps up with the *Sabbath days*, *Sabbatical Years* and *Jubilee Years*, even when they are not honored by His people. These are a part of God's calendar and *His* count of days and years.

Hopefully, this review of *Sabbatical* and *Jubilee Years* has been helpful background information in our case for using these as chronological markers in the life and ministry of Jesus. Complicated, yes, but it is helpful to understand these special years.

D. Is the Sequence of *Sabbatical* and *Jubilee Years* Now "Known"?

As stated previously, some believe that *Sabbatical Years* and *Jubilee Years* can be determined and are, in fact, "known." Related to the establishing of the sequence of *Sabbatical Years*, Ernest L. Martin, who accepts the views of Ben Zion Wacholder, has stated:

> "... only within the last 50 years (and especially the last 30—[since about 1966]), has it become possible, through archaeological discoveries, etc., to **determine with an almost certainly what the exact *Sabbatical Years'* sequence was and is.** This can be known **from 163 B.C. to the present**. Two brilliant historical studies by **Prof. Wacholder** of Hebrew Union College, Cincinnati, have solved the riddle of when the Sabbatical Years occurred in ancient times, and when they ought to be observed today."[130]

If, indeed, the above quoted statement is true, it is a great help that the sequence of *Sabbatical Years* is now known. This would be a tremendous help in determining the chronology of biblical events, including those in the life of Jesus. Remember, however, that Martin, like Wacholder, holds to a **49-year cycle** of Jubilee Years—this is certainly true for the seven *Sabbatical-Year* cycles, which are indeed on 7-year cycles within a *Jubilee-Year* cycle. As you well know, this book features much of Dr. Martin's work, and I agree with his conclusions, including his support for the 49-year cycle of Jubilee Years.

As mentioned previously, the question becomes whether the *Jubilee Year* is the first year of a new 7-year *Sabbatical-Year* cycle (resulting in 49-year cycles) or if the *Jubilee Year* occurs and *then* the first year of the *next* 7-year *Sabbatical-Year* cycle begins (resulting in 50-year cycles). Although I support the 49-year cycle position and I believe that to be correct, it is important to understand that there are "two-sides" to this controversy, with each side having supporters, and Scripture does not seem to fully clarify this controversy. It seems that this is one area where *"we see through a glass darkly,"* and we might have to await Messiah or further revelation to explain all these things.

However, as has been noted, despite the controversies about the length of the *Jubilee-Year* cycle (49 years vs. 50 years), **I do believe that the 49-year cycle is correct** and, hence, that the *Sabbatical-Year* cycles and the *Jubilee-Year* cycles are, indeed, known. Because of this, I support Ernest Martin's chronologies using these cycles; they are in conformity with all the other evidence related to Jesus' life and ministry.

E. Actual Sequence of *Sabbatical Years*

Josephus and other first-century writers mentioned *Sabbatical Years* related to the occurrence of events they had written about, and these corroborate Professor Wacholder's findings for *Sabbatical Year* (49-year cycles). Very often, large construction projects were done in Israel during *Sabbatical Years* when labor was available to be hired, as farming in Israel was not being done during those years. Per the historical records of Josephus and other Jewish records, these include the following events with their respective *Sabbatical Years* (7-year Sabbatical cycles and 49-year Jubilee cycles): [131]

- **37 BC–36 BC**: Herod's conquest of Jerusalem occurred on the Day of Atonement, at the end of this *Sabbatical Year*;
  - Josephus tells us that Herod reigned 34 years after the death of Antigonus, who was killed just months after Herod's conquest of Jerusalem; therefore, Herod reigned until 2 to 1 BC, with Herod's death in 1 BC—this confirms our chronology of Herod's death on *January 28, 1 BC* (stated in Chapter 9).

- **2 BC–1 BC**: Herod's son, Philip, started to build Caesarea Philippi;
  - The Magi coming on *Hanukkah* of 2 BC (*December 25, 2 BC*) would have been during this *Sabbatical Year*. Jesus' birth on *September 11, 3 BC* (*Tishri 1*; Feast of Trumpets) was one-year prior to the start of the *Sabbatical Year* of 2 BC, starting on *Tishri 1, Feast of Trumpets*.

- **AD 41–AD 42**: King Agrippa I started the building of the expansive third wall around the northern parts of Jerusalem;

- **AD 62–AD 63**: Agrippa II started to rebuild Caesarea Philippi;

- **AD 69–AD 70**: Temple at Jerusalem destroyed;

- **AD 132–AD 133**: *Bar Kokhba* revolt of the Jews against the Romans.

All these events happened during *Sabbatical Years,* and all are in the proper sequence, giving much credibility to Wacholder's findings (49-year cycles). Hence, according to this, all the *Sabbatical Years* in between the above terms of *Sabbatical Years* can also be known, happening at continuous seven-year intervals. This does, however, assume that the *Jubilee Year*, happening following seven *Sabbatical Years*, is either omitted or that it is also the first year of the next seven-year interval heading to the next *Sabbatical Year*—as mentioned previously, this assumes an interval of **49 years** for the *Jubilee Year* cycle, rather than a **50-year** cycle. This is the only way to maintain a consistent seven-year cycle throughout history—to follow the analogy of the Sabbath, which is a consistent seven-day cycle throughout history, and it aligns with the writings of Josephus and other Jewish writers for events they mention are in *Sabbatical Years*.

In summary, as has been stated, this book supports the 49-year cycle of Jubilee Years, with the Jubilee Year being the 50th year and it also being the first year of the next 7-year Sabbatical Year cycle. Some wonderful additional insights about the timing of the 49-year cycle, and, especially, how it relates to the prophecy of Daniel's 70 Weeks, are found in the recent books by Nelson Walters: *Revelation Deciphered* (2016) and *Rapture: Case Closed?* (2017). I highly recommend these books.

F. Timing of Jesus' First Coming—Daniel's 70-Weeks Prophecy Is in *Sabbatical Years*

The Scribes and Pharisees and the other religious leaders should have known the time of the Messiah's coming. They, however, did not. Seemingly, they did not read, study, and know the prophecy of Daniel which so clearly gave the timeframe for the coming of the *"Anointed One"* by giving the time that he would be *"cut off"* [die] in his 70-Weeks Prophecy (Daniel 9:24–27).

The Magi were looking for the coming King of the Jews, but within the court of King Herod and for the religious leaders it was nowhere on their "radar screen." Jesus stated, *"You know how to interpret the appearance of the sky, but you cannot interpret the signs of the times."* One of the *"signs of the times"* was the prophecy of Daniel as to when the Messiah was to come. Unfortunately, they were not looking for this sign from Daniel.

To correctly interpret the future timeframe of Daniel's 70-Weeks prophecy of Daniel (Daniel 9:24-27), we need to know the nature of the *"Weeks"* of which Daniel was referring. The *"Weeks"* refer to *"weeks of years"* or seven-year periods, even though a normal week is referring to a seven-day period. Hence, used here in Daniel, a *Week of years* = 7 years. In hindsight, we know this definition of *"weeks of years"* (and that these prophesied years were probably 360-day prophetic years of twelve 30-day months, as with Noah—see Genesis 7:11,24; 8:3,4) with almost certainty because the part of this prophecy which deals with the timeframe for which the Messiah would come and be *"cut off, but not for Himself"* (killed) was fulfilled with the crucifixion of Jesus in AD 30.

There are some other key things to be observed related to this prophecy in Daniel. Related to the 70-Week prophecy of Daniel, as mentioned previously, he divided the first 69 Weeks into a period of 7 Weeks and 62 Weeks (Daniel 9:25), until Messiah is *"cut off."* Why would he specify these two divisions? Understanding *God's Jubilee Calendar* from Creation (outlined in Leviticus 25) gives insight here. The first 7 Weeks (49 years) completes a *Jubilee cycle*, with the 50th year being the Jubilee Year as well as being the first year of the next 7-year cycle.

In addition, the 70-Weeks prophecy in Daniel 9 has a starting point declared, *"from the going forth of the command to restore and build Jerusalem."* When is this? It begins with the *decree of Cyrus*, setting at liberty the Jews in Babylon, ending the Babylonian captivity.[132] Others have speculated that a later decree given by another Persian king is the correct decree. However, that it is the *decree by Cyrus* is specifically stated in Isaiah 44:28, which states that his decree relates to both the rebuilding of Jerusalem and the Temple. This was confirmed by the well-known historian, Josephus.[133] Dating the 70-Weeks prophecy of Daniel from Cyrus' decree has an additional benefit in determining the chronology of Jesus—it frees us entirely from reliance on inaccurate non-biblical sources related to the Persian kings in establishing the chronology. Some commentators believe this *decree by Cyrus* was on the 70th Jubilee year from Creation—making this year of Cyrus' decree a kind of double-fulfillment of Jeremiah's prophecy related to Israel's exile and release (Jeremiah 25:8-14).[134]

So, with the start of the prophecy fulfillment beginning with the *decree of Cyrus* and the period of 69-Weeks after which the Messiah is *"cut off"* and dies (but before the destruction of Jerusalem, which happened in AD 70), to what year of His death would this equate? In other words, what is the timeframe that the Jews should have known from Daniel that their Messiah was to come, especially with the understanding of *Sabbatical Years* and *Jubilee Years* and that Daniel's prophecy was related to *Sabbatical Years* and *Jubilee Years*?

Admittedly, exact dates are difficult to presently ascertain. However, we can come close. First, a close approximation of the date of Cyrus' decree needs to be established. The year was 70 years (God-decreed period of the exile) from the destruction of Solomon's Temple [destruction in 3443 AM—(*Anno Mundi*; years from Creation—like Jewish calendar); =520/519 BC].[135] Tim Warner gives the following description of the beginning of the 70-Week chronology, starting with the decree by Cyrus:

> "The **70-weeks prophecy of Daniel** begins on the … year Cyrus decreed the end of the captivity and the rebuilding of Jerusalem and the Temple. The **first Jubilee cycle** consisted of the first *'seven weeks'* [(7 x 7 years = 49 years) … in the prophecy, and was the duration of the time from Cyrus' decree until the Temple and Jerusalem's walls were completed

by Nehemiah (covering the books of Ezra and Nehemiah). Adding the remaining **'62 weeks'** [62 x 7 = 434 years] ... we arrive at the end of the year [end of the 69-Weeks, *after* which the Messiah would be cut off]."[136]

The Jewish leaders at the time of Jesus should have known at least a close approximation of the time of the Messiah's coming from Daniel's prophecy. They could have figured from the 70-Weeks prophecy that *after* 69-Weeks (=483 years), starting from the year that Cyrus issued his decree to end the captivity and allow the rebuilding of Jerusalem and the Temple (Cyrus decree given in 3502 AM = 461/460 BC),[137] the Messiah would be *"cut off."* This would be *after* 3985 AM (3502 + 483 years = 3985 AM or AD 23/24).[138] Yves Peloquin believes that Jesus died in 3993 AM (=AD 31/32),[139] which is *after* the end of the 69-Weeks prophecy of Daniel. Taking away 30 years (for the age of a Rabbi starting his ministry) and a few years for his ministry until he would be killed, they could have come to a very close estimate of the *birthdate* of Jesus. But, unfortunately, they did not keep track of this prophecy of Daniel.

From the reaction of Herod at the meeting with the Magi, who came in search of the *"King of the Jews,"* Herod and the religious leaders were caught by surprise and had no idea of the timing of this birth event of their Messiah—foretold by their own prophet, Daniel. Shame on them, and Jesus said as much as He drew near to Jerusalem, *"You did not know the time of your visitation [His coming]"* (Luke 19:44; clarification added).

If Jesus implied that the Jews at the time of his ministry should have known the time of His coming, there must have been a way to count the years from the time of the decree by Cyrus to rebuild the Temple and the city walls to arrive at the end of the 69 Weeks of years (483 years), the timing after which Jesus was to be "cut off."

His Word is true, and He came at the appointed time. From Jesus' disappointment that the Jews did not know His coming, it is understood that they *should have* understood the prophesied time of His coming from Daniel, and to do so most likely means that they understood the *Sabbatical Year* and *Jubilee Year* cycles, upon which God based their 70-year exile. Hence, these cycles must have been known by the Jewish leaders at the time of Jesus.

G. Conclusion

From biblical evidence, we can surmise that Jesus' first year of ministry was during a *Sabbatical Year* (Luke 4:17–21; John 4:35–38), and it can be surmised that it aligned with the *Sabbatical Year* of AD 27 to AD 28. Jesus was 30 years old when he started His ministry, and this gives further confirmation of the birthdate of Jesus in 3 BC. The study of *Sabbatical Years* and *Jubilee Years* is our *Puzzle Piece #8* in solving the mystery of "When was Jesus Born?" This too aligns with all the other evidence of our case that the birth date of Jesus was September 11, 3 BC.

CHAPTER 11

Summary Sequence of Historical Events

A chronological listing of events related to this Section A of Part I should be helpful to see how events related to Jesus' life are fitting together.

Shown below is a summary of the sequence of historical events around the time of the birth of Jesus, His ministry, His death, and the destruction of Jerusalem in AD 70, as listed by Wierwille.[140]

Having the right birthdate for Jesus is key to having a correct chronology of Jesus' life, ministry, and crucifixion.

- **May, 4 BC**
  During the priestly course of *Abijah*, Gabriel appears to Zacharias serving in the Temple, telling of the upcoming conception and birth of John the Baptist. (Luke 1:5-25)

- **June, 4 BC**
  Conception of John the Baptist.

- **December, 4 BC**
  Gabriel appears to Mary in Nazareth; **conception of Jesus**; Mary travels to Judea to see her cousin Elizabeth (Luke 1:26-56), who is six months pregnant with John the Baptist at the time of Mary's visit.

- **March, 3 BC**

  John the Baptist is born to Zacharias and Elizabeth. (Luke 1:57-80)

- **August 12, 3 BC**

  Jupiter and Venus in conjunction in Leo; Magi begin noting their observations of the movements of Jupiter, the king planet.

- **September 11, 3 BC**

  Birth of Jesus in Bethlehem; in twilight period on *Tishri 1* (*Yom Teruah*—The Feast of Trumpets); sun in Virgo with the *"moon beneath her feet"*—Rev. 12:1. (Matt. 1:25a; Luke 2:1-20)

- **September 14, 3 BC**

  Jupiter (the king planet) and the star Regulus (the king star) in conjunction in Leo—Magi would have noted this.

- **September 18, 3 BC**

  Jesus' circumcision and naming—on his 8th day, for the circumcision rite is reckoned inclusively. (Matt. 1:25b; Luke 2:21)

- **October 20/21, 3 BC**

  Jesus' dedication in the Temple; purification of Mary. (Luke 2:22-38)

- **October, 3 BC**

  Jesus with Joseph & Mary return from Bethlehem to Nazareth. They did not go to Egypt immediately after the birth of Jesus but went to Nazareth after Jesus' dedication in the Temple. (Luke 2:39)

- **February 17, 2 BC**

  Jupiter and Regulus in conjunction in Leo—Magi would have noted this.

- **May 8, 2 BC**

  Jupiter and Regulus in conjunction in Leo—Magi would have noted this.

- **June 17, 2 BC**

  Jupiter and Venus in conjunction in Leo—Magi would have noted this.

- **Spring or Summer, 2 BC**

  Jesus with Joseph & Mary move into a *house* in Bethlehem. (Matt. 2:11)

- **August 27, 2 BC**

  Jupiter, Mars, Mercury, and Venus all mass together in Leo. Magi leave from Persia for trip to Jerusalem after this amazing celestial event.

- **December 25, 2 BC**

  Magi arrive in Bethlehem, after first stopping in Jerusalem. Jupiter was visible over Bethlehem before dawn as the Magi travel there. Jupiter, the king planet, came to its stationary point in mid-Virgo, the Virgin; it would have been seen as *"stopping over Bethlehem"* as viewed from Bethlehem. Jesus is more than one-year-and-three-months old (a toddler; Gk. *Paidion*); Magi present gifts (this is during *Hanukkah!—Kislev 25,* continuing for 8 days); Magi depart for Persia; Jesus taken by Joseph & Mary to Egypt. (Matt. 2:1-22)

- **Late December 2 BC**

  Herod kills all the male children, *"two years old and under,"* in Bethlehem and its vicinity (Matt. 2:16b-17); this happened about 15 months after Jesus' birth.

- **January 10, 1 BC**

  Lunar eclipse preceding King Herod's death, mentioned by Josephus; this eclipse happened shortly after two illustrious rabbis were tried and sentenced by the Sanhedrin and killed by Herod.

- **January 28, 1 BC**

  Death of King Herod, on Shevat 2 in 1 BC.

- **April 8, 1 BC**

  Archelaus, Herod's son, who became the new king of Judea when Herod died, disrupts Temple services at Passover and massacred 3,000 Jewish worshippers in the Temple; Jesus and Joseph & Mary return to Judea from Egypt and *"turn aside"* into Galilee and settle again in Nazareth. (Matt. 2:22-23; Luke 2:39)

- **Summer and Autumn, 1 BC**

  The War of Varus takes place in Israel, when Romans put down the Jewish revolt caused by the killing of the two illustrious rabbis and the massacre of the 3,000 Jews in the Temple at Passover.

- **Nisan 14 (Passover), AD 10**

  Jesus stays behind at the Temple when His parents leave after the Feast of Passover/Unleavened Bread. Jesus was 12-years old. (Luke 2:41-43)

- **October or November, AD 27**

    Jesus is baptized by John the Baptist (Matt. 3:13-17; Mark 1:9–11; Luke 3:21), at the beginning of the *Sabbatical Year* of AD 27 – AD 28, beginning His official ministry with the Passover and Pentecost seasons of AD 28.

- **Nisan 13/14 (Wednesday/Thursday) of AD 30**

    Jesus is crucified and died. He is **buried** on the evening of Nisan 13/14; (See Part II for a full discussion of these events and the chronology)

- **Nisan 16/17 (Saturday/Sunday) of AD 30**

    Jesus is resurrected at the start of Firstfruits (in evening of Nisan 16/17—the very start of Sunday, in AD 30).

- **AD 70**

    The Temple and the Jewish sections of Jerusalem are destroyed by Roman army (mainly composed of soldiers from Syria) under Titus—destruction prophesied in Daniel 9:26. The Roman fort Anatolia was not destroyed, and it was not included in Jesus' prophecy of the destruction of the Temple and (Jewish) Jerusalem, down to the foundations.

CHAPTER 12

Conclusion of *When* Was Jesus Born?

We have reviewed the *traditional* dates of Jesus' birthday and used four methods for deriving the *actual* birthdate of Jesus. It was noted that the *traditional* date of December 25, 1 BC does *not* match the evidence now available.

These four methods—incorporating biblical, historical, and astronomical evidence (using the eight *puzzle pieces* presented)—are assembled to solve the mystery of the correct birthdate of Jesus. Their conclusions all point to Jesus being born on **Wednesday, *Tishri 1* (*September 11*) of *3 BC*—**on the *Feast of Trumpets* (Hebrew: *Yom Teruah*; also called *Rosh HaShanah*).

I feel that the case for this birthdate of Jesus is very strong and is true. The *four methods* (using the eight *puzzle pieces*) for determining Jesus' birth date are as follows:

1 Evidence from Birth of John the Baptist (in Chapter 3)

Determining the birthdate of John the Baptist from the timing of the priestly service in the Temple of John's father, Zechariah (who was of the Priestly Course of *Abijah*), the ensuing pregnancy of Elizabeth, and the probable birthdate of John the Baptist. Jesus was born of Mary, Elizabeth's cousin, six months following the birth of John; this gives a reasonable month for His birth—*September*.

2   **Evidence from Astronomical/Zodiac Reference in Revelation 12:1–6 (Chapter 4)**

The date on the calendar for 3 BC that aligns with the specific positions of the sun and moon about the constellation of Virgo, described in Revelation 12:6, is uniquely *September 11, 3 BC,* from 6:18 p.m. to 7:39 p.m. of Bethlehem time. This method gives a very specific date and time for Jesus' birth.

3   **Evidence from Roman History & Death of King Herod and Life of Jesus (Chapters 8 & 9)**

The dates for the census of Quintilius Varus, the dates for The War of Varus, as well as the specific date of the lunar eclipse preceding the death of Herod (per Josephus' account), all support the date of Jesus' birth being in *September of 3 BC.*

4   **Evidence from *Sabbatical* & *Jubilee Years* in Chronology of Jesus' Birth & Ministry (Chapter 10)**

The determination that the first year of Jesus' ministry was a *Sabbatical Year* and the chronology of this first year of ministry, being approximately 3 ½ years from his crucifixion, equates to the *Sabbatical Year* of September AD 27 – September AD 28; also, that Jesus was 30 years old when He began His ministry—all supports a birthdate in *September of 3 BC.*

As has been noted, both the birth of Jesus (His *First Coming*) and the Rapture of the Church (at His *Second Coming*) occur on *Tishri 1,* the *Feast of Trumpets.* Both events occur with all the fitting symbolism of that Feast day. The Feast days are pictures—rehearsed by the Jews over the centuries, given by God through Moses (Leviticus 23)—of His plan of redemption for mankind. This plan and chronology related to Jesus' First and Second Comings is presented in my first book, *The Last Shofar!* (2014), co-authored with Donald Zoller.

God's plan of redemption of man is also pictured in His natural revelation in the sky in the "gospel in the stars," which is mankind's original witness given by God, before God revealed this plan more fully in His Written Word. Scripture reveals that both revelations are true.

Although the birth of Jesus is significant, His crucifixion (covered in Part II) with His shed blood and death to pay the atonement price for our sins is *the most significant event* in earth history. Through His birth on earth as a man and later dying for our sins as a perfect human sacrifice, we, through our faith in Him and what He has done for each one of us personally on the cross, can have eternal life with Him and the Father (John 3:16). Amen. Praise God.

Next, we can consider *Section B* of Part I of this book: "*Where* Was Jesus Born?"

SECTION B

Where Was Jesus Born?

Introduction to Section B

> Jesus was born in Bethlehem, but *where* in Bethlehem? The case is that Jesus was born at *Migdal Edar* (Tower of the Flock), where the sacrificial lambs for the temple were born, in the biblical town of Bethlehem.

Yes, of course, Jesus was born in Bethlehem. "Everyone" knows that. Of course, except for the historic King Herod the Great who lived in Jerusalem.

When the Magi visited King Herod's royal court in search of where the Messiah was born, Herod had to ask the religious authorities what the Scriptures teach. The Old Testament clearly teaches that Jesus was to be born *in Bethlehem* (Micah 5:2), and He was, of course, born *in Bethlehem*, the hometown of Jesus' relative, King David. Herod did not know what the Scripture taught and had to ask the Temple authorities.

But, *where* in Bethlehem was Jesus really born? That is the mystery and is a question which has an interesting answer. In this Section B of Part I, we are presenting a case for where I believe Jesus was *really* born in Bethlehem.

Piecing together scriptural clues, this case supports that He was born at *Migdal Edar* (mig-dawl ay-der; Heb. *"Tower of the Flock"*). OK, so what is *Migdal Edar* and where in Bethlehem is it located? We will go into these answers as part of this case study in the following chapters.

At this point, I think you have guessed that I do not support the *traditional site* for Jesus' birth, the *Basilica of the Nativity in Bethlehem*, and you are correct. I will explain why.

CHAPTER 13

Traditional Site vs. *Actual* Site

The spot where tourists are taken to see where Jesus was born is the *traditional site* of the birth of Jesus in Bethlehem.

Over the *traditional site* of a cave in Bethlehem is the present basilica—a type of Roman Catholic church—which was built by Emperor Justinian in AD 530 (6th Century). The basilica was built over the cave which Roman Emperor Constantine had originally identified as the birthplace of Jesus. At the request of Constantine's mother, Helena, Constantine built the original Basilica of the Nativity over that cave in the 4th Century. After the original basilica was destroyed, the replacement present basilica, built by Emperor Justinian, was constructed.

So, how did Helena and her son, Emperor Constantine (ruled AD 306–337), determine their site of Jesus' birth? Surely, they had good historical records to show them the correct site in Bethlehem. Well, not exactly. They found their site by relying on dreams and visions—the same way they "found" the site for the crucifixion and tomb of Jesus in Jerusalem, at the Church of the Holy Sepulcher, located to the west of the traditional "Temple Mount."

I support a totally different site of the crucifixion and burial, as presented in the case in Part II, Section B, "*Where* Were Jesus' Death, Resurrection, & Ascensions?" The site which Helena and Constantine selected for the crucifixion and burial of

Jesus, the Church of the Holy Sepulcher, was the site of the pagan Temple of Venus built by Roman Emperor Hadrian (ruled AD 117–138).

Similarly, the site of the Basilica of the Nativity in Bethlehem, the *traditional* birth site of Jesus selected by Constantine and Helena, was a pagan site—a sacred grove of Thammuz[143] of the Babylonian religion. In my humble opinion, this seems hardly a good site for God to have chosen for the birthplace of His Son. Perhaps, the dreams and visions of Constantine and Helena came from other lesser sources than from God. Just a thought.

Really, it is surprising that the present basilica built by Emperor Justinian has stood since AD 530, considering all the wars over the years in the Middle East. The present basilica was apparently spared destruction from the Persians in AD 614 because they saw the depictions of the Magi (from ancient Persia) on its walls.

All this history of the *traditional* site is "interesting," but I think the case presented for the *actual* birth site of Jesus at *Migdal Edar* in Bethlehem is even more interesting, and I believe it is biblically supportable.

CHAPTER 14

Case for *Migdal Edar*

John the Baptist exclaimed, *"Behold the Lamb of God, which takes away the sin of the world"* (John 1:29, KJV). I believe he was making a statement which even relates to His birth site in Bethlehem. How so?

It has to do with the roadmap from Scripture providing several bits and pieces of evidence which come together in this case for the birthplace of Jesus being in Bethlehem at a place called *Migdal Edar* [Heb. "Tower of the Flock;" pronounced mig-dawl ay-der].

In addition to the statement by John the Baptist equating Jesus to *"the Lamb of God,"* these bits and pieces from Scripture include several seemingly diverse subjects. These include specific statements in both the Old Testament and New Testament—about the specific shepherds who knew exactly where to find the Messiah born "in Bethlehem," the background of the lambs which were distinctly born and raised in the fields of Bethlehem to be used as sacrifices in the temple in Jerusalem, and the account of the death of Jacob's wife Rachel on the outskirts of Bethlehem. They all point to the actual birthplace of Jesus—*Migdal Edar*.

How come most of us have never heard of *Migdal Edar* in relation to the birthplace of Jesus? Well, once again because the church was led astray in the 4th century AD by Constantine and his mother, Helena, with their unbiblical dreams and visions. They incorrectly selected the birth site of Jesus as the cave under the present Basilica of the Nativity, and this became the *traditional site* of Jesus' birth.

To use the analogy presented in the introductory section "A Beginning Word" at the beginning of this book, the poor navigational aid of Constantine and Helena led the church to a "farmer's field" in the country rather than to the correct location.

Let's see where key statements in the Old Testament and New Testament lead us to find the actual birthplace of Jesus. You can evaluate the evidence for the case presented.

I give credit to Cooper P. Abrams, III for bringing together many of the details for the case for *Migdal Edar* being the birthplace of Jesus in his internet article, "Where Was the Birth Place of the Lord Jesus?"[144]

A. Old Testament Account of the Birthplace of Jesus—Micah's Prophecy

When the Magi from Persia came to Jerusalem in search of the birth of the Messiah of the Jews, they called upon King Herod as a courtesy and inquired of him where the Messiah was to be born. The Jewish religious authorities gave their answer from an Old Testament passage from Micah:

> But thou, **Bethlehem Ephratah**, though thou be little among the thousands of Judah, yet out of thee shall he [Messiah; **Jesus**] come forth unto me that is to be ruler in Israel; whose goings forth have been from of old, from everlasting" (Micah 5:2, KJV; clarification and emphasis mine).

There are several names used in connection with *Bethlehem—Ephratah* (Micah 5:2) and *Ephrath* (Gen. 35:16, 19; 45:7; 48:7). Ephrath is another name for Bethlehem (Gen. 35:19). It should be noted that Ephrath (or Ephratah) was the ancient name for the area which later was called Bethlehem. Ephrath means "ash heap" and "place of fruitfulness," and seems to have a tie-in to Isaiah 61:3 which mentions *"beauty from ashes ... "* Of course, it is widely known that the word "Bethlehem" means "house of bread." This too is a tie-in to Jesus, as He stated during the Seder with the Disciples (the Last Supper) that He is the bread which is broken for each of us (Luke 22:19), and He had previously said that He was the true bread which came down from heaven (John 6:32–33), and that He is *"the bread of life" (John 6:35)*.

The context of the visit of the Magi to Bethlehem in search of the Messiah, 15 months after the birth of Jesus, is given in Section A. 1. of Chapter 7: "Star of Bethlehem and Magi's Visit."

So, we know from Micah 5:2 that the Messiah would be born in Bethlehem. But exactly *where* in Bethlehem is the mystery, and that is our question and answer in our case presented.

One would think that the *New Testament* would tell us precisely where the Messiah would be born "in Bethlehem." However, it does not. Surprisingly, the *Old Testament* gives us the answer. An earlier verse in the book of Micah tells us *exactly* where to expect His birth:

> And thou, **O tower of the flock**, the strong hold of the daughter of Zion, **unto thee shall it come, even the first dominion; the kingdom** [the Messiah shall bring the Kingdom] shall come to the daughter of Jerusalem [God's people; the mother of Jesus is from Israel]." (Micah 4:8, KJV; clarification and emphasis mine)

This *"tower of the flock"* mentioned in Micah 4:8 is in Hebrew *"Migdal Edar"* [mig-dawl ay-der] and literally means "watch tower of the flock." Micah 4:8 tells us that the Messiah, Jesus, would be born at *Migdal Edar,* in Bethlehem. We will have more to say about this in following subsections of this chapter, which further build our case.

What is this "watch tower of the flock?" Without a doubt, this was a military tower to keep watch into the valley at the edge of Bethlehem and provide protection to the city. These types of towers are mentioned in various Old Testament references (Judges 8:71; 9:46, 51; 2 Kings 9:17, 18:8; Nehemiah 3:1). Cooper P. Abrams III states in his article related to *Migdal Edar* in Jerusalem:

> This watch tower from ancient times was used by the shepherds for protection from their enemies and wild beasts. It was also **the place ewes were safely brought to give birth to the lambs. In this sheltered building/cave the priests would bring in the ewes which were about to lamb for protection.** These special lambs came from a unique flock that was designated for sacrifice at the temple in Jerusalem.[145]

Abrams goes on to state the following:

> Typically, "Migdal Edar", (the tower of the flock) at Bethlehem is the perfect place for Christ to be born. He was born in the very birthplace where tens of thousands of lambs, which had been sacrificed to prefigure Him. God promised it, pictured it, and performed it at "Migdal Edar". It all fits together, for that's the place where sacrificial lambs were born!

Jesus was not born behind an inn, in a smelly stable where donkeys of travelers and other animals were kept. He was born in Bethlehem, at the birthing place of the sacrificial lambs that were offered in the Temple in Jerusalem which Micah 4:8 calls the "tower of the flock."[146]

This specific watch tower in ancient Bethlehem is first mentioned in Genesis in relationship to the death of Rachel, the beloved wife of Jacob, as they traveled to Bethlehem. We say more about that in Section F of this chapter.

B. Consideration of the Sheep and Shepherds of the Fields at *Migdal Edar*

What else can we say about the specific sheep and shepherds identified in the well-known passage in Luke on the birth of Jesus? Alfred Edersheim (1825 – 1889) in his classic book, *The Life and Times of Jesus The Messiah* (1883; republished Latest Edition, 1993), as a Messianic Jew, has great insights from a Hebrew-Christian perspective and references Jewish sources—the Mishnah[147] and Targum.[148] His book was the result of seven years of research and writing. In it Edersheim states:

> That the Messiah was to be born in Bethlehem, was a settled conviction. Equally so was the belief, that **He was to be revealed from *Migdal Eder*,** 'the tower of the flock' [Targum Pseudo-Jon. On Gen. 35:21]. This *Migdal Eder* was not the watchtower for the ordinary flocks which pastured on the barren sheep ground beyond Bethlehem, but lay close to the town, on the road to Jerusalem. A passage in the Mishnah (Shekelim 7.4) leads to the conclusion, that **the flocks, which pastured there, were destined for Temple-sacrifices** [footnote 15: In fact the Mishnah (Baba K. 7.7) expressly forbids the keeping of flocks throughout the land of Israel, except in the wildernesses—and the only flocks otherwise kept, would be those for the Temple-services (Baba K. 80a)], and, and, accordingly, that **the shepherds, who watched over them, were not ordinary shepherds.**[149]

We can say that the flocks which were pastured around Migdal Edar (Eder) were sheep destined for temple sacrifices, and the shepherds who tended them were special shepherds—trained to take care of these sheep from birth to the time they were ready to be used for temple sacrifice. Our case is that Jesus was born in this same "Tower of the Flock," and these are the shepherds which went to see Jesus and His mother and father in that structure after His birth.

C. New Testament Account of the Birthplace of Jesus

Luke has the most complete account of the birth of Jesus in Bethlehem, as recorded in Chapter 2:

> And Joseph also went up from Galilee, out of the city of Nazareth, into Judaea, unto the **city of David, which is called Bethlehem**; (because he was of the house and linage of David) To be taxed with Mary his espoused wife, being great with child. And so it was, that, while they were there, the days were accomplished that she should be delivered. And **she brought forth her firstborn son, and wrapped him in swaddling clothes, and laid him in a manger; because there was no room for them in the inn**. And there were in the same country **shepherds abiding in the field, keeping watch over their flock by night**. And, lo, the angel of the Lord came upon them, and the glory of the Lord shone round about them: and they were sore afraid. And the angel said unto them, Fear not: for, behold, I bring you good tidings of great joy, which shall be to all people. For unto you is **born this day in the city of David** a Saviour, which is Christ the Lord. And **this shall be a sign unto you; Ye shall find the babe wrapped in swaddling clothes, lying in a manger**. And suddenly there was with the angel a multitude of the heavenly host praising God, and saying, Glory to God in the highest, and on earth peace, good will toward men. And it came to pass, as the angels were gone away from them into heaven, the shepherds said one to another, **Let us now go even unto Bethlehem**, and see this thing which is come to pass, which the Lord hath made known unto us. And **they came with haste, and found Mary, and Joseph, and the babe lying in a manger.** And when they had seen it, they made known abroad the saying which was told them concerning this child. And all they that heard it wondered at those things which were told by the shepherds. But Mary kept all these things, and pondered them in her heart. And **the shepherds returned, glorifying and praising God for all the things that they had heard and seen, as it was told unto them.** (Luke 2:4–20 KJV; emphasis mine)

The New Testament tells us that Jesus was, indeed, born in Bethlehem, but the New Testament does not state the exact place in Bethlehem where Jesus was born. Nativity scenes displayed at Christmas time depict the birth of Jesus in a stable surrounded by donkeys, chickens, and cows. This is due to the tradition that Jesus was born in the stable behind the inn where the animals were kept, because there was no room for Joseph and Mary in the inn. However, all that is stated is that Mary gave birth to Jesus, laid Him in a manger, and wrapped Him in swaddling clothes. We know that these things occurred somewhere in Bethlehem at the time of His birth.

From Micah 4:8 we know that He was specifically born at "the tower of the flock" (*Migdal Edar*). Comments on the specifics of Luke 2:4–20 are given in the following sub-sections of this chapter.

D. Consideration of the Terms "Manger" and "Swaddling Clothes"

The account of the announcement of the birth of Jesus in Luke mentions *"manger"* and *"swaddling clothes."* What are these referring to? And why are these a *"sign"* as the angel told the shepherds in the field. Once again, here is the passage from Luke:

> And she brought forth her firstborn son, and **wrapped him in swaddling clothes, and laid him in a manger;** because there was no room for them in the inn. And there were in the same country shepherds abiding in the field, keeping watch over their flock by night. And, lo, the angel of the Lord came upon them, and the glory of the Lord shone round about them, and the glory of the Lord shone round about them: and they were sore afraid. And the angel said unto them, Fear not: for, behold, I bring you good tidings of great joy, which shall be to all people. For unto you is born this day in the city of David a Saviour, which is Christ the Lord. And **this shall be a sign unto you; Ye shall find the babe wrapped in swaddling clothes, lying in a manger**. And suddenly there was with the angel a multitude of the heavenly host praising God, and saying, Glory to God in the highest, and on earth peace, good will toward men. And it came to pass, as the angels were gone away from them into heaven, the shepherds said one to another, **Let us now go even unto Bethlehem**, and see this thing which is come to pass, which the Lord hath made known unto us. And **they came with haste, and found Mary, and Joseph, and the babe lying in a manger.** (Luke 2:7–16, KJV; emphasis mine)

The Greek word which is translated *"manger"* in our English Bibles is *Yatnh phat-ne* [pronounced: fat'-nay]. It is defined as *"stall"* where animals are kept, and in Luke 13:15 it is translated that way. In Proverbs 14:4, in the Septuagint [Greek translation of the Old Testament], the word means a *"stall"* or a *"crib."* Of course, the question becomes what kind of "stall" or "manger" is being referred to in the New Testament and what kind of animal(s) were fed or housed there?

Is there a "logical" place where God would choose to have His Son born, which would be described by the angel to the shepherds in the country as being *"… a **sign** unto you; Ye shall find the babe wrapped in **swaddling clothes**, lying in a **manger**"*?

To be a *"sign,"* it must be distinctive, understandable, and have unique meaning. From the description of the *"swaddling clothes"* and the *"manger,"* the shepherds knew right where to go to find the babe. Where was that? Our case is that they went to where the new-born lambs were typically wrapped in swaddling clothes and in a manger—in the "Tower of the Flock" (*Migdal Edar*), not far from where they were tending the sheep which birthed the lambs used for sacrifice in the temple.

The *"Lamb of God,"* as John the Baptist called Jesus, was born in the unique place where the other lambs used for sacrifice were born. Indeed, that was a unique *"sign"* to these shepherds—this baby was, indeed, the *"Savior, Christ the Lord,"* the promised Messiah, as told to them by the angel of the Lord which appeared to them and as prophesized by the Prophets of Israel.

Note what is said of the shepherds *"And they came with haste, and found Mary, and Joseph, and the babe lying in a manger."* They did not have to go into Bethlehem and search each and every stable to find which one contained this newly born baby with Mary and Joseph. The impression given is that they were able to go *"with haste"* because they knew from the descriptions of the *"wrapped in swaddling clothes"* and *"lying in a manger"* exactly where to go—to the "Tower of the Flock," *Migdal Edar*. It was not just any stable in Bethlehem, it was uniquely where the sacrificial lambs were birthed and protected. There was no need for the angel to give the shepherds directions to the place of Jesus' birth because they already knew where to go to find Him.

E. Key Statement Made by John the Baptist About Jesus

The father of John the Baptist was Zacharias, a priest who served in the temple in Jerusalem. John the Baptist was the only son of Zacharias and was also of the priestly line. In a sense, John the Baptist was the first of several things: Christian witness, Christian preacher, Christian prophet, and Christian martyr. He was the first to baptize converts, and he might have even started the first "church" as the disciples of Jesus were initially following John before they were instructed to follow Jesus (John 1:35–37; Acts 1:15–26).

Before we look at the famous statement by John the Baptist upon seeing Jesus, it is helpful to first review the problem of sin, which ties into the statement of John and gives us better understanding of the context.

The Bible teaches that mankind has a sin problem. Sin is violation of God's Word; rebellion against God. This is a big problem with God and, hence, with man. God is holy and He cannot have sin in His presence. Unfortunately, sin came into the world through the one-man Adam in the Garden of Eden, as presented in the early chapters of Genesis. But, fortunately, God already had His plan of redemption through the one-man Jesus, which He had planned from the very foundations of the world (Rom. 5:12–21; Pet. 1:18–20; Rev. 13:8; John 1:29).

The need for a substitutionary sacrifice and shedding of innocent blood to atone for sin is laid out in Scripture, beginning in Genesis 3:21, with the evidence of the garments of skin to cover the nakedness and shame of Adam and Eve following their sinful disobedience of God. A blood sacrifice is required of God, as presented in Leviticus: *"For the life of the flesh is in the blood: and I have given it to you upon the altar to make an atonement for your souls: for it is the blood that maketh an atonement for the soul" (Lev. 17:11 KJV).*

God's ultimate plan of redemption is further laid out in the account of Abraham's willingness to offer his son, Isaac, on an altar at God's command (Gen. 22). Abraham's hand was stayed and God provided an alternate substitute as a sacrifice, as He would provide in His Son, Jesus. In addition, God's ultimate plan of redemption is laid out in the Feasts of the Lord, which God gave as yearly rehearsals by the people of Israel, starting with the Feast of Passover and the shedding of the blood of an innocent lamb (Lev. 23). My first book, *The Last Shofar!–What the Fall Feasts of the Lord are Telling the Church* (2014), in Chapter 6, "The Feasts of the Lord–A Preview of Coming Events," provides a good description of God's plan of redemption in Jesus, as foreshadowed in the Feasts of the Lord. It is an interesting and valuable study.

This background of the problem of sin and God's remedy in providing a perfect sacrifice for mankind's sin in the sacrifice of His one and only son, the Son of God, now gives increased understanding to John the Baptist's statement upon seeing Jesus approaching, *"Behold the Lamb of God, which taketh away the sin of the world" (John 1:29).* Jesus is uniquely the perfect lamb sacrifice which God provided to pay the sin debt of mankind—He is, indeed, *"the Lamb of God, which takes away the sin of the world."*

The lambs sacrificed daily in the temple ceremonies, as was the Passover lamb sacrificed annually both in the temple and in the homes of the Israelites at the celebration of Passover, were but foreshadowing of the ultimate sacrifice of the Son of God, Jesus. He alone is the perfect sacrifice of God to sufficiently pay the sin-debt of mankind for all those who trust in His sacrifice. John the Baptist likened Jesus to the lambs carefully chosen and sacrificed by the Priests in the temple.

So, how does all this relate to Jesus, likened to the lambs carefully chosen and sacrificed in the temple including the place of Jesus' birth, *Migdal Edar* ("Tower of the Flock")? In fact, it has everything to do with this analogy of Jesus and the sacrificial lambs.

F. What's with Rachel, wife of Jacob, and *Migdal Edar?*

So, what does Rachel have to do with the birthplace of Jesus? It involves a veiled prophecy in Genesis, and it has to do with the first mention in Scripture of the term *Migdal Edar (Heb. "Tower of the Flock")*. It is related to the death of Rachel and where Jacob pitched his tent following her death. Let's look at it in the two passages in Genesis (Genesis 35:5–21 and Genesis 48:7):

> 5 And they journeyed: and the terror of the God was upon the cities that were round about them, and they did not pursue after the sons of Jacob. So **Jacob** came to Luz, which is in the land of Canaan, that is, **Bethel** [Heb. literally "House of God"], he and all the people that were with him. And **he built there an altar, and called the place El-beth-el: because there God appeared unto him**, when he fled from the face of his brother [Esau]. But Deborah Rebekah's nurse died, and she was buried beneath Bethel under an oak: and the name of it was called Allon-bachuth. And God appeared unto Jacob again, when he came out of Padan-aram, and blessed him. And God said unto him, Thy name is Jacob: thy name shall not be called any more Jacob, but **Israel shall be thy name**: and he called his name Israel. And God said unto him, I am God Almighty, be fruitful and multiply: a nation and a company of nations shall be of thee, and **kings shall come out of thy loins**; And the land which I gave Abraham and Isaac, to thee will I give the land. And God went up from him in the place where he talked with him. And Jacob set up a pillar of stone: and he poured a drink offering thereon, and he poured oil thereon.
>
> 16 And they journeyed from Bethel; and there was a little way to come to **Ephrath**: and Rachel travailed, and she had hard labour. And it came to pass, when she was in hard labour, that the midwife said unto her, Fear not; thou shalt have this son also. And it came to pass, as her soul

was in departing, (for she died) that she called his name Ben-oni: but his father called him Benjamin. **And Rachel died, and was buried in the way to Ephrath, which is Bethlehem**. And Jacob set a pillar upon her grave: that is the pillar of Rachel's grave unto this day. 21 **And Israel journeyed, and spread his tent beyond <u>the tower of Edar</u>** [Heb. Migdal Edal: "Tower of the Flock"]. (Genesis 35:5–21, clarification and emphasis mine)

7 And I, when I came from Padan, Rachel died on me in the land of Canaan in the way, with **only a little way to come to Ephrath. And I buried her there in the way to Ephrath. It being Bethlehem.** (Genesis 48:7, The Interlinear Bible, Vol. I; emphasis mine)

7 And as for me, when I came from Padan, **Rachel died by me in the land of Canaan in the way, when yet there was but a little way to come unto Ephrath: and I buried her there in the way of Ephrath; the same is Bethlehem.** (Genesis 48:7, KJV; emphasis mine)

Reflecting on the passages in Genesis related to the death of Rachel as Jacob and Rachel traveled from Bethel to Ephrath (Bethlehem), and where Jacob buried Rachel *"there in the way of Ephrath; the same is Bethlehem,"* it is easy to consider the gravity of the situation for Jacob. After Jacob buried Rachel, he traveled on *"… and spread his tent beyond the tower of Edar"* [Heb. Migdal Edar: "Tower of the Flock"]. We can only imaging Jacob's emotional state of grief. Jacob loved Rachel more than all his other wives; he always did from the time he first laid eyes on her (Gen. 29:17–18, 30). When she died, he was heart-broken. The love of his life had just died.

But why would Moses record that Jacob pitched his tent at *Migdal Edar* at Bethlehem? What is significant about that place? Indeed, every word of Scripture is there for a reason (Deut. 32:47). We don't know for sure, but I can offer some thoughts which I believe tie into this story.

This case is that from the Tower of the Flock would later come the birth of the Messiah who would eventually take away all death and heart-break and tears. Rachel and Jacob would eventually weep no more—Rachel would eventually be restored to life for eternity in the presence of the God of Abraham, Isaac, and Jacob. Significantly, from the place of Jacob's greatest sorrow, where his beloved Rachel died, would later come the birth of the Messiah who would bring about life and joy forever for all those who trusted in Him, including both Jacob and Rachel.

Did Jacob fully understand all these things? Probably not, but he did understand that he believed in God and knew that He was all-powerful and that He was good, holy, and righteous. I believe that Jacob trusted in God for redemption and for making all things right again, including taking away death and his heart-break.

Eventually, 1,800 years later, Jesus would be born at *Migdal Edar*, and God's ultimate plan of redemption for mankind would be set in motion, leading eventually to the Son-of-God's death on the "tree" in Jerusalem, paying the sin-debt for Rachel and Jacob and each of us who put our trust in Him.

Is the Rachel connection conclusive of *Migdal Edar* being the birthplace of Jesus? Admittedly, the evidence related to Rachel is not in itself definitive for supporting the case for *Migdal Edar*, but the other evidence provided in this chapter further implies the validity of this case—especially Micah 4:8. Once again, we leave it to you to evaluate the total evidence for the case being presented and come to your own conclusion.

CHAPTER 15

Significance of *Migdal Edar*

This specific field of the specific flock and the specific shepherds where the angel of the Lord came to announce the birth of *"the Savior, the Lord [Jesus]"* was chosen by God for a reason. A very important reason. God does not work by happenstance.

The location in Bethlehem might have been chosen to honor David, who was selected by God to be the King of Israel and who was beloved by God and was in the genetic line of the Messiah. It is likely that the shepherds in the fields of Bethlehem were in the same fields where King David as a boy tended his father's sheep and composed Psalms to honor God. The shepherds in the field to which the angel came undoubtedly knew the Psalms, especially those written by David, who grew up as a shepherd himself. Perhaps, the shepherds had recently read Psalm 8 written by David (and quoted in Hebrews 2:6–8 where it is clearly applied prophetically to Jesus):

> When I consider thy heavens, the work of thy fingers, the moon and the stars, which thou hast ordained; what is man, that thou art mindful of him? And the son of man, **that thou visitest him**? For thou hast **made him a little lower than the angels**, and hast crowned with glory and honour." (Psalm 8:3–5, KJV, emphasis mine)

But just because David had tended sheep in the same fields of Bethlehem, I don't think this is the direct reason that God selected Bethlehem and this particular field. It also might be because this was the same land which Boaz redeemed for Naomi and later passed on to Jesse, David's father. But I don't think this is the reason either.

Rather, I think God chose *Migdal Edar* as the site of the birthplace of Jesus because this was the place where the sacrificial lambs were birthed and protected, intended to be an acceptable sacrifice at the Temple ceremonies. Jesus, born at that same place, would later be that perfect and acceptable sacrifice as the "Lamb of God" to take away the sin of the world. This is why, I believe, God selected *Migdal Edar* to be the birthplace of the Messiah. He was born to die, just as the lambs born there were intended for death as temple sacrifices. The lambs had to continuously be sacrificed to temporarily cover the sins of the people; Jesus the perfect, acceptable sacrifice of God died once and once only to pay the price of our sin-debt to God. His death was acceptable to God for all those who trust in His sacrifice for his/her sins. That is the Good News of the Gospel.

Why is it important that *Migdal Edar* is the birthplace of Jesus? One simple main reason—it is where Scripture states that the Messiah, Jesus, would be born (Micah 4:8). It is stated that all Scripture is given by inspiration and is true (II Timothy 3:14, 16), and if we say that Jesus was born somewhere else, then we are saying that the Scriptures are not true. In addition, all Scripture points to this place.

There is presently no archeological evidence for the exact location of *Migdal Edar* in ancient Bethlehem at the time of Jesus. Admittedly, it *could* be at the present location of the Basilica of the Nativity but not necessarily. I rather suspect that the site selected by Helena, the mother of Constantine, by her dreams and visions, is probably not the correct location.

CHAPTER 16

Conclusion of *Where* Was Jesus Born?

Our case is that Jesus was, indeed, born in Bethlehem—in a specific structure called *Migdal Edar*, which is Hebrew for "Tower of the Flocks." I have laid out the case in the chapters of this Section B of Part I. The case is strong and is true, especially because Micah 4:8 says that the Messiah would be born there. Of course, you need to come to your own conclusion from the evidence presented.

The coming to earth of Jesus, the very Son of God, to be born of a young Jewish virgin, in an obscure structure within the town of Bethlehem in Judah, where the lambs destined for temple sacrifice were birthed, certainly seems fitting for the Christ child. That the shepherds in this specific field knew exactly where to go to find the child—wrapped in swaddling clothes and lying in a manger, having been born and announced to them by an angel sent from God—is testimony to Jesus' birth in this unique structure in this unique shepherd's field.

PART II

Mysteries of Jesus' *Death, Resurrection & Ascensions* Revealed

Introduction to Part II

This **Part II: Mysteries of Jesus'** *Death, Resurrection, & Ascensions* **Revealed** presents cases related to these mysteries. This presentation in Part II is divided into the following three sections:

- **Section A**: "*When* Were Jesus' Death, Resurrection, & Ascensions?" introduces the case for the *actual* days of the week and the *actual* year that Jesus was crucified, buried, rose again from the tomb, and ascended to heaven.

- **Section B**: "*Where* Were Jesus' Death, Resurrection, & Ascensions?" presents the case for the *actual sites* of the crucifixion, burial, resurrection, & ascensions.

- **Section C**: "*How* Did Jesus *Really* Die?" presents the case for the crucifixion and stoning of Jesus as He hung on a living tree on the Mount of Olives.

Once again, as you read these case studies, you will see that the *traditional* dates and *traditional* places are *not* supported by biblical and reliable historical evidence. In addition, there is good evidence that the actual cause of Jesus' death is different from church tradition. In summary, we believe that much of what we have previously been taught on these subjects is not true.

You can evaluate the evidence presented to make your own decision as to the validity of the conclusions.

SECTION A

When Were Jesus' Death, Resurrection & Ascensions?

Introduction to Section A

Did Jesus really die on "Good Friday" of church tradition?

Our case is that Jesus **died** per the chronology of the written Torah on the *Mosaic Pesach* (Passover) on Nisan/Abib 13 (*Wednesday*) in AD 30, between 2:30 and 3:30 PM—considered to be *"in-between the evening times"* at the beginning of Nisan/Abib 14. This is per the chronology of the original Mosaic Passover lamb sacrifice which occurred in Egypt before the Exodus, modeling the death of the future Messiah. It is not on the *Pesach* of the *Pharisaic tradition* at the time of Jesus.

Jesus was **buried** at sunset of Nisan 13, being the start ("dawning") of Nisan 14 (Thursday), which was the *Pharisaic Day of Preparation* at the time of Jesus; the *Pharisaic Passover* for that week was on Nisan 15 (Friday), which was also the first day of Unleavened Bread.

Our case is that Jesus was **resurrected** at the very start of the Feast of Firstfruits, at sunset of Nisan 16 (the ending of Saturday), being also the start of Nisan 17 (the start of Sunday). All this is in alignment with the teaching of Moses given by God and what we believe to be correct per Hebrew understanding. Evidence for this case is presented and explained.

WHEN WERE JESUS' DEATH, RESURRECTION & ASCENTIONS?

> Our case is that Jesus **ascended** to heaven on two occasions. The first was later in the day of His resurrection, fulfilling a portion of the temple ceremony of Firstfruits. His second ascension was His public ascension, 40 days after the resurrection.

The correct chronology of the crucifixion week of Jesus is a mystery. I believe that it can be correctly solved, and our case is our attempt to do that.

A case is presented for the actual *days* (and the *year*) on the Jewish calendar when Jesus died, when He was buried, when He was resurrected, and when He ascended to heaven. The details of the OT and Gospel accounts are presented, as well as Hebrew understanding of Jewish laws and customs—including the Feasts of the Lord (Leviticus 23).

This case is for Jesus' **death** being on the *Mosaic Pesach* (Passover), per the chronology of the written Torah, and specifically in AD 30 on Nisan/Abib 13 (*Wednesday*), between 2:30 and 3:30 PM—considered to be *"in-between the evenings times"* at the beginning of Nisan/Abib 14 (*Thursday*). It should be noted that by dying as the *Pesach* lamb according to the *written Torah*, Jesus was able to correct Judaism in its errors of Torah interpretation related to the timing of the Passover and Unleavened Bread.

Our case for the **resurrection** is at the very start of the Feast of Firstfruits, at sunset of Nisan 16 (the ending of *Saturday*), being also the start of Nisan 17 (the start of *Sunday*). We believe our case is in alignment with the teachings of Moses given by God at Mt. Sinai, the teachings of Jesus, and per correct understanding of Hebrew laws and customs.

In addition to what is provided herein, a good background understanding of the seven Feasts of the Lord (Leviticus 23) and their fulfillment in Jesus is important and is further provided by the authors in Chapter 6 of *The Last Shofar!*

It is also important to keep in mind the different ways that days are divided. While certainly most cultures operate on a 24-hour day, not all cultures begin and end their days alike. There are major differences in the *Roman Day*, the *Jewish Day*, and our *Modern Western Day*. The ancient *Roman Day* began at 6:00 AM and ended at 6:00 AM the next morning. The *Jewish Day* basically began at sunset and closed the next sunset—essentially about 6:00 PM to the next 6:00 PM. Our *Modern Western Day* begins, of course, at midnight (12:00 PM) and closes the next midnight.

I am seeking to harmonize Scripture and present evidence for an alternate chronology for the Passion Week of our Lord vs. what is traditionally accepted. Biblical and extra-biblical references used to support *this case* are listed in the text and in the End Notes. General references used in writing this Section A of Part II are listed in the first ten Endnotes.[150–159]

Indeed, why is this new case for the chronology of Jesus' death, burial, and resurrection important? An expanded answer to this question is given at the "Conclusion" of this Section A. Basically, with this proposed chronology, there is harmony of Scripture, and what Jesus stated as the sign of His being the promised Messiah—that of *being 3 days and 3 nights in the earth* (Matt. 12:38-42)—was *literally* fulfilled. Otherwise, it was not. Certainly, this is highly significant.

Avi Ben Mordechai, a Messianic Jewish Rabbi, provides a good Jewish perspective as to why this is important to get it right as to the day that the Messiah Jesus was crucified:

> Was His death really on a Friday? If we assume that the narratives in the *B'rit Chadashah* [New Testament] must line up with the Jewish Scriptures referred to as *Tanakh* [Old Testament], then the answer is no; **Y'shua [Jesus] could not have died on a Friday and resurrected on a Sunday**. Now you may ask, why cause a stir over a seemingly insignificant issue concerning the exact day of Y'shua's death and resurrection? Isn't this 'nit-picking'? Afterall (sic), one may say, the issue of what day He died and resurrected is not worth arguing over. What matters is that we just 'believe in Jesus,' love Him, and be faithful servants. Well, from a Jewish point of view, I have a problem with that kind of thinking.
>
> You see, **if Y'shua was supposed to be the promised Mashiach [Messiah] and yet did not order His life precisely according to the Mosaic teachings (the Torah) to the letter then it is simple: He cannot be the Messiah and we are all fools for believing He was**. But since it is my intention to show that He did live by, interpret, and teach G-d's commandments, I obviously believe that He is qualified to be HaMashiach [the Messiah]. Therefore, as I see it, it is extremely important to sort out the truth in regards to His death and resurrection, because these events meet the details of the Jewish festivals and themes set up by G-d in the beginning. **It was imperative to Y'shua's validation as HaMashiach [the Messiah] that He die and resurrect on the exact days according to the divine revelation given to Moshe [Moses] on Mount Sinai.**
>
> Before we can look at the chronology surrounding the death and resurrection of Y'shua **we must return to the first *Pesach* or Passover**

in Egypt under the leadership of Moshe [Moses]. If the *Pesach* [Passover] redemption in Egypt was supposed to be a model of the redemption to come in HaMashiach then everything about Y'shua's life should have emulated that event.[160]

For a full understanding of Avi Ben Mordechai's case, one needs to read and study Chapter 3 ("Death and Resurrection of Messiah") of his book, *Messiah–Volume 2: Understanding His Life and Teachings in Hebraic Context* (1997); pp. 41–100. Chapter 3 of his book contains key insights from a Hebrew perspective related to Jewish law at the time of Jesus—totally unknown to most Bible scholars but pertinent to understanding the correct chronology of the crucifixion week. I have included key elements of Mordechai's presentation with references provided in this Section A of Part II.

CHAPTER 17

Traditional Dates vs. Actual Dates

Historically, the Christian church has held to a *tradition* that the death and burial of Jesus was on "Good Friday" of the week of the crucifixion and the traditional date for the resurrection being on Sunday morning, before the women mentioned in the Gospel accounts arrived at Jesus' tomb. However, is this *traditional* date for the death and burial of Jesus on "Good Friday" true?

A. Traditional Dates

It should be noted that "Good Friday" was not celebrated in the early Church. For the first 200 to 300 years, the early church celebrated the death, burial, and resurrection events within the framework of the Feasts of the Lord (*Passover*, Unleavened Bread and Firstfruits), as the church was still very Jewish and Jesus was regarded as the true *Passover lamb* [*"Christ our Passover is sacrificed for us"* (1 Corinthians 5:7)].

That the early church did not celebrate the death of Jesus on "Good Friday" is significant. Proponents of the Friday crucifixion day promote that the early church did recognize the Friday date from the very beginning of the church, which is just not true. Very scholarly books such as the book by Colin J. Humphreys,

The Mystery of the Last Supper–Reconstructing the Final Days of Jesus (Cambridge University Press, New York, 2011), affirm the "Good Friday" crucifixion. Part of Humphreys' reasoning is his support of the *inclusive* method of counting days and nights. In this method, partial days and partial night are counted to attain the *"three days and three nights"* of Jesus' prophecy (Matthew 12:40). He states in his book:

> "When Jesus died at 3 p.m. on Friday this therefore counts as a whole day and [whole] night (Thursday sunset to Friday sunset). The body of Jesus was in the tomb on the second day and night (Friday sunset to Saturday sunset), and, according to the gospels, he rose from the dead on the third day and night (Saturday sunset to Sunday sunset). Counting in this way ... a Friday crucifixion and Sunday [morning] resurrection are therefore consistent with Jesus being dead for ... 'three days and three nights'." (p. 24; clarification mine)

I personally have a problem with Humphreys' method of counting. To me it seems to be a "work around" and is a distorted way of counting days and nights. But if that was the only problem with this "Good Friday" assumption for the crucifixion, I might go along with it, as strange as it seems. However, there are other significant problems with a Friday crucifixion, as are included in the 11 "puzzle pieces" enumerated in Chapter 18, and explained in the subsequent chapters of this Section B of Part II. Therefore, I personally believe that the Friday crucifixion theory is incorrect on many levels.

The early church celebration included *two days of fasting* prior to the celebration of the resurrection, and this early celebration was not anchored to a single and particular day of the week, as the Jewish *Passover* could float to various days of the week due to the lunar Jewish calendar.

So, how did the first and second day of fasting evolve eventually into a distinct day of celebration known as "Good Friday?" The history leads back to the Roman Catholic Church.

"Good Friday" evolved after AD 325 resulting from Constantine's convened Council of Nicaea, which issued the Easter Rule, making "Easter" as the day of the resurrection to be celebrated on Sunday, but did not specify the exact Sunday. The Bishop of Alexandria was to determine the exact Sunday. In the 7th century, the church ruled that Easter was to be the first Sunday that occurred after the first full moon, on or after the vernal equinox. Easter is celebrated on a Sunday between the dates of March 22 and April 25. All this set a single day for the "Easter" festival and helped to create the "Easter" festival we know today but also fostered the emergence of "Good Friday" as a separate and distinct observance.[161]

WHEN WERE JESUS' DEATH, RESURRECTION & ASCENTIONS?

Historians can trace the development of "Good Friday" as the day of Jesus' death to the Roman Catholic festivals held in Jerusalem in the 4th century. It is an invention of the Roman Catholic Church. Basically, it comes from a misunderstanding of which Sabbath that Mark 15:42 was referring to: *"And now when the even was come, because it was the preparation, that is, the day before the Sabbath."* The Roman church assumed this referred to the *weekly Sabbath* rather than understanding that the first day of the 7-day festival of the Feast of Unleavened Bread is also a Sabbath (a "High Holy Day"). This first day of Unleavened Bread is the Sabbath ("High Holy Day") following the crucifixion of which Mark is referring, rather than the weekly Sabbath.[162]

Hence, the Catholic Church misplaced the day of the crucifixion as Friday, which became "Good Friday" for the church, rather than the correct day of Jesus' death being the floating day on the Jewish calendar when the Mosaic *Passover lamb* was sacrificed. This is further explained in this case presentation.

There is much other interesting history related to "Good Friday." How did "Good" get associated with this day's celebration? From the Online Entomology Dictionary, the word "good" (adj.) comes from the Old English *god* (with a long "o"). It is a derivative of Anglo-Saxon, Proto-Germanic and Slavonic/Old Russian forms of "good," but often equated to God.[163] Today, we frequently say, *"goodbye,"* (god/b/ye). Originally, the meaning *was "God be (with) you."* The Spanish word, *"Adios,"* literally means *"to God or with God."* Along these lines, "Good Friday" was first called *"God's Friday,"* or *"God's Day."*[164]

Only in the Western church tradition is the term "Good Friday" used. The Eastern church does not call this day "good," but they better characterize the day as it is—the ignominious death of the very Son of God on the "cross." Hence, names such as "Black Friday," "Great Friday," "Holy Friday," "Sorrowful Friday," etc. are commonly used.[165]

There are major problems with the "Good Friday" designation as the day our Lord died. The case presented here does not accept this day as the day that Jesus died because, in addition to other problems which will be covered later in our case, "Good Friday" was not celebrated in the early Church, it conflicts with what Jesus said, and it does not consider the issue of floating Sabbaths—as in the first day of the Jewish Unleavened Bread celebration—in interpreting the Gospel accounts.

However, regardless of what you believe, the most important thing is that Jesus died to pay the price for our sins and rose again for our justification.

B. Other Commonly Accepted but Incorrect Dates

Aside from the traditional *"Good Friday,"* the assumed day of the crucifixion by the Roman Catholic Church, others have proposed *Thursday* for the day of the crucifixion, attempting to align the statement of Jesus that He would be in the earth for *"three days and three nights"* (Matthew 12:40), like the period that Jonah was in the belly of the great fish. A partial day is counted as a whole day in an attempt to get the three days and three nights in the grave.

As will be shown in Chapter 2, this assumed *Thursday* crucifixion day is also incorrect. It can be discussed briefly here. This *Thursday crucifixion day* assumes the crucifixion being on Passover (Nisan 14), falling on Thursday of crucifixion week. These Thursday proponents argue that this would provide the fulfillment of Jesus' statement that He would be *"… in the heart of the earth three days and three nights" (Matthew 12:40 NIV)*. This would provide all day Friday, all day Saturday and a part of Sunday—by claiming a part of the day of Sunday they claim that this fulfills the "three days." In addition, the nights of Thursday night, Friday night and Saturday night would also meet the "three nights" requirement for this scenario. However, I believe that when Jesus stated *"three days and three nights"* he meant three *full days* and three *full nights*; it is, however, fully appreciated that there are places in Scripture where partial day counts are counted as full days.

There are some other problems with a Thursday crucifixion on Nisan 14. We present the evidence for AD 30 being the year of the crucifixion in Chapter 34 of this Section A of Part II. Astronomical evidence confirms that Passover of Nisan 14 was, indeed, on Thursday in AD 30, however, the crucifixion of Jesus was not on that Thursday but on *Wednesday*—per all the evidence being presented here, including the evidence of the alignment of Jesus' crucifixion to the historical Passover and slaying of the lambs in Egypt in the time of Moses. I have shown that this historical slaying of the lambs in Egypt was actually on the afternoon of *the day before* Nisan 14, during the "between the two evenings," as I have described per Jewish understanding—presented in Chapters 19–21 of this Section A of Part II. Several reasons for a *Wednesday crucifixion* with Nisan 14 being on Thursday are given in the case.

C. The Actual Dates

The date proposed by this case for the *death* of Jesus is *Wednesday* at 2:30 to 3:30 p.m., Nisan 13/Nisan 14, of AD 30. It is important to note that the *Wednesday* afternoon death on Nisan 13 is considered a part of the Nisan 14 Mosaic Passover, due to the Hebrew definition of "twilight" (*"between the evenings"*), as further explained in Chapter 20.

The date proposed by this case for the *resurrection* of Jesus is at the division of the ending of the weekly Sabbath on Saturday and the beginning of Sunday, at "twilight," at the start of Firstfruits. The case is presented in more detail in Chapters 6 and 7 of our book, *The Last Shofar!* (2014).

Additional commentary on this case for the resurrection being at the exact division of Saturday/Sunday per the Jewish start of the new day at "twilight" is given in this Section A of Part II, in Chapter 21: "*Puzzle Piece #3*–Timing of the Spring Feasts," specifically in the discussion of "Firstfruits."

CHAPTER 18

Eleven *Puzzle Pieces* Determine the *Days*

Bringing together the evidence for this case for a different chronology of Christ's crucifixion week is like bringing together the *pieces of a puzzle*—pieces that must harmonize and fit together to make a complete and reasonable case. Each piece is important and each piece must fit together to determine truth. I invite you to evaluate each piece of evidence to come to a decision as to the overall validity of the case presented.

You will see and come to appreciate the Hebrew perspective needed to properly understand the correct chronology of the crucifixion week of Jesus. Understanding the Hebrew perspective allows us to correctly interpret the biblical account. Without understanding the correct Hebrew perspective, one will not come to the correct chronology, which, in my opinion, has been the problem with many Christian theologians over the centuries since Jesus walked the earth. Unfortunately, many Christian traditions have been developed devoid of correct biblical interpretation.

The evidence is herein represented by *eleven puzzle pieces*, each with its own distinctive story, yet assembled without contradiction with the other pieces to make a complete picture. We will examine each piece of evidence for this case and in conclusion will provide a graphic depiction of the case for the correct chronology for Jesus' death, burial, and resurrection. The eleven *puzzle pieces* are as follows:

1. *Puzzle Piece #1–Which Jewish Passover?* Among the Jewish sects there were five Passovers, with some having different dates. Which did Jesus follow in His death on the cross?

2. *Puzzle Piece #2–Hebrew timing issues re Passover.* Essential to understand the correct chronology of the crucifixion week.

3. *Puzzle Piece #3–Timing of the Spring Feasts* (Passover, Unleavened Bread, and Firstfruits) (Leviticus 23:1–22).

4. *Puzzle Piece #4–Passover lamb inspected 4 days.* Required by Jewish law for the chief priests to examine the Passover Lamb before it is killed (Exodus 12:3–6).

5. *Puzzle Piece #5–Two Sabbaths in crucifixion week (Leviticus 23:7–8; John 19:31).*

6. *Puzzle Piece #6–Sign of Jesus Being Messiah—three days and three nights in the tomb.* Statement by Jesus to the Pharisees that, as a sign for his being the Messiah, He would, like Jonah, be in the heart of the earth **"for three days and three nights"** (Jonah 1:17; Matthew 12:40).

7. *Puzzle Piece #7–Events right after Jesus' death.*

8. *Puzzle Piece #8–Chronology of the women.* Timing of the women who witnessed the burial of Christ and, subsequently, both purchased and prepared spices (both being before and after a Sabbath—two different Sabbaths—with a period of time in between) for the proper burial of Christ's body (Mark 16:1; Luke 23:54–56).

9. *Puzzle Piece #9–Tradition of visiting burial site.* During the three days after the entombment to ensure the person was truly dead.

10. *Puzzle Piece #10–Astronomical considerations.* Related to the day of the week on which Passover (Nisan 14) occurred during the crucifixion week.

11. *Puzzle Piece #11–Traditions (Christian & Jewish).* To arrive at correct chronology of events of the crucifixion week.

The remaining chapters cover each of the eleven *Puzzle Pieces* as well as some other important topics. They provide background for assembling our case to determine the most probable days for the crucifixion and resurrection of Jesus.

CHAPTER 19

Puzzle Piece #1–Which Jewish Passover?

It may surprise you to learn that in first-century Judaism, including at the time of Jesus' crucifixion week, there were five Jewish sects having their "Passovers" with distinct days for the sacrifice of their lambs—the Mosaic Passover, the Samaritan's Passover, the Essene's Passover, the Sadducees' Passover, and the Pharisaic Passover. Which one did Jesus follow in his Passover *seder* (the "Last Supper") and in His sacrificial death? This is all part of the mystery that we are examining and which many researchers have seldom adequately considered.

That there were several "Passovers" is our *Puzzle Piece #1* for determining the true day of Jesus' death.

The first Passover (Heb. *Pesach*) was, of course, in Egypt under the leadership of Moses (the "Mosaic Passover"), and involved the passing-over of the Angel of Death for those households which were protected by the blood of the lamb placed on the doorframe of those houses. Those who did not have the blood applied to the doorframe of the house, as God instructed, incurred the death of the firstborn of the family. We can see this as a part of God's plan of Redemption of mankind, with the original Passover modeling the redemption to come through the Messiah and His shed blood on the cross—for all those who put their trust in Him for their personal salvation. **Jesus came at the appointed time as the *Passover Lamb of***

God** almost 1,500 years *following the model of the original Passover in Egypt. Hence, we need to understand the proper chronology of that original Passover and apply it to the chronology of the death of Jesus.

When was the date on the Jewish calendar of the original Passover? This is clearly stated in Leviticus 23:5–7: *"In the **first month*** [Nisan/Abib], ***on the fourteenth day of the month [Nisan 14] at twilight*** *is the Lord's Passover* (clarification and emphasis mine)." This date is reiterated in Numbers 9:1–5, 28:16, and Exodus 12:6. It is essential for Jesus, as the Messiah, to die and resurrect on the exact days per the revelation given to Moses at Mount Sinai. Why is this important to state this?

It is important because there developed among factions within Judaism *other dates* for Passover as well as *other times* during Nisan 14. Avi Ben Mordechai explains that over the centuries a reinterpretation of the meaning of *"at twilight"* in, for example, Exodus 12:6 came to mean the *end* of the day of Nisan 14, opposed to the period at the *beginning* of Nisan 14—both being *"at twilight."* One would interpret the killing of the Passover lamb at twilight in-between the 13th and 14th of Nisan, and another would interpret the killing of the lamb at twilight in-between the 14th and the 15th of Nisan. In both cases, it is still the 14th but one is at the beginning of the Jewish day and one is at the end of the day.[166]

The difference between the two interpretations determines when the Passover lamb is killed and when it is eaten. From ancient Jewish sources, we know that the Sadducees and the Samaritans (on Mount Gerizim) sacrificed their lambs on Nisan (Aviv) 13/14, 24-hours before the Pharisees on Nisan (Aviv) 14/15. In addition, per the Gospel accounts, the disciples of Jesus killed the Passover lamb for Jesus and the disciples—which was registered to Jesus and the disciples according to Jewish law—on Nisan 12 (late Tuesday) and ate it that Tuesday night (after the start of the Jewish day of Nisan 13) as part of Jesus' Passover *seder* (the "Last Supper").[167] Mordechai describes it thusly:

> Here, in the mid-afternoon of Aviv 12 (Tuesday), Y'shua [Jesus] instructs his *talmidim* [disciples] to sacrifice the *Pesach* [Passover lamb] in the Temple. Then, they went to prepare it and eat it with unleavened bread that evening [after start of Nisan 13]. In order for Y'shua [Jesus] to **be** the lamb, according to the Mosaic covenant, He had to **eat** the lamb a day earlier, which one could do so long as there was no leaven in the home.[168]
>
> … The meal [John 13:1] according to the sequence of events presented is Tuesday night, Aviv 13, before Y'shua's [Jesus'] crucifixion, set to occur late the next day (Wednesday), still Aviv 13, as it was giving way to Aviv 14 at sunset.[169]

WHEN WERE JESUS' DEATH, RESURRECTION & ASCENTIONS?

... [O]n the third day of the week (Tuesday), Aviv 12, He ordered the sacrifice of a *Pesach* lamb and told His *talmidim* [disciples] to roast it and prepare it for their final meal with Him that night. These words alone could prove that Y'shua [Jesus] died on the fourth day of the week (Wednesday) because He referred to the 'preparation day' 24-hours before His own sacrifice and **not** to the Pharisaic 'preparation day' which was to begin after midday on the day of His crucifixion ... following Tuesday's sunset as Aviv 12 turned to Aviv 13 ... He celebrated His final meal with His *talmidim* [disciples].[170] See the following graphic, Fig. 19.1, to show the chronology in the crucifixion week.

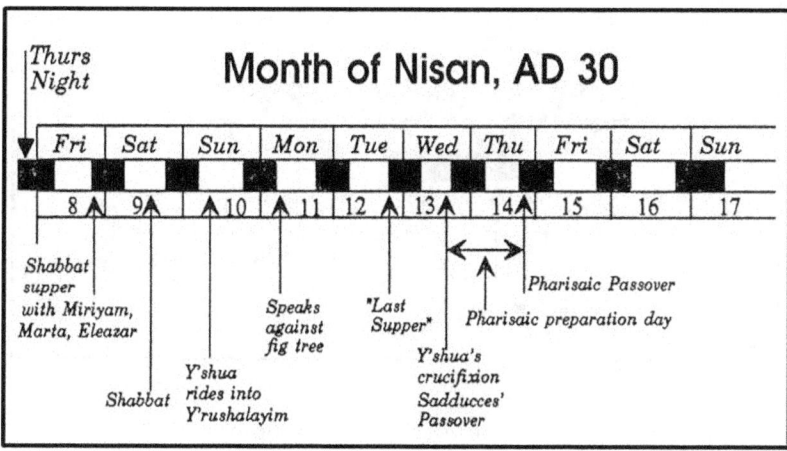

Figure 19.1. [171]Month of Nisan (Aviv), AD 30—Crucifixion Week and Days Before and After

In first-century Judaism, there were in a sense **two Passovers**: one was based on the written Torah (the one the *Tzedukim* [Sadducees] followed); one was based on the traditions of the *P'rushim* [Pharisees]. Since there were **two Passovers** celebrated on two different days in Judaism, we thus have two distinct days of 'preparation.' (Avi Ben Mordechai, op. cit., p. 77; clarification and emphasis mine)

... Y'shua [Jesus] died according to the written Torah on the Mosaic Pesach, Aviv 13/14 (late Wednesday afternoon), the narrative [John 19:31] is therefore referring to the Pharisaic day of preparation, **also** Aviv 13/14.[172]

MYSTERIES OF JESUS' LIFE REVEALED

Yes, it is a bit complicated! The quotations from Mordechai above give us a feel for the complications of the topics of the various Passovers of the sects of Judaism (*Sadducees* and *Pharisees*) going on during the crucifixion week, which Jesus and the disciples understood as well as understanding the original Mosaic Passover as described to Moses by God. Basically, Jesus and His disciples **ate** the *Mosaic* Passover lamb together on Tuesday night, Aviv 12, and Jesus **became** the Passover Lamb along with the sacrificial lamb of the *Sadducees* (who controlled Temple services per written Torah) on late Wednesday afternoon of Aviv 13/14, at *"twilight"* (*"between the evenings;"* this important *Hebrew idiom* is described in *Puzzle Piece #2*) of Aviv 14 (Thursday). See the following graphic, Fig. 19.2.

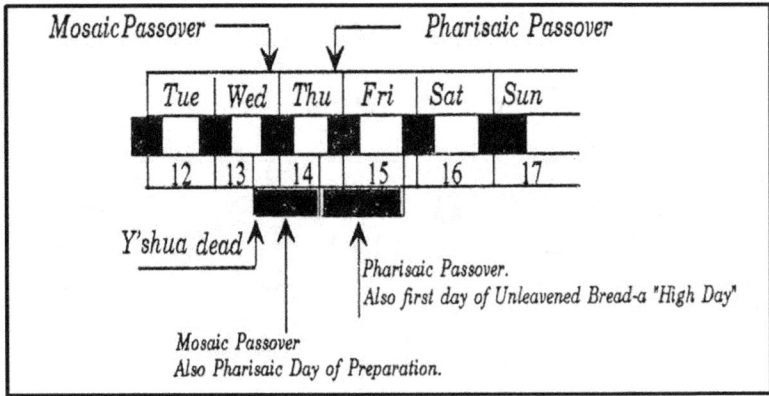

Figure 19.2. [173]Mosaic and Pharisaic Passovers of Crucifixion Week

The other Passovers celebrated by other sects of Judaism were the *Samaritan* Passover (celebrated in Samaria; was in alignment with the *Sadducees'* Passover) and the *Essene* Passover (celebrated by the Essenes located at En Gedi by the Dead Sea) in alignment with the *Mosaic* Passover.

Each of these various Passovers of the sects of Judaism had their own distinctive *Day of Preparation* prior to the sect's understanding of their first day of Unleavened Bread (a High Sabbath day; see *Puzzle Piece #5*), which complicates the proper interpretation of the Gospel accounts. In addition, there is the complication of the Preparation Day before the regular weekly Sabbath of the seventh day (Saturday).

In coming to our conclusions related to our case for the day of the crucifixion of Jesus (Wednesday of the crucifixion week in AD 30), I have considered all these aspects of the different Passovers of the various sects of Judaism.

It was understood among Judaism that the Messiah would restore Israel to proper Torah interpretation.[174]

WHEN WERE JESUS' DEATH, RESURRECTION & ASCENTIONS?

Our conclusion is that Jesus followed the Passover chronology during the crucifixion week as set forth by God *through Moses*—recorded in the Torah (Old Testament Scripture). This is our *Puzzle Piece #1*.

CHAPTER 20

Puzzle Piece #2–
Hebrew Timing Issues re Passover

Critical to the correct determination of the correct day and time of the day of Jesus' death during the crucifixion week is a correct understanding of several *Hebrew idioms* relating to timing descriptions in Scripture. These include the meanings of *"at twilight"* and *"between the two evening times."* These are part of our *Puzzle Piece #2*.

First, let's consider how *"at twilight"* is used in Scripture related to the 14th of Nisan (the first month in the Jewish religious calendar; also called Abib in Jewish literature). This is the day the *Pesach* (the Passover sacrifice) had to be sacrificed per the instructions given by God to Moses as recorded in the Old Testament:

> Take care of them [lamb or goat selected initially on the tenth day of Nisan/Abib] until the **fourteenth day** of the month [Nisan/Abib], when all the people of the community of Israel must slaughter them **at twilight**." (Exodus 12:6, NIV; clarification and emphasis mine)

> In the first month, on the **fourteenth day** of the month **at twilight** is the Lord's Passover. (Leviticus 23:5, NASB; emphasis added)

This same term, *"at twilight,"* relating to *"the fourteenth day"* of the month of Nisan is used in the first mentions in Scripture in Exodus 12:6 and Leviticus 23:5, and it is also similarly used in Numbers 9:1–5, 10–11.

What does this expression, *"at twilight,"* (Hebrew *beyn ha'arbaim*) mean? The Hebrew words are better translated as *"between the two evening times,"* which is very different from our common understanding of "twilight," meaning at the end of the daylight hours at dusk. This is a key understanding. Avi Ben Mordechai provides very helpful commentary from his unique Hebraic perspective:[175]

> For a *halachic* (Jewish legal) definition of *"between the two evenings times,"* let us refer to the ancient rabbinic writings of the Mishnah, compiled about 200 CE by Y'huday HaNasi:

> *The (afternoon) tamid (offering) is* **slaughtered at eight and a half hours** [the number of hours after 6:00 a.m., thus **2:30 p.m.**] *and is* **offered at nine and a half hours** [thus **3:30 p.m.**]. (*Mishnah, Pesachim 5, Mishnah 1*; clarification from Avi Ben Mordechai via footnote 2 of p. 43.)

> A further definition of *"between the two evening times"* is also found in Talmud tractate Pesachim which is commentary on the above quoted Mishnah:

> *The duty of the tamid (offering) properly [begins] from when the evening shadows begin to fall. What is the reason? Because Scripture saith,* **"between the evenings."** *[meaning]* **from the time that the sun commences to decline in the west.** (*Talmud Pesachim 58a; emphasis mine.*)

> According to additional *halacha* [Jewish legal teaching], **"between the two evening times"** refers to that time between noon and six o'clock. This is different from our understanding of **"twilight."** Since Mashiach Y'shua [Jesus] was to be the paschal lamb in fulfillment of the Torah, we can be certain that He was offered up precisely on schedule meaning **He died after 12 noon while it was still the 13th but before 6 p.m. when it became the 14th**, the period referred to as *beyn ha'arbaim*. However, specifically, **His death occurred between 2:30 and 3:30 p.m. on a weekday** which in Hebrew terminology means between 8.5 and 9.5 hours.[176]

Had He been crucified as the *Pesach* lamb on "**Good Friday**," as some would suppose, then this would have been the eve of the regular weekly

Shabbat [Sabbath] and therefore, His death would have been required according to Jewish *halacha*, between *12:30 and 1:30 p.m.*[177]

Above, we have the approximate time of His death conforming to *Tanakh* and Jewish *halacha* for a *Pesach* offering that happens to fall on a weekday, but certainly not one on the sixth day of the week (*Yom Shishi*)—Friday.[178]

Now, you may ask, why are we not told by the gospel writers specifically on what day of the week Y'shua died? Because it was assumed by the gospel writers in the first century that one would know, **according to the Mosaic covenant, that Jews offered their paschal lambs to G-d at the beginning of the 14th day of the first month [Nisan] as the sun was declining in the west on the 13th.** There was no need to tell the Jewish readers (including new Gentile converts) something they were expected to know. (Again, this overlap period between the **end** of the 13th and the **beginning** of the 14th is called *"beyn ha'arbaim"* or *"in between the two evening times."*)[179]

So, from the interpretation from a Hebrew perspective given by Avi Ben Mordechai, we can understand that Jesus was crucified as a parallel to the killing of the lambs of the first Passover in Egypt—during the period of time *"at twilight"* which in Jewish understanding is what is called *"in between the two evening times"* which means from 12:00 noon to 6:00 p.m. [but which for weekdays became from 2:30 p.m. to 3:30 p.m. for the Temple sacrifice and we know that Jesus died *"at the ninth hour—about 3:00 p.m."* (Mark 15:33–37)], during the overlap period between the end of Nisan 13 and the beginning of Nisan 14 of the crucifixion week of AD 30. This was on a Wednesday.

This case is that **Jesus died on Wednesday of the crucifixion week in AD 30, Nisan 13/14, at about 3:00 p.m. on Nisan 13, during the period understood by the Hebrews to be** *"at twilight"* **(also called** *"in between the two evening times"*)**. This is our *Puzzle Piece #2* and is an important Hebraic understanding.

CHAPTER 21

Puzzle Piece #3–Timing of the Spring Feasts

Understanding the timing of the Spring Feasts of the Lord (Passover, Unleavened Bread, Firstfruits and Pentecost; as presented in Leviticus 23:1–22) is important to this case being presented. This understanding of the proper timing of the Spring Feasts is our *Puzzle Piece #3*.

A. Passover and Unleavened Bread

The timing of the days in Nisan for Passover and the first day of Unleavened Bread is very straightforward. From the Leviticus text, we learn that Passover is to be observed on Nisan *14*, with the first day of the seven-day festival of the Feast of Unleavened Bread following on the next day—Nisan *15*.

How are Passover and Unleavened Bread celebrated in Israel today? It is interesting to note that the Jews in Israel today do not follow the God-given instructions recorded by Moses in Leviticus 23. Rather than having Passover on the 14th of Nisan and the first day of Unleavened Bread on the 15th of Nisan, they mix the two Feasts together. This was also the case in the time of Jesus when the two Feasts were combined and considered as one Feast, as described in the Gospel accounts as the "Feast of Unleavened Bread."

Today, on the Jewish calendar, the first night of *Pesach* (Passover), when Jews sit down to eat the Passover meal, the date always falls on the first night of *Chag HaMarzot* (Feast of Unleavened Bread) which God ordained to fall on the 15th of the first month of the religious calendar (Nisan/Abib). Hence, now the Passover meal for virtually all the Jewish people has been merged with the first night of Unleavened Bread, a seven-day festival to God. However, ***per the Scriptures, Unleavened Bread and Passover are distinct festivals with 24 hours separating the two.*** Only the Samaritans and the Karaite Jews still celebrate Passover correctly on Nisan 14.

The Jewish people developed a work-around of this problem of merging the two Feasts by adding an eighth day to the seven-day festival of Unleavened Bread.[180] Therefore, ***in attempting to correct the ancient problem of the wrongful merging of two distinct festivals of God, Judaism violates the stipulation of God to keep two separate festivals.***

How and when did the Jewish people *start* mixing together the two festivals of Passover and Unleavened Bread? Avi Ben Mordechai provides the following answer:[181]

> It appears that the two festivals, *Pesach* [Passover] and *Chag HaMatzot* [Feast of Unleavened Bread], were kept 24-hours apart from each other until sometime prior to the first century and the days of Archelaus, royal successor to King Herod. This is understood from the historical record of Yosef ben Mattiyahu (Josephus), as shown below:
>
> ... Now, upon the approach of that ***feast of unleavened bread*** which the law of their fathers had appointed for the Jews at this time, ***which feast is called the Passover***, and is a memorial of their deliverance out of Egypt (when they offer sacrifices with great alacrity; and when they are required to slay more sacrifices in number than at any other festival) ... (Ant., 9.3., sec. 213; emphasis mine.)

From the conclusion of Avi Ben Mortechai, the merging of the two festivals occurred after the death of Herod the Great (in 1 BC), and was the case during the year of the death of Jesus. This is confirmed by Josephus in his quote above related to Unleavened Bread, "which feast is called the Passover." The gospel writer Luke also refers to this mixing of the two festivals, *"Now the Feast of Unleavened Bread, which is called the Passover, was approaching"* (Luke 22:1), so we know that the mixing of the two festivals was ongoing at the time of the crucifixion of Jesus.

So, how do we make sense of all this as to the mixing of the two festivals today and extending back in the days of Jesus? Indeed, why would this unscriptural mixing of the two festivals have survived so long into modern times? The answer is clearly **tradition!** Hence, *Jewish tradition* in this case can be as unscriptural as is the case with many *Christian church traditions*, as we point out throughout this book.

It should be noted that Jesus would have correctly followed the pattern of *Pesach* (Passover) given to Moses—after all, Messiah, the lamb of God, was a prophet like unto Moses (Deuteronomy 18:15). In the days of Moses, the Israelites slaughtered the *Pesach* lamb at the beginning of the 14th of Nisan/Aviv, as the sun was declining in the west (*beyn ha'arbaim, "in-between the evening times"* of the 13th and 14th), 24-hours before their departure from Egypt. Often overlooked in study of these matters is the commandment from God to Moses and the Hebrews to stay in the house in which they ate the Passover lamb until morning (Exodus 12:22) of Nisan 14. During the daylight hours of Nisan 14, the Hebrews assembled in Rameses and received from the Egyptians their goods given to them. Then, on the night of the 15th, a full day later, they went out from the Egyptians (Deuteronomy 16:1; Numbers 33:3).[182]

Therefore, **the real Pesach, per the Torah commandment, is supposed to occur 24-hours prior to the Unleavened Bread festival.**[183]

B. Firstfruits and Feast of Weeks (Pentecost)

The third of the Spring Feasts, the Feast of Firstfruits, was not so straightforward in determining the day as it is not assigned to a specific date as is the case with Passover and the first day of Unleavened Bread. It was not given a calendar date, but Leviticus simply states that it occurs on the *"first day after the Sabbath."*

Since the dates for Passover and Unleavened Bread are based on a lunar calendar, they are *floating dates* that could occur on any day of the week of the first month of Nisan/Abib. However, by God's command and by one interpretation (this is my interpretation too), the Feast of Firstfruits must consistently fall on the *first day after the weekly Sabbath*, i.e., *our Sunday*, during the week of Unleavened Bread. Hence, by this interpretation, Firstfruits always falls on Sunday, no matter on what day of the week Passover (Nisan 14) and the first day of Unleavened Bread (Nisan *15*) fall.

There are, however, several other interpretations of when Firstfruits occurs on the calendar. In Leviticus 23: 9–11, Firstfruits is simply stated as being *"the day following the Sabbath."*

The natural question is: Does this reference pertains to the weekly Sabbath (Saturday) or about *another* Sabbath ("High Sabbath"), which occurs on some of the annual Feast of the Lord days (Leviticus 23:7, 24–25, 28, 32, 36, 39)? The official Roman church position, which has been passed down as *tradition* to the church today, is that Firstfruits was always on *the day following the "High Sabbath"* of the first day of Unleavened Bread. Therefore, the Feast of Firstfruits was assumed to always be on the 16th of Nisan, as the first day of Unleavened Bread is on the 15th of Nisan (Leviticus 23:6), while Passover is on the 14th of Nisan (Leviticus 23:5).

This position of a three-day link between Passover and Firstfruits was taken by the Pharisees in the time of Christ, was held by Josephus (a Pharisee) in his writings[184] and, later, by the Roman church.

However, the Sadducees and, later, the Karaite Jews understood *"the day following the Sabbath"* to refer to the first *weekly Sabbath* (Saturday), which followed the first day of Unleavened Bread (a 7-day Feast).[185] With this interpretation, the number of days between Passover and Firstfruits can vary from year to year, and there is *not* a three-day linkage between them.

This lack of specific number of days linkage between Passover and Firstfruits is highly significant in constructing the correct chronology of Christ's Passion Week. The Sadducees, who controlled the Temple worship protocol at the time of Jesus, may have been incorrect on several of their teachings (for example, they did not believe in a literal physical resurrection of the dead). However, in *this* interpretation of Scripture, I believe that they held the correct position.

Many commentators, of course, hold to the traditional church view of Firstfruits always being on the 16th of Nisan. *For them*—for the crucifixion week—a three-day link exists with Firstfruits being on Sunday (Nisan 16), the first day of the week following the crucifixion, with Passover being on Friday (Nisan 14) and Saturday (Nisan 15) being both the weekly Sabbath as well as the "High Sabbath" of the first day of Unleavened Bread.

Other commentators favor the interpretation of Firstfruits always being on Nisan 17, *"on the day after the Sabbath" (Leviticus 23:11 NIV)*, which would put Passover and the crucifixion on *Thursday*, with Firstfruits still falling on Sunday of the week of the crucifixion.[186]

While I agree with Firstfruits always being on Sunday for the week of the crucifixion, I feel that both positions are incorrect for the chronology of Passover, Unleavened Bread and Firstfruits. I believe that Firstfruits is neither always on, specifically, Nisan *16th* or *17th*, but is *"on the day following the [weekly] Sabbath,"* which allows for days to separate the first day of Unleavened Bread from Firstfruits.

In summary, the scriptural reasons supporting the dating of Firstfruits being the day after the *weekly Sabbath (Sunday)* are as follows:

- In Leviticus 23, God states that Passover is on Nisan 14 and the first day of the Feast of Unleavened Bread is on the 15th of Nisan. But He states that the Feast of Firstfruits is *"on the day after the Sabbath" (Leviticus 23:11 NIV)*. It seems if God intended Firstfruits to *always* be on the 16th, He would have stated this, as He did in a similar way for Passover and Unleavened Bread, giving specific dates for each of them. If He intended the Sabbath so referenced to be the *weekly Sabbath*, which I think is supported by other Scripture, He would have stated it exactly as He did. This would put Firstfruits on a different date each year, making it impossible to assign it to a specific numerical day of Nisan. I see no problem with this if, for the year of Christ's crucifixion, Firstfruits fell on a day which met the prophecy of Christ being *"three days and three nights in the heart of the earth"* after his death on the cross.

- Another significant evidence of the *weekly Sabbath* being the reference for figuring the date for Firstfruits is the mechanism mentioned in Leviticus 23 for calculating the "counting of the Omar" to arrive at the Feast of Pentecost. *"The Lord said to Moses, … **'From the day after the Sabbath, the day you brought the sheaf of the wave offering (Firstfruits), count off seven full weeks. Count off fifty days up to the day after the seventh Sabbath** [the day after is Sunday] and then present an offering of new grain (**Pentecost**) …"* (Leviticus 23:15–16 NIV, clarification and emphasis added).

The reference to the starting point being *"the day after the Sabbath"* and the reference to seven Sabbaths are clearly references, we believe, to the *weekly* Sabbaths, because there were not seven consecutive *High Sabbaths* (as the first day of Unleavened Bread is called) in arriving at the **Feast of Weeks (Pentecost).** The *"seventh Sabbath"* mentioned in Leviticus 23:16 is clearly referencing the seventh *weekly* Sabbath to arrive at the Feast of Weeks (Pentecost), and the day after *the seventh Sabbath"* is the first day of the week, Sunday. Hence, I believe that *both First Fruits and Pentecost always fall on Sunday—this is highly significant!* This deduction is from reasoning from Scripture and from not accepting the Pharisees' positions as necessarily always correct, as Jesus also pointed out during His ministry.

The above understanding that Firstfruits is *not* always on the 16th of Nisan, the day following the first day of Unleavened Bread, but is the day after the *weekly Sabbath* of the week of Unleavened Bread opens the significant possibility of another chronology harmonizing the biblical accounts.

An additional fact regarding the Feast of Firstfruits is that at sunset, the very start of the Sunday of Firstfruits, the High Priest went into a sacred field of barley at the base of the Mount of Olives and *cut free from the earth (reap)* a sheaf of barley, to be waved before the Lord as an offering of firstfruits (Leviticus 23:9–11).

This Temple ceremony of the waving of the barley occurred on the following morning of Firstfruits (Sunday). The *waving* of barley symbolized the firstfruits of the expected Spring harvest, newness of life and blessing as the barley offering ascended into heaven when burned on the altar (1 Corinthians 15:20, 23). On this day, *49 days* were to be counted to determine *The Feast of Weeks or Pentecost* (Leviticus 23:15–16), which also always falls on Sunday (Pentecost is *50 days* from the weekly Sabbath preceding Firstfruits).

As the barley sheaf was *"cut free from the earth"* at the beginning of the Feast of Firstfruits, i.e., on Saturday evening just after sunset—at the start of the new Jewish day—Jesus rose from the grave, I believe, at that time and, subsequently, became a "wave offering" of blessing to the people—parallel to the Temple ceremony by the High Priest raising the barley toward heaven on Sunday morning.

The case is made in *The Last Shofar!* (pp. 110-112), as well as in Chapter 33 of this Section ("*When Were Jesus' Two Ascensions?*") that this Temple ceremony of raising the barley toward heaven by the High Priest in the Temple on Sunday morning also coincided with the non-witnessed *first ascension* of Jesus to heaven on the day of His resurrection—to present Himself to the Father as the first-fruits of the resurrection. The later *second ascension* of Jesus to heaven was the public ascension witnessed by the disciples, 40 days following His resurrection (Acts 1:3).

The resurrection of Jesus, of course, occurred before His first ascension. E. W. Bullinger affirms this chronology for the resurrection of Christ: "Thus, the Resurrection of the Lord took place at our Saturday sunset, or thereabouts, on 'the third day'; cp. 'after three days' (Matt. 27:63; Mark 8:31)."[187]

For those having an interest in reading further, other details related to the ceremonies of the Feast of Firstfruits and the parallel with the happenings of Christ following His resurrection are presented in Chapters 6 and 7 of *The Last Shofar!*

The importance of this *Puzzle Piece #3*—*the* chronology of Passover, Unleavened Bread, and First Fruits—will become apparent as we examine the other pieces of the puzzle.

CHAPTER 22

Puzzle Piece #4–
Passover Lamb Inspected 4 Days

uzzle Piece #4 involves the Passover lamb being inspected for four days. The Jewish law required *four days* for the chief priests to inspect the Passover Lamb (Exodus 12:3–6).

The High Priest on Nisan 10, four days before the Passover on Nisan 14, selected the Passover Lamb for the nation of Israel. During the next four days, the lamb was thoroughly inspected for blemishes and defects—looking for anything that would disqualify it from being an acceptable sacrifice for the sins of the nation.

At the end of this inspection period, assuming a positive outcome, the High Priest would publicly declare, "Behold the Lamb. I find no fault in him."

This four-day inspection of the Passover lamb further confirms our case for the chronology of the death of Jesus on Wednesday, Nisan 13 [during "the twilight" (*"in-between the evening times"*) of Nisan 14]. Jesus entered the Temple on our *Palm Sunday* (*Nisan 10*).[188] From this time to when the Passover lamb was killed per the account by Moses in Exodus, i.e., during the four days (till Wednesday of the crucifixion week in AD 30), He was interrogated ("inspected") on four separate occasions by the chief priests and rulers of the Temple (Mark 11–12:34). His interrogators could find no fault (i.e., no blemish or defect) in Him. *"And after that no one dared to ask him any more questions" (Mark 12:34)*. Secular authorities (Pilate) also examined Him, all coming to the same conclusion: *"I find no fault in Him!"*

Based on the evidence, the parallel is significant between the four-day inspection of the Passover Lamb and the four encounters between the Temple rulers and Jesus, our *Passover Lamb*, during the same four-day period. It is also important to remember that on the Hebrew calendar the day begins on the evening and goes to the evening of the next day.

For the crucifixion week, holding to the significance of the four days required to inspect the Passover Lamb, starting on Sunday (Nisan 10), this would put the killing of the Passover lamb on *Wednesday*—or to be more exact per Hebrew figuring "at twilight" of Wednesday (Nisan 14), which was technically still the afternoon of Nisan 13 as was explained in Chapter 21: *"Puzzle Piece #3–Timing of the Spring Feasts."*

So, how do we know that Sunday (*Palm Sunday*) was on Nisan 10, for which to count the four days? There are two ways to confirm this. From **computer-calculated astronomy**[189] in the year AD 30, the new moon (*Rosh Chodesh*, which determines the first day of the lunar month—for example, Nisan 1) fell on the sixth day of the week—Friday, March 22 (Nisan 1). This day/date works out well as it determines that Nisan 10 would fall on Sunday (*Palm Sunday*), which correlates to the four-day inspection and the eventual death of Jesus on Wednesday [Nisan 13, during the "at twilight" (meaning *"in-between the evening times"*) of Nisan 14], per our case.

There is another way to correlate *Sunday* being Nisan 10, and that involves **Jesus' arrival in Bethany** because He would not travel on the Sabbath (Shabbat). John 12:1 informs us, *"Jesus, therefore, **six days** before the Passover, came to Bethany."* In Bethany, Jesus was hosted by Lazarus, Mary, and Martha for a lavish supper [*Gr. Deipnon*; Strong's number 1173, which is from number 1160, *dapto* (to devour); as Avi Ben Mordechai explains, the word is "defined as a costly, formal meal. In Judaism, we traditionally reserve costly, formal meals for Shabbat which always begins at sundown on the sixth day of the week, *Yom Shishi* (Friday just before sunset)."[190] Hence, we can assume that supper in Bethany was at the start of the Sabbath on Saturday (our Friday night). "Six days" from Saturday (inclusive) would take us to Wednesday, which further confirms our case that Jesus died on Wednesday of the crucifixion week.

So, how is the crucifixion week at the time of Jesus playing out? During the evening of the start of the Sadducces' Passover on Nisan 13 (after sunset of Tuesday), Jesus celebrated the eating of the Passover *seder* with His disciples and instituted the *Lord's Supper* (night of Nisan 13). Then, during the afternoon on Wednesday (Nisan 13), both the Passover Lamb (Sadducces' and Mosaic) in the

WHEN WERE JESUS' DEATH, RESURRECTION & ASCENTIONS?

Temple and Jesus were sacrificed (died) at about 3:00 p.m. (Mark 15:33). The "day of preparation" for the Pharisaic Passover/Unleavened Bread was on Thursday (Nisan 14). The Pharisaic Jewish leaders, plotting Jesus' death, were opposed to killing Him during the daylight hours of Thursday, Nisan 14, because it was still their "day of preparation" for their combined *Pesach* and Unleavened Bread festival beginning at about 3:00 p.m. of Nisan 14, and they did not want a riot by the Jewish citizens to break out around the time of their festival (Matthew 26:5).[191] All this occurred during the crucifixion week in AD 30. The case for this being AD 30 is made in Chapter 34: "*Year* of Death & Resurrection: *AD 30*." The following two graphics—Fig. 22.1 ("Passover Week, Month of Nisan, AD 30") and Fig. 22.2 ("Timing of Various Jewish Sects' Passover Sacrifice")—illustrate the chronology of these events.

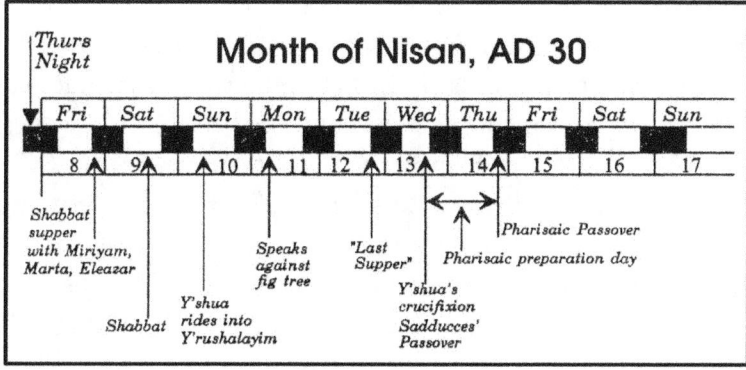

Figure 22.1. Passover Week, Month of Nisan, AD 30

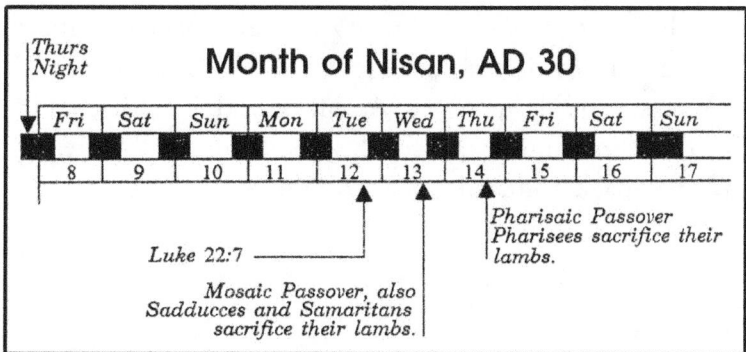

Figure 22.2. Timing of Various Jewish Sects' Passover Sacrifice

Some have speculated that this *Lord's Supper* might have been an *Essene Passover* celebration, which was done without a Passover lamb as the Essenes had distanced themselves from the Temple ceremonies in Jerusalem, which they considered corrupted by a corrupt priesthood.[194, 195]

Incidentally, the Pharisaic Passover lamb would not have been typically slaughtered until the afternoon of Passover, Nisan 14 (Thursday). This chronology has caused confusion and some commentators claim that the Lord's Supper was not really a Passover meal, the Passover *Seder*, although it is indeed so referred to in the Gospel accounts (Matthew 26:17–19; Mark 14:12–16; Luke 22:7–15). John 13:2 (NIV) simply refers to it as *"the evening meal."*

Further confusion comes from the references to *"the first day of Unleavened Bread"* (Matthew 26:17; Mark 14:12; Luke 22:7), *"when it was customary to sacrifice the Passover lamb"* (Mark 14:12; Luke 22:7). This day *"when it was customary to sacrifice the Passover Lamb"* is clearly referring to Nisan 14, which in Leviticus 23 is called the Passover. As we have seen in Chapter 21: "Puzzle Piece #3–Timing of Spring Feasts," in the time of Jesus, a distinction between a separate Passover and Unleavened Bread was not made, and the combined celebration was called either Passover or Unleavened Bread. Hence, the *"day of Unleavened Bread"* is referring to Nisan 14, which is also called the *preparation day* (the day preceding the High Holy Day of the first day of the seven-day celebration of Unleavened Bread on Nisan 15, as given in Leviticus 23). This is a bit confusing, but this understanding is the only one which makes sense and is confirmed by E. F. Bullinger: "The words in Mark 14:12 and Luke 22:7 refer to 'the first day of unleavened bread,' which was the 14th day of Nisan, and therefore 'the preparation day' [before the High Holy Day of the first day of Unleavened Bread]. That is why the Lord goes on to tell the two disciples to go and *make preparation for the Passover.*"[196]

The *"four days"* inspection of the Passover lambs, starting on Palm Sunday (Nisan 10) and the *"six days before the Passover"* for Jesus' Sabbath supper in Bethany (starting Friday evening, Nisan 8) both testify to the crucifixion on Wednesday, *"between the evenings"* of Nisan 13/14. Admittedly, this has been a bit confusing and difficult to explain, but our case for the crucifixion on Wednesday is, indeed, supported by these background understandings.

CHAPTER 23

Puzzle Piece #5– Two Sabbaths in Crucifixion Week

The fact that there were *two Sabbaths* during the week of Christ's crucifixion and resurrection is frequently overlooked, or not understood, thus making the timing of Passion Week events even more confusing (Leviticus 23:7–8; John 19:31). That there were two Sabbaths is *Puzzle Piece #5*.

The texts from Leviticus and John's Gospel show that a *special High Sabbath* was commanded by the Lord and existed during Jesus' time. This special Sabbath was in addition to the weekly Sabbath, and is referred to as a *holy convocation* or a *High Holy Day*. It is associated with the celebration of various Feasts of the Lord to emphasize their solemnity, therefore *prohibiting ordinary work*. The first day of the seven-day celebration of the Feast of Unleavened Bread is one such High Holy Day (Sabbath), starting on Nisan 15 (Leviticus 23:6–8).

The day before any Sabbath (either weekly Sabbath or High Holy Day) was called the *Day of Preparation,* when necessary tasks were done so that the following day, the *Sabbath*, could be a day of rest unto the Lord.

Understanding the existence of these special *High Holy Day*—special *Sabbaths* in connection to the Feasts of the Lord—is critical in assembling the *Puzzle Pieces*. For the week of the crucifixion in AD 30, there were two Sabbaths—the first day of Unleavened Bread and the weekly Sabbath. The first day of Unleavened Bread (Nisan 15), the day after Passover, is complicated during the time of Jesus due to the existence of multiple Passovers depending on the interpretations of the various Jewish sects; these various Passovers were covered in Chapter 19. An important insight is that Jesus' crucifixion followed the precise chronology of the killing of the Mosaic Passover lamb in Egypt.

I will cover this topic related to the *two Sabbaths* in more detail as we begin putting all the pieces of the puzzle together to arrive at our conclusion for the day of crucifixion week when Jesus was crucified.

CHAPTER 24

Puzzle Piece #6–
The Sign of Jesus Being Messiah

Jesus told the Pharisees that He would give them a sign as to His being the Messiah. The sign He gave was this: *He would, like Jonah, be in the heart of the earth for **three days and three nights*** (Jonah 1:17; Matthew 12:40). Jesus said this twice in Matthew 12:40 for emphasis. This statement by Jesus is *Puzzle Piece #6.*

Understanding the use of *cardinal numbers* within the biblical narrative is important, particularly when they are associated with *days.* When Jesus used the term *three days and three nights* about Jonah and, then about His own burial, He meant precisely what He said: *three [full] days and three [full] nights.* This is like the usage of an *ordinal number* for days (first day, second day, etc.) in Genesis 1 and the usage of a *cardinal number* for days (one, two, three … as in "six days") in Exodus 20:11 to describe the six literal days of Creation as well as to describe the six-day working week with the seventh day [full day] being the Sabbath day (Exodus 20:9–10)—showing that the creation week is the very basis of the working week. Hence, these days are inferred to be *normal 24-hour days* and *not partial days* or days of undetermined long lengths (billions of years, etc.). This is a significant understanding. After a very scholarly analysis of the Hebrew word *Yom* [day], as used in Genesis and Exodus, etc., Jonathan Sarfati, Ph.D. makes the following conclusion related to its usage in the OT:

> When modified by a *cardinal number* (for example, one, two, three …) or *ordinal number* (for example, first, second, third …), … *yom* always means a literal day of about 24 hours, or the light portion of the day-night cycle. This is true in narrative, legal writings, prophecy, wisdom literature, and even poetry.[197]

Therefore, the reference in Jonah 1:17 and Matthew 12:40 to *"three days and three nights"* in the crucifixion week would, using the Jewish calendar and according to our case, be all *night* Wednesday, all *day* Thursday, all *night* Thursday, all *day* Friday, all *night* Friday and then, finally, all *day* Saturday (*until sunset*)—*three full days and three full nights*.

Assuming Jesus said exactly what he meant to say, this *cardinal* reckoning will not work for the *traditional* chronology for Christ's death, burial and resurrection—beginning with His death on *Good Friday*. There are not enough days or nights to cover the period that Jesus said He would be entombed—*three days and three nights*. Even with an assumed "partial-day" reckoning for Friday and Sunday (partial days on Friday—with the crucifixion at about 3:00 in the afternoon—and Sunday—with resurrection early Sunday morning—both counted as a full days), there is no way to account for the *"three nights"* in this *Good Friday* scenario, as there is only the possibility of Friday night and Saturday night (only *two nights!*). **For this reason, as well as other reasons stated in this book, a Friday crucifixion simply does not work.**

Partial-day counting has been proposed for other than the *Good Friday* scenario. An example would be an assumed crucifixion on *Thursday* afternoon and the resurrection on early Sunday morning—with Sunday being a partial-day counting for a day and Thursday not counted. Another example would be the case of death on *Wednesday* afternoon and resurrection on the start of Saturday in the evening of Friday, yielding only two full days (or three days with partial-day counting of Wednesday) and three full nights.[198] We do not believe that this aligns with the teaching from the Matthew 12:40 passage and the analogous passage of Jonah 1:17, for the reasons which have been presented—especially that in the OT the Hebrew word *Yom* when used with an ordinal or cardinal number always means a full 24-hour period. Hence, we can state that we agree with Mordechai's case for the crucifixion on Wednesday afternoon, but we do not agree with his position of the resurrection at the start of Saturday in the evening of Friday.

I believe that Jesus resurrected at the very end of Saturday/start of Sunday, as Jesus stated He would (Matthew 12:40; Jonah 1:17), resulting in *three full days and three full nights* in the grave—shown in the graphic in "Conclusion of When Was Jesus' Death & Resurrection" in Chapter 35. The case being described uniquely aligns all the puzzle pieces, including this *Puzzle Piece #6* about the *three days and three nights* in the heart of the earth.

CHAPTER 25

Puzzle Piece #7 – Events Right After Jesus' Death

This *Puzzle Piece #7* relates to the timing of the events at the crucifixion site following Jesus' death on Wednesday afternoon (Nisan 13) and how these events influence the chronology of the crucifixion week which this Section A of Part II is dealing with—when Jesus' death, burial, resurrection, and ascensions occurred.

When taken together, the Gospel accounts of *Matthew 27:57–66, 28–1; Mark 15:42–16:2; Luke 23:50–56, 24:1; and John 19:38–42, 20:1* form a composite picture of the events surrounding the burial of Jesus, including the few hours after His resurrection, days later. These Scriptures give us a window through which to see when and who was involved in the burial activities, and, in summary, the following is what we have:

When it was [toward] evening of the Day of Preparation, but before the Sabbath began at twilight, Joseph, a wealthy man from Arimathea and disciple of Jesus, and Nicodemus, also a follower of Jesus, and both respected men on the Sanhedrin Council, were granted permission from Pilate to remove the body of Jesus from the cross and prepare it for burial. They washed the body and wrapped it in a clean linen cloth, a shroud which Joseph had bought—described as "... *a long linen cloth saturated or inter-leaved with about 75-pounds of myrrh and aloes—as is the Jewish custom of burial."*[199, 200] They then placed the body in a newly rock-carved tomb, belonging to Joseph of Arimathea, in a garden within the same general area where Jesus was crucified—on the Mount of Olives (Gethsemane).

The process of burying Jesus involved many steps, all of which took time. What were the steps, when did they all occur, and how much time did the total of the activities take? The following steps occurred after Jesus died on the cross up until His burial: (1) After Jesus cried out *"My God, my God, why hast thou forsaken me?"* Jesus spoke three other times; these were all after 3:00 p.m. (2) The Jews went to Pilate to request that the legs be broken for those who were crucified—to hasten their death. (3) Pilate communicated to the soldiers at the cross to break the legs. (4) Joseph of Arimathea traveled to Pilate to request that he remove the body of Jesus from the cross to bury him. (5) Before Pilate would turn over the body of Jesus to Joseph of Arimathea, Pilate sent for the Centurion to be sure Jesus was dead; once that was affirmed, he gave approval to Joseph to bury Jesus' body. (6) Joseph of Arimathea and Nicodemus took Jesus' body down from the cross, washed and wrapped the body in linen strips, packing in the 75 pounds of spices which Nicodemus brought. (7) Joseph and Nicodemus placed Jesus' body in the tomb and rolled the stone over the entrance of the tomb.

Obviously, all these steps took time and surely would have gone beyond the 6:00 p.m. start of Thursday, the Pharisaic Preparation Day. Since these steps involved burying the dead and had been started already, it was permissible according to Jewish rulings (Pesachim 55b) to continue this work on the Preparation Day (Thursday).[201] Exactly how long all these steps took to complete, we don't know. Our case, however, allows for the time frame of these steps to be completed on the Preparation Day (Thursday), either during night time or after daylight, still on Thursday. Our case allows for a day for all these activities to be completed.

Sitting outside the tomb were Mary Magdalene and Mary, the mother of Joses *(Joseph)*. We are not told if any other women were present at the tomb at the time of burial, even though many other women are said to have been present at the crucifixion (Matthew 27:55–56).

Luke's account tells us that the actual burial of Jesus was on the *Day of Preparation,* and before the beginning of the (Great) Sabbath at sunset—thus, the first day of the Feast of Unleavened Bread (Friday). The women who came with Jesus from Galilee *followed* the removal of the body of Jesus from the cross to the tomb where the body was prepared for burial. They saw the tomb and how the body of Jesus was laid in it. We are then told that these women left the tomb and, later, purchased and prepared spices and ointments for administering to the body on another day.

Who were these women and exactly when did they purchase and prepare these spices? The chronology of the women purchasing and preparing the spices is covered in the next chapter, Chapter 26: "*Puzzle Piece #8*–Chronology of the Women."

CHAPTER 26

Puzzle Piece #8–Chronology of the Women

Often overlooked is the *timing of the activities of the women* who witnessed Christ's burial and then purchased and prepared spices for the proper burial of Christ's body (Mark 16:1; Luke 23:54–56). However, this information is *critical* in properly confirming the sequence of days of the crucifixion, burial and resurrection of Christ. These activities too must fit within the chronology of this case. These activities of the women are our *Puzzle Piece #8*.

After these women (Mary Magdalene, Mary the mother of James, and Salome) purchased and prepared the spices, and during another day, they returned to the tomb (Mark 16:1–2) to anoint and further prepare the body of Jesus. These three women were involved with planning a *post-burial* anointing of the body of Jesus. We are not told specially the reason for this anointing. Many commentators believe it was the customary way of reducing the odor of a decomposing body. Some suggest it was their way of expressing devotion to the one they remembered and loved.

All this is key in assembling the pieces of the puzzle about His death, burial, and resurrection. Our case must allow for the chronology of these activities of the women, and, as you will see, it does.

A. Who Were the Women?

First, let's review who these women were. In Mark 15:40–41, we are told that among these women who were looking on at the crucifixion from a distance were Mary Magdalene, Mary the mother of James (the younger) and of Joses *(Joseph)*, and Salome. We also know that Mary the mother of Jesus was there looking on (John 19:25). When Jesus was in Galilee the women followed Him and ministered to Him. In passing, we are told that there were also many other women who came up from Jerusalem. So, now we know who these women from Galilee were—the same women who were present at his crucifixion, who witnessed His burial, and now, as we are told, purchased and prepared the burial spices.

B. Nature of Spices Purchased & Prepared by the Women

Second, let's review the nature of these spices which the women purchased and prepared. Spices were purchased in a dry state much like we find at the store today. The spices were blended with an oil base, usually olive oil, then mixed in a cooker of boiling water until a sweet-smelling unguent texture was formed. This mixture was cooled and poured into an alabaster jar or flask.[202] Mark 14:3–9 and John 12:1–8 beautifully illustrate the application of *burial* ointment in anticipation of Jesus' burial, which happened in the house of Simon the Leper in Bethany, just days before Jesus came into Jerusalem in His "Triumphant Entry":

> And being in Bethany in the house of Simon the leper, as he sat at meat, there came a woman having an alabaster box of ointment of spikenard very precious; and she brake the box, and poured it on his head. And there were some that had indignation within themselves, and said, Why was this waste of the ointment made? For it might have been sold for more than three hundred pence, and have been given to the poor. And they murmured against her. And Jesus said, Let her alone; why trouble ye her? She hath wrought a good work on me. For ye have the poor with you always, and whensoever ye will ye may do them good: but me ye have not always. She hath done what she could: she is come aforehand to anoint my body to the burying. Verily I say unto you, wheresoever this gospel shall be preached throughout the whole world, this also that she hath done shall be spoken of for a memorial of her." (Mark 14:3–9 KJV)

C. Sequence of Women Purchasing & Preparing the Spices

The women witnessed the burial of Jesus around 6:00 p.m. at the division of the Jewish days of Tuesday and Wednesday (Wednesday afternoon being the time that the Sadducees sacrificed their *Pesach*). Remember, it was important for Jesus' body to be removed from the cross and buried *before* the end of the crucifixion day (buried the same day per Deuteronomy 21:22–23) as well as before the end of the Pharisaic *Day of Preparation* (of Thursday, Nisan 14). At sunset of Nisan 14, the first day of the Feast of Unleavened Bread (Friday, Nisan 15) was to be celebrated; it was a *special Sabbath*—a *High Holy Day* in which no ordinary work was permitted. The body of Jesus was taken down from the cross on the day that the Pharisees called *"the preparation day"* (Mark 15:42). It was 24-hours before the Pharisees sacrificed their *Pesach* lambs on late Thursday afternoon (Nisan 14/15). Hence, it was already the Pharisaic *preparation day* by the time Jesus had died (for details see Chapter 20: *"Puzzle Piece #2–Hebrew Timing Issues re Passover"*).

Scripture informs us of the sequence the women followed when they *purchased and prepared spices and ointments* to anoint Jesus' body (Mark 16:1; Luke 23:54–24:1). With Jesus' burial occurring immediately before the beginning of Thursday (Nisan 14) which was the Day of Preparation before the Feast of Unleavened Bread, a High Holy Sabbath, there was not time for the women to anoint the body that day. Related to the purchase and preparation of the spices by the women to further prepare Jesus' body after he had been buried, the Gospels of Mark and Luke provide important insights into this chronology:

> **When the Sabbath was over** [High Holy Sabbath of Feast of Unleavened Bread on Friday, Nisan 15], Mary Magdalene, Mary the mother of James, and Salome **bought spices** so that they might go to anoint Jesus' body. Very early on the first day of the week [Sunday], just after sunrise, they were on their way to the tomb … (Mark 16:1–2 NIV, clarification and emphasis added)

> The women who had come with Jesus from Galilee followed Joseph and saw the tomb and how his body was laid in it. Then **they went home and prepared spices and perfumes. But they rested on the Sabbath** [the weekly Sabbath, on Saturday, Nisan 16] in obedience to the commandment. (Luke 23:55–56 NIV, clarification and emphasis added)

The women bought the spices *after a Sabbath* and then prepared the spices and then *rested on a Sabbath*. The only way this can be is that there were *two Sabbaths with either a day in between or an allowed block of time sandwiched between them when shops were open to allow for purchasing the spices,* at which time the women purchased the spices and then prepared the spices to anoint Jesus' body. **This chronology of the women buying and preparing the spices, both accomplished between two separate Sabbaths, is totally overlooked by those who adhere to an assumed crucifixion on Thursday or Friday**; it is impossible to correlate these two Scripture passages (Mark 16:1–2; Luke 23:55–56) to a scenario of the crucifixion week having just one Sabbath. There would be just one Sabbath for the case of a Friday crucifixion, with that Friday being Nisan 14, and Saturday being Nisan 15, and, hence, the first day of Unleavened Bread as well as the weekly Sabbath—not being two distinct Sabbaths to align with the Mark and Luke passages, describing the women purchasing and preparing the spices between two Sabbaths.

The case we presented in *The Last Shofar!* (Appendix III: "On What Day Did Christ Really Die?") was for two Sabbaths with a day in between being precisely the case if Jesus was crucified and buried on *Wednesday* (Nisan 14)—then on Thursday (Nisan 15; the *High Sabbath* of the first day of Unleavened Bread) and the weekly Sabbath on Saturday (Nisan 16), providing two separate Sabbath days. However, from additional research for this book, we know with high assurance that the crucifixion was on AD 30, and for that year Nisan 14 was on *Thursday* and not on Wednesday. Hence, although we still believe the crucifixion to have been on Wednesday and we still believe the resurrection to be at the very start of First Fruits at the very start of Sunday (Saturday evening), we now understand that the Wednesday of the crucifixion week was on *Nisan 13* (*"between the two evenings"* leading into Nisan 14 on Thursday). The first day of Unleavened Bread (a High Holy Day Sabbath) during the crucifixion week was on Friday. And all this is in alignment for the crucifixion week in AD 30, as further described in Chapter 34.

So, how does all this work out for the women who had to purchase the spices after a Sabbath and prepare the spices before a Sabbath, to be able to rest over the Sabbath? Indeed, how does this work for the crucifixion week in AD 30? Now, without a full day between two Sabbaths, which would have allowed them to both purchase and prepare the spices before going to the tomb to anoint Jesus' body, we now have in our chronology two Sabbaths back-to-back (Friday and Saturday) with seemingly an impossible situation of having Jewish law dictating that they cannot shop for the spices or do work such as preparing the spices during each of the two Sabbath days. Are we at an impasse where we must conclude that our case is erroneous, and we must search for another chronology to try to align with all our other evidence for our case?

The short answer is no; we are not at an impasse. The case for how the women purchased the spices and prepared the spices between two Sabbaths, which we conclude from Mark 16:1–2 and Luke 23:55–56 passages, fits within the chronology we have laid out and is understood by knowledge of Jewish Oral Law which governed the shop owners in Jerusalem. These insights related to the Jewish laws are fascinating and comprise a big "piece of the puzzle" for constructing our case for the crucifixion week and all the activities recorded in Scripture.

We believe the following is what happened. First, the women did not purchase the spices prior to the crucifixion or on the day of the crucifixion, as Mark 16:1–2 clearly states that they purchased the spices *after a Sabbath*. Nor did the women purchase the spices on the day after the crucifixion (on Thursday, the Pharisaic Preparation Day before their first day of Unleavened Bread/Passover) because the shops in Jerusalem were closed on that Preparation Day per Jewish law and they could not purchase the spices on that day (Thursday, Nisan 14).[203]

In addition, the women could not have purchased the spices on the weekly Sabbath (Saturday, Nisan 16), as all the shops were closed all day on the weekly Sabbath and no work was allowed.

So, we are left only with the Pharisaic first day of Unleavened Bread (Friday, Nisan 15) for the women to purchase the spices. Yet, how can this be as normally no work is allowed on a High Holy Day? Of course, there is provision for the priests to work in the Temple on Sabbath days, and as it turns out there is another allowance for merchants to work for a *two-hour period* on the afternoon of Nisan 15 (Friday), when that day is immediately before a weekly Sabbath day, which is our case of the crucifixion week of AD 30.

Avi Ben Mordechai provides an explanation of this key allowance in the Jewish law. Based on a technical term in Jewish Oral Law, it was possible for shopkeepers in Israel to open for *a few hours* between the end of the High Holy Day of the first day of Unleavened Bread (Nisan 15, which began Thursday, in the late afternoon of Nisan 14) and the beginning of the regular weekly Sabbath (Nisan 16, Saturday—which began at sunset at the end of Friday, Nisan 15). Mordechai provides the following explanation:

> "The Talmudic term is ... [Hebrew] *Me'et Le'et*, or 'from time to time.'[204] In other words, it was possible that the 'Great Sabbat' of *Chag HaMatzot* [Unleavened Bread] began in the late afternoon of Thursday, Aviv 14/15 [Nisan 14/15], just a couple of hours before sunset and came to an end precisely 24-hours later in the late afternoon of Friday, Aviv 15/16 [Nisan 14/15]—*me'et le'et*. Essentially, this would have shifted the 'Great Sabbat' causing it to begin a couple of hours before sunset on Thursday and

ending it a couple of hours before sunset on Friday. If this was the case, then the woman (sic) would have found merchants open **after** the 'Great Sabbat' so that they could go out and purchase spices and perfumes, according to Mark 16:1."[205]

This allowance for the shop merchants to be open on the late afternoon of the High Holy Day of the first day of Unleavened Bread (Friday) for a few hours, would provide the opportunity for the women to purchase the additional spices for Jesus' body. This is a key *puzzle piece* to unlock the chronology of the women during the crucifixion week. This chronology is shown in Figure 26.1.

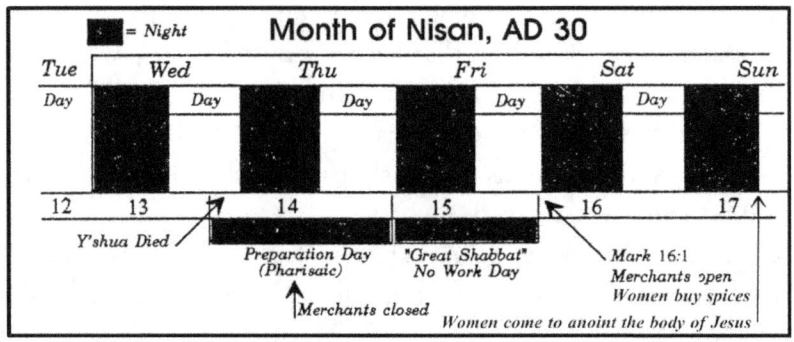

Figure 26.1. Chronology for Women to Purchase, Prepare, and Anoint Jesus' Body

Could the women have accomplished this purchase of the spices in Jerusalem during this short time of a few hours? It seems reasonable to assume that this was, indeed, possible. However, what about the problem of having time for *preparing* the spices, which would most probably extend beyond the few hours allowed for the shops to be open? There is another allowance in the Jewish Oral Law which would make this preparation possible beyond the time of the few hours when the shops were allowed open. This additional time would need to extend beyond the beginning of the weekly Sabbath on Saturday. Is this possible?

Of course, normally no work is allowed for the non-priests over the Sabbath. However, it was *halachically* (per Jewish legal law) permissible for some work to be accomplished:

"Raba said: On the first day of a Festival, [only] Gentiles may busy themselves with a corpse, [but] **on the second day**, Israelites may busy themselves with a corpse ... With regard to a dead body *the Rabbis have made the second day of a Festival as a weekday* even with respect to cutting for it (the dead body) a shroud **and *cutting for it (the dead body) a [branch of] myrtle (sweet smelling).*** "[207]

"R. Johanan, he said to them: Let Gentiles occupy themselves with him [the dead]. Raba too said: As for a corpse in the first day of Festivals Gentiles should occupy themselves with him; **on the second day of Festivals Israelites may occupy themselves with him [the dead body]** … "[208]

Nisan 16, the weekly Sabbath (Saturday), was also *the second day of Unleavened Bread* and, per the *halacha* dictates given above from the Talmud, one could tend to the needs of the dead. It certainly seems that *"preparing the spices"* by the women for the body of Jesus would have been allowed by this ruling. This provides the time after the purchase of the spices on Friday (the short time when the shops were open) to prepare the spices to derive a mixture suitable for applying to the dead body of Jesus.

So, the possible argument that "a few hours" on late Friday afternoon would not be sufficient for both purchasing and preparing the spices is not applicable. Furthermore, these two procedures of purchasing the spices *"after the Sabbath"* (Mark 16:1–2) and preparing the spices *"and then they [the women] rested on the Sabbath [weekly Sabbath]"* (Luke 23:55–56) would be literally fulfilled by the women. This too is a significant *puzzle piece* for our case for the chronology of the crucifixion week.

D. Time Needed to Prepare the Spices

So, what is a reasonable estimated length of time necessary to prepare the spices and will this timeframe fit into our case for the crucifixion week?

Scripture does not inform us as to *how long* it took the women to prepare the spices and produce ointments. However, we can reason that, although the purchase of the spices could easily have happened during the brief period allowed between the two Sabbaths, the preparation of those spices to make the *ointments* (Luke 23:56) would not fit within that short period as it probably took *most of a day*. The spices had to be cooked, blended with an oil base and reduced to an unguent texture, suitable to be applied to a body. However, with the allowance of working on the *second day* of Unleavened Bread, which in this case was on the weekly Sabbath (Saturday, Nisan 16), this long preparation time for the spices is not a problem in the chronology of the crucifixion week, and our case allows for this.

This provision in our case for the timeframe needed for the preparation of the spices is also a significant *puzzle piece* for our chronology of the crucifixion week.

E. When the Women Went to the Tomb with the Spices

It should be noted that the two Talmud references provided previously by Mordechai also would allow for the women to go on the weekly Sabbath (Saturday, Nisan 16) to the tomb of Jesus and apply the spices on his dead body on that day. Indeed, this chronology is suggested by Avi Ben Mordechai: "Early the next morning on Aviv 16 (Nisan 16; *Saturday*), before sunrise, the women (according to [Luke] 16:2) came to anoint Y'shua's corpse."[209] Mordechai also suggests that the *resurrection* of Jesus was on *Saturday*, Nisan 16[210]—rather than as the case presented here suggests the resurrection was on precisely the dividing time between the end of the weekly Sabbath and the start of First Fruits at the start of the Jewish day at sundown of Sunday, giving a full three days and three nights in the tomb.

It should be stated that I also differ from Mordechai's view that women came to the tomb on Saturday at the start of daylight. He makes a case for this, claiming translation errors of the Greek in all four of the Gospel accounts. Rather than relying on translation errors in all four of the Gospel accounts, the case presented here is that the women arrive at the tomb to anoint the body on the first day of the week (Sunday; with Sunday being the Jewish Firstfruits—this was the case presented in Chapter 21: "*Puzzle Piece #3*–Timing of the Spring Feasts." This was immediately before the sun arose when it was still dark (per Matthew 27:66–28:1, Luke 24:1 and John 20:1), many hours after Jesus' resurrection. Of course, the women found the tomb of Jesus empty at the time they arrived (John 20:1)—Jesus had already arisen.

What else can we say about when the women came to the tomb to anoint the body of Jesus? The common and traditional view is that the Resurrection occurred sometime early Sunday, sometime after mid-night. This was followed shortly by an early morning visit to the tomb of at least the three women mentioned previously, and subsequently visited by Peter and possibly John. Generally, Mark, Luke and John concur with the timing of these events, although none say exactly when the Resurrection took place. John suggests that the visit to the tomb by the women was before the light of day, i.e., "*… while it was yet dark …*" (John 20:1).

Matthew, (28:1), however, writing to the dispersed Jewish Christians, carefully constructs the events of the women who came to anoint the body of Jesus:

> Now after the Sabbath [Gk. Sabbaton: **Sabbaths**], towards the dawn of the first day of the week, Mary Magdalene and the other Mary went to see the tomb. (Matthew 28:1 ESV; clarification and emphasis mine.)

Matthew begins by telling us that it was *after* the *Sabbaths* (plural—Gk. *Sabbaton*) noting that there was more than one Sabbath that had just been completed. The phrase, *"toward the dawn of the first day of the week"* might rightly be understood by the Jewish mind as the time just after sunset at the end of the last Sabbath and the *beginning* of the first day of the week. *"Dawn,"* as well as meaning the point in a day when the light of a new day is first perceived, can also mean the beginning of any point in time, place or event that initiates something new, i.e., *the dawning of a new day or era.*

The Englishman's Greek New testament actually states, *"Now late on Sabbaths as it was getting **dusk** toward [the] first [day] of [the] week."*[211] This is based on the Greek text of Stephens, 1550.

John N. Darby, a Hebrew and Greek scholar, translates Matthew 28:1: *"Now late on Sabbath(s), as it was the **dusk** of the next day after sabbath(s), came Mary of Magdala and the other Mary to look at the sepulcher."*[212]

The Berean Literal Translation renders this verse as: *"And after the Sabbaths, it being dawn **toward** the first day of the week, Mary Magdalene and the other Mary came to see the tomb."*[213]

One possibility is that Mary Magdalene and the others were so eager to approach the tomb that even before the last Sabbath was over they went to the tomb, after sunset on Saturday night. Viewing the empty tomb and their encounter with the angel, they quickly return to tell Peter and the other disciples as to what they experienced, only to return later, early in the morning of the first day of the week. Based on the Greek text, John Gill's Bible Commentary, Exposition of Matthew 28:1 speaks very extensively of this possibility.[214]

Wikipedia's posting of an article on Matthew 28:1 indicates the verse's troubling meaning for scholars throughout the church's history, citing even St. Augustine's observations that placed the women going to the tomb sometime after the *beginning* of the first day of the week (Saturday night).[215] There is probably no clear resolution on what Matthew intended to say, comparing his account with the other Gospel writers. It is a detail that is yet to be revealed.

For further insights into the activities of these women, the reader is encouraged to investigate my findings in *The Last Shofar!* (Appendix III, "On What Day Did Christ Really Die? – What the Feasts of the Lord Tell Us," pages 286–292).

The specific events surrounding the burial and resurrection of Jesus Christ, although simplified by custom and traditional interpretation of Scripture is highly complex when the activities of the women who purchased and prepared spices for anointing the body of Jesus are inserted. In addition, the timing of the two back-to-back Sabbaths and the disparity between the Pharisees' and Sadducees' understanding of the timing for the Passover only adds to the complexity. Four Gospel writers all giving us slightly different accounts of when and what occurred further complicate the story.

Our western mind seeks a chronology that is straightforward and logical. That is not how most writers of Scripture wrote, or anyone else of that time. It did not matter if events were interposed—interrupting or transposing the chronology; whether in one case a single person is mentioned and in another case for the same event two or three are introduced—these details apparently did not matter. What mattered to the writer—what was important—were the facts that focused on the main thing—that Jesus died, was buried, and that He rose from the dead. Therein is the Gospel.

I believe that only the *Wednesday crucifixion day* of AD 30 per the evidence of the case presented here precisely fits all the scriptural requirements, including all the activities of the women to purchase, prepare the spices, and take them to the tomb to anoint Jesus' body.

F. Conclusion

In conclusion, the case presented in this book for the chronology of the crucifixion week in AD 30 is as follows: (1) The crucifixion was *"between the two evenings"* on Wednesday (*Nisan 13/14*); (2) with the Pharisaic "Day of Preparation" (*Nisan 14*) being on Thursday; and (3) the first day of Unleavened Bread being on Friday (*Nisan 16*); and (4) the weekly Sabbath being on Saturday (*Nisan 17*); and (5) the resurrection being at the precise time of both the very end of the weekly Sabbath and the start of First Fruits on Sunday (*Nisan 17/18*); (6) with the women coming to the tomb most probably on early Sunday morning (*Nisan 18*).

This case includes *Puzzle Piece #8*—what I believe to be the most probable chronology of the women from the crucifixion to the resurrection as laid out in this chapter. See the summary table in Chapter 30 and the timeline graphic Figure 35.1 in Chapter 35 in the Conclusion of this Section A of Part II for illustrations of this chronology of the crucifixion week.

CHAPTER 27

Puzzle Piece #9– Tradition for Visiting Burial Site

Ancient Jewish tradition allowed people to visit the burial site during the three days after the entombment to ensure the person was truly dead. This is our *Puzzle Piece #9*.

The women who witnessed Christ's burial were apparently following that tradition. However, because of the High Holy Day Sabbath of the first day of the Feast of Unleavened Bread (Nisan 15), their arrival at the tomb was delayed by that *High Holy Day* Sabbath. They arrived at the tomb early in the morning of the fourth day, on Sunday (Nisan 17).

Matthews account tells us: *"Now on the next day [Friday], which is the one after the preparation [Nisan 15], the chief priests and the Pharisees gathered together with Pilate..."* (Matthew 27:62). The chief priests and the Pharisees requested Roman guards be posted at the gravesite on the High Holy Day (Friday) for three days, preventing anyone from visiting the tomb, because of the fear that they might relocate the body of Jesus and declare the fulfillment of Jesus' statement that in three days He would rise from the dead. Very probably there was a combination of Roman guards and temple guards used to secure the tomb. One reason to believe that temple guards were also employed is the account in Matthew: *"While the women were on their way, some of the guards went into the city and reported to the chief priests everything that had happened"* (Matthew 28:11). It seems more reasonable that the temple guards would have reported back to the chief priests and that the Roman guards would have reported back to their Roman officials.

Matthew provides a sequential account following Jesus' resurrection. Apparently when the women arrived early at the tomb on Sunday morning, the guards were frozen as dead men, the stone sealing the grave had been rolled aside, the angel spoke to the women and, later, the presence of the resurrected Jesus confronted the women (Matthew 28:2–10).

Our case is that the women arriving at the tomb and the angel speaking to the women occurred on early Sunday morning. This chronology allows Jesus to be resurrected much earlier—on Saturday evening (which is also the start of Sunday on the Jewish calendar; Nisan 16/17) and still have the resurrection occurring at the start of the first day of the week—Sunday (Firstfruits; Nisan 17).

CHAPTER 28

Puzzle Piece #10– Astronomical Considerations

To provide a harmonious fit of Passion Week events, *astronomical considerations* are an additional *puzzle piece*, and constitute our *Puzzle Piece #10*.

Per all the evidence of the *puzzle pieces* presented in this Section A of Part II of this book, I am in agreement with Messianic Rabbi Avi Ben Mordechai as to Jesus' death being on late **Wednesday** afternoon (the *Mosaic/Sadducees'* Passover—**Nisan 13/14**; which was also the Pharisaic "Day of Preparation") during the period of time defined in Hebrew writings as *"between the two evening times"* (Nisan 13/14), which was explained in Chapter 20: "*Puzzle Piece #2*–Hebrew Timing Issues re Passover." In addition, per the evidence in Chapter 34: "*Year* of Death & Resurrection: *AD 30*," I strongly believe that Jesus died in **AD 30**.

How does this Wednesday, Nisan 13, align with astronomical software data? Because any date, such as the Passover date of Nisan 14, can float throughout a given week of any calendar year, per this case for the crucifixion being on Wednesday afternoon (Nisan 13/14), it is critical that a year be identified that shows Nisan 14 occurring on a *Thursday* (burial at Wednesday/Thursday of Nisan 13/14) to arrive at a resurrection on Saturday/Sunday, and thus allowing Jesus words, "…

three days and three nights." As already explained, this is taken literally as three full days and three full nights, which I believe strongly is implied by Jesus.

Astronomical references verify that *Nisan 14* **was, indeed, on** *Thursday* **in AD 30, and, hence,** *Nisan 13* **for AD 30 was on** *Wednesday*.[216]

This is in alignment with the case that Jesus died in *AD 30* and that He died on *Wednesday* (Nisan 13) of that year, per Chapter 34. Figures 19.1 and Figure 19.2 in Chapter 19 as well as Figure 35.1 in Chapter 35 are graphical presentations of the crucifixion week.

What about other years around AD 30? Does Nisan 13 for those years also fall on Wednesday? If so, then our case for AD 30 would not be as strong. However, they do not; so, our case for AD 30 is bolstered.

Based on the findings of Dr. James Boyer, Th.D., Professor Emeritus of Grace Theological Seminary, we know that Passover [the Passover of *Nisan 14*] occurred on Wednesdays (and not on Thursdays) in the years *AD 28, 31 and 34*.[217] These dates are confirmed by the findings of Pallant Ramsurdar in his PhD thesis, "Dating Christ's Crucifixion."[218] Boyer and Ramsurdar hold to a crucifixion on Wednesday and *that Wednesday being Nisan 14*, but they do not hold to the crucifixion being in AD 30 due to the fact that *Nisan 14 was not on Wednesday in AD 30*.

However, for our case of the crucifixion being on Wednesday (but that Wednesday being *Nisan 13*), AD 30 is, indeed, viable because astronomical findings are that in AD 30 Nisan 14 was on *Thursday*, per our case—and this was not true for AD 28, 31, and 34.

Since Jesus was crucified and died as the *Pesach* lamb on the *Mosaic/Sadducees Pesach* [Passover] on Wednesday [*Nisan 13*] of the crucifixion week, patterned after the written Torah and not on the *Pesach* [Passover] of *Pharisaic* tradition [on *Nisan 14*] in the time of Jesus, the astronomical considerations support this chronology of our case. As described, the astronomical considerations which would normally exclude a Wednesday crucifixion case *if* it was on Passover (Nissan 14) for AD 30, are **not a deterrent for our case for a Wednesday (*Nisan 13*) crucifixion date in AD 30.**

This allows for astronomical confirmation for Wednesday, Nisan 13, for AD 30 as an additional *puzzle piece—Puzzle Piece #10—*of our case to fall in place for further verification of the day that Jesus died.

CHAPTER 29

Puzzle Piece #11– Traditions (Christian & Jewish)

Both Christianity and Judaism have unbiblical traditions which are established and are passed down from generation to generation. Many of these unbiblical traditions have been around for hundreds and even thousands of years. These unbiblical traditions are our *Puzzle Piece #11*.

Unfortunately, these Christian and Jewish traditions are an impediment to many people accepting a more biblical case for the chronology of the crucifixion of Jesus, as we are presenting in this book. Their reasoning is that since the traditions have been in place for so long, in some cases for thousands of years, then they must be right. Not so!

For example, the "Christmas" and "Good Friday" teachings of the Christian church for the dates of the birth and crucifixion of Jesus do not correlate to Scripture; these traditions date to the fourth and fifth centuries AD and have been established as accepted church traditions.

In the Jewish faith, the tradition of combining of the Feasts of Passover and Unleavened Bread, which dates to first century BC—and which was in effect during the life of Jesus—is unbiblical yet is still practiced in Israel today.

The point is that religious traditions can take on a life of their own, are accepted readily as truth, and are often extremely difficult to give up. Often, when a biblical case is presented, the new case is rejected because it differs from the traditional position, and people don't want to change their entrenched beliefs. Often the thinking is that, surely, the traditional position can't be wrong.

Certainly, not all traditions are wrong. However, from our research on the birth, death, burial, resurrection, and ascensions of Jesus, we can say that virtually *all the church traditions* of the dates and places are inaccurate.

Understanding and accepting the correct chronology of the crucifixion week does depend on giving up some established traditions as to when events happened. How you either accept or reject the evidence of the cases presented in this book—and what you do with the information—is entirely up to each reader after evaluating the evidence presented.

Largely, one's salvation does not depend on this new information. God loves you either way. He is most concerned about each person's salvation and if they are trusting in the salvation available only through Jesus—Jesus said, *"I am the way, the truth, and the life. No one comes to the Father expect through me"* (John 14:6). That is what is most important.

What I am trying to do in this book is make Jesus more real to each reader—He is firmly anchored in history and in Scripture in all aspects of His life.

Unfortunately, most theories do not correctly take into account all the *puzzle pieces* being presented related to the crucifixion week—when Jesus died, was buried, was resurrected, and ascended to the Father. To come to truth, all Scripture and reliable historical truth needs to be in alignment. This is the case with the day of the week Jesus was crucified as well as the other cases presented.

Yes, I know that giving up traditions can be difficult.

CHAPTER 30

Summary Table–Days of Crucifixion Week

The following Figure 30.1 shows a summary of the days of the week of the crucifixion of Jesus. The dates (9th, 10th, 11th, etc.) refer to the days of the Jewish month of Nisan (Abib) for AD 30, the year of His crucifixion. For the specific week and year of the crucifixion, the Pharisaic Passover was on Nisan 14th (Leviticus 23:5) and Firstfruits fell on Nisan 17th (the Sadducees' Firstfruits is always on a Sunday).

See also Figure 35.1 in Conclusion of Section A of Part II for a graphic depiction of the crucifixion week.

Day	Date	Jewish Event	Jesus Event
Saturday	9th	Passover Lamb selected	
Sunday	10th	Passover Lamb brought to the Temple	Jesus enters the Temple
Monday	11th	The Passover Lamb inspected	Jesus interrogated by rulers
Tuesday	12th	The Passover Lamb inspected; lamb sacrificed for Passover *Seder* of Jesus with disciples.	Interrogation continues into 13th; Last Supper of Jesus
Wednesday	13th	Mosaic/Sadducees' Passover—Lamb sacrificed; Day of Preparation for Pharisaic Passover	Last Supper continues into night after start of Wed.; Jesus crucified
Thursday	14th	Mosaic/Sadducees' Feast of Unleavened Bread; Pharisaic Passover	Jesus buried—3 Nights and 3 Days total
Friday	15th	Pharisaic Passover/Unleavened Bread (High Sabbath)—women purchased and prepared spices	Jesus in tomb
Saturday	16th	Weekly Sabbath—no usual work, but preparation of spices by women was allowed and continued	Jesus in tomb
Sunday	17th	The Feast of Firstfruits	Jesus resurrected *(Sat. evening/start of Sunday)* Women arrived Sunday morning at tomb—Mary Magdalen spoke with Jesus

Figure 30.1. Crucifixion Week—How This Puzzle Looks When Put Together for Jewish month of Nisan of AD 30 (See also Figure 35.1 in Conclusion of Section A of Part II)

CHAPTER 31

Reference to Hard Scriptures

Another part of this proposed corrected chronology of the crucifixion week (Wednesday, Thursday, Friday, Saturday and Sunday) that needs to be addressed is the references in the Gospels to *"three days"* and *"on the third day"* (Luke 24:7) that Christ was to be resurrected. We might call these the "Hard Scriptures" which need to be accounted for by our case.

The Roman church, I believe, incorrectly interpreted these references to dictate the *Friday, Saturday, Sunday* chronology, but these can be explained within the proposed corrected chronology of our case, which also harmonizes with the *"3 days and 3 nights"* previously discussed, as well as the chronology of the women previously discussed.

We can look at the following Scripture verses:

- Mark 8:31: "And He began to teach them that the Son of Man must suffer many things and be rejected by the elders and the chief priests and the scribes, and be killed, and **after three days rise again**." (emphasis added)

- 1 Corinthians 15:4: "… and that He was buried, and that He was **raised on the third day** according to the Scriptures." (emphasis added)

- Luke 24:7: " ... saying that the Son of Man must be delivered into the hands of sinful men, and be crucified, and **the third day rise again**." (emphasis added)

With the suggested chronology, these seemingly uncorrelated statements can be reconciled by Christ's burial at sunset (division between Wednesday/Thursday) and resurrection at sunset (division between Saturday/Sunday). This represents both *"after three days"* as well as *"on the third day,"* as sundown is on both days at the division between days.

Supposedly, one of the "proofs" of the validity of the *Friday, Saturday, Sunday* tradition is the reference to *Luke 24:13–21*, which includes the verse, *"Indeed, besides all this,* **today is the third day** *since these things happened"* (v.21, emphasis added). Christ joined the two disciples as they were walking on the road to Emmaus, later, on that first day of the week after the women discovered the empty tomb, and Christ joined up with them and engaged them in conversation, although they did not recognize Him. The following is the Scripture quotation of this encounter:

> And He said to them, 'What kind of conversation is this that you have with one another as you walk and are sad?' Then the one whose name was Cleopas answered and said to Him, 'Are You the only stranger in Jerusalem, and have You not known the things which happened there in these days?' And He said to them, 'What things?' So they said to Him, 'The things concerning Jesus of Nazareth, who was a Prophet mighty in deed and word before God and all the people, and how the chief priests and our rulers delivered Him to be condemned to death, and crucified Him. But we were hoping that it was He who was going to redeem Israel. Indeed, besides all this, **today is the third day since these things happened.**' (Luke 24:17–21 NKJV, emphasis added)

The following commentary, from an article in the *Good News* magazine, gives an explanation that is in agreement with our corrected chronology:

> Here, the two disciples referred to Sunday as being *the third day* since *"these things"* happened. There were other things the Jews and Romans did after Christ was buried. Notice what Matthew included about their actions:
>
> On the next day ... , which followed the Day of Preparation, the chief priests and Pharisees gathered together to Pilate, saying, 'Sir, we remember, when He was still alive, how that deceiver said, **'After three**

WHEN WERE JESUS' DEATH, RESURRECTION & ASCENTIONS?

days I will rise.' Therefore command that **the tomb be made secure until the third day**, lest His disciples come by night and steal Him away, and say to the people, 'He has risen from the dead."' ' So the last deception will be worse that the first,' Pilate said to them. 'You have a guard; go your way, make it as secure as you know how.' So they went and made the tomb secure, sealing the stone and setting the guard (Matthew 27:62–66, emphasis added).

Christ had already been buried nearly one whole day when these things were done … The last things the Romans and Jewish leaders did were to seal the tomb and place soldiers on guard around it. **This was on Thursday, the day following that Day of Preparation. Apparently, the disciples were including *these events* in their reference to the things that had taken place. Counting from the securing of the tomb and the setting of the guards, Sunday would have been the *'third day'* since *'all these things'* happened.** [219]

With this proposed explanation, even this "hard Scripture" falls into harmony with our proposed corrected chronology. The above explanation of the *"third day"* agrees with the chronology and reasons given by E. F. Bullinger in Appendix 156 of *The Companion Bible*, which also supports a Wednesday crucifixion.[220]

CHAPTER 32

How Did the Church Err?

Jesus did not die on Friday which is the traditional view of the church. The simplest explanation for how the church could have erred to come up with Friday as the day of Jesus' crucifixion is either through ignorance or intentional disregard of their Hebrew roots.

Although the early church was increasingly distancing itself from its Jewish roots since AD 70, i.e., the fall of Jerusalem, the beginning of the fourth century AD marked a distinct departure of the church from everything Jewish.

Under the governance of the Roman Emperor Constantine, the church was to be wholly Gentile. Any remnants of Judaism that celebrated or acknowledged Jewish Feast days or a Jewish construct for biblical understanding was extracted from the practices and theology of the church. Unhappily, this led many parts of the church to become anti-Semitic—a stigma still present among some today—and led to a misunderstanding of the actual sequence of events of Jesus' crucifixion, burial and resurrection. Also, seemingly, the church did not properly understand the Feasts of the Lord—that there were two Sabbath days in the crucifixion week—with the first day of Unleavened Bread being a High Holy Day (Sabbath) in addition to the weekly Sabbath.

In summary, I have to say that the reason that the church "got it so wrong" is because the church did not follow Scripture. For one thing, the church did not consider the words of Jesus related to the *"three days and three nights"* that He would be in the heart of the earth (Matthew 12:40). This is *impossible* with a Friday, Saturday, and Sunday chronology, as there are only two nights in this sequence (Friday night and Saturday night). It just does not qualify as the correct chronology.

However, the chronology proposed in our case of a Wednesday crucifixion and resurrection on the division of Saturday/Sunday, at twilight of the start of Sunday, *does match exactly* with all the evidence related to the *puzzle pieces* presented in this Section A of Part II. See particularly Chapter 24: *"Puzzle Piece #6–*The Sign of Jesus Being Messiah" related to the *"three days and three nights."*

CHAPTER 33

When Were Jesus' *Two* Ascensions?

Few Christians understand that there were *two ascensions* of Jesus to heaven following His *resurrection*. The two ascensions of Jesus to heaven following His resurrection are the case presented here in Chapter 33.

Most Christians know about the "public ascension" of Jesus (Mark 16:19, Luke 24:50–51, and Acts 1:9–10), witnessed by His disciples, 39 days after His resurrection. This is the ascension which is talked about and written about. However, few Christians understand that this event was Jesus' *Second Ascension* to heaven.

His *First Ascension* occurred on the day of His resurrection, and, in fact, occurred shortly after His resurrection. This *First Ascension* is related to the Feast of the Lord known as Firstfruits, and, although clearly shown in Scripture, has been largely forgotten in history and in church tradition.

Why is that? The short answer is that it is due to a de-emphasis in the church, especially in the time of the Roman Emperor Constantine (fourth century), of the Jewishness of Jesus, His life, and His ministry. Chapter 6 of my first book, *The Last Shofar!*, lays out the case for Jesus fulfilling the seven Feasts of the Lord (Leviticus 23) at His First and Second Comings. The Feasts of the Lord were given by God to Moses (Leviticus 23), and they were to be celebrated annually by the Jewish people as a foreshadowing of God's plan of redemption—pointing to the coming of the

Messiah and the salvation He uniquely brings. The four Spring Feasts (Passover, Unleavened Bread, Firstfruits, and Pentecost) were literally fulfilled by Jesus at His *First Coming* in the first century, related to His death, burial, resurrection, and ascensions. The three Fall Feasts (Feast of Trumpets, Day of Atonement, and Tabernacles) will be literally fulfilled in the future at His *Second Coming*.

Jesus' resurrection and His ascensions were the fulfillment of the Spring Feast of Firstfruits. How Firstfruits ties into Jesus' resurrection and ascensions is covered in Chapter 6 of *The Last Shofar!* and the following text is taken from that book and is presented here as good background for understanding the two ascensions of Jesus. The *First Ascension*, especially, only makes sense in light of an understanding of the Firstfruits' temple-related ceremonies by the priests. Some background is helpful in appreciating this linkage to Jesus.

A. Background on Firstfruits

The purpose of Firstfruits is to present to the Lord the first sheaf (literally the "firstfruits") of the winter barley harvest. This Firstfruit offering was cut in the spring of the year—following the Passover and the first day of Unleavened Bread Feasts—from a special barley field located at the base of the Mount of Olives, to the east of the temple. The cutting was done on the evening of Firstfruits (at the *start* of Firstfruits), immediately after the weekly Sabbath, on Saturday evening, during the week of Unleavened Bread.

By Jewish reckoning, Saturday evening at sundown is also the beginning of the first day of the week, Sunday. The priest lifted the cut barley sheaf and waved it before the Lord for His acceptance.[221] According to the Talmud, the barley was then processed into fine flour throughout the night. When morning arrived, the High Priest waved the processed barley during the Temple ceremony. The waving of the barley flour symbolized God's acceptance and His pledge to His people of an abundant harvest—God's irrevocable blessing upon His people.[222]

As to the order of the resurrection of the righteous, the Apostle Paul tells us that Christ Himself is the *firstfruits*. Paul explains, *"But each in his own order:* **Christ the firstfruits**, *then at his coming those who belong to Christ"* (1 Corinthians 15:23, emphasis added).

Christ rose from the dead, having been lifted up, cut free from the earth at the same time the barley sheaf of the Firstfruits ceremony was lifted up in the field, at the *very start* of Firstfruits on Saturday evening, at the *very beginning* of the *first day of the week*, Sunday. This was the fulfillment that Jesus is the firstfruit of the resurrection. The resurrection of Jesus Christ confirms that, *"In Christ shall all be made alive"* (I Corinthians 15:22; KJV)—God's irrevocable blessing upon all who believe. As pictured in the Feast, a rich and abundant life is experienced in the resurrected Christ—who is our Firstfruits of the resurrection.

There is yet another interesting correlation of the events surrounding the crucifixion and resurrection of Jesus to the Feast of Firstfruits. This involves an explanation for something which is puzzling in the Matthew account—that of the resurrection of *"many holy people"* upon the resurrection of Jesus. Matthew states the following:

> And the graves were opened; and **many bodies of the saints who had fallen asleep were raised; and coming out of the graves after His resurrection**, they went into the holy city and appeared to many." (Matthew 27:52–53, NKJV, emphasis added)

Richard Booker, author of *Celebrating Jesus in the Biblical Feasts—Discovering Their Significance to You as a Christian* (2009)**,** has offered the following interesting correlation of these additional resurrections—*of saints*—to Firstfruits:

> The barley sheaf [group of barley stalks] wave offering consisted of a number of individual barley stalks that had been bundled together. Likewise, when Jesus offered Himself as the firstfruits from the dead, **many individual believers were raised with Him** ... When the time came to harvest the crop, the farmer would go into his field and inspect the firstfruits of the crop. If he accepted the firstfruits, then the rest of the harvest would also be acceptable to him. Since our Heavenly Father has accepted Jesus as the firstfruits from the dead, believers are also acceptable to God through Jesus. He will also raise us from the dead and give us a new resurrected body fitted for eternity.[223]

It is true that Jesus, our Firstfruits, is our representative. By presenting Himself to the Father, He consecrated the rest of us to the Father, starting with those *"saints"* who were raised just after Jesus was resurrected. Paul boldly stated to the Christians in Ephesus: *"He [God] made us accepted in the Beloved" (Ephesians 1:6).* Believers are the human stalks that have been bundled together with Jesus; therefore, *"If the firstfruit is holy,* **the lump is also holy***; and if the root is holy,* **so are the branches***" (Romans 11:16, NKJV, emphasis added).*

Therefore, Jesus Christ completely fulfilled the prophetic message of the Feast of Firstfruits. He did this by His resurrection on the very day and hour the Feast was initially observed by Israel—Saturday at sundown, which is also the beginning of the first day of the week, Sunday on the Jewish calendar. He was raised from the tomb at precisely the time when the priests cut the barley sheaf and raised it heavenly. Further information on this is presented in *The Last Shofar!*, in Appendix II—related to the Jewish calendar—and in Appendix III—related to the crucifixion week.

To fully appreciate how the Feast of Firstfruits is prophetically fulfilled, it is important to understand the sequence of events that occurred in the pre-dawn hours of the Sunday following Christ's crucifixion. Combining information from the four Gospel accounts, the following scenario emerges:

"At early dawn" (stated in Luke 24:1) [Mark states, *"when the sun had risen" (Mark 16:2)*; John states, *"while it was still dark" (John 20:1)*], two women [perhaps three] appeared at the tomb—identified as *"Mary Magdalene and the other Mary" (Matthew 28:1)*. From Luke's account (Luke 23:55–24:2), it appears to be uncertain exactly how many women came to the tomb at this pre-dawn hour; Luke mentions by name at least a third woman, Joanna (Luke 24:10).

As the women approached the tomb, the immediate concern was how they might roll away the stone that had sealed the tomb where the body of Jesus had been laid (Mark 16:3). Upon arriving at the tomb, much to their surprise, the stone had already been rolled away. In addition, they also saw an angel who said to them, *"Do not be afraid" (Matthew 28:5)* and told them that the One they were seeking was not in the tomb but had risen. The angel then instructed them to go and inform the other disciples of the things they had seen and heard. Of interest, Luke's account of this encounter gives the additional information that there were *two angels* who met the women (Luke 24:4–6). In this case, as in other Gospel accounts, details surrounding the event may vary depending on the writer's perspective and emphasis that the Holy Spirit seeks to convey to the reader.

Luke also informs us that the women [at least three] returned to the disciples and told them all the things they had seen and heard. Incredulous as it seemed, the disciples did not believe them.

Peter and *"... the other disciple whom Jesus loved" (John 20:2–3)* [presumed to be the disciple John] ran back to the tomb to verify the account of the women. After seeing the evidence of the resurrection, the two disciples believed—however, they *saw*, but did not fully *see!*—for *"... they did not understand the Scripture, that he [Jesus] must be raised from the dead."* Then the disciples *"... went back to their homes" (John 20:8–10)*.

At this point in the narrative, it appears that Mary Magdalene remained behind after the rest had returned to their homes, weeping over the empty tomb. Then, she encountered the two angels, who inquired as to why she was crying (John 20:11–12). Apparently, forgetting the words she heard from her initial encounter with the angel(s) at the tomb earlier that morning, she said, *"They have taken my Lord, and I do not know where they have laid him" (John 20:13).*

Jesus appeared to Mary and asked the same question, *"Why are you weeping?"* She gave the same reply, thinking Jesus to be the gardener. When Jesus spoke her name, *"Mary,"* she realized that no stranger could have known her name or have spoken it with a tone of intimacy that Jesus alone used. She, no doubt, fell at His feet in worship and adoration, wanting to touch Him for fear of losing Him again.

B. Specific Background of Jesus' First Ascension

At this point, Jesus said to Mary, *"**Touch me not**; for I am **not yet ascended to my Father**: but go to my brethren, and say unto them, **I ascend unto my Father**, and your Father; and (to) my God, and your God," (John 20:17, KJV, emphasis added).* The literal Greek translation is *"Jesus said to Her, **Do not touch Me**, for **I have not yet gone up to My Father**. But go to My brothers, and say to them, **I go up to My Father** ..."*[224]

While most commentators refer to *ascended* as meaning Christ's ascension to glory 40 days later, we believe that this *immediate* ascension Jesus was talking about was the fulfillment of the Feast of Firstfruits—His ascension as the wave offering of Himself and His work on the cross, that was accepted by God, as the Firstfruits offering to the Father. The evidence related to *this initial ascension* (the *First Ascension*) is followed in the narrative by Jesus meeting the other women, who apparently were traveling separately from the men, and His greeting them. The women immediately took hold of His feet, i.e., *clasped His feet* and worshiped Him— *" ... They came to him, **clasped His feet** and worshiped Him" (Matthew 28:8–9 NIV, emphasis added).* On this occasion, Jesus gave no restriction about touching Him but simply stated, *"Do not be afraid; go and tell my brothers to go to Galilee, and there they will see me" (Matthew 28:10; NIV).* Jesus had already gone up to the Father in heaven and had returned to earth again.

Also, later, when Jesus was with the disciples, He encouraged Thomas to touch Him to convince him of the reality of the resurrected Christ who stood before him. He said, *"See my hands and my feet, that it is I myself. **Touch me**, and see ... "* *(Luke 24:39 NASB, emphasis added).* There was no problem with the disciples touching Him *at this time.*

At first, all this is very puzzling. It seems obvious that something had changed between Jesus' encounter with Mary, who was told not to touch Him, and the encounter Jesus later had with the returning women, who took hold of Him, and still later with Thomas, who was invited by Jesus to touch Him. The "something" we suggest is the *first of two ascensions*—the *first* to fulfill the requirements of the wave offering of the purified barley—that ceremonial raising, *the lifting up*, of the barley offering and the waving before God by the High Priest in the temple. This was for God's acceptance and irrevocable blessing resulting from the offering. Jesus, without notice and fanfare, ascended to the Father to complete what to this point had been prophetically incomplete—the wave offering, *the lifting up* of the barley offering *(Jesus)* before God, presenting Himself to the Father as the risen, acceptable Firstfruits sacrifice—that which was uniquely special just between Him and His Father. Shortly after this *First Ascension*, Jesus returned to earth to fulfill the other encounters He had with the disciples.

Richard Booker has suggested the following explanation of Jesus' comment to Mary for her not to touch Him: "As the *barley sheaf* could **not be touched** until it was offered to God, so Jesus, the *human sheaf*, could **not be touched** until He offered Himself in the heavenly temple as the firstfruits from the dead"[225]

Due to the chronology, the ascension described above is an *earlier ascension* to the Father from that which occurred later and was witnessed by the disciples (Mark 16:19; Luke 24:31).

C. Specific Background of Jesus' Second Ascension

In the *Second Ascension* (39 days later, after Firstfruits), Jesus *publicly* ascended back to heaven. Ten days later, at Pentecost, the Holy Spirit came upon the disciples to empower them to complete His work on earth—albeit, absent physically from them until He returns in glory in the last days at the rapture of the Church.

We recognize the challenges inherit in this understanding of the text, but it is our supposition that when all of Scripture—including prophetic Scripture related to the Feasts of the Lord—are brought to bear, it is both a consistent and reasonable conclusion. (See Figure **35.1** in the Conclusion of this Section A of Part II, for our recommended biblical timeline of the week of Jesus' crucifixion and resurrection.)

I believe that the case is very strong for *two ascensions* of Jesus to heaven, following His resurrection—as we have presented in this Chapter 33.

CHAPTER 34

Year of Death & Resurrection: *AD 30*

The year of Jesus' crucifixion is a mystery, with various years suggested by Bible commentators. However, I believe the case for the year of Jesus' crucifixion and resurrection being **AD 30** is overwhelming. The case for this is presented in this chapter.

The birth date of Jesus as outlined in this book (September 11, 3 BC) as well as the life and ministry of Jesus presented in the Gospels—with His ministry starting at age 30 and encompassing three Passovers—lead us to that conclusion of AD 30. In addition, the testimonies of the Jewish writers in Jewish historical literature as to the strange happenings in the temple starting with AD 30 lend additional overwhelming evidence that something highly significant happened during that year. These evidences and others presented in this chapter point us to the AD 30 crucifixion date conclusion.

A. Not AD 28, AD 29, AD 31, AD 32, AD 33, or AD 34

Of course, other years on either side of AD 30 have been proposed by distinguished Bible commentators for the crucifixion of Jesus. So, how do we have such a wide variation in the proposed years of Jesus' death?

Simply stated, the proponents of these other years *prior to* AD 30 (AD 28 and AD 29) hold to a birthdate of Jesus *prior to* 3 BC (*i.e.*, 7 BC, 6 BC, 5 BC or 4 BC)—as explained in Section A of Part I of this book. Whereas many of the proponents of the dates *after* AD 30 (AD 31, AD 32, AD 33, etc.) hold to a birthdate of Jesus at the traditional AD 1—and counting forward 33 years (starting ministry at age 30 and having a ministry of 3 years) they arrive at a crucifixion date *after* AD 30.

By getting the birthdate of Jesus wrong, as most do, they also get the year of the crucifixion wrong as well. Once again, it is important to get all the pieces of the puzzles correct to arrive at the truth.

What about the individual who we met back in Chapter 1, the learned priest Dionysius Exiguus, who was tapped by the Roman Pope in the sixth century to determine when the original death of Jesus was—for the purpose of devising a system by which the church could announce the time of Easter. **He picked AD 33 as the year of Jesus' death/resurrection; it was the only year he could pick and stay with a Friday crucifixion date**. Theological opinion at that time was that, since Jesus was nearly 30 when He was baptized, and He had a public ministry of about 2 ½ years, He was crucified when He was in His 33rd year (in AD 33). Thus, Dionysius Exiguus arrived at Jesus' birth year of AD 1. Unfortunately, we have shown that this is impossible, because Herod died in 1 BC, and Jesus had to have been born before Herod died per the events of the Gospel account of Matthew. Exiguus might have been forced into this error, because of the hard-and-fast Roman Church tradition of Jesus having been crucified on Friday.

So, what is the wealth of evidence for the crucifixion of Jesus being in AD 30?

B. Evidence for Death and Resurrection in AD 30

We have presented the evidence for the birth of Jesus being on September 11, 3 BC, per all the *puzzle pieces* presented in Section A of Part I. Similarly, the case for the death of Jesus being in AD 30 requires putting together various *puzzle pieces* to solve this mystery. This case for the year that Jesus died is presented in this chapter.

Arriving at AD 30 is largely due to getting the birthdate of Jesus correct (3 BC) and building the chronology of Jesus' life from that starting point to arrive at AD 30 for His death.

Building on the excellent research work of Ernest L. Martin to arrive at the birthdate of Jesus on September 11, 3 BC, I believe the overall chronology for the life of Jesus developed by Martin[226] is also correct, arriving at the year of death of AD 30. All the *puzzle pieces* fit together in this chronology.

WHEN WERE JESUS' DEATH, RESURRECTION & ASCENSIONS?

1. Proposed Chronology of Jesus' Life to Arrive at AD 30

The following proposed summary of the chronology for the life of Jesus is provided by Martin in his landmark book, *The Star of Bethlehem–The Star that Astonished the World* (1996).[227] This chronology is a *puzzle piece* which leads us to an AD 30 crucifixion.

- **September 11, 3 BC**: Jesus was born.

- **September 18, 3 BC**: Circumcised (on the 8th day; the circumcision rite is reckoned inclusively).

- **October 20/21, 3 BC**: Dedicated in the temple.

- **Latter part of October, 3 BC**: Family returned to Nazareth.

- **Spring or Summer of 2 BC**: Family moved to Bethlehem; lived in a house.

- **December 25, 2 BC** (during Hanukkah): The Magi went to Bethlehem and gave the child (*toddler*) their three gifts, when the planet Jupiter came to its stationary point in mid-Virgo the Virgin.

- **Late December, 2 BC**: The family set off for Egypt to escape the wrath of Herod, following the visit of the Magi and the warning of the angel who spoke to Joseph in a dream.

- **Late December, 2 BC**: Immediately after this, Herod killed all the male children two years old and younger in Bethlehem. This slaying of the innocents was about 15 months after Jesus' birth—if the conception period were also considered, it comes to 24 months exactly. This is why the Magi saw Jesus "*standing* by the side of his mother, Mary."[228]

- **Early January, 1 BC**: Two prominent rabbis were tried and sentenced to death by the Sanhedrin.

- **January 9, 1 BC**: The two prominent rabbis were burnt alive by Herod to correspond with the lunar eclipse that was predicted for that night.

- **January 10, 1 BC**: The eclipse of the Moon occurred that Josephus mentioned as happening before the death of Herod; *this* is the eclipse related to the death of Herod, and not an earlier eclipse, which many historians claim is the one referred to by Josephus.

- About January 28, 1 BC: Herod died.

- **Spring of 1 BC**: The Passover occurred during which 3,000 Jewish worshippers were killed by the Romans in the temple precincts.

- **Summer and Autumn of 1 BC**: The *War of Varus* took place in Israel, prompted by the revolt in Israel over the slaughter of the 3,000 worshippers in the temple—as ordered by Archelaus, the successor to Herod the Great.

- **Fall (October or November) of AD 27**: About 28 years later, Jesus was baptized by John the Baptist, at the beginning of a Sabbatical Year (in the fall; happens only every seventh year)—among other evidence, close to the start of His ministry, Jesus' words spoken in the Synagogue in Nazareth related to *"acceptable year"* make reference to a Sabbatical Year (which starts in the fall, on Yom Kippur on Tishri 1).

- **Spring of AD 28**: During Passover and Pentecost season, Jesus began His ministry.

- **Spring of AD 30**: On the third Passover related to Jesus' ministry, **Jesus was crucified in AD 30**—as the Lamb of God sacrifice on Passover.

With this chronology, the birth-date details covered in Section A of Part I fit together—the many obscure passages of Josephus make sense, as well as the New Testament passages related to the birth and ministry of Jesus. In addition, the astronomical history of cosmic events happening, and the Roman history for the middle period of Augustus fit together.

In summary, with this chronology, all the puzzle pieces fit together—finally arriving at a date of Jesus' crucifixion in AD 30. But there is more evidence to bring forward.

2. Supernatural Signs in Temple Starting in AD 30

The supernatural signs in the temple precincts starting in AD 30 is the *puzzle piece* which is unknown to many of the Bible commentators who subscribe to years other than AD 30 for the crucifixion. In fact, I believe it is compelling evidence on which we can "hang our hat" related to the crucifixion date of AD 30.

Starting in AD 30, exactly 40 years before the destruction of the temple, God started to give unmistakable recurring miraculous signs in the temple precincts. These signs were a "heads up" related to the statements made by Jesus in the Olivet Prophecy in AD 30 pertaining to the destruction of the Temple and Jerusalem; Jesus said these would occur in that generation. Remarkably, the catastrophe did happen in AD 70, exactly 40 years later—a generation being 40 years.

WHEN WERE JESUS' DEATH, RESURRECTION & ASCENTIONS?

What is the background of these signs that the apostles and the Jewish people witnessed starting in AD 30? They are recorded in both the Jerusalem and the Babylonian Talmuds, showing that the Jewish authorities in the period when the Talmuds were compiled were certainly aware of them, and the four signs are exactly stated in each of the Talmuds (*Jerusalem Talmud*, Sotah 6:3; and *Babylonian Talmud*, Yoma 39b).[229]

It is important for us to spend some time on this discussion on the supernatural signs in the temple, as this *puzzle piece* is that important in the case for the crucifixion being in AD 30. And, as stated previously, these miraculous signs are not widely known and understood.

(a)   Four Miraculous Signs

What were these four miraculous signs in the temple precincts which started to happen following the crucifixion? They are as stated in the *Jerusalem Talmud*:

> "Forty years before the destruction of the Temple [starting in A.D. 30] (1) **the western light went out**, (2) **the crimson thread remained crimson**, and (3) **the lot for the Lord always came up in the left hand**. (4) They would **close the gates of the Temple by night and get up in the morning and find them wide open**. Said Rabban Yohanan ben Zakkai to the Temple, 'O Temple, why do you frighten us? We know that you will end up destroyed. For it has been said, 'Open your doors, O Lebanon [a symbol for the Temple at Jerusalem which was made from Lebanese timbers], that the fire may devour your cedars' (Zechariah 11:1)" (Sotah 6:3). (*Jerusalem Talmud*; translation is that of Jacob Neusner from his book *The Yerushalmi*, pp. 156–157; enumeration and emphasis added)[230]

It is important to note that the above four miraculous signs occurred *consistently over a period of 40 years*. This was not a random occurrence, but happened 14,400 times in a row (360 days x 40 years = 14,400 occurrances) for those events which occurred daily, and 40 times in a row for annual events (like Day of Atonement events). This is crazy impossible odds to happen by chance! For those readers with a mathematical inclination, the statistical odds for just the annual occurrence like the drawing of the black stone (the "lot") consistently over 40 years is one chance in 2^{40} (2 x 2 x 2 x 2 ... 40 times)—this reflects the power of compounding, and after multiplying 40 times it is an unbelievably large number. As stated in the *Babylonian Talmud* (Soncino Version):

"Our rabbis taught: During **the last forty years** before the destruction of the Temple (1) **the lot ['For the Lord'] did not come up in the right hand**; (2) **nor did the crimson-colored strap become white**; (3) **nor did the western most light shine** [Menorah]; and (4) **the doors of the Hekel** (the Holy Place) **would open by themselves**, until Yohanan ben Zakkai rebuked them, saying: *Hekel, Hekel,* why wilt thou be the alarmer thyself? I know about thee that thou wilt be destroyed, for Zechariah ben Iddo has already prophesied concerning thee: *Open thy doors, O Lebanon, that the fire may devour thy cedars*" (*Yoma* 39b; the bold letters, the underlined, the enumerations, and the parentheses are mine, but the words in brackets and italics are part of the Sonino text).[231]

The four miraculous signs were propitious, and need some further explanation—I am using the order for the listing of the four signs from the *Jerusalem Talmud*:

A. *The western light went out.* This refers to the western light of the seven-branched Menorah in the Holy Place; the Menorah faced to the north, and the western light was the one closest to the Holy of Holies (the most important light) and was supposed to remain lit all the time— like the eternal flame we see today at some national memorials. Despite all the efforts of the priests, this western light would, miraculously and ominously go out.

B. *The crimson thread remained crimson.* This relates to the annual temple ceremony of the Day of Atonement. A crimson-colored thread was carried into the Holy of Holies by the High Priest; although this ceremony is not mentioned in Scripture, it was associated with the Day of Atonement at least from the time of Simon the Righteous (an honorable and upright High Priest who lived in the third century BC). Up until AD 30, the crimson-colored thread turned white, showing that God approved of the Day of Atonement rituals every year and that Israel could then be assured that they were forgiven their sins as Scripture stated. However, starting in AD 30 and continuing until the temple's destruction in AD 70, the crimson thread never again turned white.[232]

C. *The lot for the Lord always came up in the left hand.* This relates to the Day of Atonement temple ceremony in which two goats were brought before the High Priest and lots were cast over them (Leviticus 16:5, 7–10, 15–22). The lots were in the form of a white and black stone, with the white stone "for the Lord," and the black stone "for the Scapegoat." The priest would use his right hand to blindly select a stone from a receptacle and place it over the right-hand goat. The Babylonian Talmud states that during the previous 200 years the stone would sometimes be white and sometimes black, per a random selection. However, beginning in AD 30, the right hand of the High Priest selected the black stone every time for 40 straight years (AD 30 to AD 70).[233]

D. The doors of the temple opened by themselves over night. The front doors behind the curtain at the entrance to the Holy Place (the *Hekel*; this was the curtain which ripped from top to bottom at the death of Jesus rather than the outer of two curtains at the entrance to the Holy of Holies) mysteriously opened every night on their own accord for 40 years (AD 30 to AD 70).[234]

(b) Another Important Historical Event

In addition to the four miraculous signs as stated in the two Talmuds, there was another important historical event—another *puzzle piece*—which occurred in the Jewish nation in that same year of AD 30. It is as follows:

> "**Forty years before** the destruction of Jerusalem, the Sanhedrin was banished [from the **Chamber of Hewn Stones** in the Temple] and sat in the Trading Station [also in the Temple, but east of its former location]" (*Sabbath* 15a the bold letters and words in brackets are from Martin; itallics mine).[235]

This move of the *Chamber of Hewn Stones* which was near the Altar of Burnt Offering in the temple precincts (see Fig. 50.1) could be accounted for by the falling stone-work over the entrance to the Holy Place of the temple which supported the curtain that tore in two at the time of the crucifixion of Jesus. Something happened to that vaulted structure of the *Chamber of Hewn Stones*, making it unsuitable to enter from AD 30 onward. Of course, the earthquake at the crucifixion death of Jesus could have caused the destruction (Matthew 27:54).

It is worthy to note that the last trial ever held by the Sanhedrin in the Chamber of Hewn Stone on the Temple Mount was that of Jesus. This could certainly be interpreted as God's displeasure over the Sanhedrin's trial and rulings on Jesus, resulting in their recommendation of the death penalty. The Sanhedrin was forced to move to other quarters inside and later outside of the temple precincts, starting in AD 30.

Ernest Martin makes a good assessment related to the commencement of these signs in the temple and the crucifixion of Jesus:

> "These signs all started with the exact year in which Jesus was crucified and anyone with any common sense should be able to tell that ***they were signs from God that had their significance beginning with that very year of the crucifixion of Jesus***. This fact is not only important for Christians to know, but it is equally significant for all the Jewish people today."[236]

The relationship to these signs and the crucifixion of Jesus was strangely missing from many of the Jewish leaders at the time. Martin makes note of an important rabbi's assessment:

> "The four signs involving the Temple were interpreted by **Yohanan ben Zakkai** (the most important rabbi at the time) **as being *warnings that the Temple was to be destroyed***. This witness of Yohanan is significant because he lived both before and after the destruction of Jerusalem and the Temple. He was the most important person in the Jewish hierarchy during the period after the destruction in AD 70. He became head of the new seat of Jewish government which was established after AD 70 at Jabneh (Jamnia) about thirty miles west of Jerusalem. His witness and interpretation is paramount to justify the reliability of the occurrence of these four signs."[237]

That these four miraculous signs related to the temple occurred is without dispute, as the evidence is plainly given in both Talmuds maintained by the Jewish authorities. Through them, we are directed to temple events of profound influence beginning in the year AD 30.

And what happened in that year of *AD 30*, which was of eternal significance? *The sacrificial death of Jesus!* Martin summarizes it well:

> "**That very year [AD 30] was the year for the crucifixion of Jesus**, and for the next 40 years there was a constant reminder by God of the coming destruction of the Temple, the city of Jerusalem and the Jewish way of life, just as Jesus had foretold on the very Mount of Olives in which he was crucified. It is time that all the world begin[s] to realize the importance of these significant events."

C. Other Commentators Supporting AD 30

This year of AD 30 is supported by Dr. Ernest Martin as well as many other biblical researchers, although it is considered a minority view—however, of course, truth is not determined by a majority position. Because our book in Section A of Part II features much from the work of Messianic Rabbi Avi Ben Mordechai, related to the Wednesday crucifixion, I want to mention that Mordechai also supports the date of AD 30 for the crucifixion of Jesus.[238] In addition, Nancy L. Kuehl, who is referenced in Section B of Part II, related to the crucifixion on the Mount of Olives, supports the date of AD 30.[239]

D. Conclusion

In addition to the biblical chronology of the events of Jesus' life including His ministry, these four miraculous signs happening in the temple, which have been described, as well as the closing of the *Chamber of Hewn Stones* are extremely important *puzzle pieces* in arriving at AD 30 for the year of Jesus' crucifixion.

How can these miraculous signs be overlooked? They can't. In short, they help greatly in making the case for the AD 30 crucifixion of Jesus.

CHAPTER 35

Conclusion of *When* Were Jesus' Death, Resurrection, & Ascensions?

What difference does all this attention to the correct chronology of Jesus' death, burial, resurrection, and ascensions make to us as individual believers and to the church at large? Since Scripture is, in fact, the Word of God, it is truth (in the original manuscripts) as He Himself is Truth. Therefore, all Scripture—being true—must harmonize and be consistent within itself.

If the traditional *Friday, Saturday, Sunday* chronology is accepted as being true, then it could be argued that the precise words of Christ— *"three days and three nights in the heart of the earth" (Matthew 12:40)* are not *exactly* true. In my opinion, this conclusion results in a dubious interpretation as to the meaning of the text, i.e., reading into the text a meaning that is not there. More to the point, it questions Jesus' means of authenticating that He is, indeed, Messiah, and, hence, the Son of God. Fulfilling the sign of Jonah to the *letter* is the confirmation that He is the *Messiah* (Matthew 12:38–42).

This is a *serious conflict*. However, with the proposed chronology presented in this book, there is harmony of Scripture, and Christ's sign of His being the *Messiah* was literally fulfilled. Praise God.

As Paul commended the Bereans on searching the Scriptures to confirm what he preached (Acts 17:11), it is, likewise, important that we also examine the Scriptures to determine if the commonly accepted *traditions* of the church are indeed true. We believe that the case for this corrected chronology for the death, burial, resurrection and post-resurrection events of Jesus, as presented in this book, is a stronger biblical case than the *traditional* chronology.

We ask each reader to be a *Berean* and search the Scriptures with eyes opened by the Holy Spirit to see if these things are true. We believe they provide for biblical harmony of all the events reported in the four Gospels and make the case for internal consistency of all of Scripture, unlike the *traditional Friday, Saturday, Sunday* chronology.

The *Wednesday* **crucifixion** and burial and the resurrection being at the very start of the Feast of Firstfruits—at sundown on Saturday evening, which is also the start of the Hebrew day of Sunday—is the best explanation of all the *puzzle pieces* provided in the Gospel accounts and as listed in this Section A of Part II of this book. Therefore, we consider the traditional understanding of the crucifixion being on *Friday* as incorrect. Only a *Wednesday* crucifixion allows *all* the *puzzle pieces* to be aligned. If this is true, and I fully believe this to be the case, then the early Roman church got it wrong and this has, unfortunately, been perpetuated down through the centuries.

This case study, with all the 11 *puzzle pieces* coming together, would propose a *"Good Wednesday"* rather than a *Good Friday* celebration of Christ's crucifixion and death on the cross, paying the sin-debt for our sins, so that we can be reconciled to God and spend eternity with Him. That is indeed Good News!

As you study Figure 35.1, remember the Jewish reckoning of a day being *the evening to evening* (nighttime followed by daylight). The bold line (night time) followed by the lighter line (day time) for each day, Wednesday through Sunday, depicts this chronology.

In support of *Wednesday* crucifixion day for Jesus, Messianic Rabbi Avi Ben Mordechai has stated the following in his insightful book:

> I have endeavored to prove that Y'shua HaMashiach died on the Mosaic *Pesach* [Passover; on Wednesday of the crucifixion week, of the year AD 30] patterned after the written Torah and not on the *Pesach* [Passover] of Pharisaic tradition. By dying as the *Pesach* lamb according to the written Torah, He was able to once again correct Judaism in its errors of Torah interpretation. Also, He was able to prove that He came to teach Torah correctly and to put it on a firm foundation.[240]

Related to the **burial** of Jesus, we have made the case for the body of Jesus having been placed in the tomb ("burial" of Jesus) being officially before the end of the Wednesday crucifixion day, by sunset of that day (to satisfy Deuteronomy 21:22–23). We believe the continuing burial activities of washing the body and applying the linen strips and spices as well as moving the stone in front of the cave entrance were accomplished the following day of the crucifixion (starting after sundown Wednesday), due to the time needed for all the steps listed in the Gospel accounts; as we have seen, this continuing activity related to burial was allowed by Jewish law.

Related to the **resurrection**, we have made the case for this happening exactly at the end of Saturday and the start of Sunday, at the start of Firstfruits. The time from the burial of Jesus precisely at the end of Wednesday/start of Thursday to the resurrection would then equate to exactly a literal *three full days and three full nights*, which Jesus likened to Jonah being in the belly of the great fish—the timeframe being an analogy to Jesus. Jesus likened this to the evidence of His being the Messiah; this is why getting this right is so important!

Finally, in conclusion to our case, there is strong evidence that there were two ascensions of Jesus to heaven. The ***First Ascension***, being on the day of His resurrection, is further fulfillment of the Feast of Firstfruits—the priest in the temple on Sunday morning raising the finely-ground Barley flour (the Firstfruits offering) up in the direction of heaven; it was not witnessed by the disciples and was accomplished on the same day of His resurrection, before Jesus met with the two disciples on the road to Emmaus. The ***Second Ascension*** is His "public" ascension, as recorded in the book of Acts, being 39 days after His resurrection, which was 10 days before Pentecost (the Feast of Weeks on the Jewish calendar). Jesus physically stayed in heaven after the Second Ascension.

Related to eschatology (study of end times prophecy), this is what I believe: Jesus will physically remain in heaven until He returns to rapture His Church to take them to heaven to be with Him; He will physically return to earth with his Church at the end of the age, to destroy His foes at the Battle of Armageddon, followed by His ruling and reigning on earth for the Millennium.

Finally, in conclusion to this case for the chronology of the crucifixion week, I believe strongly that this all occurred in ***AD 30***.

See the following graphic, Figure 35.1: *"On What Day Did Christ Really Die?,"* for a depiction of the **chronology of the crucifixion week for our case**. See also Figures 19.1, 19.2, and 26.1 and accompanying text for background information as displayed in Figure 35.1. We have laid out the evidence—the various *puzzle pieces*—for our case in this Section A of Part II, which I believe to be true, and you can evaluate the evidence and come to your own conclusion as to the accuracy of the case.

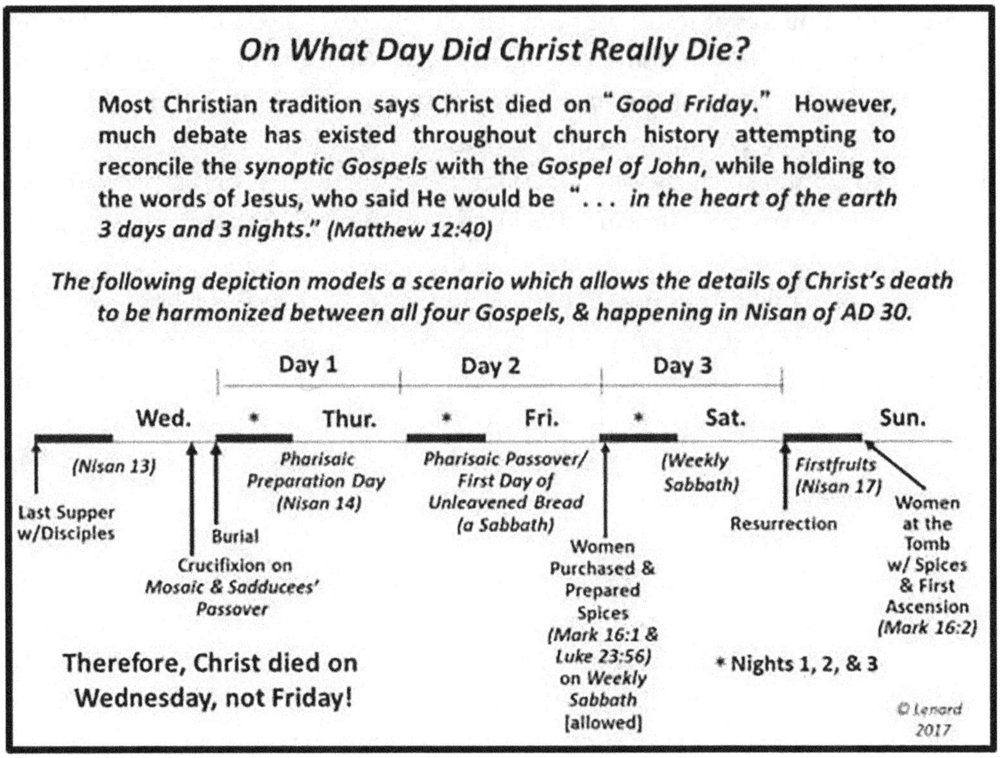

> ### On What Day Did Christ Really Die?
>
> Most Christian tradition says Christ died on "*Good Friday.*" However, much debate has existed throughout church history attempting to reconcile the *synoptic Gospels* with the *Gospel of John*, while holding to the words of Jesus, who said He would be "... *in the heart of the earth 3 days and 3 nights.*" (Matthew 12:40)
>
> *The following depiction models a scenario which allows the details of Christ's death to be harmonized between all four Gospels, & happening in Nisan of AD 30.*
>
> | | Day 1 | Day 2 | Day 3 | |
> | --- | --- | --- | --- | --- |
> | Wed. | * Thur. | * Fri. | * Sat. | * Sun. |
> | (Nisan 13) | Pharisaic Preparation Day (Nisan 14) | Pharisaic Passover/ First Day of Unleavened Bread (a Sabbath) | (Weekly Sabbath) | Firstfruits (Nisan 17) |
> | Last Supper w/Disciples | Burial | Women Purchased & Prepared Spices (Mark 16:1 & Luke 23:56) on Weekly Sabbath [allowed] | Resurrection | Women at the Tomb w/ Spices & First Ascension (Mark 16:2) |
> | Crucifixion on Mosaic & Sadducees' Passover | | | * Nights 1, 2, & 3 | |
>
> **Therefore, Christ died on Wednesday, not Friday!**
>
> © Lenard 2017

Figure 35.1. On What Day Did Christ Really Die?[241] (See also Fig. 19.1, 19.2, and 26.1)

SECTION B

Where Were Jesus' Death, Resurrection & Ascensions?

Introduction to Section B

> The case presented is that Jesus was crucified, buried, resurrected, and ascended on the **Mount of Olives**—directly east from the temple. The exact location of the crucifixion, burial, and resurrection was close to the location of the sacrifice of the *Red Heifer* on the Mount of Olives. Explanation is given as to why the *traditional sites,* which have been proposed and visited by pilgrims over centuries, are not the actual crucifixion, burial, and resurrection sites of Jesus. Strong evidence is presented in this Section B of Part II.

The case is presented for what I believe is the actual location of the place of the crucifixion, burial, and resurrection of Jesus. It is *not* the places where tour guides presently take visitors in Jerusalem, which are the two *traditional sites* offered to the tourists.

We believe a strong biblical case can be made for the crucifixion site of Jesus being on the Mount of Olives. Section B of Part II presents the supporting evidence for this location.

This case-study illustrates the importance of understanding the *Hebrew roots of our Christian faith* to correctly interpret Scripture. This includes an understanding of the sacrifice of the *Red Heifer* (located outside of the city walls and outside of the *camp*) and the Feast of Firstfruits' ceremonies related to the Mount of Olives, in addition to other biblical and historical considerations.

The primary evidence for the definitive location of the crucifixion site is deciphered from the details of the Gospel account of Matthew 27:45-56. Other supporting evidence related to this case is secondary, yet confirming in interesting ways. This case is presented in this Section B of Part II in a total of 19 chapters including a Conclusion, and their listing can be seen in the Table of Contents.

The case for the crucifixion site of Jesus being on the *Mount of Olives* is not unique to this book and references are given throughout. It is definitely a minority-held position. However, many Christians have not been exposed to the possibility and have not evaluated the case for the Mount of Olives' site. This case presentation uniquely assembles the relevant evidence. The following are some examples of others who have proposed the Mount of Olives as the site of the crucifixion (publication dates shown):

- W. J. Hutchinson (1870, 1873),[242, 243]

- Nikos Kokkinos (1980; 2007),[244]

- Ernest L. Martin proposed that the crucifixion site was on the Mount of Olives (1984)[245] and also in his subsequent book (1996).[246] In addition, his last book. *The Temples That Jerusalem Forgot,*[247] and the website article, "Updated Information on the Crucifixion of Jesus" (1992)[248] is a good summary of the reasons for supporting the Mount of Olives as the crucifixion site.

- Doug Jacoby, of Washington DC, attended Harvard Divinity School, has written a website article supporting the conclusions of this case (1997).[249]

- James Tabor, professor at the University of North Carolina at Charlotte (2008).[250]

- Nancy L. Kuehl, author of *A Book of Evidence–The Trials and Execution of Jesus*, written from a Jewish legal standpoint as well as Roman laws perspective—examining Jesus' ministry, trials, and execution.[251]

Much of the material in this Section B of Part II, related to our case for the crucifixion site of Jesus being on the Mount of Olives, is presented in the book by Ernest L. Martin, *Secrets of Golgotha–Second Edition* (1996). In Section A of Part I, and Section A of Part II, I have referenced another book by Martin, *The Star That Astonished the World–Second Edition* (1996). I consider Martin, now deceased as of 2002, to be an excellent Bible and historical researcher—he was a scholar who had a knack for assembling scriptural and historical evidence for non-traditional positions related to the birth and death of Jesus. His cases pertaining to dates and places constitute remarkable works and have been most helpful in assembling the information in this book.

In addition, the landmark book by Nancy L. Kuehl, *A Book of Evidence–The Trials and Execution of Jesus* (2013)[252] is a treasure trove of research into the Jewish and Roman laws as well as early historical writings. Kuehl's book is also important in assembling this case presented on Jesus' crucifixion on the Mount of Olives.

Admittedly, there is presently no *archeological evidence* to support the case for the Mount of Olives being the location for the crucifixion of Jesus, although much documentary historical evidence is available. However, it is well to remember the statement applicable to archeology, "Absence of evidence is not evidence of absence." Perhaps, archeological evidence will be found in the future.

Some might ask, "Why is it important to determine the correct site of the crucifixion and burial of Jesus?" The short answer is that the pursuit of truth is always important. A longer answer is that church-held positions which do not align with biblical positions, such as overlooking what Scripture has directly stated or reading into Scripture what is not there (*eisegesis*), are a deception which might lead some believers down a road where their faith might be jeopardized. Their next question might be, "What else have I been misled about?"

CHAPTER 36

Traditional Sites vs. Actual Site

Of course, the *traditional sites*, which have been widely suggested by the church and others, are vastly different from the Mount of Olives' location of which evidence will be shown is the actual place of Jesus' crucifixion, burial, resurrection, and ascensions.

One of the competing two *traditional sites* is the *Church of the Holy Sepulcher*, widely supported by the Catholic and the Orthodox Churches and dating back to the time of Roman Emperor Constantine. The other is what has been termed *Gordon's Calvary* (the *"Garden Tomb"*), a site suggested by an Englishman, General Charles George Gordon, upon visiting Jerusalem in the late 1800's and is widely supported by Protestants.

There are archeological, historical and other problems with the *traditional sites*. From the work of Dr. Gabriel Barkay and Gordon Franz, the site of *Gordon's Calvary* (the *"Garden Tomb"*) has a basic problem. Although the site has a tomb carved from a rock face, with an adjourning garden, and the site was outside of the city walls at the time of Jesus, the tomb has archeological evidence that dates it to Iron Age II, and, hence, is dated *prior* to the time of Jesus.[253]

In like manner, the archeological evidence for the site of the *Church of the Holy Sepulcher*, although potentially stronger and also being outside of the city walls at the time of Jesus, is not convincing. This site largely originates from the location chosen by Constantine's mother, Helena, who came to the Holy Land in AD 326 in search of holy artifacts and with a desire to venerate various *holy sites*. This site was the location of the pagan Temple of Venus, the goddess of love, erected by Emperor Hadrian in the late AD 130s. Indeed, the site was *sacred*—but sacred to the spirit of paganism rather than as the place of Jesus' crucifixion.[254] However, it is acknowledged that some feel that Hadrian built his pagan temple over the site of the crucifixion. Others have speculated that another site west of the city wall might have been the crucifixion site.[255]

Jacoby states that there is a lack of attestation related to the site of the *Church of the Holy Sepulcher*, as there is " … no mention of it in records of Christian writings before the 4th century."[256] Jacoby also sites Eusebius, the church historian of Caesarea, who was familiar with Jerusalem and served in the court of Constantine, who " … expressed surprise that the 'tomb' of Jesus was found at the [western] location of a pagan shrine."[257] Eusebius lived in the Jerusalem area and knew this site was not the site of the crucifixion, but due to strong political pressure it was tantamount to a death wish to disagree strongly with Emperor Constantine's decreed location.

Integral to this case, the basic problem with the *traditional sites* is that they do not fully meet the test of Scripture. This is, of course, a necessary condition for determining the true location of Calvary. In addition, there are other critical historical considerations mentioned by extra-biblical Jewish and early Christian writers which are problematic for the traditional sites and are addressed in this case presentation.

The *actual site* for the crucifixion, burial, resurrection, and ascensions of Jesus is on the Mount of Olives, directly east of the location of the temple, and a strong case is laid out for that in this Section B of Part II and in Part III of this book. As reference, the following Figure 36.1 shows the two *traditional sites* of the crucifixion and burial of Jesus: *Church of the Holy Sepulchre* and the *Garden Tomb*, neither of which hold up to scrutiny. The "First Wall," "Second Wall," and "Third Wall" refer to city walls constructed at various times in history. The *traditional site* of Calvary is outside of the historic Second Wall, and the Third Wall was built in AD 41, after the crucifixion. The "intermediate wall," which still stands today dates to the Turkish times. Of course, all potential sites on the Mount of Olives are outside all Jerusalem city walls.

WHERE WERE JESUS' DEATH, RESURRECTION & ASCENSIONS?

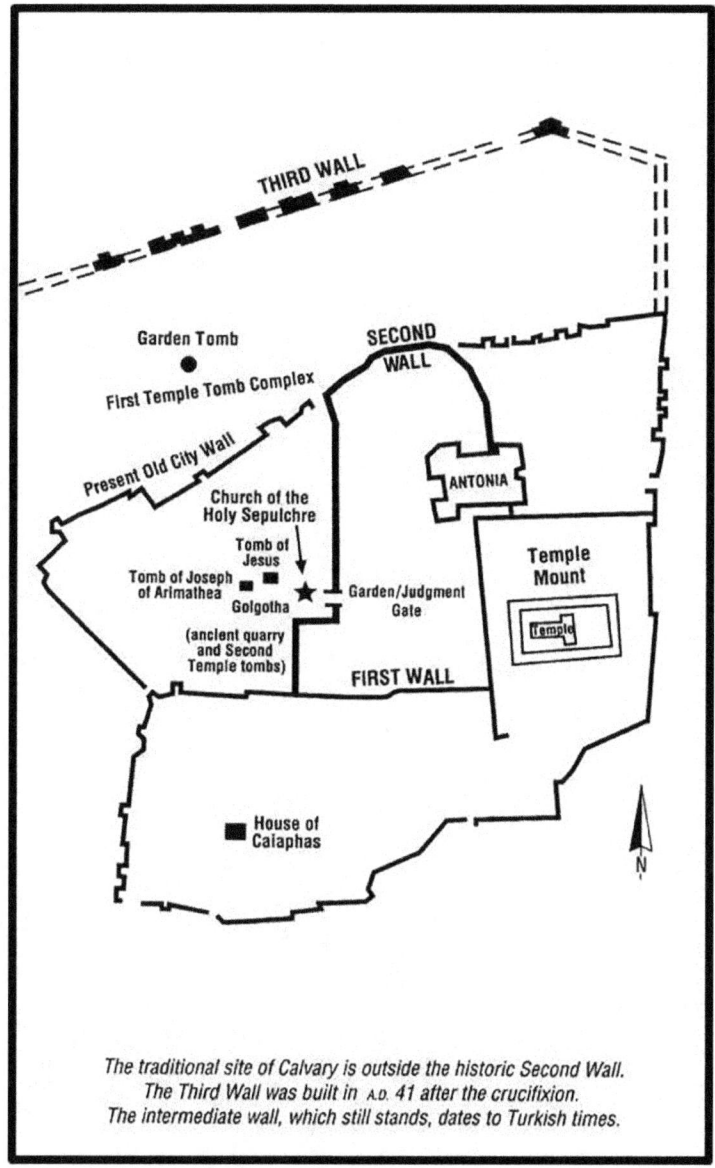

Figure 36.1. The Two Traditional Sites of Calvary in Jerusalem (Church of the Holy Sepulchre and the Garden Tomb)

CHAPTER 37

Eight *Puzzle Pieces* Determine Sites

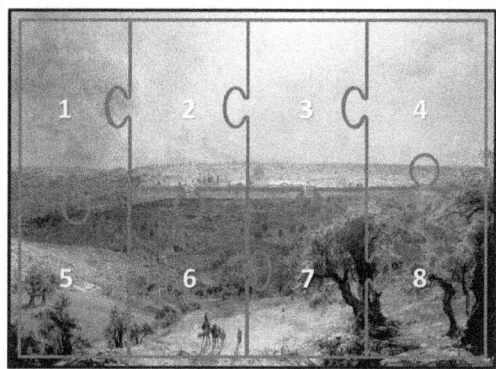

I am presenting a case using various evidences presented, once again as *puzzle pieces*, to solve the mystery of the true locations of Jesus' crucifixion, resurrection, and ascensions. *Eight puzzle pieces* are presented.

Most Christians do not understand that this is a mystery. The overwhelming teaching in churches presents the *traditional sites* as the true locations of Jesus' death, resurrection, and ascensions. The *traditional* sites are the tourist sites in Jerusalem where guides take tourists and give their spiel. In my humble opinion, these *traditional sites* are not where these historic events *really* happened.

In this book, I am presenting the case for the true sites being on the Mount of Olives, essentially directly east of Herod's Temple.

The eight *puzzle pieces* to solve the mystery of these true locations of the crucifixion, resurrection, and ascensions of Jesus are presented in separate chapters as follows:

1   *Puzzle Piece #1*–Crucifixion Accounts in the Gospels

2   *Puzzle Piece #2*–Plausibility on Mount of Olives?

3   *Puzzle Piece #3*–Red Heifer Sacrifice

4 *Puzzle Piece #4–Area Designated for Executions*

5 *Puzzle Piece #5–Executions Outside the Camp*

6 *Puzzle Piece #6–Firstfruits' Barley Sheaf*

7 *Puzzle Piece #7–Pattern of West-to-East Movement (Mount of Olives)*

8 *Puzzle Piece #8–True Temple Location is Key Factor*

I think you will find the investigation of the various pieces of evidence interesting. As in determining truth in Scripture, all Scripture needs to align to determine truth—even small seemingly obscure passages. Similarly, **all** these *puzzle pieces* must be properly considered, and they must all align to determine the true locations of Jesus' death, resurrection, and ascensions. Commentators often go astray by not properly considering **all** the *puzzle pieces* in coming to their conclusion; by doing that, they come up with incorrect locations.

In the following chapters, we will consider the evidence in each *puzzle piece*, starting with "*Puzzle Piece #1*–Crucifixion Accounts in the Gospels" to see specifically how the account in the Gospel of Matthew provides evidence in solving the mystery of the place of Jesus' crucifixion.

As is typical throughout the book, the graphic at the start of each upcoming chapter illustrates the *puzzle piece* being examined.

CHAPTER 38

Puzzle Piece #1 –
Crucifixion Accounts in the Gospels

The crucifixion account of the death of Jesus is contained in the following Gospel accounts: *Matthew 27:45-56; Mark 15:33-41; Luke 23:44-49; and John 19:28-37*. They are complementary and each contain various bits of information related to the death of Jesus. From our understanding of the inerrancy of Scripture, the crucifixion site must be in alignment with all the details of the Scriptural accounts. Specifically, Matthew provides the details on the definitive location of the crucifixion site which is at variance with the *traditional sites*. The account in Matthew—our *Puzzle Piece #1*—is as follows:

> "And when Jesus had cried out again in a loud voice, he gave up his spirit. At that moment **the curtain of the temple was torn in two from top to bottom**. The earth shook and the rocks split. The tombs broke open and the bodies of many holy people who had died were raised to life. They came out of the tombs, and after Jesus' resurrection they went into the holy city and appeared to many people. **When the centurion and those with him who were guarding Jesus saw the earthquake <u>and all that had happened</u>** [including the tearing of the curtain], they were terrified,

and exclaimed, 'Surely he was the Son of God!'" (Matthew 27:50-54; NIV; clarification and emphasis mine)

The biblical account of the death of Jesus in Matthew, given above, states that the centurion and the others who were with him at the crucifixion site *"**saw the earthquake and all that had happened.**"* The preceding verses describe the events which happened and which the centurion and the others observed (note two or more witnesses!), including the following events: (1) the *curtain torn* from top to bottom; (2) the *earthquake*; (3) the *opening of the tombs* and the bodies of many holy people raised to life. Seeing these events would surely cause the centurion to exclaim, *"Surely he was the Son of God!"*

It should be noted that only if the crucifixion was on the Mount of Olives and the centurion was standing on the Mount of Olives, east of the temple, could he have viewed the temple to see the curtain at the entrance to the temple torn from top to bottom.

From the traditional sites, to the west and to the north of the temple, the centurion would not have been able to look at the entrance to the temple to see the curtain being torn, as the Matthew account so states. This is our *Puzzle Piece #1*, and is extremely important in solving the mystery of *where* Jesus was crucified—it totally rules out both of the *traditional* crucifixion sites.

CHAPTER 39

Puzzle Piece #2– Plausibility of Mount of Olives?

Our *Puzzle Piece #2* is the very plausibility of the crucifixion being on the Mount of Olives, as deduced from the descriptions in Scripture—as mentioned in Chapter 38 related to Matthew 27.

A. The Tearing of the Temple Curtain

Included in the list of events which the centurion and others observed was the tearing of the curtain from top to bottom (Matthew 27:50–54). It seems plausible that the centurion and others at the crucifixion site on the Mount of Olives might have initially been alerted to the tearing of the curtain by the loud sound of the curtain being ripped in two, resounding across the Kidron Valley. Some extra-biblical Jewish sources state that the curtain was several inches thick. Ritmeyer notes that it was "… one handbreadth thick … as stated in the mishnaic tractate *Shekalim* 8.5,"[259] which one could imagine caused quite a tearing sound when it was ripped apart by God. At any rate, the Scripture account alludes to the fact that the centurion and others *saw* this event.

B. Seeing the Tearing of the Curtain

The account of the centurion and others *seeing* the tearing of the curtain is very significant, because the location of the crucifixion had to allow them to actually *see* this event. This could only be from a vantage point which would allow for sighting directly into the temple. Only from an elevated easterly direction would this be possible. Of course, directly east of the Temple Mount and of the entrance of the temple is the Mount of Olives. Hence, in spite of others making a case for other plausible locations of the crucifixion site of Jesus, Scripture strongly *implies* that it was on the Mount of Olives, as only from an elevated easterly direction from the temple would it be possible to have looked into the temple to have *seen* the curtain.

But, of course, a question arises as to the plausibility of the centurion and others actually *seeing* the curtain from a site on the Mount of Olives. This is answered by Leen & Kathleen Ritmeyer in their book, *Secrets of Jerusalem's Temple Mount*, which shows an illustration with a cross-section of the temple and enclosure, including the large *Nicanor* Gate as well as the lesser wall of the entrance into the Court of the Women as well as the Eastern Wall of the Temple Mount. Ritmeyer's description is as follows (emphasis mine):

> "A VERTICAL SLICE. This section drawing cuts through the Temple Mount from west (left) to east (right) and shows the relative positions of Temple structures … Es-Sakhra [Arabic name for the rock inside the present Dome of the rock] is the highest point of the Temple Mount, located at the center of the Dome of the Rock and in the innermost (and westernmost room of the Temple, the Holy of Holies. This most sacred enclosure was walled on the south, west and north sides; **a veil hung over the opening on its eastern side. The Temple's eastern orientation allowed the High Priest to look directly into the sanctuary while sprinkling the blood of the red heifer on the Mount of Olives** across the Kidron Valley from the Temple."[261] (emphasis mine)

The *Mishnah*, the rabbinic interpretation of the Hebrew Bible, in *Middoth* 2:4, states that the priests, offering the sacrifice of the *Red Heifer*, needed to be able to see the altar of burnt offerings in the temple from their vantage point on the Mount of Olives:

> "All the [Temple] walls were high, save only the eastern wall, because the priest that burns the Heifer and stands on top of the Mount of Olives

should **be able to look directly into the entrance of the sanctuary** when the blood [of the Red Heifer] is sprinkled."[262] (emphasis mine)

Hence, not only has Scripture stated that the centurion and others saw the curtain rent [*"**When the centurion and those with him who were guarding Jesus saw the earthquake and all that had happened ...**" (Matthew 27:54 NIV)*], but the *Mishnah* also states this possibility. In addition, the Ritmeyers have verified that it was, indeed, plausible to sight from the Mount of Olives directly into the Holy Place to see the curtain; this was done also by the High Priest at the sacrifice ceremony of the *Red Heifer* on the Mount of Olives. More related to this *Red Heifer* sacrifice is given in Chapter 40: "Red Heifer Sacrifice," which provides strong support for the crucifixion of Jesus on the Mount of Olives, possibly at or close to the site of the sacrifice of the *Red Heifer*.

Of course, a very good question is **which curtain** in the temple complex was rent. There were *two curtains* in the Temple, one being in front of the Holy of Holies and the other being in front of the double doors leading into the Holy Place. The usual commentary is that it was the inner-most curtain, between the Holy Place and the Most Holy Place, which was rent. The usual conclusion is that this renting opens the way to God and that all are available, through Christ, to go in to God. Certainly, through Jesus Christ we have access to God in our prayers and our relationship, but does this necessarily mean that the *inner* curtain of the Temple was the one which was rent by God? Maybe not.

There is a little-known complication related to the *inner-veil* theory. Actually, there were *two curtains* rather than a single curtain separating the Holy Place from the Most Holy Place! As mentioned in both the *Rose Guide to the Temple*[263] and in Ritmeyer's *Secrets of Jerusalem's Temple Mount – Updated & Enlarged Edition*,[264] the *Mishnah* (*Yoma* 5.1) describes this veil as a *double construction* (*two veils*) with about half a meter between the *two curtains*, to allow the High Priest to travel between them to arrive into the Holy of Holies chamber. The Ritmeyers describe the High Priest's path as follows: "He would first have gone in via the south side of the outer curtain which was left slightly open, then passed through a gap on the north side of the inner curtain."[265] If indeed the *inner veil* was rent, then God would have had to rent *two curtains* rather than a single curtain. Certainly, God could have done this, but it is an additional *messy detail* related to the *inner veil* theory.

However, the case for the renting of the *outer curtain* seems compelling. An interesting view is presented in an article entitled, "The Heavenly Veil Torn: Mark's Cosmic 'Inclusio'" by David Ulansey. He makes an interesting case for the analogy of the *"tearing of the heavens"* at the baptism of Jesus (Mark 1:10) and the *"tearing of the temple veil"* at the death of Jesus (Mark 15:38). Ulansey also makes the case for the *outer veil,* at the entrance of the Holy Place, being the one which was torn. He makes the following points for this conclusion:

- "Many interpreters have assumed that it was the **inner veil**, and have understood the tearing of the veil to have been Mark's way of symbolizing the idea that the death of Jesus destroyed the barrier which separated God from humanity. Recently however, **favor seems to have shifted to the view that it was the outer veil**, the strongest argument for which is that Mark seems to have intended the awestruck response of the centurion to the manner of Jesus' death (Mk 15:39) to have been inspired by his **seeing** the miraculous event of the tearing of the veil, but he could only have seen this event if it was the **outer** veil that tore, since **the inner veil was hidden from view** inside the temple." (emphasis added)

- The interesting reason for his conclusion is the analogy of the *"tearing of the heavens"* at the baptism of Jesus and the *"tearing of the temple veil"* at the death of Jesus. (emphasis added)

- In support of this analogy is the following from the article, including the accounts from Josephus: "The evidence to which I refer consists of a passage in Josephus's Jewish War (sic) in which he describes the **outer veil** of the Jerusalem temple as it had appeared since the time of Herod. According to Josephus, this outer veil was a gigantic curtain 80-feet high. It was, he says, a 'Babylonian tapestry, with embroidery of blue and fine linen, of scarlet also and purple, wrought with marvelous skill. Nor was this mixture of materials without its mystic meaning: **it typified the universe** …' Then Josephus tells us what was pictured on this curtain: 'Portrayed on this tapestry was **a panorama of the entire heavens** …' In other words, the outer veil of the Jerusalem temple was actually one huge image of the starry sky! Thus, upon encountering Mark's statement that *'the veil of the temple was torn in two from top to bottom,'* any of his readers who had ever seen the temple or heard it described would instantly have seen in their mind's eye an image of **the heavens being torn**, and would immediately have been reminded of Mark's earlier description of the heavens being torn at the baptism. This can hardly be coincidence: the symbolic parallel is so striking that Mark must have consciously intended it. We may therefore conclude (1) that Mark did indeed have in mind the **outer veil**, and (2) that Mark did indeed imagine a link between the tearing of the heavens and the tearing of the temple veil – since we can now see that in fact in both cases the heavens were torn – and that he intentionally inserted the motif of the *'tearing of the heavenly veil'* at both the precise beginning and at

WHERE WERE JESUS' DEATH, RESURRECTION & ASCENSIONS?

the precise end of the earthly career of Jesus, in order to create a powerful and intriguing symbolic inclusion."[266] (emphasis added)

It is also interesting to note from Josephus that *the outer curtain was on the outside of the actual doors*, unlike one would imagine, and that the curtain and the doors were set back in the gate. The *outer curtain*, being on the *outside* of the doors into the Holy Place, would allow the curtain to be seen by the centurion even if the doors to the Holy Place were closed. This full Josephus citation states the following:

> "4. (207) As to the holy house itself, ... (208) Its **first gate** [into the porch before the Holy Place] was 70 cubits high, and 25 cubits broad; but **this gate had no doors**; for it represented the universal visibility of heaven ... and through it the first part of the house, that was more inward did all of it appear; which, as it was very large, so did all the parts about the more **inward gate** [into the Holy Place] appear to shine to those that saw them; (209) but then, as the entire house was divided into two parts within, it was only the first part of it that was open to our view. Its height extended all along to 90 cubits in height [vs. 60 cubits height of the Holy Place], and its length was 50 cubits, and its breadth 20; ... the inner part was lower than the appearance of the outer, and had **golden doors** of 55 cubits altitude, and 16 in breath; (212) but **before these doors [into the Holy Place] there was a veil** of equal largeness with the doors. It was a Babylonian curtain ... Nor was this mixture of colors without its mystical interpretation, but was a kind of **image of the universe** ... "[267] (clarification and emphasis added)

Another interesting consideration related to the opposing argument that the *inner curtain* (veil) was rent, and might have been seen by the centurion from the Mt. of Olives, is the following observation made by Alfred Edersheim in his classic publication from the late 1800s:

> "Indeed, everything seems to indicate that, although the earthquake might furnish the physical basis, the rent of the Temple Veil was—with reverence be it said—really made by the Hand of God. As we compute, **it may just have been the time when, at the Evening-Sacrifice, the officiating Priesthood entered the Holy Place**, either to burn the incense or to do other sacred service there."[268] (emphasis added)

Admittedly, it might well have been at the precise time that the Priesthood opened the outside curtain and opened the doors leading into the Holy Place that God rent the inner curtain, such that the centurion might have seen the *inner curtain* in front of the Holy of Holies being rent. This is a possible explanation for how the centurion could have seen the *inner curtain* being rent, although it is doubtful that the Priesthood could have sufficiently opened the *outer veil* (due to the extreme bulk and weight) to have offered a clear view all the way back to the *inner veil*. Hence, the *outer-curtain* theory is still favored.

In conclusion, we must say that we do not know for sure which curtain was rent, the outer one or the inner one. However, the possibility of the *outer curtain* being the one that was rent for the reasons given above by Ulansey seems to have validity. In addition, that there were actually *two curtains* separating the Holy Place from the Holy of Holies (with a space between them, for the High Priest to travel down along the curtains) seems to lend support of the *single outer veil* (at the entrance to the Holy Place) as the veil which was rent by God and witnessed by the centurion at the crucifixion site of Christ.

In any case, accepting the scriptural account that the centurion **saw** *the curtain rent in two* is the important point to make, and this supports the Mt. of Olives as the crucifixion site.

Other supporting points for the Mt. of Olives are contained in subsequent sections of this chapter.

C. At Site Well Traveled by the Jews

What are some of the other considerations about the crucifixion site being on the Mount of Olives? Obviously, the site is *outside the city walls* (per Heb. 13:12) but near the city and *on a site which was well traveled* by the Jews, as mentioned in *John 19*:

> "Pilate had a notice prepared and fastened to the cross. It read: 'JESUS OF NAZARETH, THE KING OF THE JEWS." **Many of the Jews read this sign**, for the place where Jesus was crucified was **near the city**, and the sign was written in Aramaic, Latin and Greek." (John 19:19-20; NIV; emphasis added)

A related question is would *"many of the Jews"* have read the sign above the cross of Jesus if the site of the crucifixion was on the Mount of Olives? Indeed, this would be the case as the Mount of Olives was the location of a major pilgrim route, with one of the entrance sites for the Jews going to the Temple Mount via a *causeway* from the Mount of Olives to the Eastern Wall of the Temple Mount. This is based on a reference in the *Mishnah* (*Parah* 3:6) as mentioned by Ritmeyer in *The* Quest (where he also shows an illustration of the causeway):[269]

> "They made a **causeway** from the Temple Mount to the Mount of Olives, an arched way built over an arched way, with an arch directly above each pier [of the arch below], for fear of any grave in the depth below."[270]

Some might contest that a causeway completely across the Kidron Valley might not have been practical, as Ritmeyer states, due to the depth of the Kidron Valley, and, instead, he suggests a ramp:

> "Ramp or Bridge? The Hebrew word for causeway is *kevesh*, which is usually translated as '**ramp**' and not bridge, which is *gesher*. I suggest therefore that the stepped approach to the Golden Gate, just described, was the beginning of this arched ramp that continued down into the Kedron Valley and up again to the Mount of Olives. There is therefore no reason to suggest that an actual bridge was built over the Kedron Valley. Such a bridge would have had to span an enormous distance, as the valley is located some 180 feet (55 m) below the level of the sill of the Golden Gate. The so-called bridge thus would have been 20 feet (6 m) higher than the famous Pont du Gard in France, which is 160 feet (49 m) high!"[271] (emphasis mine)

However, whether a causeway or a ramp, the extra-biblical evidence supports *an approach road* from the Mount of Olives to the Temple Mount. Especially at Passover/Unleavened Bread and the other Pilgrim Feasts (Pentecost and the Feast of Tabernacles), when a large number of Jews from all of Israel came up to Jerusalem, many would approach the Temple Mount from the Mount of Olives and would cross over this connecting roadway. Hence, the Mount of Olives as a site of the crucifixion would potentially meet the Scriptural imperative of *"many of the Jews read this sign."*

D. Site with Adjacent Graves

What about the other Scriptural imperatives of *adjacent graves*, for the centurion and others to have seen the graves opened, and for a *near-by garden tomb* site for the actual burial site, to allow for Jesus' body to have been moved quickly from the cross to the tomb? The tomb had to have been located fairly close by to the crucifixion site, as there was limited time—from when Joseph of Arimathea asked Pilate for the body of Jesus, for Joseph and Nicodemus to have moved Jesus' body to the tomb, and wrapped the body with spices. Indeed, the Gospel account states, *"At the place where Jesus was crucified, there was ... a new tomb" (John 19:41; NIV; emphasis mine).*

The Mount of Olives, known to have numerous Jewish graves, is an extremely desirable burial site due to the prophetic Scripture reference for the initial site for the return of the Messiah being the Mount of Olives (Zechariah 14:4). It is very plausible that a Jewish man at the time of Jesus would seek to have a burial site on the Mount of Olives, especially a *"rich man,"* as Joseph of Arimathea is so described in the Gospel accounts (Matthew 27:57; NIV).

E. Site with Garden Nearby

In addition, the Gospel account in John states, *"At the place where Jesus was crucified, **there was a garden**, and in the garden a new tomb ... they laid Jesus there" (John 19:41-42; NIV; emphasis added).* Is the Mount of Olives plausible for having a garden? Certainly, as Jesus often visited Gethsemane, described as an olive grove (garden), on the Mount of Olives. Therefore, we can say that the Mount of Olives had what might have been described as gardens.

We have considered our *Puzzle Piece #2.* In summary, the case has been presented for the plausibility of the events and the descriptions of the location related to the crucifixion of Jesus. The Mount of Olives not only meets the conditions as stated in the Gospel accounts, but, due to the sighting requirement of seeing the curtain in front of the Holy Place of the temple, the case has been made that the Mount of Olives is *uniquely situated* to allow for this sighting at the entrance of the Holy Place of the temple. Neither of the *traditional sites*, being on the western and north-western sides of the *traditional* Temple Mount, allow for this sighting at the entrance of the Holy Place of the temple. This, alone, negates the possibility for the traditional sites being the actual site of the crucifixion.

CHAPTER 40

Puzzle Piece #3–Red Heifer Sacrifice

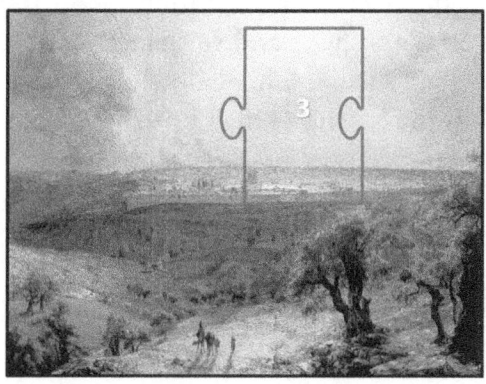

There is an additional support for the crucifixion of Jesus to have been on the Mount of Olives. As has been mentioned previously, the parallel of the rare ceremony of the sacrifice of the *Red Heifer* to the sacrifice of Jesus on Calvary is noteworthy and constitutes our *Puzzle Piece #3*.

A. Background of the Sacrifice of the Red Heifer

Ritual purity is a necessary condition for temple worship and has nothing to do with physical cleanliness. *Lack* of *ritual purity* is a spiritual state which can be caused by a variety of factors, but the most severe form is caused by exposure to death. As explained by Rabbi Chaim Richman, of the Temple Mount Institute, "Once life has departed, it is not the stuff of death itself which renders impurity, but the absence of God-given life."[272] Rabbi Richman further explains:

> "Several methods of restoring purity were used in the Holy Temple, most notably immersion in water, but the Bible's exclusive remedy for defilement caused by exposure to death was sprinkling with the **ashes of**

the red heifer. Many of the thousands who arrived at the Holy Temple had to undergo this process before they could enter into the court."[273] (emphasis mine)

The origins of the *Red Heifer* sacrifice go back to the Exodus, almost thirty-five hundred years ago, and are given in the book of Numbers, as follows:

"And the Lord spake unto Moses and unto Aaron, saying, 'This is the ordinance of the law which the Lord hath commanded, saying, Speak unto the children of Israel, that they bring thee a **red heifer** without spot, wherein is no blemish … and ye shall give her unto Eleazar the priest … and one shall slaughter her before his face … **And shall burn the heifer in his sight** … and it shall be kept for the congregation of the children of Israel for a water of separation: it is a purification for sin … and it shall be unto the children of Israel, and unto the stranger that sojourneth among them, for **a statute forever**.'" (Numbers 19:1-10; emphasis mine)

Rabbi Richman further explains the tradition which links the *Red Heifer* to the golden calf:

"There is a tradition which **connects the concept of the red heifer with the sin of the golden calf** which Israel, under the influence of the Mixed Multitude, committed in the desert 40 days after the revelation at Mount Sinai, and it must be red, on account of the verse which promises *'though your sins be as scarlet …" (Isaiah 1:18)*, for sin is alluded to as 'red.'"[274] (emphasis mine)

As listed by Jacoby, per Jewish tradition, nine Red Heifers had been sacrificed since the time of Moses (*Mishnah; Parah* 3:5). However, also according to Jacoby, Ory Mazar, Professor Emeritus of Hebrew University, "… believes, perhaps rightly, that this was in fact an annual sacrifice."[275]

B. Importance of the Ashes of the Red Heifer to Temple Worship

The ashes of the *Red Heifer* are essential to Temple worship as they must be available for the purification of the actual building, the implements, and the priests themselves. As stated in *Numbers 19:21*, the ordinance was to be a perpetual statute unto the Jewish people.

Related to the annual service of the Day of Atonement (*Yom Kippur*), it was crucial to the nation that the High Priest maintain his ritual purity so as not to be disqualified from performing his *Yom Kippur* duties. Twice during the week preceding *Yom Kippur*, the high priest was sprinkled with the mixture of water and ashes of the Red Heifer to circumvent the possibility that he had become ritually impure through touching a dead body.[276]

C. Location of the Red Heifer Sacrifice/Procedures

The following explanation is given by Rabbi Richman and relates to the location of the sacrifice of the Red Heifer and the procedures involved:

> "The heifer was prepared on the Mount of Anointment, **on the Mount of Olives, directly opposite the eastern entrance to the Sanctuary**. After slaughtering the heifer, the priest sprinkled its blood seven times while facing the Temple. Afterwards, the heifer burned on a pile of cedar and hyssop wood, tied together by a scarlet band. A small amount of **the ashes was placed in a vessel containing natural spring water** and this was sprinkled with a branch of hyssop onto the body of anyone who had become impure."[277] (emphasis added)

Please note that there was a *ceremonially clean place* outside the temple walls, yet was considered an extension of the holy temple. The *Red Heifer* sacrifice was accomplished outside the camp, on the Mount of Olives, unlike the sacrifices offered on the altar of burnt offerings in the temple. The *Red Heifer* was led alive by the high priest and the other priests eastward through the Miphkad Gate (Nehemiah 3:31), just outside the limits of the Camp of Israel, as was also the case with *the scapegoat* as part of the Yom Kippur ceremonies. Martin states that "the details of these matters can be found in the Jewish *Mishnah* (*Middoth* 1:3, 2:4; and *Yoma* 7:2) along with the *Talmud* (*Yoma* 68b and *Zebahim* 105b ... "[278] Ritmeyer states that the complete temple ritual concerning the sacrifice of the Red Heifer is described in *Parah*, one of the mishnaic tractates.[279]

Martin states that the location of the sacrifice of the Red Heifer was the same as the *Miphkad* Altar,[280] the *third* altar of the temple, located *outside the camp* and devoted to the incineration of the bodies of sacrificial animals (Leviticus 4:12, 6:11). Jacoby states that the *Miphkad* Altar was technically a pit, according to the

Mishnah (*Parah* 4:2), and he estimates that it was 2,000 cubits from the temple on the Mount of Olives, with this distance being a *reasonable inference* from Numbers 35:5.[281] Another author, James Tabor, states, "The *Talmud* and *Mishnah* are clear that this altar was located 2,000 cubits [3,000 feet], outside the Eastern Gate, on the slopes of the Mount of Olives (*bYoma* 68a, *mSanhedrin* 6:1)."[282]

Interestingly, the gate and path of the Red Heifer being led out from the Temple Mount, through the *Miphkad* Gate (Nehemiah 3:31-32) and over the *special bridge* connecting the Temple Mount with the Mount of Anointment (Mount of Olives), was the same as that for the *scapegoat*, as part of the Yom Kippur ceremonies.[283] Ritmeyer states that the *Miphkad* Gate of Nehemiah's time could have been located outside the temple, and may, therefore, have been a gate in the eastern city wall, near the approach to the eastern gate of the Temple Mount, the Shushan Gate.[284]

D. Red Heifer Sacrifice Corresponds to the Sacrifice of the Messiah

The writer of Hebrews alludes to the remarkable correspondence between the *Red Heifer* sacrifice and the sacrificial death of Jesus, as given below:[285]

> "When Christ came as high priest of the good things that are already here, he went through the greater and more perfect tabernacle that is not man-made, that is to say, not a part of this creation. He did not enter by means of the blood of goats and calves; but he entered the Most Holy Place once for all by his own blood, having obtained eternal redemption. The blood of goats and bulls and **the ashes of a heifer [Red Heifer]** sprinkled on those who are ceremonially unclean sanctify them so that they are outwardly clean. How much more, then, will **the blood of Christ,** who through the eternal Spirit offered himself unblemished to God, cleanse our consciences from acts that lead to death, so that we may serve the living God!" (Hebrews 9:11–14; emphasis added)

The writer of Hebrews also alludes to the *Red Heifer* sacrifice in Hebrews 13 and to the death of Jesus outside the city gate:[286]

> "We have **an altar from which those who minister at the tabernacle have no right to eat [Red Heifer]**. The high priest carries the blood of animals into the Most Holy Place as a sin offering, but the bodies are

burned outside the camp [Miphkad Altar]. And **so Jesus also suffered outside the city gate** to make the people holy through his own blood. Let us, then, go to him outside the camp, bearing the disgrace he bore." (Hebrews 13:10–13; clarifications and emphasis added)

Many Christians, early on, realized the symbolism of the Red Heifer sacrifice to the death of Christ, with the allegorical image of Jesus' own cleansing sacrifice, with the "sprinkling" of His blood likened to that of the water prepared with the ashes of the Red Heifer. *The Epistle of Barnabas*, written around AD 100, made this connection:[287]

> "Now what type do you think was intended, when he commanded Israel that the men whose sins are complete should **offer a heifer** [Red Heifer], and slaughter and burn it, and then the children should **take the ashes** and place them in containers, and tie the scarlet wool around a tree [observe again the type of the cross and the scarlet wool], and the hyssop, and then the children should sprinkle the people one by one, in order that they may be purified from their sins? Grasp how plainly he is speaking to you: **the calf is Jesus**; the sinful men who offer it are those who brought him to the slaughter ..." (*Epistle of Barnabas* 8:1–2; emphasis added)

It is true that Jesus is the *Lamb of God*, as noted by John the Baptist (John 1:29). His death on the cross, as a sacrifice, is acceptable and efficacious as the sacrifice to atone for our sins (Hebrews 9:26–28). Jesus is a *lamb* insofar as His blood, paralleling the Passover sacrifice, *covers* us (1 Corinthians 5:7). Yet the *Passover Lamb* was not specifically a sin offering. Although the people are saved by virtue of its blood, the lamb did not in any sense *bear sin*. There are other biblical sacrifices which foreshadow the sacrificial death of the Messiah. For example, the crucifixion of Jesus parallels the *sacrifice of Isaac*, which took place on *a mountain in Moriah*, although it too does not mirror an offering for the forgiveness of sins. In addition, the atoning sacrifice of Jesus parallels the *Red Heifer* sacrifice, the ashes of which were used for purification.

Interestingly, the *two goats* used in the Yom Kippur (Day of Atonement) ceremonies were considered *sin offerings* (Leviticus 16:5–8). One of the goats, selected by lots, was *chosen for the Lord* and was sacrificed on the Temple altar, and the other goat was *the scapegoat* (Leviticus 16:8–10), which was led across the same causeway as for the *Red Heifer* and into the desert, where, according to some accounts in Jewish literature, it was destroyed by being pushed backwards over a cliff.[288]

But why was the death of Jesus not in the temple, as is the case with the sacrificial lambs on the altar, but, instead, occurred outside the city walls? Prophecy had stated that the Messiah was to have His hands and feet pierced as specified in Zechariah 12:10 and Psalm 22:16. In addition, the fact that the Messiah was to be *hung on a tree* is alluded to in *Deuteronomy 21:23*: *"…because anyone who is hung on a tree is under God's curse."* But why was the Messiah to die outside the city walls? Could this be to fit the pattern of *the sacrifice of the Red Heifer*, which was done outside the city wall and on the Mount of Olives?

Doug Jacoby suggests that Jesus' death is also symbolically connected with the *Miphkad Altar* outside the temple, where the sacrifices from the altar inside the temple were taken to be completely incinerated. However, he states that the crucifixion did not necessarily take place *at* this altar.[289] In addition, he states that the *Red Heifer* sacrifice was the " … approximate site of Jesus' death and burial."[290] Both are outside the city walls and on the Mount of Olives.

Hence, there is scriptural support, as well as support from early Christian writings like the Epistle of Barnabas, correlating the *Red Heifer* sacrifice and the sacrificial death of Jesus, and, by correlation, it might be argued that both occurred on the Mount of Olives, where, unquestionably, the Red Heifer sacrifice was located.

This is our *Puzzle Piece #3*—the Red Heifer sacrifice was on the Mount of Olives. Related to all the various blood sacrifices, both in the temple and of the Red Heifer outside the temple, it is well to keep in mind that they all prefigured the (*singular and complete*) sacrifice of Jesus Christ.

E. Mount of Olives Location of Sacrifice of Isaac?

There are several reasons that the Mount of Olives might also have been the site that Abraham offered his son Isaac on an altar which he constructed. Admittedly, the evidence is anecdotal, but it is worth looking at it.

It should be noted that the place where Abraham was to sacrifice Isaac was a high place. God told Abraham:

> "… go to the region of Moriah. Sacrifice him there as a burnt offering **on one of the mountains** I will tell you about … On the third day **Abraham looked up and saw the place in the distance … We will worship** and then we will come back to you [the servants]." (Genesis 22:2, 4–5 NIV, emphasis added).

In addition, it is written:

> "When they reached the place God had told him about, Abraham built an altar there and arranged the wood on it. He bound his son Isaac and laid him on the altar, on top of the wood. Then he reached out his hand and took the knife to slay his son ... Abraham looked up and there in a thicket he saw a ram caught by its horns. **He went over and took the ram and sacrificed it as a burnt offering** instead of his son. So Abraham called that place **'the Lord will provide.'** And to this day, it is said, '**On the mountain of the Lord it will be provided**.'" (Genesis 22:9–14 NIV, emphasis added)

From the verses in Genesis 22, we can see several things which are interesting related to the possibility of this site of the sacrifice of Isaac being also the site of the later sacrifice of Jesus. First, it is stated that Abraham had to *"look up"* to see the mountain *"in the distance,"* where God intended for Abraham's son, Isaac, to be sacrificed. Compared to Mount Zion, where David later built his City of David, the Mount of Olives is higher and, indeed, Abraham could have seen it *"in the distance"* because of its height. Less so for seeing Mount Zion, being across the Kedron Valley from the Mount of Olives and at a lower elevation.

Notice too that this place on the mountain is the place where God said *"the Lord will provide ... On the mountain of the Lord it [God's sacrifice] will be provided."* Two thousand years later, God did provide the perfect sacrifice—God's son, Jesus, to be the sacrifice for the sins of the world. It is on the Mount of Olives that our case holds that Jesus was sacrificed—at the same place where I believe Isaac was to be offered up to God, but God provided His own sacrifice. The author of the book of Hebrews draws a parallel to the willingness of Abraham to offer Isaac and God offering His son (Hebrews 11:17–19).

There is something else which is interesting and possibly relates to the Scripture verses in Genesis relating to the offering of Isaac by Abraham. It is said of Abraham, related to that mountain, that, *"We will worship [there] ... "* I believe there is an interesting tie-in related to what King David did when he was forced to flee Jerusalem because of Absalom pursuing him, as David headed over the Mount of Olives:

> "But David **continued up the Mount of Olives**, weeping as he went; his head was covered and **he was barefoot** ... When David arrived **at the summit** [of Mount of Olives], **where people used to worship God**. . ." (2 Samuel 15:30, 32 NIV, clarification and emphasis added)

It appears that David may have paused at the summit of the Mount of Olives, *"**where people used to worship God**,"* for him to worship God there. Although just conjecture, this might have been at the same place where, 1,000 years previously, *Abraham worshiped God*—Abraham said, ***"We will worship God [there]."*** If so, then this would be an interesting tie-in to the Mount of Olives being both the site of Abraham's "sacrifice" of Isaac and Jesus' sacrificial death, both being acts of ***worship*** to God by their obedience (Romans 12:1).

Most of the time, I am presenting facts. However, with this presentation related to the possible tie-in of the account of Abraham and Isaac and the crucifixion death of Jesus, I am presenting an interesting conjecture—but I believe it has some merit and I feel compelled to share it.

In summary, what do we know for sure? With the parallel of the sacrifice of the Red Heifer being on the Mount of Olives, foreshadowing the death of Jesus (Hebrews 9:13–14), this is supportive that Jesus' death was also on the Mount of Olives. This is our *Puzzle Piece #3* for solving the mystery of where Jesus was crucified.

CHAPTER 41

Puzzle Piece #4 – Area Designated for Executions

We can look at the areas designated for executions from the Roman perspective as well as from the Jewish perspective. This is our *Puzzle Piece # 4*.

A. Execution Site from the Roman Perspective

James Tabor, in his website article, "The Place of Jesus' Crucifixion," states the following related to the Roman's preference for the *Mount of Olives* for their crucifixion sites:

> "Josephus says that during the Jewish revolt (66–70 AD) thousands of Jewish victims were crucified **'before the wall of the city,'** in order to terrorize the population. This description fits perfectly with the **Mt. of Olives**, before the main city gate, with the Romans camped just to the north on Mt. Scopus. This was the only location that could be seen by anyone in the city of Jerusalem, thus providing a visible warning to those who might be tempted to sympathize with rebels."[291] (emphasis added)

B. Execution Site from the Jewish Perspective

Ernest L. Martin states that the region of Jerusalem where the Jewish authorities considered the official site for executions of criminals was the eastern area. This region was also the symbolic place where they considered the whole world would one day be judged by God and where Moses had so indicated. Martin states the following:

> "The authorized place of execution for criminals in the time of Jesus had to be **east of the Temple Mount**, but it had to be in a place where the condemned could see the entrances to the Temple located in a westward direction. The biblical examples for judicial sentencing of people for their criminal acts in the time of Moses show they took place on the **east** side of the Sanctuary. Women accused of adultery were brought for judgment *'before the Lord'*, that is, to the **east** entrance of the Sanctuary (*Numbers 5:16–31*; emphasis added). The two sons of Aaron were judged *'before the Lord'* on the **east** side of the Sanctuary (*Leviticus 10:1–7*; emphasis added). Korah and his Levites were also punished **east** of the Tabernacle (*Numbers 16:41–50*; emphasis mine).
>
> "It was important for **official judgments to be rendered and executed east of the Temple**. This allowed the judgments to be made 'in the presence of God,' who figuratively faced **east** from his Sanctuary. Because of this, both the Sanhedrin and the lesser courts at Jerusalem in the time of Jesus were located in the Temple to the **east** of the Holy Place (Cohen, *Everyman's Talmud*, 299) (sic). It was reckoned that while God was symbolically sitting in the Holy of Holies, he could watch the proceedings going on in the law courts. God supposedly faced **east** while sitting on his Temple throne. Thus God in a figurative way had a panoramic view of all the ritualistic and judicial duties of his people which were being conducted **east** of the Sanctuary. This allowed all ceremonies (both religious and secular) to be done 'in the presence of God.'"[292] (emphasis mine)

The *eastern* location was significant in judicial matters involving capital crimes. The preferred execution site from both the Roman and Jewish perspectives, for different reasons, was the *Mount of Olives* and not the *traditional sites* to the north or west of the Temple Mount area (or any other proposed non-eastern site).

Our *Puzzle Piece #4* supports the Mount of Olives, east of the Sanctuary, as the execution site of Jesus.

CHAPTER 42

Puzzle Piece #5–Executions Outside the Camp

From the Jewish perspective, Moses stated that the place of executions had to be *"outside the camp" (Numbers 15:35, 36)*.

Ernest Martin states that in Jewish practices, heinous criminals were required to be their own *sin offerings* in paying for their sins, without having the benefit of an animal sacrifice as a substitute,[293] and all ritual sacrifices were offered *east* of the Sanctuary, outside of the camp, and in full view of God, who figuratively dwelt in the Holy of Holies.[294]

In Jerusalem, this eastern area which is outside the camp would be the Mount of Olives. This is our *Puzzle Piece #5*.

Jesus was, in fact, crucified both *outside the city walls (gates)* as well as *outside the camp*, as is stated in Hebrews:

> "And so Jesus also suffered **outside the city gate** to make the people holy through his own blood. Let us, then, go to him **outside the camp**, bearing the disgrace he bore" (Hebrews 13:12, 13; emphasis added).

What does the significance of *outside the camp* have on the determination of the site for Jesus' crucifixion? The answer is "a great deal!" This is also a *deal-breaker* for the *traditional sites* and supports the location as being on the Mount of Olives. In fact, this, in itself, disqualifies the present sites of the *Church of the Holy Sepulchre* and the *Garden Tomb* from being the place of Jesus' crucifixion, even though they were outside the city walls, as they were by the definition not *outside the camp*.[295] The next question becomes, "What is the definition for being *'outside the camp?'*"

In addition to the specification that all ritual sacrifices were to be offered east of the Sanctuary and in full view of God, who figuratively dwelt in the Holy of Holies, Moses specified that the place of executions had to be *"outside the camp" (Numbers 15:35,36)*. Martin states:

> "The limits of the camp, in the time of Jesus, were determined to be **a radius of 2,000 cubits** (approximately 3,000 feet) from the Court of the Sanhedrin in the Temple (*Rosh ha-Shanah* 2:5; see also *Sanhedrin* 1:5 and *Shebuoth* 2:2 for the authority of the Sanhedrin to set the limits of the camp."[296, 297] (emphasis added)

As Martin has observed, both of the *traditional sites* were *within* the official region of the *camp*,[298] hence, by this definition, they would be disqualified as possible sites of the crucifixion.

A very interesting event happened around Jerusalem which is compelling additional evidence against the *traditional sites* for the crucifixion of Jesus. Tabor states the following:

> "In the time of Jesus, **Jewish tombs**, other than the tomb of David, **had been moved at least 2000 cubits 'outside the city,'** (Tosephta *Baba Bathra* 1:2), to avoid ritual contamination. This indicates that **the tomb in which Jesus was temporarily placed by Joseph of Arimathea, was, of necessity, far outside the area where the Church of the Holy Sepulchre stands today**—just a few yards from the city wall. That is why we find the tombs of Helena, the high priests Annas and Caiaphus, and the Sanhedrin tombs, well beyond this 2000 cubit parameter. No one was carving a 'newly hewn tomb' that close to the city wall in the 1st century, and the tomb area there today most likely dates back to Hellenistic times."[299] (emphasis added)

Outside the camp in the time of Jesus would seem to be good evidence for the *traditional sites* not qualifying as possible sites for the burial site of Jesus. In addition, the movement of the Jewish tombs away from the city by a distance of 2,000 cubits would also eliminate the *traditional sites*.

Conversely, the Mount of Olives potential sites would qualify as being *outside the camp* as well as being at least 2,000 cubits outside the city, and this lends credence to this possibility for the *burial site of Jesus* being on the Mount of Olives—our *Puzzle Piece #6*.

As has been discussed, the *crucifixion site* and the burial site were most probably close-by due to the timeframe to move the body and to bury Jesus before sundown, hence also being on the Mount of Olives.

CHAPTER 43

Puzzle Piece #6–Firstfruits' Barley Sheaf: Represents Resurrection of Jesus

Our *Puzzle Piece #6* involves the Feast of Firstfruits and how it ties in to the Mount of Olives and the analogy of the death of Jesus on the Mount of Olives.

The final part of the Feast of Passover is called the "Feast Day of the Sheaf of Firstfruits" and is referred to in Leviticus 23:9-14. The New Testament mentions this Feast on seven occasions and Paul correlates this Feast day to the *resurrection* of the Messiah: *"But now Christ is risen from the dead, and has become the firstfruits of those who have fallen asleep" (1 Cor. 15:20; cf. Rev. 1:5).*

In addition, the day of the Sheaf of Firstfruits is a remarkable prophetic type of His *ascension to heaven* to the Father and is also symbolic of the coming resurrection of all saints of all ages. As one author has stated, "… Christ fulfilled the reality and spirit of it [Feast of Firstfruits] in His resurrection and glorified body. The empty tomb testified to the fact that the sheaf of firstfruits had been reaped and waved before the Lord in His heavenly sanctuary."[300]

Interestingly, there is a connection of the ceremony involving the sheaf of Firstfruits to the *Mount of Olives*, east of the temple, and, hence, to the proposed location of the resurrection of Christ, which, of course, from all of our evidence is also the location of the crucifixion.

A. The Meaning of Firstfruits

Firstfruits marked the beginning of the barley harvest in Israel, the first grain to ripen of those sown in the winter months. A sheaf (Heb. *Omer*, meaning "measure") was harvested and brought to the temple as a thanksgiving offering to the Lord for the harvest to come. The priest at the temple would wave the sheaf before the Lord for acceptance and for His blessing.

Firstfruits (the third Feast of the Lord mentioned in Leviticus 23) was also seen as a time-marker for the Feast of Pentecost, also called the *Feast of Weeks*. The Lord commanded: *"And you shall count for yourselves from the day after the Sabbath, from the day that you brought the sheaf of the wave offering: seven Sabbaths shall be completed.* **Count fifty days to the day after the seventh Sabbath**" *(Lev. 23:15–16).* Much more can be said about the date of Firstfruits—which always, per our case, falls on Sunday—and other details of the Feast.[301, 302, 303, 304]

B. Preparations for Firstfruits (Location of Special Barley Field)

An interesting description of the national ceremony of Firstfruits is provided by Howard and Rosenthal in their outstanding book, *The Feasts of the Lord–God's Prophetic Calendar from Calvary to the Kingdom* (1997):

> "In Temple days, Nisan 14 brought the painstaking preparations for the Passover season to completion: lambs had been chosen for Passover sacrifices, houses had been purged of all leaven in preparation for the Feast of Unleavened Bread, and barley sheaves had been marked in the fields for the Feast of Firstfruits.
>
> … Looking eastward from the Temple, one could see the breathtaking panorama of the **Mount of Olives** and the intervening **Kidron Valley** basking in the bright golden rays of the springtime sun. Across the Kidron in an area known as the **Ashes Valley**, a small, open field of amber barley nestled itself against a background of grassy, green slopes and misty gray olive trees … At one end of the field, several bundles of barley were conspicuously marked and tied together, still uncut, in anticipation of

the coming Feast of Firstfruits.

This barley field was a special field, cultivated solely for the national Firstfruits offering and kept strictly in accordance with all rabbinic traditions. It had been plowed in the autumn and sown with barley some seventy days earlier during the winter months. Constant oversight assured that the crop had grown naturally, with no artificial watering or fertilization. In the days leading up to Passover, several sheaves were selectively marked and bundled by representatives from the Sanhedrin, Israel's ruling religious body. With that, the preparation for Firstfruits was complete."[305] (emphasis mine)

C. Temple Processions at Firstfruits

As described by Howard and Rosenthal, *at sundown, at the start of the day of Firstfruits*, a three-man delegation from the Sanhedrin emerged from the temple area, accompanied by a multitude of interested observers, and made their way down to the barley field to perform the Firstfruits reaping ceremony. The marked sheaves were then reaped and taken to the temple to be waved before the Lord.[306]

D. Significance of the Sheaves' Harvest on Mount of Olives

The Messiah fulfilled the prophetic meaning of this holy day by rising from the dead to become the *firstfruits of the resurrection* (*1 Cor. 15:20*), and He did it on the very day of Firstfruits. It can be argued that the resurrection was at the exact time of the harvesting of the sheaf in the barley field, at sundown at the start of Firstfruits on the start of Sunday—to align precisely with the *3 days and 3 nights* prophecy by Jesus as to the extent that He would be in the heart of the earth (Matt. 12:40; see also Section A of Part II of this book).

The cutting of the sheaf of Firstfruits was done east of the temple on the Mount of Olives, and the crucifixion and resurrection of the Messiah was also on the Mount of Olives, per this case.

This *Puzzle Piece #6* related to the Firstfruits offering, undoubtedly, supports a further correlation between the two events having ties to the Mount of Olives.

CHAPTER 44

Puzzle Piece #7– Pattern of West-to-East Movement

The *Pattern of West-to-East Movement* related to the Mount of Olives is our *Puzzle Piece #7*. This involves an interesting observation from Scripture related to the Mount of Olives, and it also supports our case for the crucifixion having been located there.

As James Tabor has stated, "The basic case for the Mt. of Olives being the site of Jesus' crucifixion rests on several interrelated arguments of varying evidential strength."[307]

This last covered evidence might be considered of lesser rank in the *evidential strength* offered in this case. However, it is an interesting correlation which further supports the case for the crucifixion being on the Mount of Olives, and it does tie together well.

This other biblical consideration relates to the case for what might also be called *The Place of the Pattern*—it is our *Puzzle Piece #7*. This involves the biblical significance of the pattern of west-to-east movement from Jerusalem vs. east-to-west movement to Jerusalem as relating to the Mount of Olives. There is a definite correlation of west-to-east movement from Jerusalem having a negative connotation and just the opposite for east-to-west movement, having a positive connotation. The biblical examples are interesting. Here are some illustrations:

A. Leaving Jerusalem (West-to-East Movement), Having Negative Connotation

- David, forced to leave his son, Absalom, and leave Jerusalem, left by way of the Mount of Olives, traveling west to east—"David went up by the Ascent of the Mount of Olives, and wept as he went up; and he had his head covered and went barefoot … " (2 Samuel 15:30).

- Shekinah glory of God left the Temple and went to the mountain to the east of the city. "And the glory of the Lord went up from the midst of the city and stood on the mountain [Mt. of Olives], which is on the east side of the city" (Ezekiel 11:23 NKJV).

- Red Heifer was led from the temple to Mount of Olives for sacrificial death.

- Scapegoat was led to Mount of Olives and eastward into the wilderness where it was killed.

- Jesus going to Gethsemane on the Mount of Olives, following the Passover dinner with disciples in Jerusalem, to pray and cry out to the Father before His arrest and crucifixion.

- *Jesus was led to Calvary* for His death on the Cross on the Mount of Olives, per our case.

B. Entering Jerusalem (East-to-West Movement), Having Positive Connotation

- Ashes of *Red Heifer* are brought from the Mount of Olives to the temple for use in purification of temple, instruments, and people.

- Sheaf of barley harvest was harvested from the foot of the Mount of Olives and brought into the temple, as part of the Feast of Firstfruits' ceremony, as anticipation of a later full harvest.

- Triumphal entry of Jesus entering Jerusalem from the Mount of Olives.

- Resurrected Old Testament saints enter Jerusalem, after the resurrection of Jesus (Matthew 27:52–53), from the Mount of Olives, as part of the resurrection with Jesus—the Firstfruits of the resurrection.

- Future coming of the glory of the God of Israel from the east—the glory of the Lord enters the temple through the gate facing east (*Ezekiel 43:2,4*).

The *Place of the Pattern*, being the Mount of Olives, supports the crucifixion of Jesus being on the Mt. of Olives—this constitutes our *Puzzle Piece #7*. We see this with the sacrifice of the Red Heifer as well as the scapegoat—with their movement west-to-east from the temple to the Mount of Olives. This pattern of movement would not be the case with the two *traditional* crucifixion sites.

CHAPTER 45

Puzzle Piece #8–True Temple Location Is Key Factor for Location of Crucifixion

As has been established in our case, the crucifixion site was on the Mount of Olives, directly east of the true temple location. This case is made in the previous chapters of this Section B of Part II.

So, now the question becomes: Where in Jerusalem was the true temple location?

Of course, the *conventional* answer is that the temple location was on what is now *traditionally* called the "Temple Mount." But is that really the true location of all the temples in Jerusalem, including the original temple built by King Solomon in the City of David?

Specifically, in Part III, *"New Insights–Where Was Herod's Temple?–Martin's Proposed Location,"* we look at the alternate case for the true location of the temples being in the City of David, over the Gihon Spring, and located to the south of the presently so-called "Temple Mount." Indeed, I know this sounds utterly preposterous. However, this interesting case was introduced by Ernest L. Martin, following his extensive biblical and historical research, and presented in his landmark book, *The Temples That Jerusalem Forgot* (2000). Admittedly, this is a highly controversial case and is not presently accepted by virtually all historians and archeologists. However, I strongly suggest you read the case that is made in Part III and make your own decision.

Whatever the true location for Herod's Temple in Jerusalem, either on the *traditional* "Temple Mount" or in the more southern location over the Gihon Spring (per Martin), the locations of the crucifixion, burial, resurrection, and ascensions of Jesus were on the Mount of Olives, with the crucifixion site being directly east of the temple.

Hence, the *true location* of Herod's Temple determines the location on the Mount of Olives that these events surrounding the death of Jesus occurred. Since the Mount of Olives is basically a ridge which runs from north to south, either possible location of the temple "works" for the death of Jesus to still be on the Mount of Olives.

CHAPTER 46

Conclusion of *Where* Were Jesus' Death, Resurrection, & Ascensions?

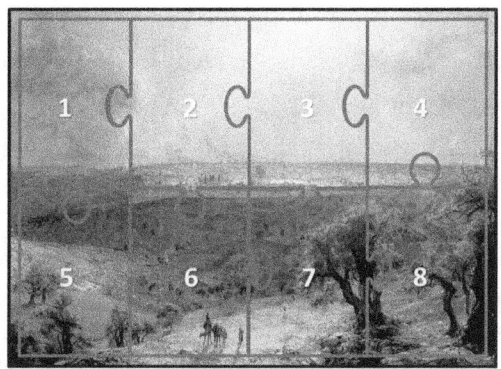

I have now examined the evidence representing eight different *puzzle pieces* of *Where Were Jesus' Death, Resurrection, and Ascensions?* I believe the evidence strongly supports that Jesus was crucified, buried, and resurrected on the Mount of Olives, rather than at one of several more *traditional sites* elsewhere in Jerusalem. The primary evidence for this case is found in the biblical account of the crucifixion in the Gospel of Matthew, in the records of first-century historians, and in certain extra-biblical writings.

In addition, an understanding of the Hebrew roots of the Christian faith, including an understanding of the details of the temple and the Feasts of the Lord, assists in building the argument for the location of what were arguably the most significant events in the history of the world.

In this presentation, I have evaluated eight different *puzzle pieces,* and through each I have sought to expose the problems posed by *traditional* thinking regarding the events that occurred at the end of Jesus' life. For centuries, the church has maintained the *traditions* regarding the crucifixion, burial, resurrection, and ascension of Jesus without properly considering that many of these traditions were based on hearsay, misinformation, and pure speculation. Hopefully, we can see more clearly now.

In this search for truth, I have wrestled with how the *puzzle pieces* fit together. I believe the puzzle is now complete, ultimately assembled by examining the critical pieces of information related to the following:

- The problems associated with the *traditional sites* for the crucifixion

- Scriptural support for a new crucifixion location, based upon the account in Matthew, in which the Centurion and others witnessed the tearing of the curtain in the temple—something which would only have been possible from the Mount of Olives

- The alignment of the gospel accounts with the Mount of Olives

- The correlation of the sacrifice of the *Red Heifer* on the Mount of Olives with the sacrificial death of the Messiah—as recorded in Scripture, Jewish literature, and early Christian writings

- The understanding that the official area designated for executions was east of the temple, on the Mount of Olives

- The understanding that at the time of Jesus executions were *only* performed *outside the camp,* at least 2,000 cubits (about 3,000 feet) from the temple Court of the Sanhedrin

- Recognizing that, in God's perfect plan, the cutting of the barley sheaves in the special field on the Mount of Olives at the start of the Feast of Firstfruits coincided with the resurrection of the Messiah, which by design was also on the Mount of Olives (at evening of start of the first day of the week, our Sunday)

- Realizing that a biblical pattern of movement of people and key events exists related to the Mount of Olives—*West-to-East* movement having a negative connotation; and an *East-to-West* movement having a positive connotation—favoring Jesus' movement from Jerusalem eastward to the Mount of Olives for the crucifixion

It should be noted that if the crucifixion of Jesus occurred on the Mount of Olives—as I believe this study has shown—then the *Via Dolorosa* (the *Way of the Cross*) must run to the *east* from Jerusalem, across the Kidron Valley and on to the Mount of Olives, and *not* along the *traditional* path through Old Jerusalem. This might be difficult for some to accept. Furthermore, if my case is accurate—and I believe it is—then the following activities associated with the final week of Jesus' life and of his eventual physical Second Coming back to earth are all associated with the Mount of Olives:

- Triumphal Entry
- Prayer at Gethsemane
- Arrest
- Crucifixion
- Burial
- Resurrection
- Ascensions (first and second)
- Physical Second Coming to earth (Zechariah 14:4)

Although I believe this study has sufficiently resolved that the crucifixion, burial, resurrection, and ascensions of Jesus all occurred on the Mount of Olives, it is fair to ask the question: *"Where* on the Mount of Olives did these events occur?" This, of course, would depend on the location of the temple. As we have shown, the location of the crucifixion in particular was dependent on the temple being located precisely due west of the crucifixion site.

Virtually all present-day historians and archeologists believe that Herod's Temple was located on the site of the *traditional* "Temple Mount." This, then, would have placed the crucifixion, burial, and resurrection sites of Jesus close to the *southern summit* of the ridge on the Mount of Olives. According to Nancy Kuehl in her insightful book, ***A Book of Evidence–The Trials and Execution of Jesus*** (2013),[308] there is historical evidence that this site east of the temple on the Mount of Olives was the location of *Beth Pagi,* an area situated at the intersection of the path from Bethphage and the Jericho Road. Kuehl states that *Beth Pagi* served as an extension of the temple's administrative functions and was the place for executions by the temple officials.

Dr. Ernest Martin makes a case for a different southern location of the crucifixion in his book, ***The Temples That Jerusalem Forgot*** (2000).[309] According to Dr. Martin, the more likely location of the crucifixion site would have been on the *southern spur* of the Mount of Olives, somewhat further south of the *southern summit*. This *southern spur* of Olivet would have been what is referenced in I Kings 11:7 as the place where Solomon sinfully built a high place for Chemosh, the detestable god of Moab, and Molech, the detestable god of the Ammonites. The author of the *Book of Enoch* referred to this area of the Mount of Olives as " ... the **Mount of Offense,** eastward from Zion across the Kedron Valley ..."[310] Although not part of the Holy Scriptures, Enoch is referenced favorably in the New Testament Book of Jude. It was written near the time of Simon the Hasmonean (about Second Century BC).

In II Kings 23:13, the *southern spur* of Olivet—the **"Mount of Offense"**—is referred to as the **"Hill of Corruption."** The passage from I Kings states: "The high places that were *before* Jerusalem [that is, *east* of Jerusalem], which were *on the RIGHT HAND* [southern part of Olivet] on the **Hill of Corruption** ..."[311] Martin believes this is likely the area where Jesus was crucified, to the east of the southern location of the temple.

In Part III, "Where Was Herod's Temple?", I look more closely at the details of the temple location and present the case espoused by Dr. Martin that the temple was located over the Gihon Spring in the original City of David. As you will see, the case is highly controversial. In his book, ***The Temples That Jerusalem Forgot***, Dr. Martin references a topographical map from the late 1800's from which he supports his position regarding the original location of the Jewish temple. According to Dr. Martin, up until the time of Simon the Hasmonean a crescent-shaped southeastern ridge defined the limits of the city of Jerusalem. Dr. Martin's proposed location for the temple was the original Mount Zion area of the former City of David, within this crescent ridge.

Regardless of the location of the temple—whether on the *traditional* "Temple Mount" or at the more southern location—Dr. Martin makes the case in his book, ***Secrets of Golgotha (Second Edition)–The Lost History of Jesus' Crucifixion***,[312] that Jesus was **buried and subsequently resurrected at a cave at the site of the current Pater Nostra Church** at the summit of the southern hill of the Olivet ridge.[313]

However, I have several problems with this proposed location of the burial of Jesus. The first problem is that the Pater Nostra Church is located very near the *southern summit* of the ridge on the Mount of Olives. This proposed burial location would not have been in close proximity to Martin's proposed crucifixion site on the *southern spur* of the Olivet ridge, a distance of several thousand feet to the south from the present Pater Nostra Church location. We know that close proximity of the tomb to the crucifixion site is a requirement from the gospel account of John:

> "At the place **where Jesus was crucified, there was a garden**, and in the garden a new tomb, in which no one had ever been laid. Because it was the Jewish day of Preparation and since **the tomb was nearby**, they laid Jesus there" (John 19:41–42 NIV; emphasis added.)

The second problem arises from the fact that we know that Jesus' body was claimed by Joseph of Arimathea and Nicodemus (John 19:38–40). No others are mentioned. It would be unreasonable to presume that these two men could transport the body of Jesus several thousand feet up the Mount of Olives to the supposed burial site at the cave at the Pater Nostra Church and somehow accomplish this feat prior to sunset on the day of crucifixion. It fails both the test of Scripture (proximity to crucifixion) and the test of logic (time and distance).

Now if the crucifixion was on the *"Southern Spur"* of the Olivet ridge—as Martin proposes—the tomb of Jesus would have been in the same vicinity. In support of this position, I have included Figure 46.1, which depicts the route of the Bethany Jericho road crossing the *"Southern Spur"* of Olivet. In my mind, this location would be more in keeping with both Scripture as well as Martin's proposed crucifixion site.

In addition, a crucifixion site on the *"Southern Spur"* near this road would have more properly aligned with accounts that the crucifixion site was close to a main thoroughfare. From this road, Jewish pilgrims traveling to Jerusalem for the Passover/Unleavened Bread Feasts would have been able to pass by, see the crucifixion as well as the written notice posted by Pilate, and ridicule Jesus as he hung on the "cross" (Matthew 27:39, Mark 15:29, John 19:20). Additionally, this site for the crucifixion and burial would have been directly east of Martin's proposed southerly temple location (see Part III)—at the location of the Gihon Spring and basically straddling the crescent-shaped ridge which defined the old City of David, located to the south of the *traditional* "Temple Mount."

This is also illustrated in Figure 46.1. In order to magnify the writing on the map, I have rotated the map 90 degrees; hence, "north" is to the left and east is to the top in this rotated map.

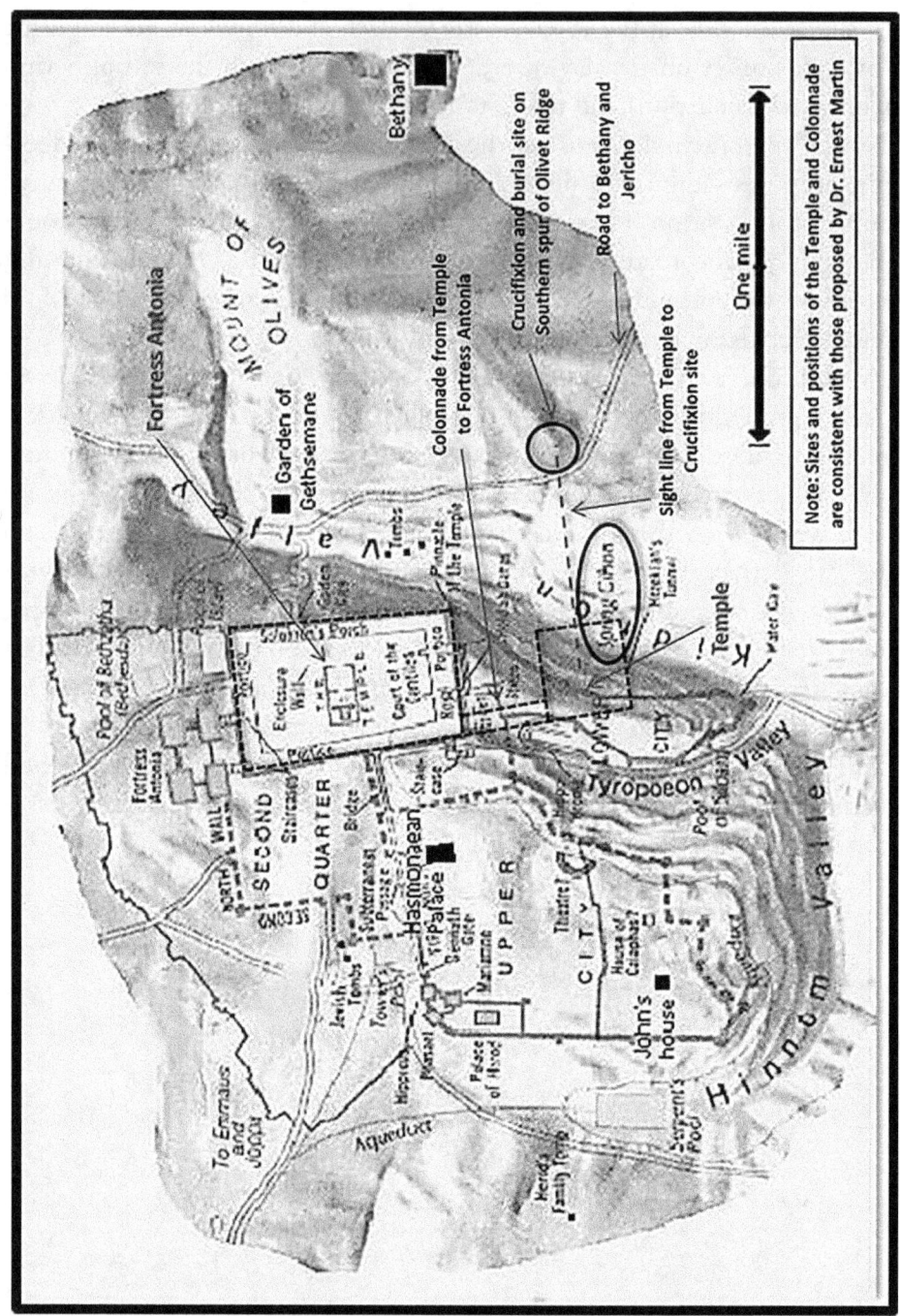

Figure 46.1. (Copyright with enhancements) Ancient Jerusalem and Mount of Olives with Martin's location of the Temple at Gihon Spring, located to the west of the Bethany Jericho Road crossing of the southern spur of the Olivet Ridge—possible location of crucifixion and burial of Jesus

Robert Cornuke, the author of *Temple–Amazing New Discoveries that Change Everything About the Location of Solomon's Temple* (2014; LifeBridge Books), has written another follow-up book, *Golgotha–Searching for the True Location of Christ's Crucifixion* (2016; Koinonia House). Cornuke also supports the location of the crucifixion being on the "*Southern Spur*" of the Olivet Ridge. He builds the case for the present Silwan hillside of the Muslim village of Silwan, opposite the City of David, being the location of the crucifixion and burial of Jesus. This follows from Martin's proposed location of all the temples being in the City of David.

However, I have a problem with this crucifixion site shown in Figure 46.1—it is not outside the "Camp of Israel" which is demarked by a distance of 2000 cubits outward from the threshold of the Holy of Holies in the temple. I need to refer you to Figure 64.2 in Chapter 64 for a possibly better placement of the crucifixion site on the southern part of the Olivet Ridge and not on the "*Southern Spur*" of the Olivet Ridge. That location meets the requirement of being outside the "Camp of Israel."

In short, we can state that the vast majority of present-day theologians and religious archaeologists believe that Herod's Temple during the time of Jesus was located on the *traditional* "Temple Mount." Still, there is a small—but growing—number of scholars who now argue that the temple was actually located 600 feet south of the southern wall of the Haram, within the ancient City of David in the "Mount Zion" area, and where the Gihon Spring is still located today.[314] This is the location advocated by Dr. Martin and the one which I will explore in more detail in Part III. Presently, we might say that "the jury is still out" on this.

Yes, with all of the controversy surrounding the death, burial, resurrection, and ascensions of Jesus—and now including the latest mystery involving the true location of the Jewish temples—it is as if God has placed a veil over the eyes of mankind regarding these things.

As you continue to explore this case with me, you will come to appreciate even more why I believe it is so important to study Scripture, read reliable history of eye-witness accounts, and research reliable religious writings in an effort to "lift the veil," as best as we can—so that we might behold the truth, with eyes and minds open.

However, of course, there are some things which, admittedly, God will need to reveal in His time.

SECTION C:

How Did Jesus *Really* Die?
(Not Just Crucifixion!)

Introduction to Section C

> The case presented is that Jesus along with the two thieves were **crucified** on a living tree, and that Jesus was additionally **stoned** to death per *Jewish law and custom* practiced by the Sadducees priesthood at the time of His death. The offense was ***blasphemy*** by leading the nation of Israel astray from the teachings of the scribes and from worship in the temple. Jesus also received the **lashes** from Pilate's soldiers, but this was *not* a major contributor to the death of Jesus. Death by ***crucifixion*** is a relatively slow process; the main cause of death was the ***stoning***, causing His death to be quicker than the other two thieves and quicker than expected by Pontius Pilate. Also, crucifixion alone would not fulfill the prophecies of the "Suffering Servant" of Isaiah 52, 53 and Psalm 22; the effects of ***stoning*** would meet the biblical descriptions of the "Suffering Servant."

Ask most Christians how **Stephen** was killed following the resurrection and ascension of Jesus and they will get it right—***stoning*** by the Jewish leaders and the Jewish citizens (Acts 7:54–60).

Ask them if the Jews had the authority to inflict capital punishment, and they will say "No, only the Romans could carry out the death sentence." However, this is not totally correct. Obviously, that was not the case with Stephen. There is more to it than that, and we will look at both Roman and Jewish laws which governed this execution procedure during the first century at the time of the trial of Jesus.

We want to look at this question: Was just the process of **crucifixion** what really killed Jesus?

There is a strong case for the **stoning** of Jesus while He hung on the "tree" being the contributing cause of the physical death of Jesus. You most probably have never heard of this case for the stoning of Jesus under Jewish law for blasphemy by "leading the nation astray"—and allowed by Roman authorities. However, the evidence is very strong. The case for this is laid out for your consideration.

Much of the material presented in this case is from the significant book by Nancy L. Kuehl, *A Book of Evidence–The Trials and Execution of Jesus* (2013)—specifically, Chapter 6: "The Execution;" and the landmark book by Ernest L. Martin, *Secrets of Golgotha, Second Edition–the Lost History of Jesus' Crucifixion* (1996)—specifically, Chapter 22: "The Surprising Cause of Jesus' Death." Both books contain many scriptural references as well as much historical research into the details of the Jewish and Roman laws as well as historical documents of the first century. Information from the book by Nancy L Kuehl is used by permission of Wipf and Stock Publishers (*www.wipfandstock.com*), and information from all the books and materials by Ernest L. Martin is used by permission of Associates of Scriptural Knowledge (ASK) [www.askelm.com] and David Sielaff, Director of ASK.

This **Section C of Part II** presents the case for exactly how I believe Jesus *really* died as He hung on the "tree." And, yes, Jesus and the two thieves were nailed to a *yoke [Gk. patibulum]* and attached to a *living tree [Gk. xulon]*, unlike what has been depicted by the church for centuries—He was not hung on a traditional "Roman cross," as has been commonly depicted. The case for this is presented.

Additionally, something caused Jesus to die earlier than the two thieves on the "cross," as the legs of the two thieves needed to be broken by the soldiers to allow them to expire before sundown (*they* were not stoned by the Jews as they were not guilty of blasphemy). Yes, Jesus suffered the lashes of Pilate's soldiers before being placed on the "cross," but, despite common belief, that was not sufficient to cause such an early death, as Pilate intended to release Jesus following the lashing; Pilate did not want to kill Jesus—the Jewish authorities did—so, I believe, the lashings inflicted by the Romans at Pilate's instruction were significant but not the major contributor to the early death of Jesus.

What else was involved with Jesus' death which ties into the prophecy of Isaiah about the *"Suffering Servant"* (Isaiah 52, 53 and Psalm 22)? This prophetic description of the Messiah, Jesus, is largely not given sufficient weight and understanding. This description in Isaiah and other very strong evidence is that Jesus died mainly from *stoning* while on the "cross." Recall that Stephen and Paul were stoned due to their blasphemy per the Jewish religious laws.

This Section C of Part II lays out the case for the *combined* crucifixion and stoning of Jesus for your consideration—you can evaluate this evidence for yourself and come to your own conclusion.

This information, which you have probably never heard before, will, I believe, cause you to love and appreciate even more what Jesus did for each of us on the "cross." I suspect that some will find this information on the punishment inflicted on Jesus to be the most profoundly emotionally impacting of all the information presented in this book.

Why is this understanding important? Obviously, it is part of the case we are presenting related to the "death" of Jesus.

In addition, if Jesus is the Jewish Messiah—and He fulfilled all the relevant prophecies of the Old Testament—He would have also fulfilled the important prophecy related to the *"Suffering Servant"* as prophesized in Isaiah 52 and 53 (and Psalm 22). The fact is that mere crucifixion would not have caused the fulfillment of the description of the Messiah in these prophecies. It just would not have caused the described injuries. We will look at this in more detail.

I have laid out the case for this fulfillment of Isaiah's prophecy as well as presenting other evidence for the exact cause of Jesus' death—*stoning* of Jesus while He was hanging on the "tree," all per Jewish law and customs and Roman law at the time of His death. This is my understanding of the events of Jesus' death.

Please read all the evidence. I ask that you come to your own decision after evaluating the totality of this evidence.

CHAPTER 47

Traditional Cause vs. Actual Cause

The *traditional* cause of Jesus' death is by crucifixion under Roman law, on a Roman-style cross, with the scourging by the Roman guards prior to the crucifixion having a *major* contributing role in His death. This is the story and the scene depicted by the church over the ages and handed down to its members today. Admittedly, it is partially true, but I believe it is largely inaccurate.

The *actual* cause of Jesus' physical death, as presented here, is that He died mainly from *stoning* while He was hanging on a living tree. This occurred at the place for executions on the Mount of Olives, directly to the east of Herod's Temple. This punishment by stoning was per the law of Moses (Leviticus 24:15–16). Yes, the scourging and the crucifixion were contributing factors, but the *stoning* was the chief cause of Jesus' early death and ties into the "Suffering Servant" prophecy of Isaiah.

Crucifixion alone would not cause the injuries to fulfill Isaiah's prophecy. This is largely "lost history," just as we have been presenting related to the other mysteries of Jesus' life. Unfortunately, time and folklore have a way of changing accounts of the true events of history.

The question put forth is this: "Did Jesus primarily die from stoning by the Israelites, as He hung on a living tree?" We can look at the following case for the evidence of this happening.

CHAPTER 48

Four *Puzzle Pieces* Determine Cause of Death

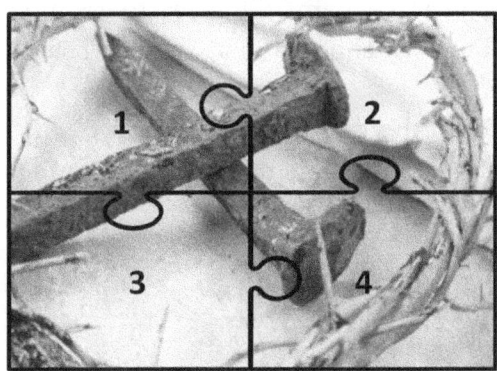

Various evidences are presented, once again as *puzzle pieces*, to solve the mystery of how Jesus *really* died. Specifically, four *Puzzle Pieces* are presented.

The overwhelming teaching in churches today presents the *traditional* cause of Jesus death—dying mainly due to Roman-style crucifixion on a traditional Roman cross.

The four *puzzle pieces* help us solve the mystery of how Jesus *really* died. They are presented in separate chapters and are as follows:

1 *Puzzle Piece #1*–The Stoning of Stephen, Paul, and James

2 *Puzzle Piece #2*–Jewish Law vs. Roman Law

3 *Puzzle Piece #3*–Suffering-Servant Considerations

4 *Puzzle Piece #4*–Place of Stoning Matches Crucifixion Site

All these four *puzzle pieces* must be properly considered, and they must all align to determine the true cause of Jesus' death. Commentators often go astray by not properly considering **all** the *puzzle pieces* in coming to their conclusion; by doing that, they can come up with incorrect conclusions.

In the following chapters, we will consider the evidence in each *puzzle piece*, starting with "*Puzzle Piece #1*–The Stoning of Stephen, Paul, and James." This evidence shows specifically how the Roman government allowed the Jewish authorities to execute Jewish individuals for breaking Jewish laws per the ruling of the Sanhedrin at the time of Jesus. In addition, this first *puzzle piece* shows that the punishment under Mosaic Law for "blasphemy by leading the nation of Israel astray from the teachings of the scribes and from worship in the Temple" was punished by death—by stoning.

I believe that biblical and historical evidence support the case that Jesus was stoned while he hung on a tree. I am asking you to examine all the evidence provided and come to your own conclusion as to what really happened to Jesus to cause His early death.

I suspect that much of this evidence may startle you but will also cause you to love Jesus even more for what he suffered to pay the sin-debt to the Holy Father for our sins.

CHAPTER 49

Puzzle Piece #1 –
The *Stoning* of Stephen, Paul, and James

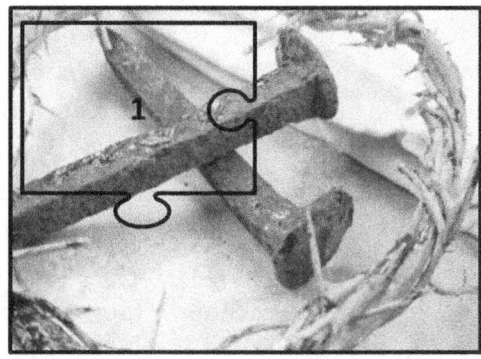

You might be thinking, "Surely Jesus could not have been *stoned to death*! After all, the Bible clearly states that He was *crucified*!"

Those statements are typical thoughts of most Christians today. Of course, Jesus was crucified, but, in fact, there is much more to the factual historical accounts related to His death.

Another statement frequently heard is this: "Jesus was sentenced and executed under Roman law, and the death penalty under Roman law was by crucifixion. Hence, Jesus was crucified and was not subjected to stoning under the Jewish law." Once again, there is more to the story than that.

The purpose of this chapter is to just illustrate examples of death by stoning under Jewish law, allowed by the Roman authorities. This is *puzzle piece # 1*. It is to ease you into considering the case for the stoning of Jesus while He hung on a tree, as I do not want you to dismiss this case "out of hand."

As horrible as it sounds, please do not shut yourself off from considering the evidence for this case. I strongly believe the evidence will cause you to appreciate even more what Jesus did for each one of us as He hung on the tree on the Mount of Olives at the appointed execution site. We are pursuing truth. That is why this is important.

Stephen (Acts 7:57–60), the ***Apostle Paul*** (Acts 14:19), and ***James* the brother of Jesus** (Josephus, *Antiquities* 20.9.1; and discussed in Kuehl, *op. cit.,* pp. 113–114) illustrate the Jewish practice of *stoning to death* under Jewish law for crimes of blasphemy, which was allowed by the Roman government in Jerusalem as well as in other Roman-controlled regions. Yes, even Paul was seemingly stoned to death in the Province of Lystra (Asia Minor) during his first missionary journey [the Jews in Lystra *"... **stoned Paul** and dragged him outside the city, thinking he was dead." (Acts 14:19b NIV; emphasis mine)*]. However, it seems that Paul miraculously recovered (Acts 14:19–20), although he bore *"... the marks (scars) of the Lord Jesus" (Galatians 6:17).*

Please note that since Paul was not crucified, he was referring to the *stoning* he suffered, and he compared his scars to that of Jesus! Paul's description of his own marks from his being stoned as being the marks of Jesus gives important support for the case of Jesus having also being stoned. Stephen and James suffered the same punishment by stoning as Paul did, but both incurred death from the stoning.

Detractors of this case for Jesus having been stoned to death will undoubtedly say, "There is not a single verse in the Bible which says that Jesus was stoned—therefore, to teach that Jesus was stoned is error, and anyone who says that He was stoned to death is guilty of 'false teaching.'" However, please note that this is implicitly taught by Paul in his teaching of Galatians 6:17 related to his *"marks [scars] of the Lord Jesus,"* most probably related to his own stoning—which we know occurred as taught in Acts 14:19-20. Therefore, it can be inferred that Jesus was also stoned since Paul likened his "marks" on his body to that of Jesus, and we know that Paul was stoned.

Many Bible commentators make the claim that Jewish authorities had no authority to execute prisoners and that executions were done under Roman law. However, the examples of Stephen, James, and Paul belie that claim. In each of these cases, the Jewish law (Mosaic Law) against blasphemy was applied seemingly without Roman consultation or objection.

Before the trial and execution of Jesus in Jerusalem, even **Jesus** was subjected to the threat of stoning, *"At this [Jesus' statement, '... before Abraham was born, I am!'],* **they picked up stones to stone him**, *but Jesus hid himself, slipping away from the temple grounds" (John 8:58–59; clarification and emphasis added).* Except for a miraculous escape, Jesus would have been stoned to death at that time. On another later occasion, the Jews picked up stones to stone him, but, once again, " *... he escaped their grasp" (John 10:30–33, 39).*

The point to be made is that the Jews were after Jesus to stone him to death under the Mosaic Law as punishment for what they considered to be *blasphemy*, and the Roman government allowed for that punishment.

Next, we will look at the historical record of specific Jewish law and Roman law at the time of Jesus related to His trial and execution. It seems that this is rarely fully considered by commentators but is, of course, appropriate to what really happened with Jesus' execution.

CHAPTER 50

Puzzle Piece #2–Jewish Law vs. Roman Law

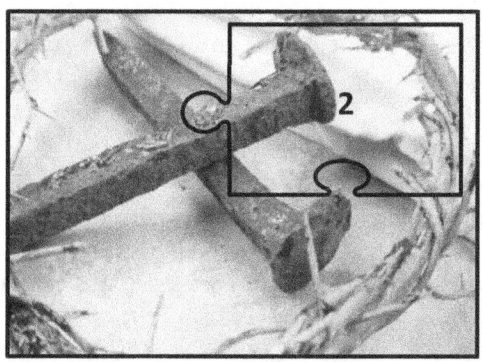

The Apostle Judas Iscariot had been paid off by the temple authorities to betray Jesus into their hands. Then, on the night of Jesus' execution day (the day runs from evening to evening by Jewish reckoning), Judas guided a detachment of temple soldiers and some officials from the chief priests and the Pharisees to an olive grove in the Garden of Gethsemane on the Mount of Olives. They went there to arrest Jesus.

Judas gave Jesus the infamous kiss as a sign to identify Jesus. After a small ruckus and the Apostle Peter doing some "ear surgery" on the High Priest's servant named Malchus, Jesus was bound and lead away. He was headed first into the Jewish legal system and then, later, into the Roman legal system.

In the Jewish legal system, He was taken first to **Annas**, who was the "father-in-law" (*ab bet din*) of **Caiaphas**, the High Priest that year (AD 30). Then, Jesus was taken to Caiaphas.

To put this in context, the Creator of the Universe stood before them in their courtrooms. Someday, Annas and Caiaphas will stand before Jesus in His courtroom where He will be Judge over everyone and will pass His judgment as King of kings and Lord of lords. However, at that time in Jerusalem, they viewed Jesus as a *criminal,* and He was, finally, in their courtroom per God's plan.

So, where did they go and what is going on? It helps to know some background, including some specifics about both ***Jewish law*** and ***Roman law,*** both of which come into effect during Jesus' trial, sentencing, and execution.

Jewish law and Roman law comprise *puzzle piece # 2*. Some of this story is familiar to us, and other parts not so much. At least that was my experience before studying these things.

A. Jewish-Law System

First, it helps to understand about Annas and Caiaphas and the robust Jewish legal body and legal system of which they belonged and how they operated at the time of Jesus' trial and execution.

1. The Background of Annas and Caiaphas

Who were this **Annas** and **Caiaphas** to whom Jesus was taken? **Annas** (Ananus), an Alexandrian Sadducee, was originally appointed High Priest in AD 7 by Coponius, the Roman Procurator. Annas held power in and about the temple for the next 50 years via the influence of his high priestly family (*the House of Annas*). Five of his sons were High Priests during that period, and, at the time of Jesus, his "son-in-law" **Caiaphas** was the High Priest. They were all part of the Sadducean aristocracy who controlled the temple during this time.[315]

The Gospel of John states that Annas was the "father-in-law" of Caiaphas (John 18:13), but little else is known about this Caiaphas. Rather than a family relationship through marriage, it is possible that "father-in-law" might have been a reference to the *title* of Annas to which John was referring. Annas, as "father of the court" of law (title of *ab bet din*), might in this way have been considered the "father-in-law" of Caiaphas.[316] Specifically, there is no mention of Caiaphas being the *son-in-law* in the gospels. Whatever the case, the two of them were the Jewish government rulers and were influential in the Jewish trial of Jesus.

Actually, there were *two* High Priests who ruled over the government of Israel at the time, extending back to the time of the Hasmonians and lasting until the Sanhedrin was abolished by the Romans in the centuries following the destruction of Jerusalem. This dual role is stated in *The Jewish Encyclopedia*:

> Two persons were at the head of the bet din [Lesser Sanhedrin]: one, the actual president [Caiaphas] with the title "nasi" [prince, high priest]; the

other, the second president or vice-president [Annas], who bore the title "ab bet din" (father of the court).[317]

Although there is controversy about this, **Annas**, as the *ab bet din*, was the more powerful of the two priests, as evidenced that the Annas family served the priesthood until AD 70; his kinsmen were present at the trials of Peter and John (Acts 4:5–6), Stephen (Acts 6:15), Paul (Acts 23:2), and James (Josephus, *Ant.* 20.9.1). It is assumed that Annas was the supreme authority of the criminal court. The high priest who was the president of the assembly of Sanhedrin (**Caiaphas**) was merely a figurehead who rubber-stamped the decisions of the higher authority.[318]

The whole lot of them were corrupt and incredibly wealthy through control of the temple bazaars which sold the sacrificial offering of the temple and controlled the temple tribute. Jesus described the temple at the time as a *"den of thieves."*

Another influence of Annas was his effective control of the Sanhedrin, due to all those allied in interest with the family of Annas; hence, he had a sufficient number to constitute at least a quorum of the Sanhedrin to do his bidding.

2. The Arrest of Jesus

The Jewish temple officials intensely kept a watch on Jesus during His three-and-a-half-year ministry. The Gospel of John provides the background and the developments.

After the Feast of Dedication (*Hanukkah*), which occurs during the ninth month on the Jewish calendar (*Kislev*—December on the Julian and Gregorian Calendars), the rulers had sought to *"stone him" (John 10:31)* and were *"seeking to take him" (John 10:39)*. Therefore, Jesus and His disciples went into hiding. When they heard that Lazarus was sick, the disciples were concerned that Jesus was considering a trip to Bethany of Judea, which was less than two miles from the Jewish seat of government, to visit Lazarus. They knew this would be dangerous to them. They posed a question to Jesus, *"But Rabbi ... a short while ago **the Jews tried to stone you**, and yet you are going back there?" (John 11:8 NIV; emphasis mine)*.

To bring Jesus to trial, it was necessary for the Sanhedrin to first deliberate among themselves, form a consensus of guilt, and formally issue a warrant of arrest. Similarly, Paul had sought such arrest warrants from the Sanhedrin in Jerusalem against the followers of Jesus, prior to his own conversion (Acts 9:1–2). These high-council deliberations (John 11:47) would have occurred about forty days prior to Passover,[319] and *"then from that day forth [the day of the high council], they took council together for to put him to death" (John 11:53)*.

The Sanhedrin waited for an opportunity to find and arrest Jesus. This was provided by Judas Iscariot, immediately before Passover. It was a legal requirement for the execution of one found to be *"leading the nation astray"* to be put to death during *"the festival"* (Passover), to act as a deterrent to others.[320] *"The festival"* mentioned in the Mishnah passage (*Sanhedrin* 11:4a–c), related to Deuteronomy 17:13, is always Passover.[321]

3. Appearance before Annas in the "Temple House"

After Jesus' arrest, the temple officials and guards brought Jesus from the Mount of Olives to the temple. Jesus was first taken to Annas. Simon Peter and *"another disciple"* (the *disciple* John) followed the entourage there.

The temple was open. Since it was Passover, the gates of the temple were opened at midnight, and it was acceptable for people to enter the temple after that time.[322]

It was convenient that Annas was so readily available at about 3:00 a.m. at the temple when the temple guards arrived with Jesus. What was that all about?

This is because the High Priests were not at that time in their normal residences in western Jerusalem but were in their temporary *temple residence*, referred to as *"the house of the high priest"* (Luke 22:54).

The Mishnah (earliest part of the Talmud) provides additional information about this *"house of the high priest"* at the temple. It called this "house" the *"Counselor's Chamber,"* as the High Priest was the "Counselor" or President of the Sanhedrin. The Mishnah also states that the residence was at or near the "Wood Chamber," located to the west of the "Chamber of Hewn Stone" (*Mid.* 5:4) and next to the "House of Abtinas" where the incense for the temple was prepared. The *"house of the high priest"* was in the Upper Chamber of this "Temple House" on the second story around and above a courtyard of columns below.[323]

The Gospel of Mark states specifically that Jesus was taken into the Upper Chamber of the High Priest's house while Peter had to stay below near the vestibule of the *"courtyard"* (Mark 14:66). This is precisely in agreement with the Misnah's description. This high priest's courtyard as mentioned in the gospels (Matthew 26:58; Mark 14:54; Luke 22:55; John 18:15) was located between the temporary temple residences of Annas and Caiaphas.

This residence is where the High Priests spent seven days in the temple compound prior to the Passover Feast and other major Feasts—to avoid being contaminated, for meditation, and to study the temple procedures related to the upcoming Feast. Therefore, both Annas and Caiaphis were at the temple during the night that Jesus was brought to them.

The residence of the High Priests in the temple complex was different from the "Chamber of Hewn Stone" (*Lishkat Hagazit*), both of which were part of the temple on the true Temple Mount in AD 30. This "Chamber of Hewn Stone" was where the Sanhedrin met and where Jesus was tried.[324] It was operational up until Jesus' death in AD 30, at which time the accompanying earthquake destroyed the "Chamber of Hewn Stone" with its domed ceiling.[325]

When Jesus was brought before **Annas**, he *"questioned Jesus about his disciples and his teaching" (John 18:19 NIV).* One might think that he would question Jesus about the details of his blasphemy or other aspects about his ministry, but per the arrest warrant crime of "leading the nation astray" this was the focus of Annas inquiry about who he kept company with and his teaching.

As to His teaching, Jesus replied to Annas that He had *"spoken openly to the world,"* and had *"said nothing in secret."* A temple official struck Jesus in the face, and Jesus replied, *"... If I said something wrong ... testify as to what is wrong. But if I spoke the truth, why did you strike me?" (John 18:20–23; NIV).* The Gospel of John records no answer to Jesus' question. Jesus always spoke the truth, and He was not guilty of blasphemy. Instead, it was the temple officials who spoke blasphemously—*"And many other things blasphemously spake they against him" (Luke 22:65 KJV).*

Following Jesus' arrest about midnight, it was Annas' duty, as *ab bet din*, to interrogate the accused and form an accusation. What was the accusation brought against Jesus? Kuehl sums up the considerations:

> "The accusations against Jesus were many and varied, but the **crime of blasphemy** was not the 'vain oath' or the utterance of the ineffable name. It was not the breaking of the Sabbath, claiming equality with God, nor the crime of the rebellious son; neither was it false prophesy or 'desecration' of the Temple which formed the specific accusation. But each of these charges played a role in the final verdict. Jesus was, instead, **sentenced for blasphemy as one leading the nation of Israel away from the large body of pseudo-pious Pharisaical scribal interpretation of the Oral Torah, and from the economic and political aspirations of the Sadducees.** Furthermore, Jesus had interpreted the Torah in an innovative manner that conflicted with their own self-serving interpretations ... It became politically and socially expedient to them to bring him to trial and execution in order to secure their positions and status within the government of Israel."[326]

Hence, Jesus was legally accused of **"leading the nation astray,"** which was the gravest crime and the worst form of ***blasphemy*** with which Israel might charge an individual. Because of this, Jesus was deemed a *mesith,* a revolutionary, a sorcerer, and a false prophet. As such, He would be tried in a Jewish court for Jewish crimes and, as it turned out, pay the ultimate Jewish penalty for his apostasy through

Jewish execution. This execution was by stoning to death by the community while being hung on a tree (crucified). More on this follows later.

4. Appearance Before Caiaphas

Next, Jesus was taken to the other High Priest, **Caiaphas**, and, as stated in the Gospel of Mark, *"and **all the chief priests, elders and teachers of the law came together** ... The chief priests and the **whole Sanhedrin** were looking for evidence against Jesus so that they could put him to death" (Mark 14:53,55 NIV; emphasis mine)*. Testimony was given by witnesses, but their testimonies did not agree. The High Priest then asked Jesus again:

> **'Are you the Christ, the Son of the Blessed One?' 'I am,' said Jesus**, 'And you will see the Son of Man sitting at the right hand of the Mighty One and coming on the clouds of heaven.'
>
> The high priest tore his clothes. 'Why do we need any more witnesses?' he asked. **'You have heard the blasphemy.** What do you think?' **They all condemned him as worthy of death.** (Mark 14:61b–64 NIV; emphasis mine.)

When daylight came, Luke informed us that the chief priests and the teachers of the law *"met together, and Jesus was led before them" (Luke 22:66)*. The group would have left the house of Caiaphas and **walked next door to the building in which the Sanhedrin normally held their official trials and judgments**—the "Chamber of Hewn Stone." Luke makes it clear that this was done *"at daybreak,"* because the law required that trials and judgments involving capital crimes had to be accomplished within the hours of daylight and within the "Chamber of the Sanhedrin" (the "Chamber of Hewn Stone") itself.[327]

It was Jesus' claim before the Sanhedrin that He was the Son of God that made the Jewish authorities proclaim him a ***blasphemer***, and that was the official legal charge brought against Him. This was the most heinous of crimes imaginable to the people of Judea, and the official judgment against Him made him worthy of death in despicable fashion (Matthew 26:65–66).

What can be said about the Jewish legal proceedings? It can be said that everything that happened to Jesus that day was within the Law of Moses, although the Jewish authorities did not precisely follow their normal rules. The disciple John in his gospel account makes it clear that Pontius Pilate, at the time that the Sanhedrin brought Jesus to him, tried his best to prevent the execution of Jesus. Martin offers the following opinion:

> "Had Pilate found the slightest illegality in the manner of his trial even from the Jewish point of view (and it is only reasonable that Pilate had a bevy of lawyers around him trained in Jewish jurisprudence), he would have dismissed their charges against Jesus or demanded that they hold another trial under *legal* circumstances."[328]

It is important to note that it was essential that Jesus was tried and convicted in an overall legal-manner proceeding to fulfill all the laws and types of the Old Testament, and such might be perceived to be the case. However, other commentators including William Barclay make the point that " ... the Sanhedrin, when it tried Jesus, was far from keeping its own rules and regulations" (William Barclay, *The Gospel of Luke, Revised Edition,* p. 276). For example, the Sanhedrin sought for false witnesses, and the sentence of death, as with Jesus, was to be carried out on the day after the sentence was given; a night was to elapse so that the court might sleep on it, so that perhaps their condemnation might turn to mercy. A day did not elapse with Jesus.

Figure 50.1: "The Temple at the Time of Christ," is an illustration by Norman Tenedora from Martin's book, *Secrets of* Golgotha (p. 118) and shows the location of the "Chamber of Hewn Stone," the "Counsellor's Chamber," "House of Abtinas," and the "Chamber of Wood."

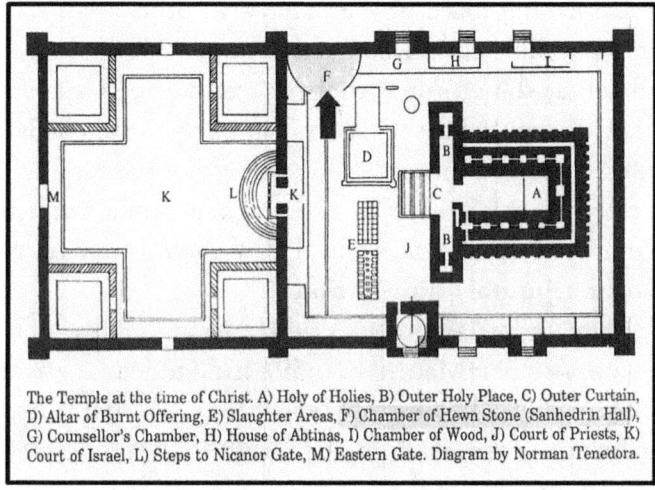

The Temple at the time of Christ. A) Holy of Holies, B) Outer Holy Place, C) Outer Curtain, D) Altar of Burnt Offering, E) Slaughter Areas, F) Chamber of Hewn Stone (Sanhedrin Hall), G) Counsellor's Chamber, H) House of Abtinas, I) Chamber of Wood, J) Court of Priests, K) Court of Israel, L) Steps to Nicanor Gate, M) Eastern Gate. Diagram by Norman Tenedora.

Figure 50.1. Temple at the Time of Christ Showing "Chamber of Hewn Stone" where Jesus was tried by the Sanhedrin

Before we move on to consideration of the proceedings under Roman law when Jesus was led to Pilate, it is helpful to have a better understanding of the Sanhedrin as well as the Jewish laws controlling the punishment of a blasphemer who has been found guilty of *"leading the nation astray."* We will consider these things in the next two sections of this chapter.

5. The Sanhedrin

Some additional background on the Sanhedrin, the Jewish Supreme Court within the Jewish law system, is helpful to know related to where the Jewish trial of Jesus took place as well as some of the other mysteries related to the Sanhedrin.

It should be stated that a correct understanding of the locations of the Jewish trial proceedings before the Sanhedrin is dependent on the correct understanding of the *date* for Jesus' trial and death. As covered in Chapter 34: "*Year* of Death & Resurrection: *AD 30*," I believe strongly that the correct date for Jesus' trial and death was AD 30.

Parts of Herod's Temple in AD 30 were destroyed from the effects of the earthquake which happened upon the death of Jesus. The meeting place of the Sanhedrin in the "Chamber of Hewn Stone," located in the temple complex at the time of Jesus' trial, was destroyed sufficiently to render it unfit for the meeting of the Sanhedrin. As mentioned in Jewish sources, the Sanhedrin moved to other locations on and off the Temple Mount in the ensuing years.

If a commentator assumes a crucifixion date of AD 31, AD 32 or later, he/she will assume a meeting place of the Sanhedrin other than the "Chamber of Hewn Stone" in the temple complex on the Temple Mount. For example, Nancy L. Kuehl assumes that the criminal trial proceedings of Jesus occurred on the Mount of Olives ("during the first century") in a region called **Beth Pagi**, which was, indeed, an extension of the ecclesiastical areas of the temple on the Temple Mount. Kuehl refers to this area as "… the regular public meeting place at the Plaza of Gulgoleth within the parameters of **Beth Pagi**, where the **Sanhedrin was known to meet for criminal adjudication.**"[330]

However, it is my understanding that *in AD 30*, at the time of the trial of Jesus before the *"whole Sanhedrin"* (Matthew 26:59), the Sanhedrin was still meeting on the Temple Mount in the "Chamber of Hewn Stone." At that time, the Sanhedrin had *not* moved from the temple-complex location to the possible ecclesiastical district of *Beth Pagi* on the Mount of Olives. Hence, at the time of Jesus' trial, the Sanhedrin was meeting in the temple complex on the Temple Mount—that is where Jesus was tried by Annas and Caiaphas, per the gospel accounts.

We are informed from Jewish sources that, in the year that Jesus was crucified

(AD 30), the Sanhedrin ceased holding its sessions in the official "Chamber of Hewn Stone." They were "banished" to an insignificant section of the temple called "the Trading Post," located a little further to the east of their former location. Josephus tells us that the meeting place of the Sanhedrin moved again—this time outside the temple area within a common part of the city of Jerusalem. This was at a gymnasium inside the city of Jerusalem just to the west of the temple, next to a building called the Xystus (*War* V.144; comp. *War* II.344). Then, after the destruction of Jerusalem and the temple, the Sanhedrin moved to a city called Jamnia (Jabneh), located about 30 miles west of Jerusalem. The Sanhedrin suffered a total of ten removals, ending up in Tiberias (along the Sea of Galilee).[331]

This is important information as it indicates that at the time of the trial of Jesus in AD 30 the Sanhedrin was, indeed, meeting in the "Chamber of Hewn Stone." It was from there that Jesus was taken to meet with Pilate in the Roman praetorium.

Later, at the death of Jesus—on the same day of His trial—the accompanying earthquake damaged the "Chamber of Hewn Stone," making it unusable. This has previously been covered in Chapter 34. Hence, God caused the trial of Jesus to be the last trial by the Sanhedrin in that chamber.

6. Jewish Penalty for Blasphemy

What was the punishment under the Mosaic Law for blasphemy? Indeed, the only type of execution specified for capital crimes in the Old Testament is *stoning to death*; this is not widely known by Christians. This applies to the crime of blasphemy per the Mosaic Law:

> And **he that blasphemeth the name of the Lord [Yahweh], he shall surely be put to death**, and **all the congregation shall certainly stone him**: as well as the stranger, as he that is born in the land, when he blasphemeth the name of the Lord, shall be put to death. (Leviticus 24:16 KJV; emphasis mine)

With the official charge of *blasphemy* brought against Jesus, the leaders went to Pilate and asked him to allow Jesus to be killed according to the Law of Moses. They stated to Pilate, *"We have a law, and **by that law he ought to die**, because he has made himself the Son of God"* (John 19:7; emphasis mine). Note that Pilate granted approval for this to happen: *"You take him and crucify him"* (John 19:6b).

The law as stated in Leviticus 24:16 was death by stoning by *"all the congregation."* Hence, all the residents of the land, both Jews and Gentiles, were required to cast volleys of stones upon the blasphemer. Similarly, as the congregation was to stone Achan (Joshua 7:25) for his sin, so it was the duty of the congregation to perform "justice." In the case of Jesus, the person bearing witness to the blasphemy was to cast the first stone—in this case, the High Priest Caiaphas and members of the Sanhedrin.

The Jewish concept of capital punishment follows Chapter 7 of Joshua (stoning of Achan) and Deuteronomy 21:21–23 (stoning and hanging on a tree). In them are the elements related to the execution of Jesus under Mosaic Law:[332]

1 The 'accursed thing' or individual who caused the 'curse' upon the land (Joshua 7:13);

2 The confession of the accursed (Joshua 7:20);

3 Stoning performed by the 'whole congregation' (Joshua 7:25);

4 The 'sin unto death' (Deuteronomy 21:22); and stoning and hanging upon a tree (Deuteronomy 21:21–22);

5 One who is hanged on a tree is 'accursed of God,' and the corpse of the accursed was not to remain on the tree overnight, defiling the land (Deuteronomy 21:23)

It is interesting to note the order of events related to the stoning and the hanging on a tree as stated in Deuteronomy 21:21–23:

> And all the men of his city shall **stone him with stones**, that he die: so shalt thou put evil away from among you; and all Israel shall hear, and fear. And if a man have committed a sin worthy of death, and **he be to be put to death, and thou hang him on a tree**: His body shall not remain all night upon the tree, but thou shalt in any wise bury him that day; (for he that is hanged is accursed of God that thy land be not defiled, which the Lord thy God giveth thee for an inheritance. (Deuteronomy 21:21–23 KJV; emphasis mine.)

While the original Mosaic legislation stated that the Israelites should first stone the blasphemer to cause his death and then hang him on a tree until near sunset, in the case of Jesus it is possible that it was Pilate's soldiers who first nailed Jesus to a tree, and then he allowed the people to stone him—all done under the watchful eyes of the temple authorities. This "reverse technique" was being utilized in Jerusalem within the first century. One of the Dead Sea Scrolls, *The Temple Scroll*, has verified that the Jewish authorities in the first century had re-evaluated the strict wording of Deuteronomy 21:21–23, interpreting it in the reverse order. With this interpretation, the hanging could take place before the stoning, but according to *The Temple Scroll*, the person must be dead before sunset. In the case of the two robbers crucified with Jesus, the Roman soldiers needed to break their legs, preventing their pushing up to exhale and, hence, speeding up their death. Jesus was already dead from the stoning, which was not inflicted on the two thieves.

The execution of Jesus involved both the hanging on a living tree (*"green tree"*—Luke 23:31 KJV; Acts 5:30; Acts 10:39; Acts 13:29; I Peter 2:24) as well as stoning to death while hanging on the tree. In the time of Jesus, anyone who was sentenced to death by stoning was also hanged on a *living tree* (Gk. *xulon*; Heb. *'ets*, derived from *'atsah*).[333]

It should be noted that because Pilate handed Jesus over to the Jewish authorities to accomplish his death *under Jewish law*, Jesus did not carry a *Roman cross* and was not hung on a *Roman cross* (Gk. *stauros*), as is depicted in church traditions. His wrists were nailed to a gibbet (yoke—like a yoke of an ox; Latin *patibulum*), which was then hung on a living tree; the yoke would have been attached either by ropes or by nails to a living tree. All the evidence for these things are presented by Kuehl in her well-researched book, *A Book of Evidence–The Trials and Execution of Jesus* (2013), in Chapter 6: "The Execution," as well as by Ernest Martin in his book, *Secrets of Golgotha (Second Edition)* (1996), in Chapter 21: "The Manner of Jesus' Crucifixion."

In Jewish culture, anytime the term "hanged on a tree" was used, stoning was automatically assumed. It was used as a Hebrew idiom. Kuehl states the following:

> "When the disciples accused the Sanhedrin of 'hanging' Jesus on a 'tree,' it was simply a **Hebrew idiom** for the terminology implying the entire execution process, **both stoning and hanging.** For instance, in the Talmud (b. Sanh. 43a) a herald goes forth announcing that Jesus was to be 'stoned'; the passage then goes on to state that he was 'hanged'. **The writers meant that he was both stoned and hanged, and this was a Jewish mode of execution, not a Roman one**. Not one aspect of the 'hanging' indicated a Roman crucifixion. Likewise, when the Jewish writings indicate that an individual has been stoned and that stoning resulted in his death, it was automatically assumed that he had been hanged afterward."[334]

> "And if not, stoning him is [the duty] of all Israelites, as it is said, 'The hand of the witnesses shall be first upon him to put him to death, and afterward the hand of all the people (Dt. 17:7). **'All those who are stoned are hanged on a tree,'** the words of R. Eliezer." (*Mishnah Sanhedrin* 6:4 g–h; emphasis mine.)[335]

During Jesus' ministry, many of the people tried to carry out this Mosaic Law against Him—it is written by John, "***Then they took up stones to cast at him**: but Jesus hid himself, and went out of the temple, going throughout the midst of them, and so passed by*" (John 8:59; emphasis mine). It is further stated in the Gospel of John:

> "Then **the Jews took up stones again to stone him**. Jesus answered them, many good works have I showed you from my Father; for which of those works do you stone me? The Jews answered him, saying, **For a good work we stone you not; but for blasphemy; and because you, being a man, make yourself God**" (John 10:31–33 KJV; emphasis mine.)

Time and again, the authorities were trying to kill Jesus by stoning. "*His disciples say to him, Master, **the Jews of late sought to stone you**; and go you [to Jerusalem] again?*" (John 11:8; emphasis mine). The Jewish authorities finally got their wish when they went to Pilate and stated, "*We have a law, and **by our law he ought to die**, because he made himself the Son of God*" (John 19:7; emphasis mine).

The Gospel of John records the appeal of the Jewish authorities to Pilate to have Jesus killed according to the Law of Moses, which was by stoning. This is what the Jewish authorities were petitioning Pilate for permission to do.

Death by stoning took *two forms* over the course of Jewish history according to whether the Pharisees or the Sadducees were in power in the temple administration. This explanation is given by Kuehl:

> "The Pharisaic and Sadducean methods of stoning an individual were, however, entirely different. Whereas the ***Pharisees* used only one large stone** and threw the individual [and the stone] down from a great height, the ***Sadducees* demanded the whole congregation of Israel have a part in putting the accused to death**. Each person passing by the execution site would have been required by law to **pick up a stone and cast it at the accused**, thus "casting out" that individual from the nation of Israel. It was a process similar to the placing of hands on the Sinbearer Goat [Scape Goat in Day of Atonement ritual by the High Priest] to be 'cast out' into the 'wilderness' as a 'curse' of God. **Since the *Sadducean priesthood* was the powerful sect during the lifetime of Jesus, we must assume it would have been their law that carried the day**."[336]

The Sadducean method of stoning involved hanging an individual alive on the tree and the congregation casting small stones until death of the person. The

Pharisees, as did the Essenes, found this method abhorrent; they hanged individuals on the tree only after being stoned to death, and they used a single heavy stone dropped from a height to cause rapid death. The Pharisees gained power after AD 70, after the Sadducean priesthood was deposed upon the destruction of Jerusalem at that time; from that time on, the Pharisaic method of stoning was used.

It was no coincidence that the Sadducean priesthood was in power at the time of Jesus. This was orchestrated by God to fulfill the cause of death of Jesus according to the prophecies of the Old Testament. These prophecies include Psalm 22:16–18 (pierced His hands; seeing His bones), Psalm 34:20 (no bones broken), and Isaiah 52–53 ("Suffering Servant")—more on this in Chapter 51.

In the Talmud (*Sanhedrin* 43a) we have the following account of the crucifixion and stoning of Jesus:

> On the eve of the Passover Yeshu the Nazarean [Hebrew for Jesus the Nazarean] **was hanged**. For forty days before the execution took place, a herald went forth and cried, 'He is going forth **TO BE STONED** because he has practiced sorcery and enticed Israel to apostasy. Any one who can say anything in his favour, let him come forward and plead on his behalf.' But since nothing was brought forward in his favour he was hanged on the eve of Passover.[337]

What we find in this Jewish historical reference is confirmation that Jesus was both hanged [on a tree] as well as stoned, fulfilling the Jewish penalty for blasphemy under the Law of Moses.

Following the deliberations in the "Chamber of Hewn Stone" by the Sanhedrin and after reaching a decision, **Jesus was taken to Pilate**:

> Very early in the morning, the chief priests, with the elders, the teachers of the law and the **whole Sanhedrin**, reached a decision. They bound Jesus, **led him away and handed him over to Pilate**. (Mark 15:1 NIV; emphasis mine.)

We can now look at the trial of Jesus under the Roman law system, after Jesus was taken from the Sanhedrin to Pilate at the Roman *praetorium*.

B. Roman-Law System

Following the appearances of Jesus before Annas and Caiaphas and the Sanhedrin, Jesus was taken from the temple to the *praetorium* to meet with Pontius Pilate. Jesus then fell under the Roman law system and its proceedings.

1. The Background of Pilate and Roman Rule in Israel

The Roman Senate had given authority to King Herod the Great to rule and reign in Judea up until his death in 1 BC. Herod the Great possessed exclusive rights in trying political legal cases and governing in general, and the Sanhedrin's authority was limited exclusively to religious issues.

At Herod the Great's death, the Sanhedrin sent a delegation to Rome requesting complete autonomy under the rule of one of Herod's sons. Rome agreed to joint rule over Judea, with a Roman prefect ("governor") and a son of Herod ruling the country. Rome had little interest in the internal affairs of the Jewish nation, if order was kept and taxes were paid.

This Roman administration over Judea effectively began in AD 6 with the appointment of Coponius, the first Roman "governor" with the title of "prefect" in Judea. Following the death of his father, Herod Antipater (Herod Antipas), son of Herod the Great, reigned as tetrarch ("king") of Galilee and Perea. **The prefect in Judea was expected to respect Jewish religious law and customs with little interference**. He was not very powerful and was overshadowed by the Roman governor in Syria.

Pontius Pilate, before whom Jesus appeared, was appointed prefect in Judea in AD 26, largely through the influence of Sejanus (*Aelius Seianus*), the all-powerful minister in the Roman emperor Tiberius' court, and Pilate served as prefect until AD 36—six years after Jesus' death.

Pilate was specifically sent to Judea to end the self-rule among the Jews. He was in an awkward position of having to juggle favor with Tiberius, Sejanus, the Syrian governor, Antipas, and the Sanhedrin. Such was the political situation in Judea in AD 30, the year of Jesus' trial and execution.[338]

2. Roman Trial Proceedings in Roman Praetorium

Jesus was brought by the temple guards, along with the high priests and chief priests of the Sanhedrin, to **Pontius Pilate** at the Roman *praetorium* in Fort Antonia. This Greek term means both judgment hall and palace, and the location was in the Roman Fort Antonia, which was located close to the temple.

The Jewish authorities wanted Pilate to "do the dirty work" and execute Jesus in order for the Jewish authorities to not be blamed for this by the people of Judea, many of whom had followed Jesus, respected His teaching, seen His miracles, and had waved palm branches before Him as He rode the colt of the donkey into Jerusalem just a few days prior to the arrest and trial. The fact is that the Jewish authorities were afraid of the people's reaction on them (Mark 11:18).

To avoid ceremonial uncleanness, the Gospel of John explains that the Jews did not enter the palace, as they wanted to be able to eat the Passover, *"So Pilate came out to them and asked, 'What charges are you bringing against this man?'" (John 18:29 NIV)*.

The temple officials verbalized the accusations against Jesus:

> We have found this man subverting our nation. He opposes payment of taxes to Caesar and claims to be Christ [Messiah], a king. (Luke 23:2 NIV; clarification mine.)

The Sanhedrin, in direct reply to Pilate about the charges against Jesus, stated, *"If he were not a criminal ... we would not have handed him over to you" (John 18:30; NIV)*. Then, Pilate makes a key statement to the Jewish authorities, **"Take him yourselves and judge him by your own law"** *(John 18:31 NIV; emphasis mine)*. It is important to note that Pilate's statement was in accordance with Emperor Tiberius' policies in Judea—to allow the Jews to handle their religious affairs and rulings themselves.

The Jewish rulers replied to Pilate, **"But we have no right to execute anyone"** *(John 18:31b NIV; emphasis mine)*. This indicates that the Jewish authorities needed Roman approval to execute Jesus. However, this may not be entirely true, as they seemingly did not receive Pilate's approval when they later executed Stephen by dragging him from the Sanhedrin and stoning him to death (Acts 7:58). In the case of Jesus, the Jewish authorities were attempting to place the burden of the execution on Pilate.

Pilate found no reason to try Jesus in a Roman court for crimes against Rome. He stated to the Jewish leaders, **"I find no basis for a charge against him"** *(John 18:38 NIV; emphasis mine)*. However, when Pilate found out that Jesus was a Galilean, he sent Jesus to Herod Antipas, who had jurisdiction over the region of Galilee. Finding no basis for the charges against Jesus deserving death, Herod Antipas sent him back to Pilate (Luke 23:13–15) and Pilate reported back to the *"chief priests, the rulers and the people."*

It was not Pilate's intention to crucify Jesus, but to release Him. However, "for good measure," Pilate took Jesus and had him flogged; his intention was to have him flogged and then release Him. I believe the church tradition that Pilate had Jesus flogged almost to the point of death is, perhaps, an exaggeration; Pilate was sympathetic to Jesus and did not want to kill Him but to release Him. Indeed, the scourging of Jesus was severe enough to elicit a comment by Pilate, *"Behold the man!" (John 19:5 KJV)* when Jesus stood again before Pilate. Church tradition has relied on this Roman flogging to produce the excessive blood loss to fulfill prophecy, not understanding that Jesus was stoned to death while hanging on the tree—this produced copious blood-loss and completely fulfilled prophecy. We will discuss this further in Chapter 51: "Suffering Servant-Servant Considerations."

Following the flogging, Pilate said again to the Jewish officials, *"I find no basis for a charge against him." (John 19:4b NIV)*. After the Jewish officials shouted, *"Crucify! Crucify!" (John 19:6)*, Pilate answered, **"You take him and crucify him. As for me, I find no basis for a charge against him"** *(John 19:6b NIV; emphasis mine)*. Still, Pilate tried to set Jesus free (John 19:12), but the Jewish officials used the "Caesar card" on Pilate and kept shouting, *"If you let this man go, you are no friend of Caesar. Anyone who claims to be a king opposes Caesar" (John 19:12b NIV)*.

If Pilate did not comply with the wishes of the Jewish officials for crucifixion, he risked their informing Caesar—and Pilate might have, himself, been executed by Caesar. When Pilate heard this accusation against him by the Jewish leaders, he *"... brought Jesus out and sat down on the judge's seat at a place known as The Stone Pavement (which in Aramaic is Gabbatha). It was the day of Preparation of Passover Week ..." (John 19:13–14)*.

"Finally, Pilate handed him [Jesus] over to them [temple officials] to be crucified. So, the soldiers took charge of Jesus" *(John 19:16 NIV; clarifications, emphasis, and commas mine)*.

We should note that Jesus is handed over to the Jewish temple authorities to be crucified according to Jewish law, as previously described. The soldiers mentioned were both Roman and Jewish temple soldiers, as both were involved in the crucifixion proceedings as stated in the gospel accounts. The crucifixion included the Jewish sentence of stoning to death according to Jewish law. All this was done in proper fashion under both Jewish and Roman laws.

C. Timing of Jesus' Last Words

Although not specifically stated in the Gospel accounts, my supposition is that after Jesus was hung on the tree, before the stoning began, the soldiers at the foot of the "cross" took Jesus' clothes and divided them (John 19:23–24).

My further speculation is that following the period of crucifixion and period of stoning, nearing Jesus' death, when Mary and the other women came to the foot of the tree, Jesus uttered His last words, including *"It is finished"* (John 19:30 NIV) and *"Father, into your hands I commit my spirit"* (Luke 23:46 NIV). After these words, following Jesus' death, the soldier *"... pierced Jesus' side with a spear ... (John 19:34 NIV).*

D. Conclusion of Jewish vs. Roman Law & Jesus' Sentence

All was accomplished in the execution of Jesus according to the Jewish and Roman laws. And especially, all was accomplished according to Mosaic Law, in fulfillment of the prophecies of the Old Testament.

The Roman prefects, like Pontius Pilate, often allowed the Jewish officials to administer their own punishments according to Jewish religious law and customs.

Pilate sent a small execution detail, as was customary, to oversee the Jewish execution of Jesus. It was, however, possibly *not* those Roman soldiers who hanged Him on the tree but the Jewish temple captains. John 19:16–18 states that it was the Jewish authorities who executed Jesus. Kuehl provides helpful commentary embedded in this Scripture:

> "Then **therefore he [Pilate] delivered him [Jesus] up unto them [referring to the High-priests and the Sanhedrin], that he [Jesus] might be crucified [hanged on a tree].** They [the Jewish authorities] took possession, therefore of Jesus. And bearing for himself the cross [gibblet, that is the yoke that was to be attached to the tree] he [Jesus] went forth unto the so-called Skull-place [sic, "ridge", ha-Rosh on the Mount of Olives, the bet haSeqilah or "Place of Stoning"], which is named in Hebrew Golgotha [this is the Greek transliteration of the Hebrew Gulgoleth, place of the mountain ridge]; where him **[Jesus] they [the Jewish authorities] crucified [hanged] him [on a living tree].**" (John 19:16–18 KJV)[339]

A fuller understanding of the Jewish law and Roman law at the time of Jesus' execution helps us to appreciate how the execution of Jesus occurred to fulfill all that is written in the Scriptures. Jesus, following His resurrection, met two of His disciples on the road to Emmaus *"And beginning with Moses and all the Prophets, he [Jesus] explained to them what was said in all the Scriptures concerning himself"* (Luke 24:27).

Undoubtedly, part of the Scriptures which Jesus explained to the two disciples on the road to Emmaus were those Scriptures which presented prophecy about the "Suffering Servant." Our next chapter explains these important Scriptures which Jesus fulfilled.

CHAPTER 51

Puzzle Piece #3–
Suffering-Servant Considerations

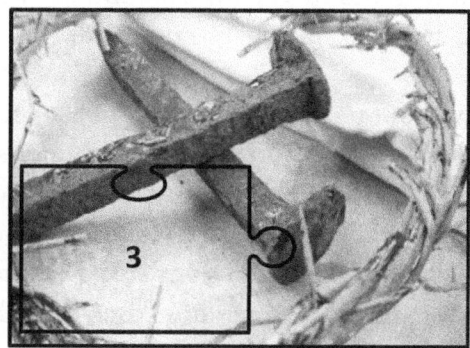

There are some prime Scriptures which are totally overlooked in most commentaries related to the crucifixion of Jesus. Without correctly considering the details of these passages of Scripture, we will miss what really caused the early death of Jesus. Unfortunately, this has been missed by most people. This prime Scripture relates to Isaiah's prophecy about the **Suffering Servant.**

A. Scripture Related to the Suffering Servant

Scripture relating to the *Suffering Servant* are Isaiah 52:13 to 53:12—particularly **Isaiah 52:14**—as well as **Psalm 22:6–7,17**. These *Suffering-Servant* prophecies comprise *Puzzle Piece #3* related to "How Did Jesus *Really* Die?"

This information may not be easy for those who are squeamish by nature, but I urge you to stay with it in reading the material in this chapter. Some of these points have been covered in previous chapters, but this chapter brings together our case related to the fulfillment of the vitally important *Suffering-Servant* prophecies.

Ask most Christians if they believe that Jesus either fulfilled or will fulfill all prophecies related to Him in the Old Testament, and you will get a fast response,

"Yes, of course." Well, these *Suffering-Servant* prophecies were also precisely fulfilled, and this makes all the difference in our understanding of how Jesus really died.

Here are the passages of Isaiah with highlighted principal verses related to the *Suffering Servant, especially Isaiah 52:14, which I have made bold and underlined*:

52 [13]See, my servant will act wisely; he will be raised and lifted up and highly exalted. [14]**Just as there were many who were appalled at him— his appearance was so disfigured beyond that of any man and his form marred beyond human likeness—**[15]so will he sprinkle many nations, and kings will shut their mouths because of him. For what they were not told, they will see, and what they have not heard, they will understand.

53 Who has believed our message and to whom has the arm of the Lord been revealed? [2]He grew up before him like a tender shoot, and like a root out of dry ground. [3]**He had no beauty or majesty to attract us to him, nothing in his appearance that we should desire him. He was despised and rejected by men, a man of sorrows, and familiar with suffering. Like one from whom men hide their faces he was despised, and we esteemed him not.** [4]Surely, he took up our infirmities and carried our sorrows, yet we considered him **stricken by God, smitten by him, and afflicted**. [5]**But he was pierced for our transgressions, he was crushed for our iniquities; the punishment that brought us peace was upon him, and by his wounds we are healed**. [6]We all, like sheep, have gone astray, each of us has turned to his own way; and the Lord has laid on him the iniquity of us all. [7]He was oppressed and afflicted, yet he did not open his mouth; he was led like a lamb to the slaughter, and as a sheep before her shearer is silent, so he did not open his mouth. [8]By oppression and judgment, he was taken away. **And who can speak of his descendants? For he was cut off from the land of the living**; for the transgression of my people he was stricken. [9]He was assigned a grave with the wicked, and with the rich in his death, though he had done no violence, nor was any deceit in his mouth. [10]Yet **it was the Lord's will to crush him and cause him to suffer**, and though the Lord makes his life a guilt offering, he will see his offspring and prolong his days, and the will of the Lord will prosper in his hand. [11]After the suffering of his soul, he will see the light of life, and be satisfied by his knowledge my righteous servant will justify many, and he will bear their iniquities. [12]Therefore, I will give him a portion among the great, and he will divide the spoils with the strong, because **he poured out his life unto death, and was numbered with the transgressors.** For he bore the sin of many, and made intercession for the transgressors. (Isaiah 52:13–53:12 NIV; added two commas—after "So" and after "Therefore"; emphasis mine.)

Here are the verses of Psalm 22 which I am also highlighting related to the *suffering Servant*, with the principal verse being Psalm 22:17, which I have made bold and underlined:

> ⁶But I am a worm and not a man, scorned by men and despised by the people. **⁷All who see me mock me; they hurl insults, shaking their heads** ... ¹⁶ ... they have pierced my hands and my feet, **¹⁷I can count all my bones; people stare and gloat over me**. (Psalm 22:6–7, 16b–17 NIV; emphasis mine.)

While David applied Psalm 22 as belonging to himself in an allegorical sense, it was seen by the apostles as having a literal fulfillment in the person of Jesus. Martin gives the following commentary related to these passages:

> It is interesting, however, that these verses are usually not fully applied today in connection with Jesus' crucifixion. But let us do so. **Coupling these two sections of the Bible together (as certainly was done by the writers of the New Testament) gives us a further indication to the type of death that Jesus encountered**. Had there been no literal application of these verses ... to Jesus it is difficult to see how the apostles could have defended them as describing the role of Jesus at his crucifixion (which, of course, was quite *literal*).[340]

If these prophetic descriptions in Isaiah and the Psalms are to be literally interpreted and applied to Jesus—and it appears they were by the apostles—then we have the description of a man who was not only crucified but one who had his flesh so torn away from his bones that people looking upon him after his ordeal could hardly even tell he was a human being (Isaiah 52:14). Let me ask you a question. Do you think that the descriptive words of Isaiah, *"... his appearance was so disfigured beyond that of any man and his form marred beyond human likeness ..."* apply to someone who has undergone crucifixion by itself? I don't believe they do. However, someone who was stoned to death as well as crucified could very well match that description!

In addition, **even the bones of his body could be seen *by him* penetrating outward through his skin (Psalm 22:17).** *"Seen by him"* **indicates on the *front* of his body, and *not* on his back where this could not be seen by him—therefore, this could not be referring to the results of the lashing by the Roman solders as ordered by Pilate, which were administered on the back.** This can be interpreted that even his bare bones themselves on the *front* of the body were being exposed because so much skin and flesh had been rent away from the bones.[341]

This is what the prophet Isaiah was communicating in his description of the *Suffering Servant.* His flesh was to be so mangled and his form so disfigured that it was almost impossible to recognize him as a human being (Isaiah 52:14). What would have caused this much skin and flesh to be torn away from the *front side* of his body? It should be recognized that **Roman scourging and simple crucifixion would not have caused this.**

Scourging was primarily on the back, and, it is true, the whips could curl around and mangle the rib cage. However, I do not believe that scourging alone fully accounted for David's prophetic description in Psalm 22:17 of the front side of Jesus' body where his bones were seen by Him (*"I can count all my bones . . ."*). Stoning, however, could have caused that.

The prophet Isaiah described the *Suffering Servant* with his visage marred more than any man. That is quite a statement! Of course, some of us find this description distasteful to imagine Jesus in this fashion, but that is what is described by Isaiah and the apostles and disciples certainly did, and several were eye-witnesses of the crucifixion and saw Jesus in this state.

The question we should ask is what type of punishment under Jewish law could produce such an awful description of the *Suffering Servant*? The scourging that Jesus was subjected to before his crucifixion cannot account for such a description since Pilate fully intended to let Jesus go after the Roman soldiers had chastised him, and from this it shows that Pilate fully believed that he would recover. Pilate did not wish him to die (Luke 23:22). In addition, the scourging was on the back side of Jesus' body as was typical and would not relate to the description of Psalm 22:17 of *"seen by him,"* which relates to the front side and not the back side of his body.

The common judicial punishment at the time of Jesus that would cause these scriptural descriptions is being pelted repeatedly with small stones—*stoning to death*. Also, it is important to note that ***stoning was the only kind of punishment for capital crimes (like blasphemy) under the Mosaic Law.*** This is incredibly significant. The description in Isaiah 52:14 is consistent with stoning to death by the Saducean method of stoning, which makes sense as the Saducean priesthood was the powerful sect in the temple administration during the lifetime of Jesus. The

Pharisaic method of stoning—with a single large stone dropped from a height—would have caused broken bones, which according to John 19:36 did not happen (and supported by the analogies of Exodus 12:46, Numbers 9:12, Psalm 34:20).

While we presently view stoning to death as a barbaric and inhumane practice and we cannot imagine that our Messiah might have been stoned, this execution method was entirely legal for **blasphemy** (Leviticus 24:13–16) and was fully accepted during the time of Jesus.

Martin gives the following commentary related to Jesus being stoned:

> There is no doubt that Jesus experienced the torment of volleys of small, sharp stones thrown at the front parts of his naked body while he was nailed to the tree of crucifixion. **The stones were hurled at his face, at his mid-section and his legs. These must have been like sharp flintstones (many of which are on the Mount of Olives) that would break the skin and dislodge the flesh but without the force to break his bones. Such volleys of stones hitting his body persistently for almost six hours could produce the description of Isaiah**: 'As many were astonished at thee: his visage [his outward appearance] was *so marred* more than any man, and his form [*so marred*] more than the sons of man.'[342]

Pontius Pilate was the Roman authority to approve the execution of Jesus (John 18:31), but **Pilate gave permission to the Jewish authorities in Jerusalem to kill him according to their biblical law**. Pilate told them, *"take ye him and judge him according to your law"* (John 18:31). This subjected Jesus to suffer the Jewish method of execution of hanging on a tree and the people of Jerusalem pelting him with stones in the scriptural (Mosaic) manner (Leviticus 24:16). Moses commanded that all Israelites and aliens in sight of a blasphemer should take up stones and stone the profane and ungodly person to death. The Hebrew understanding was that Israel was to overwhelm the criminal with countless volleys of stones being thrown at his naked body (Rashi, *Commentary*, volume II, p. 111).

When one was charged with the most heinous of crimes, such as blasphemy, it was common for the stoning to be done with as much humiliation upon the person as possible. Initially, in the process of stoning, it was to the head and eyes that the stones were predominately thrown. This is illustrated in the Parable of the Tenants in the Gospel of Mark: *"And again he sent unto them another servant: and at him **they cast stones**, and **wounded him in the head** shamefully handled"* (Mark 12:4 KJV; emphasis added). No doubt that sometime during the six hours of being barraged by stones, several of the stones hit his eyes and Jesus was probably blinded by them.

Most people will not like the description of Jesus' appearance, and this is what the prophet Isaiah stated. The description of the *Suffering Servant* is so unknown in most churches—that Jesus was an unrecognizable bloody mass of flesh—this can hardly be believed by many people. This is precisely what Isaiah said would be the reaction to his prophecy:

> Kings shall shut their mouths at him [keep silent in astonishment]: for that which **has not been told them** shall they see and that which **they had not heard** shall they consider. (Isaiah 52:15 KJV; emphasis mine.)

Isaiah knew that most people, even the kings of the world, would *not* believe his report. He recognized that people would miss the full force of what he was saying—that Isaiah's *Suffering Servant*, with whom the apostles identified with Jesus, was an unrecognizable bloody mass of flesh whose outward appearance was so altered by his ordeal that almost no one seeing him near the time of his death would have thought him as having a normal human form.

B. Passover Seder & Communion–Analogy to Jesus's Body Broken

When Jesus instituted the Lord's Supper on the eve of His crucifixion, he took bread and *broke* it and He said this *breaking* was like his body which would be *broken* for them (Matthew 26:26). He spoke of the *breaking* of His body in the same context as the wine which represented His blood which was shed for the remission of sins. From the bread and the wine of the Jewish Passover Seder came the Lord's Supper which developed in the Christian church.

It has been a mystery to scholars how *breaking off* pieces of flat and crispy bread like the unleavened bread that Jews eat at Passover today—called *matzos*—could represent the body of Jesus at his crucifixion. Indeed, the New Testament specifically states that no bones in His body would be broken (John 19:36). Many scholars can see no reference whatever to the death of Jesus in the *breaking* of the unleavened bread. Many feel that the breaking of bread must only refer to the ceremony at fellowship meals without any significance to the crucifixion of Jesus. However, many early Christians did not see it that way at all.

Several Greek manuscripts and writings of several Church Fathers provide an explanation related to First Corinthians 11:24 concerning the *breaking* of the bread at the Lord's Supper and the association of the *breaking* of Jesus' body at his crucifixion. **They made comments that there were early beliefs that the *broken***

bread in the ceremony of the Lord's Supper did indeed represent the *broken* body of Jesus at the time of his crucifixion. In the prophecy of the *Suffering Servant* in Isaiah 52:13 to 53:12 there was the statement in Hebrew that the person of the prophecy would be *broken* for our iniquities [*bruised* in KJV]. The Hebrew word *dahchah* in Isaiah 53:5 means *broken* (*cf.* Isaiah 19:10).[343]

Thus, we have both the writings of early Christians as well as the prophecy of Isaiah that the body of Jesus would indeed be *broken* like *breaking off* pieces of unleavened bread. **The normal scourging of the Roman soldiers before His crucifixion as well as the simple act of crucifixion itself would not account for such *breaking off* of pieces of Jesus' body on his front side**. It just would not. However, the act of *stoning* with small sharp stones would fit this description precisely. The impacting of small and sharp stones hurled at his body would tear away pieces of his flesh like pieces of unleavened bread being torn from a larger piece. After six hours of such pummeling, Jesus would have been hanging on the tree of crucifixion as the person described by Isaiah as the *Suffering Servant*—so marred that he would not have resembled a normal human any longer.

Let's mention one other thing related to Jesus' death. It relates to Jesus' blood and the importance of the shedding of blood. The book of Hebrews has important insights related to this:

> When Moses had proclaimed every commandment of the law to all the people, he took the blood of calves, together with water, scarlet wool and branches of hyssop, and sprinkled the scroll and all the people. He said, 'This is the blood of the covenant, which God has commanded you to keep.' In the same way, he sprinkled with the blood both the tabernacle and everything used in its ceremonies. **In fact, the law requires that nearly everything be cleansed with blood, and *without the shedding of blood there is no forgiveness*.** (Hebrews 9:19–22 NIV; emphasis mine.)

It has been a mystery to some about this importance of the shedding of blood in redemption and the death of Jesus. **In simple crucifixion, there is relatively little shedding of blood**. This is important. Yes, the lashings of Jesus' back by the Roman soldiers would account for *some* shedding of blood—but remember that Pilate did not want a scourging to the point of death; he wanted to release Jesus as he felt Jesus was not guilty of crimes warranting death. Also, the pounding of nails into Jesus' wrists would have accounted for *some* shedding of blood. However, the spear thrust into Jesus' side would not have resulted in much blood loss as Jesus was dead at that time and his heart was not pumping blood; in addition, the spear would not count in a theological sense as that happened after his death.

All these aspects of the traditionally accepted punishment of Jesus did not result in the amount of blood loss even as illustrated in the Passover lamb whose blood was applied to the door frame and lintel of the front doors of the Israelites in Egypt before the Tenth Plague.

However, **the act of stoning to death, per the description of the *Suffering Servant,* would have resulted in *copious* shedding of blood.** This fits the Old Testament description and requirement as well as the New Testament emphasis on the shedding of blood.

I can't help but interject a comment in reaction to all this—all this is what Jesus did for us as the *Suffering Servant* to pay the price for our sins! He paid the gruesome penalty of death for our sins according to the Mosaic Law, being acceptable to the Father as the perfect substitutionary sacrifice. Thank you, Jesus, and praise God for His gift to each one who trusts in the salvation which is only available in Him through His payment of our sin-debt. Amen.

All this is further evidence that Jesus physically died from *stoning*. His body was torn to shreds in its frontal areas. The conclusion presented in this case is that he did not die from crucifixion alone.

You should evaluate this evidence presented and come to your own conclusion.

I believe that you will never look at holy communion in the same way again. I certainly don't.

C. Jesus' Body Healed at His Resurrection

It is well to remember that at the *resurrection* from the grave into which he had been placed, Jesus was healed from the effects of the whipping, stoning, and the crucifixion injuries. Except for the nail holes in his "hands" [wrists] and the hole in his side from the spear of the Roman soldier—as eternal reminders of the punishment He underwent for us (John 20:27) and for his identity (John 20:24–28)—his flesh was restored and he was once again recognizable to the disciples. The disciples were overjoyed at the sight of Him in his restored body (John 20:20).

At first, He was not recognized by the women at the tomb and the two disciples on the road to Emmaus, because after the stoning, who would expect to see his form restored to better than "normal?" His whole body was restored, even His vision. He is the "firstfruits" of the resurrection, and He has a resurrection body for eternity.

The same restoration of the body will be experienced by Stephen and Paul from the effects of their stoning, and for each of us from whatever physical conditions we have presently. This will, of course, occur following the resurrection from the grave and the Rapture at the Second Coming of Jesus. Because of Jesus' faithfulness as the *Suffering Servant,* the dead in Christ will rise and bodies will be healed (I Corinthians 15:42–58). We too will be given resurrection bodies as Jesus received and have His likeness (I Corinthians 15:49). In addition, all those who are *"in Christ"* will see Him as He is. Praise God.

Jesus is the first-fruits of the resurrection, and that is *Good News* for us.

CHAPTER 52

Puzzle Piece #4– Place of Stoning Matches Crucifixion Site

An offshoot of making the case that Jesus was sentenced to stoning by the Jewish authorities is that this is further evidence for our case of the crucifixion of Jesus having occurred on the Mount of Olives.

The specific Jewish place of legal stoning to death, as sanctioned by the Sanhedrin, and the place of the crucifixion of Jesus is the same place. This is *puzzle piece #4* of our case for how Jesus really died—it was by stoning while hanging on a tree, at *The Place of Stoning*.

The crucifixion and stoning occurred at a specific place where the punishment of stoning, as authorized by the Sanhedrin, was carried out—this was true for Jesus and it was true for Stephen. That place was called *"The Place of Stoning"* and was located possibly near the summit of the Mount of Olives, slightly downslope towards the temple and directly east of the temple, so that the criminal could be killed in the presence of God in the Holy of Holies of the temple.[344]

We know that it was outside the city of Jerusalem from the account of the **stoning of Stephen**: "… [T]hey dragged him ***out of the city*** and began to stone him" (Acts 7:58 *KJV; emphasis mine*). We know also that the location was "**outside the camp**," as the Mishnah states: "*The Place of Stoning* was outside [far away from] the court [located in the Temple], as it is written, Bring forth him that hath cursed **without the camp**"

(*Sanhedrin* 6:1 and also see sections 2–4).³⁴⁵ This makes the location outside of a radius of 2000 cubits (about 3000 feet) from in front of the Holy of Holies in the temple.³⁴⁶

So, where did these three parameters of (1) being outside the city and (2) outside the camp as well as (3) directly east of the temple put *The Place of Stoning* on the Mount of Olives? A fair answer would be that it was located directly east of the temple possibly at close to the top of the Mount of Olives ridge, at what is called the southern summit. This was also close to the place of the **sacrifice of the Red Heifer** ceremony on the Mount of Olives, as this was also directly east of the temple. The writer of the book of Hebrews likened the sacrifice of the Red Heifer to that of Jesus (Hebrews 9:13–14).

What else can we say about the site of Stephen's stoning? In the fifth century, Christians built a Martyrium for Stephen inside the colonnade area of what is today called the ***Imbomon*** (the suspected place of Stephen's martyrdom). This is mentioned by John Wilkinson in a book he wrote, *Egeria's Travels, Third Edition* (1999), based on the translation of the travelogue reports (AD 381 to AD 384) of a Spanish nun from Spain called Egeria; she wrote back to her fellow nuns in Spain on her travels to the Holy Land. Wilkinson states: "The Martyrium of St. Stephen, built by Melania the Younger, and dedicated in [AD] 439, was inside the colonnade of the Imbomon … and **the Martyrium on the Mount of Olives was probably the principal sanctuary of St. Stephen**."³⁴⁷

Where is the *Imbomon* (the suspected place of **Stephen's Martyrium**) located? It was at the southern summit of the Mount of Olives. It is associated with the area called Golgotha, the suspected place where Jesus was also stoned and crucified. Both the execution of Jesus and Stephen occurred in the legal site for stoning called by the Jews *The Place of Stoning*.

There is another reference to be made about this place of stoning and it oddly relates to **King David** and events which happened to him. The events which happened to King David when he was ousted from his kingship and was excommunicated from the society of Israel at the time of Absalom's rebellion (II Samuel Chapters 15–16) typified Jesus at his crucifixion! It was on the Mount of Olives where David experienced his humiliation and was stoned (II Samuel 15:30, 32; 16:1; and II Samuel 16:5–14). This is also where David composed **Psalm 22**, which Jesus cited as referring to himself at the time of his crucifixion, *"My God, my God, why have you forsaken me?"* (Matthew 27:46; Psalm 22:1 NIV).

Note that this humiliation and stoning of King David, almost 1000 years before Jesus, was prophetic of Jesus being accursed, stoned, and forsaken on the same Mount of Olives.

All this gives support for the punishment of Jesus being *stoning to death* on the Mount of Olives, at the place designated for stoning to death.

CHAPTER 53

Conclusion of *How* Did Jesus *Really* Die?

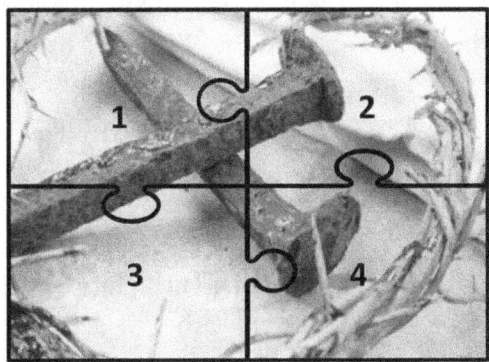

These four *pieces of the puzzle* as to how Jesus really died so quickly fit together in the case for Jesus having been *both crucified and stoned to death* for the Jewish crime of blasphemy—all according to Mosaic Law. Scripture, historical evidence, and Jewish religious law all point to this, and this is our conclusion in this case study.

It seems to me that those who hold to the *traditional* view of how Jesus died, by just scourging and hanging on a Roman cross, ignore the biblical account that Pontius Pilate turned Jesus back over to the Jewish temple authorities for *them* to crucify Him (John 19:6); this would be by the method of crucifixion by the Sadducees—hanging on a live tree and stoning to death according to Mosaic Law.

Once we accept that Jesus died quickly principally from *stoning* during the act of crucifixion, we can fully appreciate how truly awful His crucifixion was. History is important; and I fully believe that the conclusion of this case is consistent with Jewish law and customs at the time of Jesus' life, with Scripture, with the commentary of first century travelers, and—consequently—with history.

I understand that this conclusion is at odds with the *traditional* church view of how Jesus died, and I acknowledge that this conclusion will not sit well with some. But as we have seen in other *traditional* views—many of which have been addressed in various chapters in this book on the ***Mysteries of Jesus' Life Revealed***—*tradition* is often the enemy of truth. In spite of clear and convincing Scriptural and historical evidence, we often find that *tradition* replaces real truth with half-truths, fanciful stories, and wishful thinking, passed down through the centuries, from one generation to the next. Unfortunately, once *tradition* has taken hold, it can be very difficult to dislodge.

You may ask, "What's the big deal? These are not salvation issues." This is true. Regardless whether you believe that Jesus was scourged to within an inch of his life or received a milder form of lashing at the direction of Pilate, in anticipation of His release; regardless whether you believe He was nailed to a Roman cross or to a living tree somewhere on the Mount of Olives; regardless whether you believe He suffered the painful and humiliating punishment of being stoned to death by passing strangers or was allowed to hang relatively unmolested for six excruciating hours from the spikes penetrating his wrists and feet—regardless what you ultimately believe, your salvation will not depend on your understanding of these specific details.

Even so, we owe it to ourselves, to our faith, and to the One who sacrificed Himself for our salvation to make every effort to determine the truth of these things. To do less would be a disservice to the sacrifice of our Savior and to the Scripture which reveals all things to those who seek with open eyes and an open heart.

I have made every effort to be both thorough and truthful in presenting my understanding of the punishment which Jesus endured for blasphemy in accordance with Mosaic Law—*stoning*. Surely, it was all part of God's plan that Jesus would ultimately be punished by Jewish Temple officials according to Jewish law and that He would ultimately fulfill the Isaiah and Psalm 22 prophecies of the *Suffering Servant*.

Certainly, we could wish that *tradition* was true, that Jesus was executed just as we have been taught since we were in Sunday school. But the evidence is quite strong that this was simply not the case. At least, that is my conclusion.

I sincerely hope that the evidence presented in this case study has been helpful to you, that it has caused you to re-think what you have always believed to be true about the crucifixion of Jesus. God's Grace is such that you will not be penalized if you get the execution details wrong, but it is my hope that perhaps you will now be better positioned to get the details right to more fully appreciate what all Jesus possibly endured for the salvation of those who trust in His sacrificial death.

I earnestly believe that a more complete and factual understanding of our Lord Jesus and of his sacrifice for you will lead you into a deeper relationship with Him and to a greater appreciation of the pain He endured to deliver each one of us from our sin. Indeed, we can praise Him for eternity. He is God in the flesh; and He humbled Himself enough to be born as a man, to minister under duress during His brief time on earth, and to die a humiliating and agonizing death—all to pay the price for our sins before the Father. His death is fully acceptable in payment by the Father. Now, Jesus lives forever as our risen Savior and Lord. Praise God.

I have presented a great deal of evidence on a number of topics related to Jesus' trial and death. It remains only for you to evaluate this evidence, to be a good Berean, and to come to your own conclusions.

Admittedly, since Scripture does not state explicitly that Jesus was stoned while He was hanging on the cross/tree, we can't say with absolute assurance that was the case, although much evidence supports it. I pray that the Holy Spirit will guide each of us in our understanding of these important truths.

So … **what do you think?**

PART III

New Insights–
Where **Was Herod's Temple?**

—Ernest L. Martin's Proposed Location

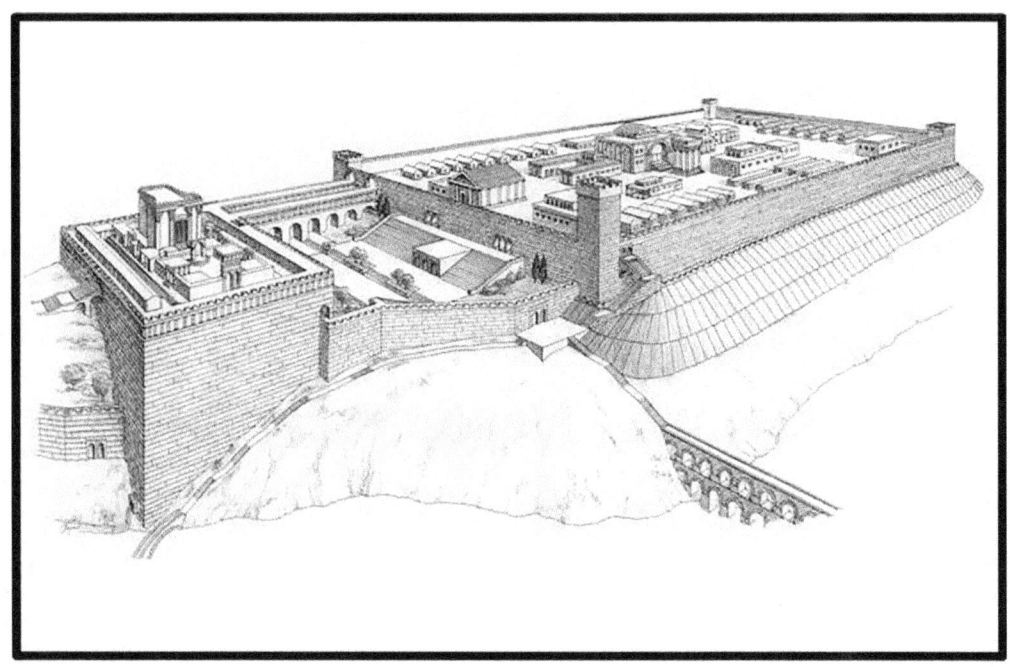

(Graphic from *www.askelm*.com)

Introduction to Part III

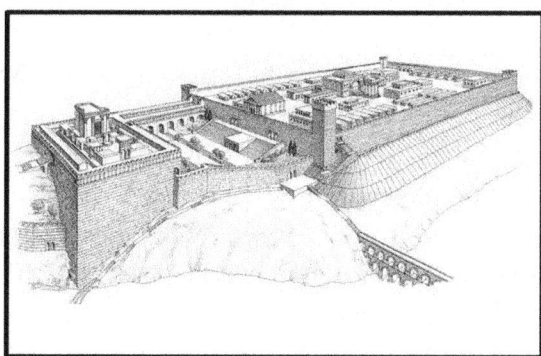

> According to the eye-witness descriptions of Josephus and others, Ernest L. Martin has presented the case that the true Temple Mount was to the south of the *traditional* "Temple Mount," on the *southeast* ridge of Jerusalem—the true location of "Mount Zion" in the City of David. In addition, the case is presented for the entire presently so-called "Temple Mount" being the former location of the *Roman Fort Antonia*—another important complex of buildings constructed and enlarged by Herod the Great.
>
> This case includes that Fort Antonia was much larger and in a different location than is depicted on current models of ancient Jerusalem, where it is depicted as a much smaller structure attached to the *traditional* "Temple Mount" at the northwest corner of the Mount.

It seems that even the location of the former temples in Jerusalem is a mystery. Were the temples of Solomon, Zerubbabel (the rebuilt temple following the Babylonian exile), and Herod really located on the present *traditional* "Temple Mount" location?

Almost everyone has assumed that to be true. However, Dr. Ernest L. Martin has proposed a *non-traditional* temple location—*which is not what you think!* He makes an interesting and compelling case based on biblical and eye-witness historical accounts as well as a literal interpretation of Jesus' prophecy related to the temple's destruction and what we see today.

So why is the correct location of the temple important in determining the correct location of the crucifixion and burial of Jesus? The answer is that the location of the temple is important because the crucifixion site of Jesus is directly east of the location of the temple—on the Mount of Olives, as has been established in previous chapters. Hence, we need to correctly locate the temple, which, as it turns out, is no small task as it has largely been "forgotten" according to Ernest Martin.

If the temple was on the traditionally accepted Temple Mount or in a more southerly location, the exact location determines where—on the crescent-shaped Mount of Olives—Jesus was crucified, buried, and resurrected. Therefore, the correct location of the temple is an important *puzzle piece.*

I want to give you fair notice. The case presented in this chapter is extremely controversial, and I want my readers to fully understand this. The present religious, scholarly, and archaeological opinion is that the ancient temples were located on what is presently called the "Temple Mount" in Jerusalem. The case of another site as presented in this chapter, is not accepted by the overwhelming proportion of Christian and Jewish historians or by Christian and Jewish archeologists. I want to be very clear about this.

However, as you know, truth is not a factor of current popularly-held positions. In this book, I have been emphasizing that the *traditional* dates and places related to the birth, death, and resurrection of Jesus are largely not true, and the cases and evidence have been presented for what I believe *really* happened. For example, I am presenting the case for the crucifixion site being on the Mount of Olives. This too is not the popular traditional position, but I believe the evidence is overwhelming. The bottom line is that the popularity of a position does not make it true.

Are you ready to consider **another *non-traditional* and, certainly, highly-controversial view?** We will be considering that the ancient temples, both the First and Second Temples, including the temple which Herod built, did not actually reside on what is now called the *"Temple Mount,"* which is the *traditional* site.

Proponents of this new case for *a more southerly location for the temples* incur the wrath of the traditionalists who *positively* have concluded that the ancient temples *did* reside on the "Temple Mount." After all, where would the temples be other than on the so-called *"Temple Mount?"* And in their minds, their case is so overwhelming that they do not by-and-large even consider another location, even though there is strong historical and scriptural evidence for that being true—it is for them "case closed!" This is the case with most scholars and archeologists who have already taken a position and have published on the topic—for them, particularly, it is usually very difficult to change positions.

But, is the case *really "case closed?"* There are some who do not think so. However, to even suggest otherwise, is to incur ridicule and a "pity him" condensational attitude from almost the whole of the Christian and Jewish communities. Martin provides a good illustration of the usual response to his case presentation:

> "An illustration: On an airplane between London and Tel Aviv, I explained to a distinguished looking man who appeared to be an orthodox Rabbi the basic historical research of this book [*The Temples That Jerusalem Forgot*]. My conclusion to him showed that the Bible and history revealed the 'Wailing Wall' was *not* a wall of the Temple but is the western wall of Herod's Fort Antonia. He retorted vociferously and vigorously with a single English word: '**PREPOSTEROUS**'!"[348]

Presently, admittedly, there is not definitive archeological evidence to back up Martin's claims, and it has to be said that some archeological evidence *seems* to point to the present Temple Mount as being the site of the temples.[349] However, as Dr. Randall Price has stated, "It must be remembered in archaeology that the absence of evidence is not evidence of absence ... As a friend of mine who works as a curator at the Rockefeller Museum in Jerusalem put it: 'Absolute truth in archaeology lasts about 20 years!'"[350]

After this introduction, I think you "get" the situation. However, I want you to make up your own mind on this evidence presented.

If, indeed, the past temples were never located on the present "Temple Mount" but at another location, then the consequences are astonishing to consider. It would mean that, if accepted by the Jewish people, any rebuilt temple would *not* need to be built at or near the same general location of the present Muslim's Dome of the Rock. What would this mean? It would mean that the Jewish people could tell the Muslims, "Fine, you can keep your Dome of the Rock on its present location; we are rebuilding our temple in a southern location, where the original temples were built." One would have to say, "Wow, that's an interesting prospect!"

What else would a different temple location mean to the Jewish people? Sadly, it would mean that the Jewish people have been praying at the wrong location of the temple for centuries; they have been praying at the "Wailing Wall," but there is a strong possibility that it is really a western wall of the ancient Roman Fort Antonia—and not the western retaining wall of the ancient temples.

Well, you might say, "The Jews could not have gotten this wrong, for surely they would know their own temple location!" However, if the true temple location has been *lost in history*, this is not totally different from all the Christians who have for centuries been praying at the *traditional* site of Jesus' crucifixion—the Church of the Holy Sepulcher—located to the *west* of the *traditional* "Temple Mount," when the true location of the crucifixion and burial sites of Jesus is to the *east*—on the Mount of Olives (per the case given in Section B of Part II).

I will readily say that I am *not 100% convinced* of the truth of Martin's case which is presented in this chapter. I am just saying that the case is, in my opinion, strong and should be considered seriously. It's implications, if true, are astounding. I have to say that the more I look into it, the more I am coming to accept the case as true.

OK, so who is saying that the true temple location is further to the south of the *traditional* Temple Mount—where tourists today are paraded to see and hear the spiel of tourist guides? Well, how about reliable eye-witnesses who lived in the first century BC and first century AD and are validated by Jesus' prophecy? For example, such eye-witnesses as the Jewish historian Josephus and Eleazar, who commanded the remnant Jewish forces at Masada some three years after the temple and Jerusalem were demolished by the Romans. At least this is some of the evidence of the case which is presented here. You will see where eye-witness descriptions of the temple and Jerusalem were given which clearly don't align with the present "Temple Mount" location. In addition, in Chapter 64: "How Could the Rabbis Forget?" you will see a case for just how the proposed correct sites got *lost in history*.

As in all the cases presented in this book, you can evaluate the evidence and come to your own conclusions. Consider me just the messenger presenting the evidence for this case.

So, who is this person who proposed this "crazy" theory that the true location of the temples in Jerusalem were over the Gihon Spring, in the City of David in Zion, to the south of the *traditional* Temple Mount?" Dr. Ernest L. Martin has presented this case in his book, **The Temples That Jerusalem Forgot** (2000).[351] Martin died in 2002, at the age of 70, just two years after writing this landmark book. Unfortunately, the book is now only available from third-party sellers on *www.Amazon.com*, and the demand has pushed the price high. However, presently, it can also be purchased through the website *www.askelm.com* , which is dedicated to Martin's findings, for a more reasonable price.

Robert Corneke's book, **Temple–Amazing New Discoveries That Change Everything About the Location of Solomon's Temple** (2014),[352] supports Martin's findings in a condensed manner and presents some archeological evidence; however, in my opinion, the full case is best presented by Martin in his book as well as on the website which features Martin's work: *www.askelm.com* . Cornuke also has a follow-up book, **Golgotha–Searching for the True Location of Christ's**

Crucifixion (2016; Koinonia House), which proposes the present Muslim village of Silwan on the southern spur of the Mount of Olives, to the east of the City of David, as the crucifixion and burial site of Jesus.

By way of background, Ernest L. Martin, PhD, had an interesting academic career in England and the U.S., as well as an interesting ministry career in general. Specifics can be referenced from Wikipedia ("Ernest L. Martin"). He does have a background in archeology—between 1969 and 1973 he worked on a five-year archeological program with students from Ambassador College, under the direction of Dr. Benjamin Mazar (the legendary Jewish biblical archeologist), involving excavations near the Western Wall of the "Temple Mount."

In my opinion, Martin is best described as a brilliant historian who is insatiable in his research to uncover truth. He has the uncanny ability to research primary-source historical documents and Scripture in building a case, going where the evidence leads him, and taking a stand for what he has uncovered and believes to be the truth.

Who else supports this temple location? One person is **George Wesley Buchanan, Ph.D., Litt.D., D.S.L.**, Professor Emeritus of New Testament, Wesley Theological Seminary, Washington, D.C., and the author of 17 books and 63 articles on both testaments of scripture, theology, and rabbinic literature. As of 2013, he was on the Editorial Advisory Board of the *Biblical Archaeological Review*. His insightful paper, "In Search of King Solomon's Temple" (June 2009), is available at *www.askelm.com*.

Dr. Buchanan became aware of Martin's work after reading his book soon after its publication in 2000. It is noteworthy that Buchanan had been working on similar research about the temple being over the Gihon Spring and came to the same conclusion as Martin, but beginning from a different perspective. In Buchanan's paper, it mentions that he had known Ernest Martin "for about 30 years."[353] In this article by Buchanan, he also mentioned that in 1961 Martin visited Jerusalem where he met Israeli archeologist **Benjamin Mazar and his son, Ory.** The article states that, "It was Ory who told him that both he and his father believed that the Temple of Solomon was located on the Ophel mound to the north of the original Mount Zion [over the Gihon Spring]."[354] Martin worked closely with Dr. Benjamin Mazar from 1969 to 1973 on the archaeological excavations near the Western Wall of the *traditional* "Temple Mount."

Others have given favorable reviews of Martin's book, including Dr. **Michael P. Germano**, Editor of *www.bibarch.com*, Professor Emeritus Ambassador University, a graduate of the University of Illinois at Urbana-Champaign, and holds earned doctorates from the University of Southern California and the University of La Verne.[355] **Prof. James D. Tabor**, Department of Religious Studies, The University of North Carolina at Charlotte (NC), has written:

"Having now read his [Martin's] arguments I am convinced this thesis, however revolutionary and outlandish it first appears, deserves careful, academic and critical consideration and evaluation. I am not yet convinced that Martin has ironed out all the problems or handled all the potential objections, yet he has set forth a case that should be heard."[356]

Please note that what I am presenting here is only a small portion of the extensive biblical and historical evidence which Martin lays out in his 585-page book, *The Temples That Jerusalem Forgot* (2000). Interested seekers will want to read his full account.

In addition to Martin's case for a southern location of the temple, there is another case recently presented by **Nancy L, Kuehl** which is interesting and worth considering. It is presented in her landmark book, *A Book of Evidence–The Trials and Execution of Jesus* (2013).[357] Which case is correct? I will discuss this additional case by Kuehl further in Chapter 63: "Nancy L. Kuehl's 'Temple.'"

Now, let's look at the case for the temple not being on the *traditional* Temple Mount (also called by Muslims, "*Haram esh-Sharif*") but, rather, at a more southern location. Martin's case is that the true Temple Mount was down the hill so to speak from the *traditional* Temple Mount, on the *southeast* ridge of Jerusalem—unquestionably the true location of "Mount Zion" of King David's time. Mount Zion was definitively located 130 years ago by Professor Birch; this is significant because "Mount Zion" and "Temple Mount" are acknowledged as identical in several biblical contexts.[358] Psalm 65:1–4 states that God's Temple is *"in Zion;"* Psalm 99:1,2 states that God dwells between the Cherubim *"in Zion;"* and Joel 3:17,21 shows the temple *"in Zion."* Martin's case is that the temples were slightly north of Mount Zion, over and around the Gihon Spring—a source of *running water* which was essential for temple sacrifices and for ritual bathing of the priests. He makes the case to *"follow the water!"*

In addition, the case is presented for the entire *traditional* Temple Mount being the former location of the *Roman Fort Antonia*—another important complex of buildings constructed and enlarged by Herod the Great. The case is made that Fort Antonia was much larger and in a different location than is depicted on current models of ancient Jerusalem, where it is depicted as a much smaller structure attached to the "Temple Mount" at the north-west corner of the *traditional* Mount.

This evidence presented by Martin helps in determining the true location of the temple and, hence, the true site of the crucifixion and burial of Jesus—on the Mount of Olives, to the east of Herod's Temple.

CHAPTER 54

Nine *Puzzle-Pieces* Determine Validity

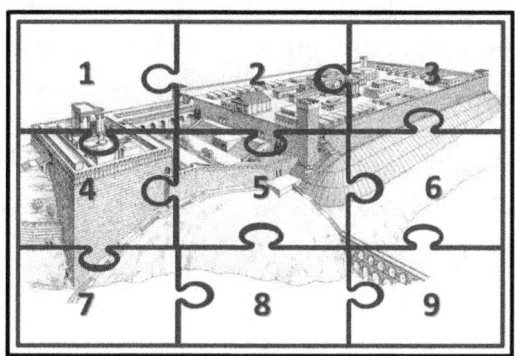

N ine *puzzle pieces* are used to determine the validity of Ernest L. Martin's proposed locations of Herod's Temple and Fort Antonia, and they are presented in separate chapters in this Part III, as follows:

1   *Puzzle Piece #1–Jesus' Prophecy*
2   *Puzzle Piece #2–Eye-Witness Accounts*
3   *Puzzle Piece #3–City of David/Gihon Spring/Temple*
4   *Puzzle Piece #4–Can Spring Push Water Up to Temple?*
5   *Puzzle Piece #5–Fort Antonia on "Temple Mount"?*
6   *Puzzle Piece #6–What About the Rock on "Temple Mount"?*
7   *Puzzle Piece #7–Martin's Graphic*
8   *Puzzle Piece #8–Critiques by Ritmeyer and Franz & Rebuttals*
9   *Puzzle Piece #9–Nancy L. Kuehl's "Temple"*

I think you will find this investigation of the various pieces of evidence interesting. As in determining truth in Scripture, all Scripture needs to align to determine truth—even small seemingly obscure passages. Similarly, **all** these *puzzle pieces* must be properly considered, and they must align to determine the true locations of Herod's Temple and Fort Antonia. In my humble opinion, commentators and even archeologists often go astray by not properly considering **all** the *puzzle pieces*, including the critically important eye-witness descriptions, in coming to their conclusions; by doing that, they can come up with incorrect locations.

In the following chapters, we will consider the evidence of each *puzzle piece*, starting with "*Puzzle Piece #1*–Jesus' Prophecy." We will see specifically how the prophecy given by Jesus to His disciples on the Mount of Olives provides evidence in solving the mystery of the location of Herod's Temple and Fort Antonia.

The graphic at the start of each upcoming chapter illustrates the *puzzle piece* being examined to determine the validity of Martin's proposed locations of Herod's Temple and the Roman Fort Antonia. The *puzzle pieces* are shown overlaid on a drawing which Martin had produced by an artist he commissioned to follow the exact descriptions of Flavius Josephus, an eye-witness of Herod's Temple and Fort Antonia before they were destroyed in AD 70.

CHAPTER 55

Puzzle Piece #1–Jesus' Prophecy

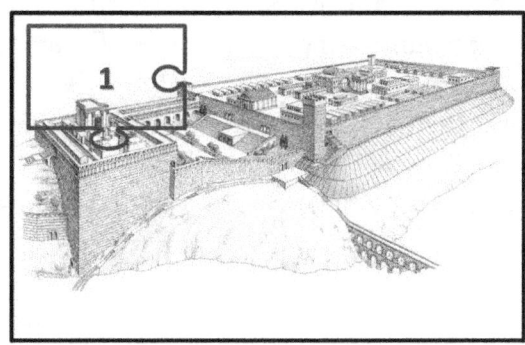

Of preeminent importance in the interpretation of the true location of Herod's Temple in the time of Jesus is Jesus' prophecy of what was to happen to the temple and, indeed, all of Jerusalem because the Jews did not recognize the time of His coming.

Jesus' prophecy in the Olivet Discourse related to the destruction of the temple (Matthew 24:1–2, Mark 13:1–3, and Luke 19:43–44 and 21:5–6) is *Puzzle Piece #1* for the solution of the true location of Herod's Temple.

In fact, the proper interpretation of Jesus prophecy helps greatly to determine the true location of the temple. Here are two passages from the Gospel of Luke of what Jesus told his disciples:

> For the days shall come upon thee, that thy enemies shall cast a trench about thee, and compass thee round, and keep thee in on every side. And **shall lay thee [*Jerusalem*] even with the ground**, and thy children within thee; and **they shall not leave in thee one stone upon another**; because thou knewest not the time of thy visitation. (Luke 19:43–44, KJV, clarification and emphasis added)

> As some spake **of the *Temple***, how it was adorned with goodly stones

and gifts, he [Jesus] said: 'As for these things which ye behold, the days will come, in the which **there shall not be left one stone upon another, that shall not be thrown down**.' (Luke 21:5–6, KJV, clarification and emphasis added)

We know from the parallel passages from Mark 13:1–3 that Jesus' prophecy was *given by Jesus as the disciples and Jesus sat on the Mount of Olives, looking back on the temple, its retaining walls, and Jerusalem*. Just for clarification, Jesus prophesized that not one stone would be left on one another, either in the city of Jerusalem and its walls, or the temple and its walls. This is stated in a total of four passages in three of the Gospel accounts—the two passages of Luke (previously quoted), Matthew 24:1–2, and Mark 13:1–3.

Jesus' prophecy was that total destruction, including the foundations, would happen to every building as well as every wall in Jewish Jerusalem. Indeed, this happened during and after the Roman/Jewish war of AD 66–73. Josephus stated the following related to the destruction of the temple and the buildings of Jewish Jerusalem:

> "… Caesar gave orders that they should now demolish the entire city and Temple … but for all the rest of the wall [surrounding Jerusalem], **it was so thoroughly laid even with the ground by those that dug it up to the foundation, that there was left nothing to make those that came thither believe it [Jerusalem] had ever been inhabited**. This was the end which Jerusalem came to by the madness of those that were for innovations; a city otherwise of great magnificence, and of mighty fame among all mankind."[359]

Indeed, what is seen today as one stands on the Mount of Olives and looks to the west at the city of Jerusalem? Most notable is that the gigantic walls of the *traditional* Temple Mount (the *Haram esh-Sharif*) are still standing in all their glory with the 10,000 Herodian and pre-Herodian stones in place in their lower courses.[360] If these walls were retaining walls of the temple and its buildings, then we must say that Titus did not completely destroy these walls, which would call into question Jesus' explicit prophecy as well as the accuracy of Josephus' eye-witness account.

So, why do these walls now exist? The usual answer given by most scholars who are conciliatory to Christian principles is that Jesus could only have meant the stones of the *inner* temple and its buildings and *not* the *outer* temple and its surrounding walls. However, this is simply not true. The exterior building of the temple including its walls were always reckoned within the meaning of "temple" that Jesus used concerning the total destruction of the temple. Note that in Matthew 4:5 related to the account of Satan taking Jesus to the *"pinnacle of the Temple,"* this pinnacle section was the southeastern corner of the *outer retaining wall* that surrounded the whole of the temple complex. Martin explains it:

> The wording in the New Testament shows that **this southeastern angle was very much a part of the Temple—it was a pinnacle [a wing] 'of the Temple.' That area was a cardinal attachment to the sacred edifice itself and an integral section of the Temple Jesus referred to when he prophesied that not one stone would remain on another.**[361]

Another important point in understanding Jesus' prophecy is the consideration of the location on the Mount of Olives and the view back to the west at the temple and Jerusalem when Jesus gave his teaching to the disciples on the Mount of Olives. Martin gives the following commentary:

> Another important geographical factor proves this point. When Jesus made his prophecy [about the temple destruction], Matthew said that Jesus and his disciples just departed from the outer precincts of the Temple. This means **all of them were viewing the *exterior sections of the Temple and its walls*** (the *heiron [Gk.]*) when he gave his prophecy (Matthew 24:1). The Gospel of Mark [Mark 13:1–2] goes further and makes it clear the ***outside walls of the Temple*** were very much in Jesus' mind when he said they would be uprooted from their foundations. *'And as he [Jesus] went out of the Temple'* [note that **Jesus and the disciples were standing *outside* the Temple walls and looking back toward the Temple enclosure**].
>
> Without doubt, **when Jesus spoke in his prophecy about the destruction of the Temple, he included the stones of the outer walls enclosing the Temple as well as the buildings of the inner Temple.**[362]

Indeed, everything hinges on what Jesus meant in His prophecy about the temple and Jerusalem. Without preconceived notions, all indications are that Jesus meant the temple and all the walls, *including the outer retaining walls of the temple complex.* There is really no ambiguity about Jesus' meanings.

The prophecies about the temple and the city of Jerusalem either happened exactly as Jesus predicted, or those prophecies must be reckoned as false—simple as that. The utter destruction as Jesus prophesied necessarily included the temple and the retaining walls, down to the foundations. Since we see the outer retaining walls of the *traditional* Temple Mount still standing, a natural conclusion is that the "Temple Mount" is not the location of the temple which stood at the time of Jesus. This is an important part of the case which Ernest Martin has presented, and I think it is quite convincing.

Those scholars who hold firmly to the *traditional* Temple Mount being the actual site of the temple must employ a *work-around* and exclude the outer retaining walls of the temple complex from Jesus' prophecy. In my humble opinion, this is a strained view (*eisegesis*—reading into Scripture; rather than *exegesis*—reading out of Scripture) and is not what Jesus intended.

If this is the correct view that Jesus did intend to include the retaining walls of the temple in his prophecy, then one would have to say that the *traditional* Temple Mount is *not* the site of the temple at the time of Jesus.

Let's look at some of the other evidence which Martin has presented in his book, starting with important eye-witness accounts of the temple in the time of Jesus.

CHAPTER 56

Puzzle Piece #2—Eye-Witness Accounts

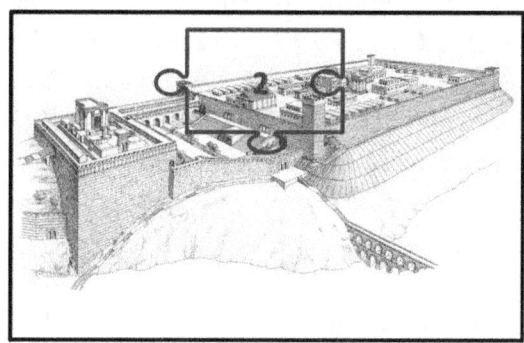

Reliable eye-witness accounts are the "gold-standard" of historical proof of happenings. This is true in crime investigations as well as in a correct view of history.

We are fortunate to have several eye-witness accounts related to the temple and Jerusalem before the destruction in AD 70. These should carry considerable weight.

Two important eye-witnesses of the temple and its location are ***Josephus*** and ***Eleazar.*** Flavius Josephus is, of course, the Jewish historian who defected to the Romans during the early part of the Roman–Jewish War. Eleazar was the head of the Jewish forces on Masada who withstood the assault of the Roman army before finally succumbing in AD 73. Both witnessed firsthand the destruction of the temple and of Jewish Jerusalem. However, with Eleazar's account, written by Josephus, we have his unique testimony of how the Roman camp was preserved among the ruins of Jerusalem.

These eye-witness accounts are important *puzzle-pieces* which bear heavily on the temple's true location and the true location of the Roman Fort Antonia. They comprise *Puzzle Piece #2.* They are important evidence and are, in my opinion, too often overlooked. We can evaluate these eye-witness accounts to see how they contribute to our evaluation of the true site of the Jewish Temple.

Eleazer gave an eyewitness account in AD 73 of the survival of the Camp of the Romans, which was the lone facility which survived the utter destruction of Jerusalem. Here are his words:

> And where is now that great city [Jerusalem], the metropolis of the Jewish nation, which was fortified by so many walls round about, which had so many fortresses and large towers to defend it, which could hardly contain the instruments prepared for the war, and which had so many ten thousands of men to fight for it? Where is **this city** that was believed to have God himself inhabiting therein? ***It is now demolished to the very foundations, and hath nothing left but THAT MONUMENT of it preserved, I mean THE CAMP OF THOSE** [the Romans] **that hath destroyed it, WHICH [CAMP] STILL DWELLS UPON ITS RUINS;*** some unfortunate men also lie upon **the ashes of the Temple** [then in total ruins—burnt to ashes], and a few women are there preserved alive by the enemy, for our bitter shame and reproach.[363]

Eleazer presented the account of utter ruin of the city and the temple, except for the Camp of the Romans. He further stated that God "**abandoned His most holy city to be burnt and razed to the ground.**"[364] Eleazer completed his eyewitness account with the following words:

> I cannot but wish that we had all died before we had seen that holy city demolished by the hands of our enemies, or **the foundations of our Holy Temple dug up**, after so profane a manner.[365]

It should be noted that **in Eleazer's eye-witness account, the foundation stones of the temple complex (including its walls) had been "dug up" and the very foundations destroyed.** According to Eleazar, the only thing that survived was a single Roman Camp; that camp was the *Roman Fort Antonia*. *This is incredibly significant!*

That camp site was not part of Jewish Jerusalem and was Roman imperial property which Roman General Titus' troops did not destroy—he only destroyed Jewish buildings, including walls of the temple and the city. With its four substantial walls and the 37 cisterns and special aqueduct supplying it with water, Titus decided to keep it and continue to use it as the Roman Camp after the war to house the Tenth Legion. **That camp was located on the *traditional* "Temple Mount" site, and this was the reason Titus did not destroy the massive retaining walls.** It had been a Roman fortress since AD 6. All other walls of the city and the temple were destroyed. ***This is powerful evidence that the Jewish temple was not at this site.***[366]

According to Martin, as expected, the temple which was located to the south and above the Gihon Spring was totally destroyed and the Fort Antonia on the *traditional* "Temple Mount" was preserved by Titus. Admittedly, this is what is seen today as the *Haram esh-Sharif*.[367]

The eyewitness account of Josephus supplies powerful evidence for the *Haram esh-Sharif* being Fort Antonia and not being the Temple Mount where the temple was located. The *Haram* had originally been built by King Herod as a military fortress, was used by the Romans, and continued to be used as such after the Roman War and destruction of Jerusalem.[368]

Josephus' physical descriptions of the temple and Fort Antonia are further convincing evidence for the temple being to the south of Fort Antonia, which was *not* on the *traditional* "Temple Mount."

His physical descriptions are forgotten and overlooked history. These physical descriptions are discussed in more detail in the following chapters: Chapter 59: "Fort Antonia on 'Temple Mount?'", Chapter 60: "What About the Rock on 'Temple Mount'?", and Chapter 61: "Martin's Graphic."

CHAPTER 57

Puzzle Piece #3– City of David/ Gihon Spring/Temple

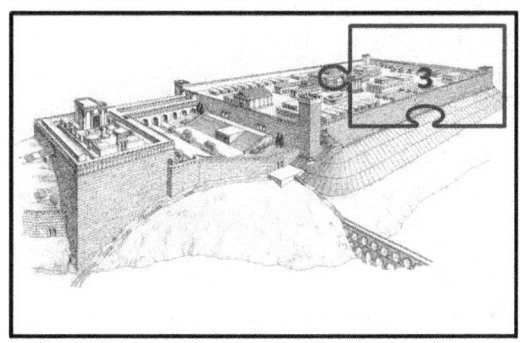

The relationships and the locations of the City of David, the Gihon Spring, and temples constitute *Puzzle Piece #3* in determining the true location of the temples.

The First Temple was built by King David's son, King Solomon, between 960 BC and 953 BC. It was destroyed by the Babylonians in 586 BC. The temple was rebuilt under the leadership of a Jewish governor named Zerubbabel, with the foundations laid in 538 BC and the temple dedicated in 515 BC. This Second Temple was a modest reconstruction of the truly magnificent First Temple built by King Solomon.

This Second Temple existed for almost 500 years until it was completely replaced by a new temple by Herod the Great, beginning in 19 BC.

The Second Temple was built on the same site as the First Temple, and the new temple of Herod was also built at the same location, adjacent to the then existing temple. Upon completion of Herod's Temple, the previous temple was deconstructed. There seems to be agreement on this.

So, the key question becomes: Where was the original temple built? Was it at the location of the *traditional* "Temple Mount" or was it over the Gihon Spring at a different temple mount, in the City of David—about a third of a mile south of the presently so-called "Temple Mount"?

Incredibly, there is historical and biblical evidence that the temples were all located in the City of David over the Gihon Spring. First, let's review the location of the City of David and the evidence for the temples being located there. Then, we can summarize the evidence that they were constructed uniquely and necessarily over a source of spring water—the Gihon Spring, which is the only fresh-water spring within five miles of Jerusalem; this is the case presented by Ernest L. Martin, and is supported by eye-witness testimonies.

The location of the City of David was for centuries "lost in history." It seems that the Christian church might have had a large part in this by changing the manuscripts of Josephus related to his descriptions of the location of first-century Jerusalem as well as the City of David.

Josephus describes first-century Jerusalem as having been built on two mountains.[369] One mountain, which he called the Upper City, encompassed the western area. The other mountain, which Josephus designated as the Lower City, was the ridge east of the Tyropoeon Valley. The whole extent of the eastern ridge was called the "**Lower City**," with the Tyropoeon Valley—a center ravine—dividing the "**Upper City**" from the "Lower City."[370]

Josephus, in his description of first-century Jerusalem contained in *War* V.4.1, has a statement which has thrown off modern historians for centuries. It is stated that the *western mountain* comprising the southern part of the Upper City was formerly the site where King David built the City of David, which is also called the *Akra* or Citadel. However, this is not true, and it contradicts what Josephus stated in *Antiquities* VII.3.1, where he *correctly described* the original City of David on the *south<u>east</u>* ridge.

How did this error in Josephus' writing come about? As all manuscripts of Josephus fell into Christian hands, it seems that the former statement is an editor's insertion presenting Christian opinion in the fourth century that the *south<u>west</u>* hill was "Mount Zion" to justify the belief that the Church of the Holy Sepulchre was the site of Herod's Temple. This was an alien insertion into Josephus' writing, and, as Martin emphatically states, Josephus would never have made such a false statement related to the true location of the City of David.[371]

So, the City of David was located on the *crescent*-shaped *south<u>east</u> ridge*. This Lower City consisted of two elevated areas which Josephus called "hills"—known as the *"**Second Hill**"* and the *"**Third Hill**."* The *"Second Hill"* was the southeast section of first-century Jerusalem and was called the *Akra*.[372]

See Figure 57.1 (same as Figure 61.4) which shows a photograph with the location of the ancient City of David to the south of the traditional Temple Mount and surrounding areas. The photograph is from an article by Dr. George Wesley Buchanan [*Washington Report on Middle East Affairs*, August 2011, pp. 16, 64.

(*http://www.washingtonreport.me/2011-august/misunderstandings-about-jerusalem-s-temple-mount.html*)]. Additional sites and descriptions have been added to this photograph by the author to help the reader visualize all that has been described.

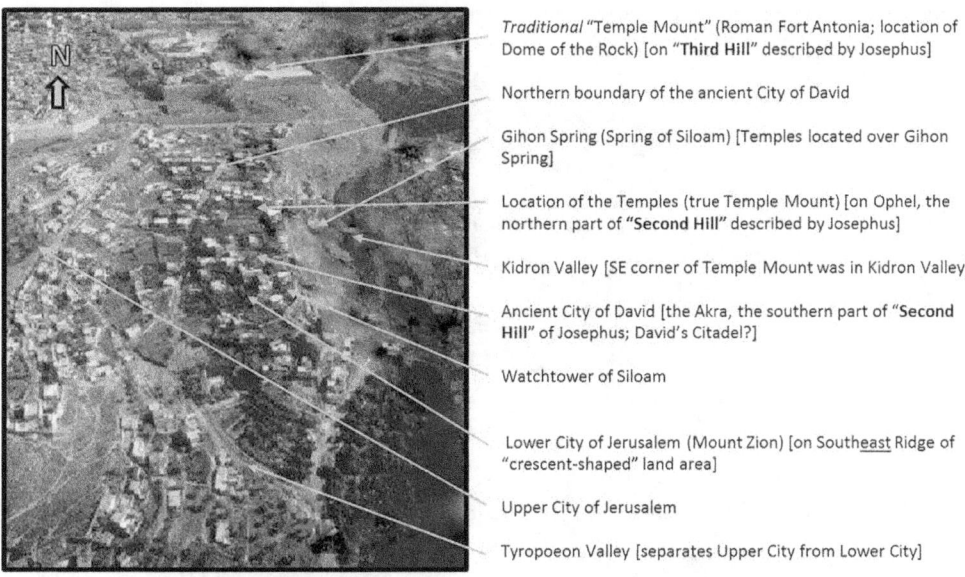

Figure 57.1. Photograph with ancient City of David located south of the traditional Temple Mount (Fort Antonia) with labels for locations of historical structures

The Second Mountain (*"Second Hill"*) had two summits (like the case of the ridge of the Mount of Olives having three summits). **The northern summit of this *"Second Hill"* was called the *Ophel* area, and this is where the temple was located—over the site of the Gihon Spring.** At the time of King David/Solomon up until the time of Simon the Hasmonean (when he completely cut down the southern summit), the southern summit was slightly higher than the northern summit.[373] The southern summit was the site of the Citadel (which was the *Akra* or the *City of David*). This *Akra* is what David conquered from the Jebusites in about 1003 BC.

The *"Third Hill"* was north of both the *Akra* and *Ophel,* and to Josephus this *"Third Hill"* would be the hill on which the Dome of the Rock now rests. It was on the *"Second Hill"* that the City of David was located. This true location of the City of David has been confirmed archeologically, so there is now agreement on this.

Figure 57.2 is a topographic map which shows the original "**Mount Zion**" ("Lower City") with its *Ophel* extension, to the south of the *traditional* "Temple

Mount." I have also rotated this map 90 degrees, with North shown pointing to the left on the page, to be able to show the map in a larger size to make it easier to read the writing on the map.

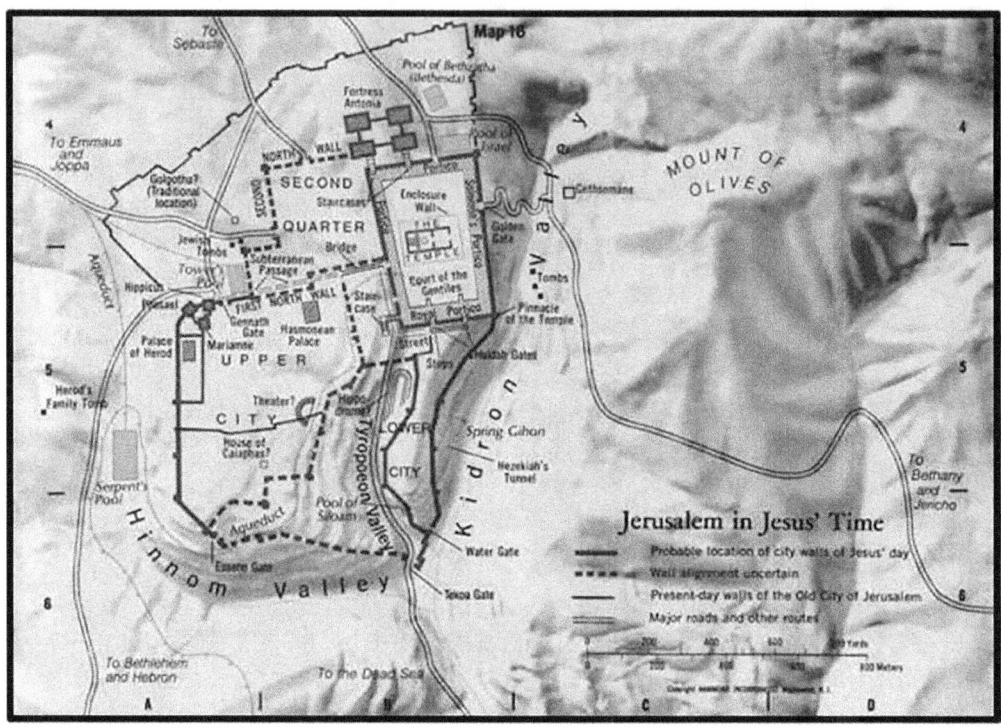

Figure 57.2. Topographical Map of Jerusalem at Time of Jesus with City of David to the South, within the crescent of the ridge south of the traditional Temple Mount; Mount of Olives is to the East

Figure 57.3 shows ancient Jerusalem and surrounding area in 64 BC, and clearly shows the old City of David down (south) from the *traditional* Temple Mount location. The Mount of Olives is to the east of the Kidron Valley. The graphic of Figure 57.3 has also been rotated 90 degrees and expanded to make it easier to read. For orientation, the labeled "Mount of Olives" is to the East.

NEW INSIGHTS – WHERE WAS HEROD'S TEMPLE?

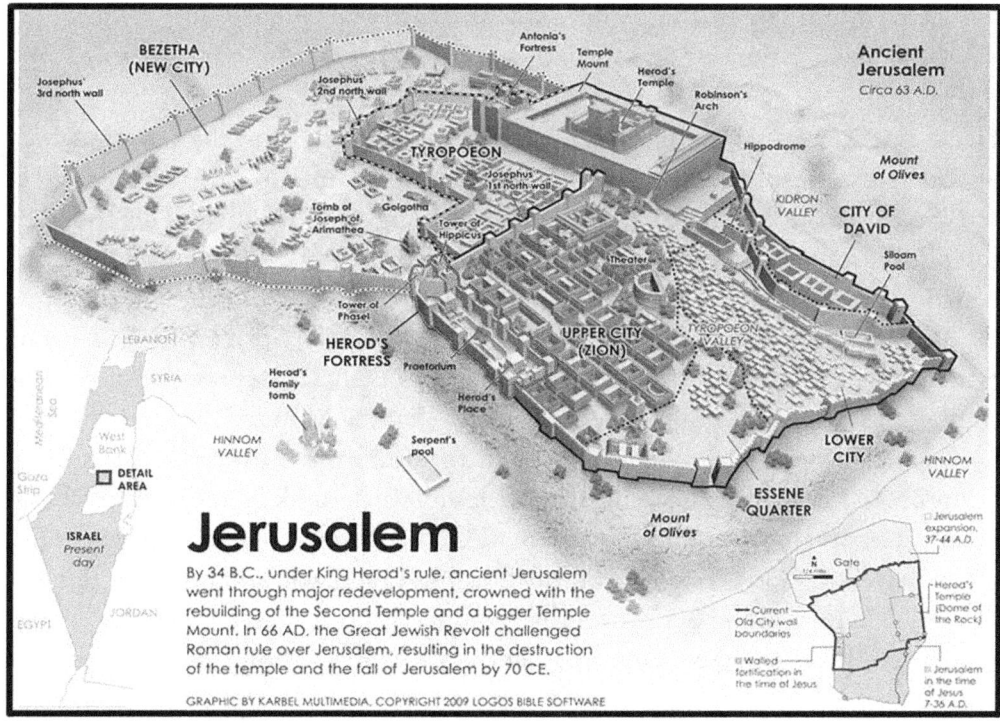

Figure 57.3. City of David, Traditional Temple Mount, Traditional Fort Antonia at NW corner

But what do we have that links the site of the first temple to the City of David, the original Jerusalem? We have an eye-witness report about the temple having been located on a crescent-shaped mountain in this early Jerusalem. The eye-witness is **Aristeas**, who wrote *"The Letter of Aristeas,"* penned more than 300 years before the time of Josephus, in the second century BC. This early author described Jerusalem of his time as being shaped like a theatre—*crescent-shaped,* and *on a [single] mountain*:

> The size of the city [of Jerusalem] is of moderate dimensions. It is about forty furlongs in circumference, as far as one could conjecture. *It has its towers arranged **in the shape of a theatre**."* [376]

> When we arrived in the land of the Jews we saw the city [Jerusalem] situated in the middle of the whole of Judaea *on the top of a mountain* [a single mountain] of considerable altitude. On the summit the Temple had been built in all its splendor. It [the Temple] was surrounded by three walls [a wall on the south, one on the west, and one on the north—the

325

eastern rampart of the Temple was the east wall of the City] ... The Temple faces the east and its back is toward the west.[377]

Hence, Aristeas is telling us that all of Jerusalem, including the temple which was in Jerusalem of that day, was on the crescent-shaped southeastern ridge of the "**Second Hill**" [a single mountain ridge having two summits] as described by Josephus. Note that this is not the location of the *traditional* "Temple Mount," which is located on the "**Third Hill**," located further to the north.

What about the temple being located over the Gihon Spring? There is strong evidence that this is the case, and, if so, this absolutely locates the temples in the southern location and not on the *traditional* "Temple Mount."

Indeed, what other evidence is there to locate the temples over a spring? Scripture has numerous references to the temple at Jerusalem and its furnishings being a physical representation on earth of God's official residence in heaven; this was reflected in God's residence on earth in the Tabernacle and the later Temples of God. We read in the Scriptures that God has "spring waters" in His heavenly residence. This is reflected, among other places, in Revelation:

> And I John saw the holy city new Jerusalem, coming down from God out of heaven, prepared as a bride adorned for her husband ... I will give to him that is *athirst* of the *fountain* [*spring*] of the *water of life* freely ... And he showed me ***a pure river of water of life*, clear as crystal, *proceeding out of the throne of God*** and the [throne of the] Lamb ... And let him that is athirst come. And whosoever will, let him take the *water of Life* freely.[378]

As Martin states, "The symbolism on earth of the heavenly House of God would not be complete without *spring waters* being within the earthly temple. It was believed by the early kings and prophets of Israel that if God's House had no *spring within it,* it would not be supplied with an appropriate water supply to perform the rituals of purification, and provide other life-giving therapeutic features that issue from the throne of God."[379]

The description of God's House in heaven as well as its counterpart on earth shows that the Sanctuary has (or must have) *spring waters* emerging from within its interior. Related to the temple in Jerusalem, the **Psalmist** indicates there were springs within Zion:

> His [God's] foundation is in the holy mountains. The Lord loveth the gates of Zion more than all the dwellings of Jacob. Glorious things are spoken of thee, O city of God. Selah ... The singers as the players on

instruments shall be there [in the Temple]: **ALL MY *SPRINGS* ARE IN THEE** [Zion]. (Psalm 87:1–3, 7)

With the temples located over the Gihon Spring, this would provide a spring within each of the temples. The Gihon Spring is the only spring within a five-mile radius of Jerusalem, including none on the present so-called "Temple Mount."

Before the temples, there was the Tabernacle constructed by Moses per God's plans (Exodus 25:8–9). There is another significant example of water coming from the House of God related to the *Tabernacle* during the 40-year wilderness journey of the Israelites in the desert. Where did the whole massive group get their water during this desert trek? Paul gives us the answer in I Corinthians 10:4, where Paul tells us the water came from *"the spiritual rock that accompanied them, and that rock was Christ."* He associated the rock with *"the cloud,"* which was the Shekinah (the Glory of God) that accompanied them during the Exodus. It hovered over the Holy of Holies in the Tabernacle (Exodus 13:21–22).

Ezekiel gives us a picture of a great cloud and fire and a throne, made from a solid piece of sapphire stone. On it sat the Glory of the Lord who appeared like a man (pre-incarnate Jesus) suspended above the cherubim who carried the sapphire stone. (Ezekiel 1:26–28). This sapphire stone is the "rock" which Paul writes about, from which the water came during the Exodus. The stream of water went forth from the Tabernacle eastward to give the Israelites water to drink. This shows us how *spring waters* were connected to God's dwelling places, both the Tabernacle and the later temples.

You might wonder how sufficient water supply could come out from the Tabernacle, sufficient for perhaps two-million Israelites plus animals. I believe this happened in a similar fashion as described related to the future Temple of Ezekiel—starting as a trickle and becoming a mighty river (Ezekiel 47:1–5), coming forth from the Holy Place and going out the right side of the Altar of Burnt Offering and into the Dead Sea to make those waters clean and fresh (Ezekiel 47:1–12). In other words, a miracle supplied the water daily for all the Israelites in the desert! In a similar way, God supplied the manna as daily food, which was also a miracle.

There is much evidence that the temples were located above the Gihon Spring. The evidence goes back to King David. Before David brought the Ark to the City of David, he built a Sacred Tent to house the Ark. Where was the location where King David positioned the Sacred Tent? We know from the account of Solomon that the Sacred Tent was placed on the terrace directly at and just above the Gihon Spring. When Solomon was crowned "King," Zadok the priest took a horn of oil out of the Sacred Tent wherein was the Ark and anointed Solomon.[380] From the example of Zadok, the Rabbis learned that Kings are only anointed by the site of a spring.[381] Martin explains the significance of this:

> So, the first "Temple" at Jerusalem erected by King David (before Solomon finally built the permanent Temple) was placed on the terrace directly at and just above the Gihon spring ... [and] all Israel resorted to this holy spot at the Gihon Spring to worship God and to offer sacrifices. And what was this place called? Look at **Second Samuel 12:20**. "Then David arose from the earth, and washed, and anointed himself, and came *into the House of the Lord*, and worshipped." David was in Jerusalem when this event occurred. It was at the Tent of the Ark of the Covenant. **Wherever the Ark was located was called the "House of the Lord" — another name for the Sanctuary** [Exodus 34:26; Deuteronomy 23:18; Joshua 6:24; 9:23; Judges 18:31]. David also called the place of the Ark "his [God's] habitation"—**it represented the "House of God"—the Temple** [II Samuel 15:25].[382]

From the case laid out by Martin, the Gihon Spring was within the area of the Sacred Tent of King David, as were the Temples of Solomon, Zerubbabel, and Herod; it was called the *"fountain of Israel."* What is the evidence for this? We have an eye-witness account!

A detailed eye-witness description of the temple is given by **Aristeas**, the Gentile from Egypt who visited Jerusalem over a hundred years before the time of Simon the Hasmonean (who ruled 142 BC to 135 BC). We have his actual written words of his descriptions of Jerusalem and the temple of his day. In his description of the temple, Aristeas tells us that in the interior of the temple there was an important geographical feature that serves as a topographical benchmark for the temple's location. He stated, "**There is an inexhaustible reservoir of water, as would be expected from an abundant spring gushing up naturally from within [the temple]. . .**"[383]

The description of the distinctive water source within the temple is verified by another eye-witness, the Roman historian **Tacitus**, in his description of the temple as it existed just before its destruction in 70 AD. He states, "**The temple ... contained an inexhaustible spring . . .**"[384]

Excuse me, but I feel compelled to ask a question. Where is the consideration of these multiple eye-witness historical accounts—that the temple had a spring associated with its location—in the theories of current historians and archeologists? The only spring in a five-mile radius is the Gihon Spring. The *traditional* "Temple Mount" had NO SUCH SPRING. This is strong evidence in my mind for the temple location to be at the Gihon Spring. It seems that **experts of today who support the *traditional* "Temple Mount" conveniently overlook these historical eye-witness accounts of a spring associated with the temple location.**

The temples had to have spring water available. An example is the mixing of the **ashes of the red heifer**, to be used for purification ceremonies. This required spring water—as stated in Numbers: *"And for an unclean person they shall take of the ashes of the burnt heifer of purification for sin and* **running water** [spring water] *shall be put thereto in a vessel"* (Numbers 19:17, KJV; clarification and emphasis added). This is further reason that the temples required a source of pure spring water, which the Gihon Spring supplied.

This spring is a most important feature in locating the area in the Jerusalem region where the temples were located. **When we *"follow the water,"* there is only one spring in all of Jerusalem, and that is the *Gihon Spring*.** This is exactly where Martin's case for the temple location is situated—*not* on the *traditional* "Temple Mount," which is a third of a mile to the north of the only spring in Jerusalem, the Gihon Spring.

CHAPTER 58

Puzzle Piece #4 –
Can Spring Push Water Up to Temple?

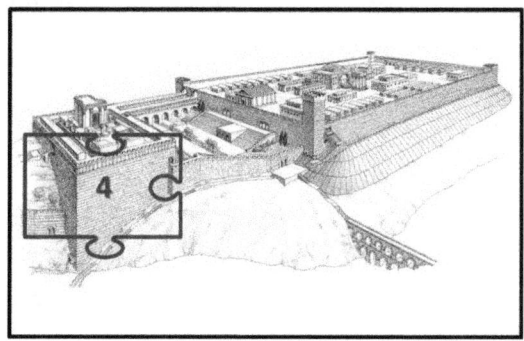

T he fact that the Gihon Spring could send water flowing all the way up to the level of the temples is *Puzzle Piece #4* for solving the mystery of the temple location.

King David originally conquered the Jebusites who then lived in what was later to become the City of David. The account given in 2 Samuel 5:8 is that David told his men to use the *"water shaft"* to conquer the fortress of the Jebusites. This "water shaft" led from the fortress of the Jebusites down to the Gihon Spring, the only water source in the whole area of Jerusalem. It, hence, provided a way to climb up to get into the Jebusite city, and David's men did just that.

This water shaft exists today and provides important archeological evidence of the location of the City of David. It is now called "Warren's Shaft" after the man who discovered it in the middle of the 19th century. Some archaeologists have dated the carving of the shaft to the 10th century BC, around the time of Solomon. However, if this is the water shaft which is referred to in 2 Samuel 5:8, then it would have been carved earlier by the Jebusites.

What is interesting about the Gihon Spring is that it is a *karst-type* of spring, also called a siphon-type of spring, thrusting out its water with great pressure as much as five times a day in the Springtime when water is plentiful. Hence, it is an intermittent spring, and in the dry season it may flow only a few minutes once a day.[385] The oscillating action of the Gihon may be why the ancients called this single water source with the plural "springs." Be that as it may, both **Aristeas** and **Tacitus** state that the temple at Jerusalem had an inexhaustible spring in its interior, and this must be the Gihon Spring.[386]

The oscillating nature of the Gihon Spring undoubtedly allowed David's men to climb up the water shaft when the water was not gushing forth. This was rather convenient for them in gaining entrance, surreptitiously, into the Jebusite city.

With the Gihon Spring blocked off and all its water channeled up through the "water shaft" mentioned in 2 Samuel, there was ample pressure to push the water up into the temple, as is described by Aristeas and Tacitus and others.

CHAPTER 59

Puzzle Piece #5–
Fort Antonia on "Temple Mount"?

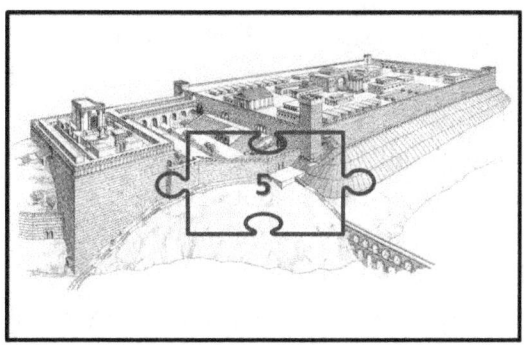

The case being made by Ernest Martin is for the temples being located over the Gihon Spring. This was located near the northern foot of the original Mount Zion (the *Akra*) and just below the *Ophel* summit, on the crescent-shaped original city of Jerusalem. Much evidence of this has been presented.

Accordingly, the fact that the *traditional* "Temple Mount," located a third of a mile north of the Gihon Spring, is not over a source of spring water is strong evidence that this is not the site of the temples. As reported in previous chapters, the eye-witness accounts of Aristeas and Tacitus state that there was spring water associated with the temples.

There is much other specific evidence against the *traditional* "Temple Mount" site being the location of the temples, which is covered in depth in Martin's book, *The Temples that Jerusalem Forgot*. Martin's case is that the *traditional* "Temple Mount," the *Haram esh-Sharif* (Muslim name), was the site of the Roman Fort Antonia in Herod the Great's day and following.

Overall, we will now look at the case that this Haram is *not* the site of the temples of Jerusalem. This constitutes *Puzzle Piece #5*.

Martin's case is that, next to the temple, Herod reconditioned and enlarged an existing fortress formerly called the *Baris*, originally built by the Hasmonean

John Hyrcanus in about 107 BC. Herod renamed it Fort Antonia after Mark Anthony. The presently-seen, massive retaining walls of the Harem were built by King Herod, using Herodian stones, which can be identified with their distinctive raised border design. It is estimated that there are between 8,000 to 10,000 Herodian and pre-Herodian stones still in place as they were 2,000 years ago. In the Western Wall, often called the "Wailing Wall," there are seven courses that are visible; in addition, eight courses of Herodian stones lie under the soil down to the ground level which existed in the time of Herod and Jesus; and an additional nine courses of foundation stones lie below that—a total of 24 courses of stone. This equates to an estimated 96 feet height of stones in the Western Wall.[387] That's a lot of stone walls still standing.

I have previously covered Jesus' prophecy related to *"... not one stone here will be left on another; every one will be thrown down"* (Matthew 24:2 NIV).

Certainly, that did not happen to the stones of the retaining walls of the *traditional* "Temple Mount," unlike every other wall of Jewish Jerusalem.

This is still a haunting question about why these walls were left standing after the Roman-Jewish War of AD 70. Admittedly, if these retaining walls of the Haram were part of a Roman fort structure, which had value to the Romans after the war, we can see why these walls were preserved by the Romans. Despite the attempted "work-arounds" of contemporary historians and archaeologists, this is still a haunting question in my mind.

Those enormous Roman military facilities of the Haram which resided within the massive retaining walls are well defined in the eyewitness accounts of *Josephus* and other historical narratives. *Eye-witness* accounts are a gold-standard of investigative detective work. Let's look at some of those accounts.

First, a few words about a bias against **Josephus** by some scholars because Josephus' descriptions of buildings and sites do not seem compatible with present-day preconceived notions. For example, Josephus' descriptions of the temple and the site of the temple do not align with the Haram esh-Sharif being the site of Herod's Temple. This is, understandably, the case if Josephus is giving dimensions of a *different* building with very *different* measurements. This has led many scholars to discount the descriptions of Josephus. However, maybe it is not Josephus who is wrong but the scholars with their incorrect presumptions in trying to force his measurements on the Haram esh-Sharif.

Professor Benjamin Mazar (1906–1995), often described as the "dean" of biblical archaeologists, aptly showed in his many writings that his appreciation of the accounts of Josephus grew in admiration over the years. Dr. Mazar was a witness to the validity of Josephus' descriptions in several archaeological areas when many modern scholars thought that Josephus had it wrong.[388]

NEW INSIGHTS – WHERE WAS HEROD'S TEMPLE?

While the Haran retained its four retaining walls, **Josephus** was clear on telling his readers that all the walls around Jerusalem were leveled to the ground: "Now, the Romans set fire to the extreme parts of the city [the suburbs] and burnt them down, and **entirely demolished its [Jerusalem's] walls**."[389] We can conclude that the walls surrounding the Haram were not city walls but walls which protected something else, and a Roman fortress would be something else, being not a part of *Jewish* Jerusalem.

Martin presents the following case scenario to explain the preservation of the walls of the Haram:

> With its walls left intact the Haram made a perfect complex of buildings, protected by four substantial walls, to be the **Camp of the Romans** for the Tenth Legion. When Titus viewed the Haram esh-Sharif (Fort Antonia) and saw its walls relatively unscathed (especially its eastern, southern and western walls) and with its 37 cisterns and special aqueduct supplying it with water, he decided to retain that strategic area (with its military advantages) as his Camp for the /tenth Legion. It had been the Roman Camp before the war, and Titus decided to keep it as the Roman Camp after the war. What the Romans did was to permit this former Camp to remain as the principal fort to quarter the Tenth Legion for the security of the Empire. **This is why the Haram esh-Sharif was left by Titus to dwell upon the ruins of Jerusalem**.[390]

> But what happened to the Temple and its walls? Just as Jesus prophesied, there was not one stone left on another of the Temple buildings or walls. And as **Eleazar** observed, even the very foundational stones of the Temple and it walls had been completely "dug up" and the site was left in thorough ruins. In a word, **nothing was left of the Temple once located just to the south and above the Gihon Spring. All that remained of Jerusalem was the Camp of the Romans** (Fort Antonia), the Haram esh-Sharif.[391]

What other evidence is there to support the Fort Antonia being on the Haram? The necessary size of the fort to house and provide for the number of Roman soldiers is a strong point of evidence.

What can we say about the largeness of Fort Antonia? First, it must be realized that the size was much larger than most people imagine today. Because scholars have mistakenly identified the large area of the Haram as the site of the temple, they had to invent a new location for the Fort and greatly diminish its size for the camp to fit into Jerusalem.

MYSTERIES OF JESUS' LIFE REVEALED

Scholars positioned Fort Antonia just outside the *northwest corner* of the Haram and greatly diminished the size from the dimensions reported by Josephus. The usual *traditional* placement of Fort Antonia is over or around a rock pavement found in that area. That pavement area was indeed a Roman camp, but archaeological investigation has shown this to be a camp which flourished in the time of Hadrian, not during the earlier period of King Herod and Pilate.[392] So, that location which is shown on virtually all maps and models of Jerusalem depicting the time of Herod and Jesus does not "work," and that concept should be discarded.

Figure 59.1 shows the incorrect *traditional site* of Fort Antonia as an appendage to the NW corner of the traditional Temple Mount. Note that the graphic is rotated 90 degrees clockwise, and North is shown to the right.

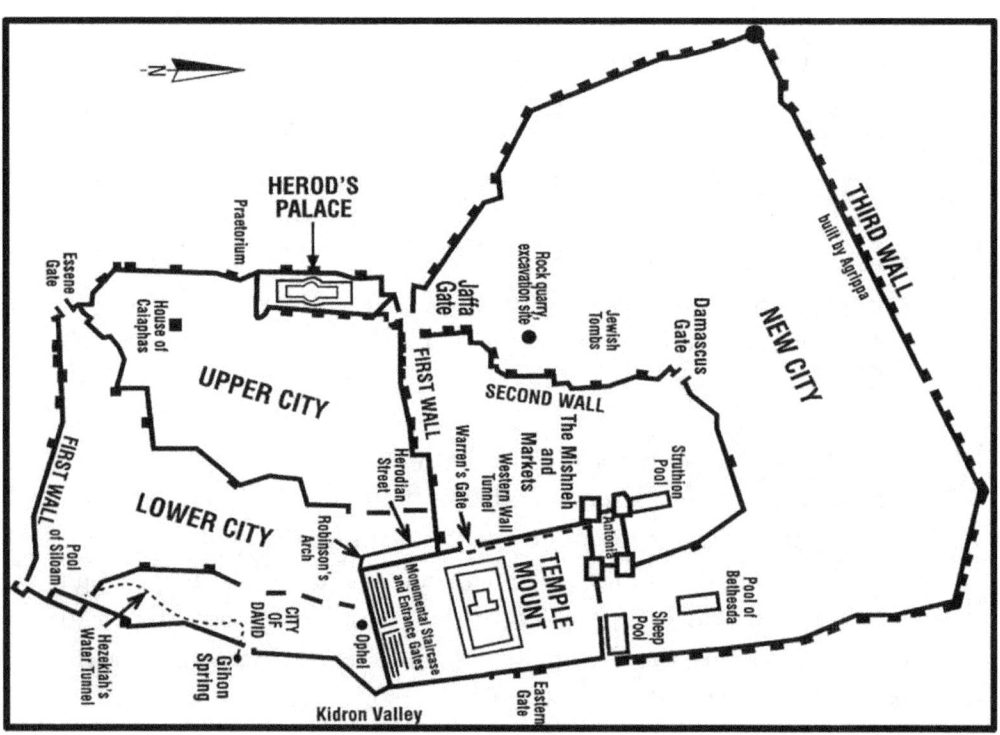

Figure 59.1.[393] *Traditional* Depiction of Jerusalem During Second Temple Period; note *traditional* location of Fort Antonia at NW corner of *traditional* Temple Mount

So, how large was Fort Antonia? **Josephus'** eye-witness account is that there were spacious grounds inside the fort and that it was *like a city in size*.[394] It housed a legion of troops, which means at least 5,000 men, and about 5,000 support personnel who serviced the legion.

336

A fort to hold 10,000 military personal takes a massive area, and, as a matter of fact, exactly the size of the Haram! The Roman fortresses scattered throughout the empire typically followed the general design of the fortress in Rome. What is seen there? The Praetorian Camp in the northeastern part of Rome was a square of two *stadia* on each side (1,200 feet by 1,200 feet).[395] The Haran, although not a square but a trapezoid, was similar in size—with the Haram being about 15 percent larger than the main military camp in Rome. The Haram is large, a total of 36 acres.[396]

What else did **Josephus** state about the massive size of Fort Antonia? He stated that the fortress was so prominent that "Antonia dominated the Temple."[397] It was large enough to guard the city of Jerusalem, the temple, and the fortress at King Herod's former palace, which later became the personal residence of General Titus. Josephus' description is that Fort Antonia was so large it obstructed the view of the temple from those approaching Jerusalem from the north.[398] This is the case if Fort Antonia took up the whole area of the Haram, but would not be the case with the presently popular theory that the Fort was confined to a small appendage to the northwest corner of the Haram—in no way could the Fort in that location obstruct the view of the temple from those approaching Jerusalem from the north.

It should be noted that these eye-witness observations of **Josephus** scream out to us that the popular opinions of Herod's Temple being on the Haram and that Fort Antonia was confined to a minor structure at the northwestern corner of the Haram are blatantly false. That was never true.

Although present day scholars and archeologists attempt to make the case that the ancient *temples* were located at the site of the Haram, it just does not correlate with historical eye-witness accounts. This is a major problem in my opinion. It makes sense that Josephus reported accurately; he reported directly to General Titus in Jerusalem during the Roman-Jewish War, and his reports would not have been blatantly inaccurate—as Titus was right there and would have not accepted inaccurate descriptions. Josephus valued his head too much to have reported inaccurately. The conclusion according to the eye-witness accounts is that Herod's Temple was not located on the *traditional* "Temple Mount" but Fort Antonia was.

Another question might be asked. If one does not locate the massive Antonia Fort at the Haram, then where in Jerusalem—that is adjacent to the true location of the temple—would one place it? There is no good other answer to this. The size and lack of another logical location in Jerusalem adjacent to the true site of the temple (assume for now at the Gihon Spring) argues strongly for Fort Antonia being on the Haram, north of the Gihon Spring.

As such, I believe that General Titus was very pleased with the size, location, and security provided by his fort on the Haram; King Herod had designed it well. This is my opinion after looking at all the evidence, including the eye-witness testimony of Josephus.

CHAPTER 60

Puzzle Piece #6–
What About the Rock on "Temple Mount"?

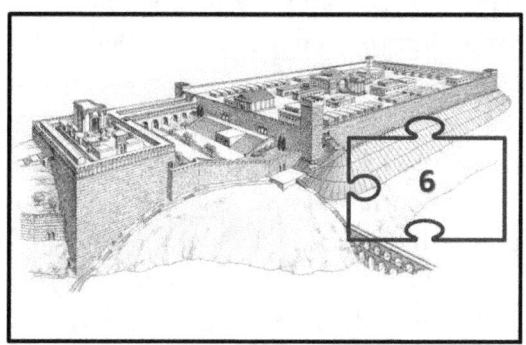

Much more evidence for the *traditional* "Temple Mount" being Fort Antonia and not the true temple location can be presented, and all this is carefully laid out in Ernest Martin's book, *The Temples That Jerusalem Forgot* (2000).

Among the problems, there is a big problem with the huge rock being on the *traditional* "Temple Mount." Josephus stated there was *a huge rock* associated with *the location of Fort Antonia*, but he made no mention about a rock being on the Temple Mount. This is *Puzzle Piece #6*.

Once again, we can look to the eye-witness accounts of ***Josephus*** in the first century. He was intimately aware of the locations and descriptions of Fort Antonia as well as the Herod's Temple. Another eye-witness is the ***Bordeaux Pilgrim***, known in historical literature as one who traveled from Bordeaux in what later became France to Jerusalem during the fourth century AD. He recorded his journey in his *Itinerarium Burdigalense*, written in Latin, and in it the *Pilgrim* wrote of his visit to Jerusalem in AD 333. He is the only ancient eyewitness from AD 70 to AD 370 who referred to the walls of the Harem esh-Sharif as then existing in Jerusalem.[399]

So, what did these two eye-witnesses say related to the temple and Fort Antonia? They had much to say, but, unfortunately, these descriptions have been forgotten or overlooked by historians and archeologists.

First, let's look at the description given by **Josephus** related to the location of Fort Antonia. He spoke of a ***prominent rock*** associated with the location of the Roman fort; this is additional evidence for the location of Fort Antonia.

What about this massive rock? The most prominent geographical feature associated with Fort Antonia was the rock around which the Fort was built. Josephus mentioned it as *dominating* other geographical features of the area. Josephus used the Greek word *huper* in giving the location of Fort Antonia. Rather than meaning "on top of" the rock itself, which is the Greek word *epi*, the word *huper* used by Josephus indicates the fortress was built *over and around* a rock.

Josephus said: "**The tower of Antonia ... was built upon [around] a rock fifty cubits high [75 feet] and on all sides precipitous ... the rock was covered from its base upwards with smooth flagstones**"[400] Before the construction of Fort Antonia, we learn from Josephus' description that the rock was originally 75 feet high. Herod built the present four massive retaining walls and filled in the region, covering most of the massive rock and then placed smooth flagstones on top of the fill; this created the present surface of the *Haram esh-Sharif* which is seen today.

Much later, in the fourth century, Helena, the mother of Constantine, ordered that a small Christian Church called "St. Cyrus and St. John" be built over that "Rock." This church was enlarged, probably in the fifth century, becoming a major church, "The Church of the Holy Wisdom." What is particularly significant about the location of this church and the location on the Haram is a comment made by the ***Piacenza Pilgrim*** in a sixth-century work:

> We also prayed at **the *Praetorium*, where the Lord's case was heard: what is there now is the basilica of Saint Sophia [the Holy Wisdom Church], which is in front [north] of the Temple of Solomon [located] below the street [east and downslope] which runs down to the spring of Siloam outside of Solomon's porch [the eastern wall of Solomon's Temple]. In this basilica is the seat where Pilate sat to hear the Lord's case**, and there is also the ***oblong stone*** [I emphasize this to identify the spot] which used to be in the center of the ***Praetorium*** [the *Praetorium* tent was movable]. The accused person whose case was being heard was made to mount *this stone* so that everyone could hear and see him. The Lord mounted it when he was heard by Pilate, and *his footprints* [italicized for emphasis] are still on it. He had a well-shaped foot, small and delicate."[401]

As *Josephus* stated, the "Rock" was the most prominent part of Fort Antonia; this is also the *Praetorium* area, which ***Piacenza Pilgrim*** connects to the "oblong stone," being the central feature of the "Church of the Holy Wisdom." That church was destroyed by the Persians and Jewish soldiers in AD 614. That "Rock" [oblong stone] is now under the Dome of the Rock on the Haram esh-Sharif, the former location of Fort Antonia.[402]

Now, we can get back to the statement by the **Bordeaux Pilgrim** about the location of Fort Antonia, per his visit to Jerusalem in AD 333. He was the first to give a systematic view of the Jerusalem of his time, although it was not an extensive report. Yet, the *Bordeaux Pilgrim's* account is important in recognizing the location of Fort Antonia and the temple which existed prior to his time. From the location of the unfinished Church of the Holy Sepulchre, the *Bordeaux Pilgrim* viewed a "walled facility" with its foundations within the Tyropean Valley; he identified that "walled facility" as the *Praetorium* and further described it as the former residence of Pilate in the time of Jesus' trial. As Martin comments:

> So, the walled area east of the Holy Sepulchre [Church of the Holy Sepulchre] was an edifice that had remained in existence from the time of Pilate and Jesus. In other words, this structure survived the Roman/Jewish War of 66–70 C.E.
>
> Since we are assured from earlier eyewitness records that *nothing* of 'Jewish Jerusalem' or the Holy Temple (either their inner or outer walls) survived the war, **the only candidate that remains to tally with the description of the Bordeaux Pilgrim is the former Fort Antonia—which in the time of Pilate and Jesus had the same technical name *Praetorium* connected to it**.
>
> This shows that the Bordeaux Pilgrim was looking at the broad view of the western side of the *Praetorium* with its walls (the southern and western walls making the *southwestern* angle) that we called today the Haram esh-Sharif. It must be emphasized that the Pilgrim observed the *Praetorium's* walls (plural) with their foundations that reached downward to the lower areas of the Tyropoeon Valley. His description can only refer to the southwest corner of the Haram ramparts at the junction of the southern and western walls near what we call 'Robinson's Arch' being directly in front of him.[403]

The *Bordeaux Pilgrim* in the early fourth century AD was aware that the walls of the Haram were those of the *Praetorium—Fort Antonia*, the former Camp in Jerusalem of the Romans.

In conclusion, the massive rock located on the Haram, which was covered up with fill material and smooth pavement stones by Herod the Great, plays a prominent role in the historical descriptions of *Fort Antonia*—not related to the description of Herod's Temple in any way. That massive rock is presently located under the Dome of the Rock on the Haram, the location of Fort Antonia. This supports the location of the temple being to the south, in the City of David, according to the evidence given by Ernest Martin.

CHAPTER 61

Puzzle Piece #7–Martin's Graphic

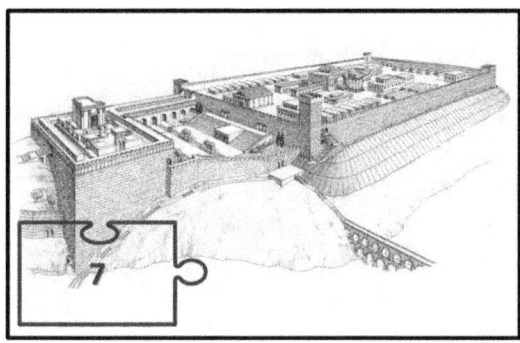

What would Herod's Temple and Fort Antonia look like if we followed the eye-witness descriptions of *Flavius Josephus,* who lived in Jerusalem during the first century AD? This is a surprisingly a novel question asked by Ernest L. Martin.

When we do follow the eyewitness descriptions of Josephus, we get an entirely different picture than what is presented in the maps and models shown in Jerusalem today. Why is that? We will go into the reasons for this variance later in this chapter.

As is well known, Josephus, the Jewish priest/historian, recorded his observations and commentary on Jerusalem and the Jewish/Roman war of AD 70, and he dedicated his works to the Roman **General Titus** and to **Harold Agrippa II**. Indeed, both Titus and Agrippa II were eyewitnesses also, and Josephus would not have given inaccurate descriptions of Jerusalem. He valued his neck too much to do that. Hence, I think it serves us well to pay heed to the descriptions given by Josephus.

Figure 61.1 shows Martin's graphic of Herod's Temple attached to the massive Fort Antonia, according to the *eye-witness* descriptions of Josephus. The graphic is rotated 90 degrees and enlarged to make the graphic and text more readable. For Martin to construct this graphic, which I am using at the start of each chapter of this Part III, he commissioned a professional artist. Working with Dr. Martin, the artist incorporated all sections of Josephus' literary works in which he describes Herod's Temple and Fort Antonia, including what Josephus said about their positions and precise measurements. In the words of Martin, "[This drawing] is simply a replica of the Temple and Fort Antonia complex as precisely described by Josephus."[404]

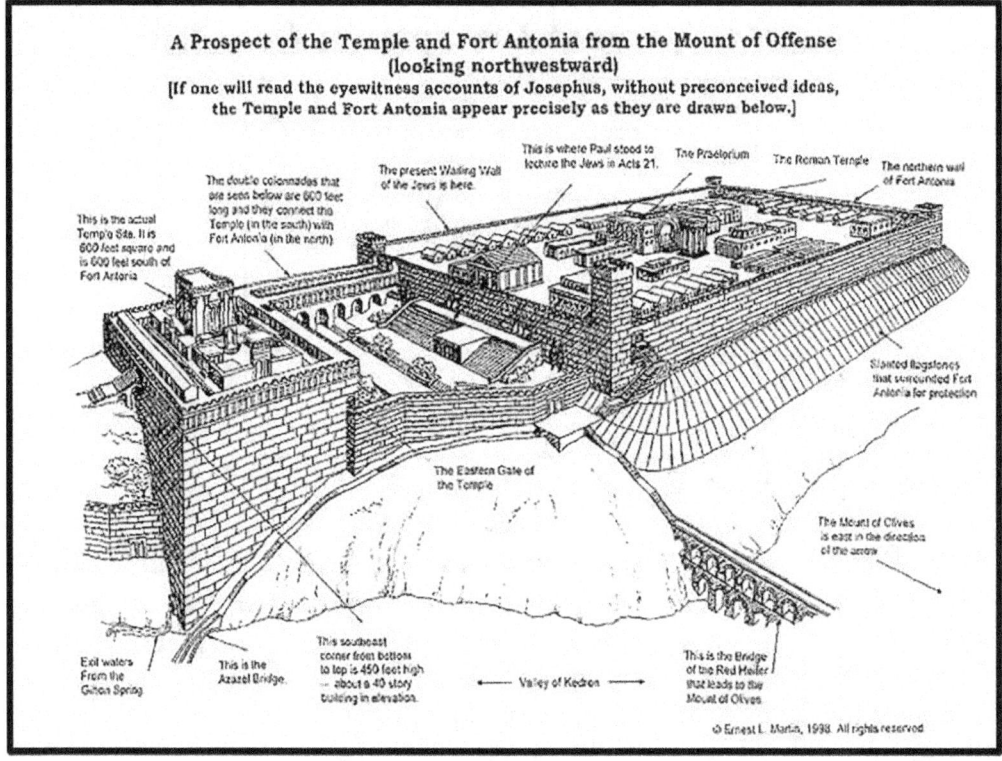

Figure 61.1. Ernest L. Martin's Diagram of Herod's Temple & Fort Antonia, looking from south-east from temple. [From internet search "Temple and Fort Antonia graphics;" credit to Ernest L. Martin]

This Temple Mount and Fort Antonia, described by Josephus, have a separation of a *Roman stade* (600 feet) with two parallel, connecting, 600-foot-length colonnade roadways extending from the temple to Fort Antonia.[405] These two connecting colonnades extended from the northwestern corner of the true Temple Mount to the southwestern corner of Fort Antonia.

NEW INSIGHTS – WHERE WAS HEROD'S TEMPLE?

A. Present Traditional Location of Fort Antonia

It should be noted that these eye-witness accounts of Josephus and others absolutely destroy the notion that Fort Antonia was a relatively small appendage to the presently so-called "Temple Mount" at the north-west corner of the "Temple Mount," which is the way it is depicted on present-day diagrams and models of Jerusalem. This is shown in Figure 61.2.

Figure 61.2. Model of Herod's Temple, on *traditional* "Temple Mount," and Fort Antonia in upper right (NW) corner[406]

It should be realized that in no way does the *design* of the buildings shown in Figure 61.2 incorporate the clear descriptions of Josephus. For example, there are no 600-foot-length roadway appendages connecting the temple to Fort Antonia, as Josephus so clearly indicated. In this diagram, Fort Antonia is shown in the upper right corner (north-west corner) of the *traditional* "Temple Mount." There are numerous problems with this location. As has been covered in Chapter 59, this depiction of Fort Antonia is way too small to accommodate a legion of Roman soldiers. In addition, it does not match the eye-witness accounts related to the Roman fort and the temple.

B. Josephus' Descriptions of Temple

Josephus supplied eye-witness descriptions of the location and design of Herod's Temple, which are critical for a proper understanding of the temple's location and design. This information is fully covered in Part Four: "The Position and Description of Herod's Temple" (Chapters 31–34), of Martin's book, *The Temples That Jerusalem Forgot* (2000).[407] Interested readers should consult his book for complete coverage of this topic.

These eye-witness descriptions of Josephus are, unfortunately, overlooked and discounted by present-day tour-guides, commentators, biblical historians, and archeologists. Here are some of Josephus's descriptions of Herod's Temple and Fort Antonia as listed in Martin's book (with references back to original sources), which I have assembled in logical groupings. You can observe how these descriptions are depicted in Martin's graphic of the Herod's Temple and Fort Antonia.

- The distance between the southern wall of Fort Antonia and the northern wall of the temple was one *stade* (600 feet). (*War* VI.2,6; Martin, p. 413; emphasis added).

- There were two parallel, connecting, **600-foot-length colonnade roadways extending from the temple to Fort Antonia**. (*War* VI.2,6; Martin, p. 413, 468; emphasis added).

  - The entrance to Fort Antonia from the temple was from the northwest corner of the outer walls that formed a square around the temple. Josephus stated, "Now as to the Tower of Antonia, it was situated at the corner of two cloisters [colonnades] of the court of the Temple, of that on the west, and that on the north." (*War* V.5,8; Martin, p. 428).

  - The two connecting colonnades (military roadways) are integral part of the temple. They were likened to two "limbs attached to a body." (*War* VI.2,9; Martin, p. 415).

  - He stated that the temple was likened to a "body" and the side-by-side colonnades represented the two "limbs," like two straight outstretched "arms" attached to a human body. They were reckoned part of the temple itself. (*War* VI.2,9; Martin, p. 425).

  - Related to the roofs of the two connecting colonnades, Josephus said, "The usual crowd had assembled at Jerusalem for the Feast of Unleavened Bread, and the Roman cohort [i.e., 2000 troops] had taken up its position on the roof of the portico [colonnade] of the Temple; for a body of men in arms invariably mounts guard at the feasts, to prevent disorders arising from such a concourse of people." (*War* II.12,1 Loeb translation; Martin, p. 414).

- In Josephus' description of the battle scene witnessed by Titus in the war of AD 70, the whole battle scene shows there was the **space of 600 feet between Fort Antonia and the Temple**; it was a "narrow space" in an east/west direction within which the Romans and Jews were fighting with one another [**this fits the description of the colonnades**]. (*War* VI.1,7–8 and VI.2,6; Martin, p. 417; emphasis added).

- The **temple was located on an elevated platform with four walls surrounding it that formed a perfect square**. Each of the four temple walls was exactly a *stade* (600 feet) in length. (*War* V. V.5,2 with VI.5,4; and *Antiquities* XV.9.3; Martin, p. 412; emphasis added).

  - He said, "The whole enclosure [of the Temple], having a circumference of four *stades,* each side taking up the length of a *stade* [600 feet]." (*Antiquities* ZV.9,3 Loeb translation; Martin, pp. 425–426; emphasis added.)

  - Speaking of the four colonnades around the periphery of the true Temple Mount, Josephus said: "The colonnades were thirty cubits broad [45 feet wide], and the complete circuit of them, embracing [the colonnades to] the Tower of Antonia, measured *six stades*." (*War* V.5,2; Martin, p. 426). Note that Josephus in reaching the dimensions of *six stades* includes the two colonnades of one *stade* in length each (two *stades* in all) that extended up to Fort Antonia. He added these two *stades* to the four *stades* of the colonnades surrounding the square-form true Temple Mount. The flat roofs on the top of the colonnades were the "roadways." (Martin, p. 426–427).

- **Fort Antonia** was so vast it actually dominated the temple on its northern flank in all aspects. (*War* V.5,8. Loeb translation; Martin, p. 411.)

  - He said that the whole of the temple precincts could be observed by anyone who was standing on top of the **SE tower of Fort Antonia**. (*War* VI.2,6; Martin, p. 416; emphasis added).

- Josephus tells us in his description of the temple and its walls that most of the eastern wall of the temple (existing in the time of Herod and Jesus) was constructed by Solomon. (*War* V,5,1; Martin, p. 465) He also stated that **the eastern wall was constructed of gigantic stones which were "bound together with lead."** (*Antiquities* XV.11,3; Martin, pp. 465–466; emphasis added).

- He stated, "The Temple [original Temple of Solomon] was seated on a **strong hill, the level area on its summit originally barely sufficed for shrine** [the Holy of Holies and the Holy Place] and the altar [the Altar of Burnt Offering], the ground around it being precipitous and steep." (*War* V.5,1; Martin, p. 435; emphasis added).

  - Josephus stated related to the height of this "**strong hill**" on which Solomon built his Temple, his palace, and government buildings, that Solomon built an **east wall that reached upward from the very base of the hill (that is, from the bottom of the Kedron Valley)** for 300 cubits (**450 feet**). (*War* V.5,1; Martin, pp. 436–437; emphasis added.). [This eastern wall was completely back-filled in, called the "Millo," and most of the eastern part of the Temple was built over this filled-in area.]

  - Josephus in his account of the Roman General Pompey in his attack against the Temple in 63 BC (this was before Herod and his rebuilding activities) confirms that Solomon placed the foundation of the east wall in the floor of the Kedron Valley. Josephus wrote, "He [Pompey] saw the walls [of the Temple] were so firm, that it would be hard to overcome them. **The valley before the walls was terrible [for depth]; and that *the temple, which was within that valley,* was itself encompassed with a very strong wall** …" (*War* I.7,1; Martin, p. 439; emphasis added).

  - After Solomon, the Israelites built the north, west, and south walls. The **final temple platform of Herod was shaped like a square block, 600 feet by 600 feet in size**; Josephus said Herod doubled the size of the Temple from what existed before. (*War* I.21,1; Martin, p. 444; emphasis added.) [The whole structure was the height of a modern skyscraper, some 40 to 45 stories above the extreme depths of the Kidron Valley on the east.] Josephus said **the eastern wall of the temple "exceeds all descriptions in words … The wall was itself the most prodigious work that was ever heard of by man …** He [Solomon] also built *a wall below, beginning at the bottom ['at the foot' of the eastern hill, Loeb translation] which was encompassed by a deep valley [the Kedron].*" (*Antiquities* XV.11,3; Martin, pp. 439, 445; emphasis added).

Josephus' description of the precipitous eastern wall of the temple complex was wonderful almost beyond belief, **and the foundation of this eastern wall was placed in the Kidron Valley**. From Josephus' descriptions of the eastern wall of the temple being in the extreme bottom of the Kidron Valley—right in the very floor of the valley—is strong evidence that the *traditional* "Temple Mount" (the

Haram) is *NOT* the mount of the true location of the temple, as its eastern wall is located over half way up the west slope of the Kedron Valley. This is an important "marker" given by Josephus related to the temple and should not be overlooked.

The perfectly square temple platform was at the top of the steep walls surrounding it and was viewed as perched on a "tower" that reached upward 40 to 45 stories, much like a modern skyscraper occupying a square block in New York City today. This square-shaped "tower," per Josephus' descriptions, was located 600-feet south of the southern wall of Fort Antonia and was connected to the Fort by two parallel bridges, connecting the northwestern corner of the temple platform with the southwestern corner of Fort Antonia. This is as shown in Martin's graphic of the Herod's Temple and Fort Antonia.

Another key feature described by Josephus that distinguishes the true temple retaining walls from the Haram esh-Sharif is that the stones that made up the wall on the east side of the temple were "bound together with lead" and on the inside of the wall they had "iron clamps" that fused them together permanently in Josephus' reckoning. Note that the stones of the eastern wall of the Haram, which some attribute to Solomon because they think it is the Temple Mount, are stacked one on top of another and do not have any of these lead and iron features.[408] In the words of Martin, "This fact is, again, a clear indication the walls surrounding the Haram are NOT those that encompassed the Temple of Herod as described by Josephus, our eye-witness historian."[409]

One can easily see in reading over Josephus' listing of descriptions of Herod's Temple and Fort Antonia that they are *NOT* met in the model of the Temple and Fort Antonia being shown today in Jerusalem (see Figure 61.2), supposedly representing the conditions during the first century AD. For example, in the model, the Fort and the temple are not separated by 600 feet and there are no double-colonnaded roadways connecting the Fort and Herod's Temple. In summary, this is not what was observed by Josephus.

It should be noted that modern historians and archeologists have willfully chosen to ignore the clear eye-witness observations of Josephus related to Herod's Temple and Fort Antonia.

C. What Is Modern Opinion of Josephus' Descriptions?

Unfortunately, scholars today have a very low view of the accuracy of the descriptions of Josephus. It seems to me that the basic reason for this low view of Josephus is that they are so convinced that the temple was located on the *traditional* "Temple Mount" and that Fort Antonia occupied the relatively small space at the north-western corner of the *traditional* "Temple Mount." With these assumptions about the locations, the dimensions given by Josephus related to the temple do not line up with the present dimensions of the *traditional* "Temple Mount." These scholars are not willing to abandon their conclusions as to the location of the temple on the Haram, so they have chosen to disregard the eye-witness testimony of Josephus. That is the way I see it.

This lack of trust in Josephus' stated dimensions is evident with the eminent Israeli archeologist Leen Ritmeyer, former chief architect of the Temple Mount excavations and today director of Ritmeyer Archaeological Design in England. Ritmeyer had assisted Benjamin Mazar, the eminent director of the Temple Mount excavations before Mazar's death. Ritmeyer is also the author of *The Quest–Revealing the Temple Mount in Jerusalem* (2006).[410]

Ritmeyer writes the following:

"... It is not any easier to understand the Herodian Second Temple. The root of the problem lies in the fact that the two major historical sources we have at our disposal, namely the writings of **Josephus** and *massechet middot* (the tractate called **Middot** or 'measurements' of the Mishnah), **seem to contradict each other ... The subject becomes even more complicated if one tries to impose the conflicting measurements given in these works onto the Temple Mount as we know it today.**"[411]

Of course, the presupposed present ideas of the location of the temple and Fort Antonia do not match the descriptions given by Josephus and other eye-witnesses. Instead of unilaterally questioning the accuracy of the eye-witness descriptions of Josephus, it might be suggested that the presupposed location of the temple on the so-called "Temple Mount" might also be questioned. Of course, this is presently considered *heresy* to raise any such questions.

There seems to be an understandable reason for the "discrepancy" between measurement of the temple given by Josephus and in the *Middot* which Leen Ritmeyer points to in the quoted text above. *Josephus* gives the measurement of the walls of the Temple as 400 cubits on each side (600 feet), while the *Mishnah* (*Middoth 2:1*, Danby's translation) in its description of the "Temple Mount" gives the measurement of 500 cubits on each side (750 feet). Why this discrepancy of these two sources? Martin provides what seems to be a reasonable explanation for this. He states that the larger dimension of 500 cubits (750 feet) on each side " ... was the size of the 'Camp of the Levites,' being a legal definition which goes back to the Mosaic Law. This square area of the specific 'Camp of the Levites' (known also as the 'Temple Mount') had no walls surrounding it."[412] Therefore, there is no discrepancy between the measurements of Josephus and as stated in the *Mishnah* (Middoth 2:1), as these are referring to two different entities—specifically the physical temple and the "Camp of the Levites" per Mosaic law.

With the above insight, the *seeming* discrepancy is not a reason to throw out the testimony of Josephus. It appears to me that this understanding is key to this whole discussion of the true locations of the temple and Fort Antonia. The conclusion is that the case for Josephus being a reliable witness of what he observed as well as his specific descriptions is strengthened; his testimony cannot be so easily thrown out of worthy consideration.

So, by the testimony of Josephus, where would the temple and Fort Antonia be in relation to ancient Jerusalem and the Mount of Olives? Figure 61.3, which was also used in Chapter 46 as Figure 46.1, shows this relationship. [Both Figure 46.1 and Figure 61.3 have this map rotated 90 degrees (with North to the left of page) and expanded to enlarge the figure and text to make it more readable].

Note the temple extending out into the Kidron Valley. Some have criticized Ernest Martin for depicting this location of the temple in his drawing, but this is exactly as described by Josephus, as given previously—he said **the eastern wall of the temple "exceeds all descriptions in words … The wall was itself the most prodigious work that was ever heard of by man … He [Solomon] also built *a wall below, beginning at the bottom ['at the foot' of the eastern hill, Loeb translation] which was encompassed by a deep valley [the Kedron].*"** (*Antiquities* XV.11,3; Ernest Martin, *The Temples that Jerusalem Forgot,* pp. 439, 445; emphasis added).

As was presented in Chapter 46, this Figure 61.3 also presents the possible location of the crucifixion and burial sites of Jesus—if, indeed, this is the correct site of the temple! However, there is a problem with this depiction of the possible crucifixion site of Jesus. Jesus was crucified "outside of the Camp of Israel" (Hebrews 13:10–12) as has been described in Chapter 42: "Executions *Outside the Camp,*" with a distance along the ground of 2000 cubits from the threshold of the Holy of Holies in the temple. The problem with Figure 61.3 is that it shows a site which is less than the required 2000-cubit distance. See Figure 64.2 for a more accurate depiction of the crucifixion site, incorporating the 2000-cubit limit of the "Camp of Israel." That places the crucifixion site on the southern part of the Olivet Ridge and *not on the southern spur* of the Olivet Ridge. That seems to be a better depiction of the crucifixion site.

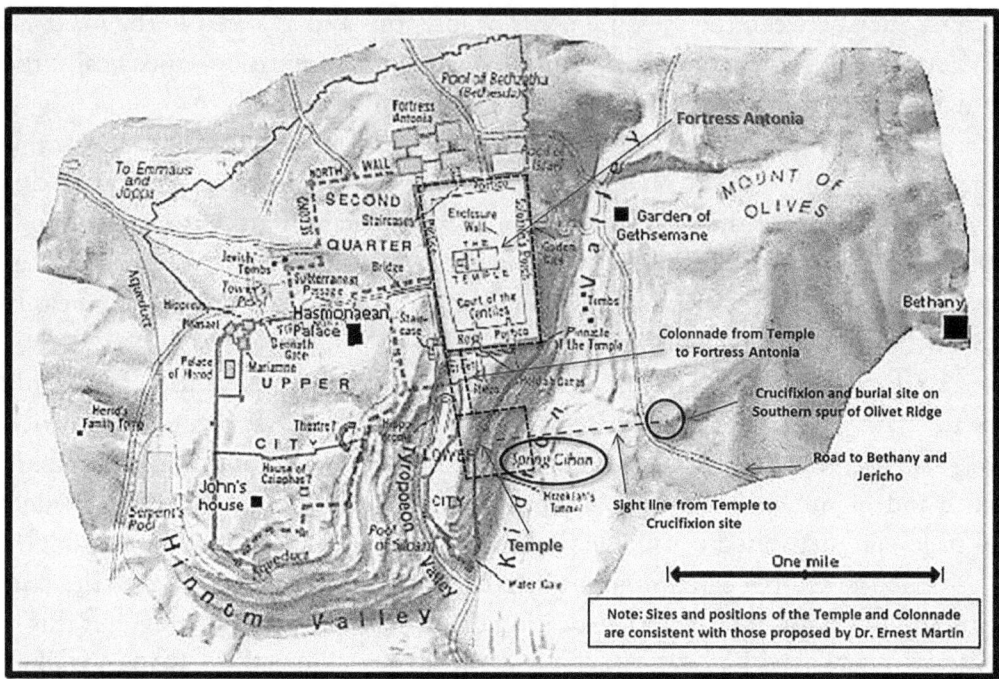

Figure 61.3. (Copyright; with enhancements) Ancient Jerusalem and Mount of Olives with Martin's location of the temple at Gihon Spring, located to the west of the Bethany Jericho Road crossing of the *southern spur* of the Olivet Ridge—possible location of crucifixion and burial of Jesus

See also Figure 61.4 (which is same as Figure 57.1), which shows a photograph with the location of the ancient City of David to the south of the traditional "Temple Mount" and surrounding areas. The photograph is from an article by George Wesley Buchanan [*Washington Report on Middle East Affairs*, August 2011, pp. 16, 64. (*http://www.washingtonreport.me/2011-august/misunderstandings-about-jerusalem-s-temple-mount.html*)]. Additional sites and descriptions have been added by the author to help the reader visualize all that has been described.

NEW INSIGHTS – WHERE WAS HEROD'S TEMPLE?

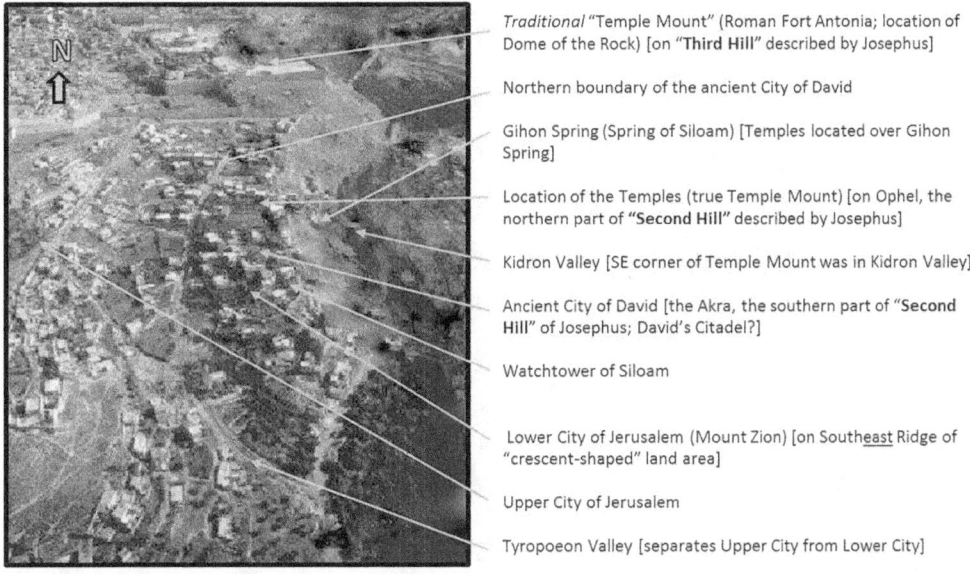

Figure 61.4. Photograph with ancient City of David located south of the *traditional* Temple Mount (Fort Antonia) with labels for locations of historical structures

D. Conclusion About Martin's Temple & Fort Locations

In conclusion, Josephus' descriptions favor the locations and designs of Herod's Temple and Fort Antonia as shown in Ernest Martin's graphic—which is based directly on Josephus' eye-witness descriptions. So, in my mind, the case for the temple being on the *traditional* "Temple Mount" is not "case closed." Josephus would agree.

Indeed, have modern scholars selected the wrong site for the former temples?

CHAPTER 62

Puzzle Piece #8–Critiques by Ritmeyer and Franz & Rebuttals by Martin and Sielaff

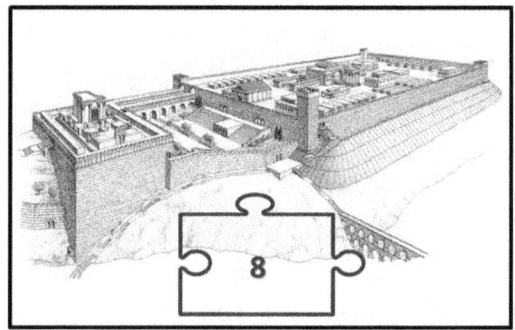

Dr. Ernest L. Martin and his case for the temples being over the Gihon Spring south of the *traditional* "Temple Mount" is certainly not without his vociferous critics. If surveyed, his critics would include virtually all the present-day historians, biblical commentators, Jewish religious leaders, and archaeologists.

Martin's critics would also include the usual group which parrots many of the *traditional* dates and sites related to the birth and death of Jesus in Jerusalem, which we have been considering in this book.

A. Ritmeyer's Critique and Martin's Rebuttal

One noteworthy critic of Martin's proposed location of the Temple and Fort Antonia is **Dr. Leen Ritmeyer**, whose impressive credentials as an archeologist in Jerusalem were presented in the previous chapter. Dr. Ernest Martin has stated about Dr. Ritmeyer, "He could rightfully be called one of the top representatives of the traditional school of Temple experts that place the Temple within the confines of the Haram esh-Sharif (that all scholars have accepted as true, and this also includes me until I started to look extensively into the subject in 1995)."

Dr. Martin goes on to opine, "It can properly be stated that Dr. Ritmeyer could legitimately be considered a proper and qualified spokesman for all the *traditionalists* throughout the world who insist that the Temples were located within the precincts of the Haram esh-Sharif. As for me and my research, I am the lone *anti-traditionalist* who has brought forth the research to prove dogmatically that the world is thoroughly and totally *wrong*."[413]

We have available to us on Dr. Martin's website (Associates for Scriptural Knowledge: *www.askelm.com*) a very interesting and helpful critique of Dr. Martin's book (*The Temples That Jerusalem Forgot*) by Dr. Leen Ritmeyer, with an accompanying rebuttal by Dr. Martin. This highly colorful exchange is available at *http://www.askelm.com/temple/t010513.htm*, and it provides a "point and counter-point" of many of the elements of Dr. Martin's case. In his rebuttal, Dr. Martin first gives a section of Dr. Ritmeyer's critique (shown in italics) and then Martin comments on that portion.

Dr. Leen Ritmeyer starts out by writing the following:

> *"In the last few issues of Biblical Archaeology Review (BAR) an advertisement appeared under the heading "Who moved the Temple" advertising a book called "**The Temples that Jerusalem Forgot**" by a certain Ernest Martin. Part of the advertisement is **a strange drawing**, which shows the Temple outside the Temple Mount. Many people have asked me to comment on this and below you will find my critique of **this outrageous idea**."*[414]

Dr. Martin responded with the following colorful rebuttal:

> "Leen Ritmeyer in his beginning statement says that my descriptive picture of the Temple and Fort Antonia complex which has appeared in *BAR* for the past two years is '**a strange drawing**' based on an '**outrageous idea**.' This response is because of Ritmeyer's ignorance or disbelief at what Josephus (the first century Jewish historian) describes about the Temple and Fort Antonia in his writings recorded in his *Antiquities* and *Wars*. **Josephus** as an eyewitness in 70 A.D. gave an adequate description of how those buildings appeared on the eve of Jerusalem's destruction by the Romans. **All I did was to depict in a drawing what Josephus said about the positions and dimensions of the Temple and Fort Antonia.** This drawing that provokes Ritmeyer's ire is simply a replica of the Temple and Fort Antonia complex as precisely described by Josephus … Josephus made some cogent and profound observations that scholars today avoid believing and they normally consider Josephus as an unreliable observer

and recorder. This is because what Josephus describes as the Temple and Fort Antonia does NOT fit any part (or in any way) the Haram esh-Sharif that scholars believe today to be the remains of the Temple. The truth is, **Josephus as an eyewitness was describing the Temple in a very different manner than that found in the Haram esh-Sharif that Ritmeyer and other scholars accept today ...** Consequently, it is NOT my drawing in *BAR* that is 'strange' and 'outrageous' as Ritmeyer states, but it would be Ritmeyer's Temple (using Josephus' eyewitness measurements) being located inside the Haram esh-Sharif that would be totally outrageous ..."[415]

The 16-page critique and rebuttal document provides a good summary of the main points of Dr. Martin's case in an entertaining "take-off-the-gloves" exchange between the two. I recommend it highly.

Regarding locating the Temple on the *traditional* "Temple Mount," Dr. Ritmeyer claims the high ground of having convincing archeological evidence, but Dr. Martin contests that, stating the following observations:

"There is not one bit of identifiable archaeological evidence that suggests the Haram esh-Sharif is the Temple Mount. Oh yes, there is **a piece of stone that was discovered near the southwest corner of the Haram that says an elevated spot (apparently above its *in situ* position) was the place for 'blowing the trumpet.'** To say this refers to the blowing of the Shofar for Temple rituals is pure guessing. In fact, the stone site could equally refer to the place for blowing bugles for denoting time periods and military commands associated with Fort Antonia ... Listen folks, let us be honest about this matter. **There is NOT ONE archaeological item found in or around Jerusalem that denotes without doubt that the Haram is indeed the site of the former Temples**. Pure speculation is reigning supreme in this matter. For any archaeologist to say differently is stepping far out of line. It is time that this subjective reasoning of the modern interpreters comes to a halt and that the modern archaeologists return to stating the truth that all the Temples were built over the Gihon Spring as the eyewitness evidence dogmatically states. As I have abundantly pointed out in my book, it is really without doubt that the architectural and geographical evidence supplied to us by Josephus, the Holy Scriptures and other historians shows that the Temple square was located over the Gihon Spring."[416]

Towards the end of the exchange between the two, Dr. Martin makes the following prognosis of his research and the case he has presented to the world:

> "The historical and biblical research I am offering to the world is based on the eyewitness accounts of many people. There can be no doubt that I am right in my conclusions and I will counter effectively any alternative view that supports the present erroneous teaching that the Haram esh-Sharif is the site of the Temples of God in Jerusalem. **It is the archaeological evidence that has been misjudged by Ritmeyer and other scholars that is flawed and a lot of wishful thinking.** I have not the slightest doubt that my conclusions will be (in the main) accepted by the scholarly world. This will be done simply because they are true."[417]

The final statements made by Dr. Ritmeyer in his critique are as follows:

> *"Jan Simons, wrote in his scholarly work, 'It has been said that all authors on ancient Jerusalem, though disagreeing among themselves about every aspect of their subject, are so much at one about a single point that they usually do not even trouble to prove it, viz., the fact that the temple of Solomon and Herod stood on the same middle part of the eastern ridge which is now occupied by Haram esh-Sharif. Indeed, a demonstration of this localization formulated in such general terms might be dispensed with because, at any rate to my knowledge, nobody has ever ventured to suggest another place for it.' Martin's ideas fall therefore outside the scope of main stream scholarship regarding the Temple Mount."*[418]

Dr. Martin responds with his last rebuttal to the above critique statement by Ritmeyer:

> "Ritmeyer is correct in one of his judgments. No one in modern times has suggested that the Temples of God were all located over the Gihon Spring. **All scholars and historians since the time of the Crusades (for the past 600 years) and no matter who they are or of what religious persuasion they proclaim, have held steadfastly and religiously to the belief that the Temples were located within the precincts of the Haram esh-Sharif. What I have done with my research is to prove otherwise.** And folks, there is not the slightest doubt that I am right. All I can say, in closing, is that the truth will triumph, and triumph soon. When the truth is finally accepted, it will help all parties in the Middle

East (and especially those in Jerusalem) to put down their guns and rocks and to turn them into plowshares and into monuments of peace. I hope that day may soon emerge."[419]

CONCLUSION: If this exchange between Dr. Ritmeyer and Dr. Martin had been a formal debate, and I had to pick the "winner," in my humble opinion, I would have to say that Dr. Martin held his own very well against "the top representative of the *traditional* school of Temple experts that place the Temple within the confines of the Haram esh-Sharif." In my opinion, it is hard to refute historical *eyewitnesses* who have clearly stated their observations compared to "lesser questionable historical and archeological evidence."

What do you think?

B. Franz's Critique & Sielaff's Rebuttal

Another vocal critic of Dr. Ernest Martin's theory of the location of the temples in Jerusalem being over the Gihon Spring in the ancient City of David and Fort Antonia being on the *traditional* Temple Mount is **Mr. Gordon Franz**. Robert Cornuke in his recent book, *Temple: Amazing New Discoveries that Change Everything About the Location of Solomon's Temple* (Charlotte, NC: LifeBridge Books, 2014) fully supports the theory of Dr. Ernest L. Martin about the location of the temples and Fort Antonia, and Mr. Franz directs his critique against Robert Cornuke and his book.

Gordon Franz has posted a recent three-page Internet article, "Eight Reasons Why the Temples of King Solomon and Herod the Great Were NOT Over the Gihon Spring in the City of David" (posted on November 1, 2015 in "Cracked Pot Archaeology I" in Life and Land–http://www.lifeandland.org). This posted article is a summary of Franz's 46-page essay: "Cornuke's *Temple* Book: 'The Greatest Archaeological Blunder of All Time'" (*http://www.lifeandland.org/2015/11/cornuke-temple/*). This article by Franz represents much of the criticism of Dr. Martin's theory found on the Internet. But are the criticisms well founded?

David Sielaff, Director of Associates for Scriptural Knowledge—ministry founded by Dr. Ernest Martin, has written a point-by-point rebuttal to Gordon Franz's article. Sielaff's article, "Temple Mount Controversy," is published in the monthly magazine *Prophecy in the News.com–with Bible Archeological Updates* (Volume 36, Number 6, June 2016; *www.prophecyinthenews.com*). David Sielaff is Dr. Martin's successor and is well qualified to provide this response to Franz's article in keeping with the theories of Ernest L. Martin.

So, who is Gordon Franz? His background is provided from his website (*www.lifeandland.org*). He is a Bible teacher with an MA in Biblical Studies from Columbia Biblical Seminary, SC. He has engaged in extensive research in archaeology and has participated in excavations in and around Jerusalem. He has taught the geography of the Bible and led field trips in Israel for the Jerusalem Center for Biblical Studies, the Institute of Holy Land Studies and the IBEX program of Master's College. He also co-teaches the Talbot School of Theology's Bible Lands Program and is on the staff of the Associates for Biblical Research (ABR). Mr. Franz has been involved with the Temple Mount Sifting Project under the leadership of the eminent Israeli archeologist Dr. Gabriel Barkay and Mr. Zachi Dvira of Bar-Ilan University in Israel.

On a personal note, my wife and I have participated in the Temple Mount Sifting Project on an ABR-sponsored tour of Israel led by Mr. Franz in January 2010. I have high personal regard for Gordon Franz. He is referenced in Chapter 36 related to an article related to one of the *traditional* burial sites of Jesus in Jerusalem.

I wish to thank David Sielaff and Associates for Scriptural Knowledge as well as *Prophecy in the News.com* for permission to reprint this article by David Sielaff in this book. The comments made by Mr. Franz in his posted article are shown below under *"**COMMENT**" and presented in italics* whereas the responses by Mr. Sielaff are shown in regular-type font under "**RESPONSE**."

> "**COMMENT:** *In his latest book, Temple: Amazing New Discoveries that Change Everything About the Location of Solomon's Temple (2014), Robert Cornuke advocates that the Temples of King Solomon and Herod the Great were not located on the Temple Mount as vast majority of scholars believe but were situated over the Gihon Spring in the City of David. Mr. Cornuke identifies the traditional Temple Mount with the Antonia's Fortress, home to 10,000 troops and support personnel of the Tenth Roman Legion. Cornuke's theory is simply a restatement of an old theory by Dr. Ernest L. Martin, The Temples that Jerusalem Forgot (2006).*
>
> **RESPONSE:** The author's first error regards Dr. Martin's book. It was published in 2000, not 2006; he should check his own bibliography. Bob Cornuke did **not** claim to originate the evidence that all the Jewish Temples were above and west of the Gihon Spring, but he powerfully popularized and contributed evidence with such force that he has threated 'tradition.'[1]

NEW INSIGHTS – WHERE WAS HEROD'S TEMPLE?

Dr. Martin died in January 2002, so critics attack Cornuke who strongly emphasizes that Zion **is equivalent** to the city of David which **is equivalent** to the site of all Israelite Jerusalem Temples. Supporters of the 'alleged' temple mount conveniently ignore that the Temples were in the City of David. In fact, they ignore what Scripture often states so that a false tradition can be preserved. Yes, Fort Antonia did hold a *tagma* of troops as Josephus says. A *tagma* in Greek is a *legio*, a 'legion' in Latin.

COMMENT: *Here I offer eight reasons why the Temples of King Solomon and Herod the Great could NOT have been located over the Gihon Spring in the City of David.*

(1) The Temple Mount platform built during the First Temple period and supported the Temple of King Solomon will not fit in the City of David. *Josephus, the First-century AD Jewish historian, and the Mishnah gives the dimensions of the platform supporting Solomon's Temple was built on as 500 x 500 cubits (861 feet x 861 feet, almost three football fields long!), a size much too large for the narrow hillock comprising the City of David.*

The square platform would have extended over the Kidron Valley and up the slopes of the Mount of Olives and would have covered known buildings and tombs that have been excavated by archaeologists. This understanding reveals that the maps and drawings in the book are inaccurate. Bottom Line: ***Cornuke's Square Temple Platform is way too small for the ancient literary sources and the 500 x 500 Square Platform is way too big for the City of David.***

RESPONSE: Not true. The hillside of the original Solomonic Temple was cut down to bedrock by Simon the Hasmonean. The topography and the geology from the time of Solomon and Zerubbabel was changed by Simon. No one claims the Solomonic Temple was 500 cubits square. He also does not point out that Solomon's Temple went **into** the Kidron Valley, something the Haram site does not do. All authors supporting the Gihon location quote Josephus who cites Hecatus, who wrote about the time of Alexander the Great, regarding the size of the Solomonic and Zerubbabel temples.

Hecatus gives different dimensions than what the Internet author erroneously cites as a dimension in the Mishnah of 500 x 500 cubits. 'The

Jews have only one fortified city; ... they call it Jerusalem. ... Nearly in the center of the city stands a stone wall [of the Temple], enclosing an area about 500 feet long and 140 feet broad, approached by a pair of gates. Within this enclosure is a square altar, built of heaped up stones, unhewn and unwrought; each side is 30 feet long and the height is 15 feet. Beside it stands a great edifice, containing an altar and a lampstand, made of gold, and weighing two talents; upon these is a light which is never extinguished by night or day' (Josephus, *Against Apion,* 1:197–198).

The Solomonic Temple was identical in size with the Zerubbabel Temple, built by the returnees from Babylon. They were poor and could not afford to enlarge it. Simon the Hasmonean later enlarged the Temple, and Herod enlarged it yet again. Josephus nowhere cites a 500-cubit square for Solomon's Temple. The Herodian Temple was 600 x 600 feet on the outside. The Mishnah was written hundreds of years later than Heratus and Josephus (both eyewitnesses in their times), and their comments on the size of the Solomonic Temple. However, Dr. Martin explains that the 500 x 500 cubit square perimeter of the Mishnah had to do with ritual purity, a point reinforced by archaeologist Yigael Yadin. [The 500-cubit square perimeter referenced in the Mishnah refers to the "Camp of the Levites," a non-physical boundary of this definition of the "camp" in Moses' time, mentioned in Exodus 32:26–27. There were three "camps:" (1) "Camp of the Priests"; (2) "Camp of the Levites"; (3) "Camp of Israel" (2,000 cubits radius). The second camp, the "Camp of the Levites," was analogous to the zone around the Temple that was called in the first century the 'Temple Mount.' (Editorial comment by author of this book based on Martin's statements in pp. 458–459 of *The Temples that Jerusalem Forgot*)].

COMMENT: (2) The Lord Jesus did not prophesy the destruction of the Temple platform. *When the Lord Jesus prophesied that 'not one stone would be left upon another' of the buildings of the Temple (Matt. 24:1–2; Mark 13:1–2; Luke 21:5–6), He was referring to the Temple of Herod, the surroundings buildings, and the Royal Stoa; but not the lower retaining walls that supported the Temple platform. These retaining walls were not buildings!*

RESPONSE: Not true. The author **should** support Jesus' prophecy as fulfilled. Jesus said to His disciples, *'There shall not be left here one stone upon another that shall not be thrown down'* 'Matt. 24:2). No exclusions, no exceptions. Josephus was specific in confirming the Romans dug up the foundation stones of the Temple (*Wars of the Jews,* 7.379) as Jesus predicted. There are thousands of stones both above and beneath the ground of the Haram (which is actually Fort Antonia). '*Not ... one stone upon another*' **includes** the foundation stones, *if* the Temple was on the Haram (it was not). No Herodian stones are upon another for the Gihon site of the Temple, although there are remains of Jebusite and Solomonic structures.

Many who go to the alleged temple mount ask when they first visit that site, 'What are all these stones doing here 'one upon another'? I asked that question when I went in 1983 to the Haram esh-Sharif. Haven't you done the same? Those stones were (and are) in reality the remains of the stones from Fort Antonia.

COMMENT: (3) The normal locations of threshing floors are always outside the city, and generally on top of hills. *This fact contradicts Cornuke's proposal to locate the threshing floor of Araunah the Jebusite downslope near the Gihon Spring inside the City of David. A threshing floor near the Gihon Spring would not catch the gentle evening breeze for winnowing the wheat and chaff. The ideal location for a threshing floor in Jerusalem is the area of the Temple Mount, the place where the ancient sources have always placed it.*

RESPONSE: Wrong again. First, note that he admits the alleged Haram temple site is **not** in the City of David.

Second, the alleged Temple site on the Haram was **not** originally a flat area. I am surprised he claims that to be true. The entire structure is a raised platform of filled-in earth around a massive rock, supported by massive retaining walls. Originally the rock under the 'Dome of the Rock' was part of the bedrock. It is smoothed but it is not flat like a threshing floor should be. However, that rock does fit Josephus' description of the 50-cubit stone under Antonia.

For him, Mount Moriah must be one-half mile north of the nearest source of water, the Gihon Spring. Did the Levites have a bucket brigade to transport water that far on the Sabbath and Holy Days? Yes, threshing floors are near the tops of hills, which fits the site of Solomon's Temple.

The original site of the threshing floor was on top of Mount Zion on the north portion of the City of David (1 Chron. 21:15–18), not outside of it.

The Solomonic and Zerubbabel Temples were on a hill taller than what existed later. Simon the Hasmonean **cut down** the hill (with approval of the religious leaders and help of the people) to bedrock, and rebuilt the Temple on the bedrock of a lower hill, but still above the Gihon Spring. Therefore, the height of Herod's Temple was also lower.

COMMENT: (4) The book misrepresents what the Pilgrim of Bordeaux wrote in his travel-log. *By ignoring the fact that the Pilgrim had already described his visit to the Temple Mount, Cornuke incorrectly identifies it as the Pilgrim's location of the Praetorium.*

RESPONSE: Not true. He assumes facts not in evidence. The Bordeaux Pilgrim described the Temple as being desolate and abandoned, not the center of Aelia. Quoting Martin: 'The first place the Bordeaux Pilgrim visited was the site of the former Temple. Remarkably, the Pilgrim says **nothing** about going through a gate in the city wall to reach the site of the Temple. The Pilgrim speaks of the Temple as being **outside** the City of Aelia [Constantinian Jerusalem]. Indeed, he did not enter what he called 'Jerusalem' until **after** viewing the site of the Temple and the area around it. ... then he walked northward to a gate in the city's southern wall, through which he entered the city, then called Aelia. Once through this southern gate, he walked directly north and noted two buildings, the only two **inside** the walls of Aelia that he thought fit to describe. On his left [to the west] was the new and unfinished Church of the Holy Sepulchre. On his right [to the east], directly opposite the Church of the Holy Sepulchre, was a structure surrounded by walls ['walls' in the plural] with their foundations in the Tyropoeon Valley. The Bordeaux Pilgrim identified that 'walled facility' as the *Praetorium,* the residence of Pilate at the time of Jesus' trial. If his information was correct, this structure had survived the Roman/Jewish War of 66–70 C.E.'[2, 3]

COMMENT: (5) Eleazar Ben-Yair, the commander of Masada during the First Jewish Revolt and a non-eyewitness to the fall of Jerusalem, was misunderstood in the book. *Cornuke's theory wrongly attributes Eleazar Ben-Yair's description of the Citadel near today's Jaffa Gate with an* *alleged Praetorium on the Temple Mount. Only by confusing these building does Cornuke find support for his proposal.*

RESPONSE: Not true. Eleazar's statement (recorded from statements of women survivors at Masada, Josephus had access to all the Roman records) must refer to Antonia, not some fortress in the western part of the city, which is on the site of what is today called David's Citadel fits the location of Herod's palace. Eleazar was definitely speaking about Antonia, which Josephus describes (as an eyewitness present at its destruction) as larger and more massive than the Temple.

COMMENT: (6) Cornuke's 600-feet bridge between the Antonia's Fortress and the Temple Mount is a misreading of Josephus. *A careful reading of the passage shows that Josephus is describing porticoes around the entire Temple Mount and the stairs leading down from the Antonia's Fortress to the Outer Courts of the Temple. Josephus never wrote of a bridge between the Temple and Antonia Fortress.*

RESPONSE: Not true. Josephus says there were two (not one) bridges 'like arms' (different translations call them colonnades, porticos, or cloisters) between the northwest corner of the Temple and the southwest corner of Antonia (*Wars of the Jews,* 5.238, 243, 6.164). Cornuke simply reports what Josephus says.

Cornuke makes an extremely important point in his reading of the text of the apostle Paul's arrest (Acts 21:27–40). Note the 'up' and 'down' descriptions in the narrative of Paul's arrest. When the Roman tribune (commander of 1,000 troops), several centurions, and troops took Paul into custody, they came 'down' to the Temple, seized Paul, who spoke to the crowd from stairs going up (v. 40). Then Paul was taken into 'the castle' Antonia which was at a higher level than the Temple. The traditional (and erroneous) site of the Temple makes the plain reading of Scripture to be impossible. Again, is Scripture wrong and tradition correct?

I am thankful to Bob Cornuke for stimulating interest in the powerful biblical and eyewitness evidence of the site of all the Israelite Temples being located above and west of the Gihon Spring, at the top of the City of David.

COMMENT: (7) The alleged evidence of a coin dated to AD 20, recently found under the Western Wall, does not prove that Herod the Great did not build the Temple on the Temple Mount. *To the contrary, it disproves Cornuke's theory that the whole Temple Mount was the Antonia's Fortress. This is because Herod built and finished the Antonia's Fortress in his lifetime, but the coin only indicates that the enclosure of the Temple Mount was not completed during his lifetime.*

RESPONSE: Not true. Whether the coin is under Antonia or the Temple is the issue in dispute. All the lower courses of the original stones on the Western Wall of the Haram are ***retaining walls***. You do not build retaining walls last, around an existing supposed temple. You build the retaining walls first. The truth of the matter is that the portion of the 'seam' (going from west to east 107 feet extending north from the southern wall of the Haram), was an addition constructed by Emperor Constantine for the Nea Church constructed in the mid-6th century AD (Martin, "Major Keys" in *Discovering the Lost Temples of Jerusalem*). The original terminus of the southern wall of Antonia was 107 feet further north.

COMMENT: (8) The book misunderstands the early Muslim history of the Temple Mount. *The Dome of the Rock was built by the Umayyad Caliph 'Abd al-Malik (AD 685–705). Its octagonal shape indicated that it was commemorative building, and not a mosque. 'Abd al-Malik constructed the Dome of the Rock as a commemorative building over the site of the Solomon's Temple that had been identified for him by the Jewish people who came to Jerusalem with 'Abd al-Malik. Bottom line:* **The Muslims built the Dome of the Rock because it was the place of the former Temple of Solomon.**

RESPONSE: Not true. Cornuke correctly describes the process of the Dome of the Rock's construction. In fact, the octagonal shape of the Dome of the rock was continued from a ***previous*** Christian Byzantine church at that location (see James Tabor, "The Dome of the Rock Is Not a Mosque; Originally a Christian Church"). It was a common feature of Muslim constructions to appropriate existing structural patterns and put them to use for their religious purposes.

Bob Cornuke is not alone in his understanding that the Temple was located above and west of the Gihon Springs. Besides Dr. Ernest L.

Martin (and myself as Dr. Martin's successor), Professor George Wesley Buchanan began his research on the Temple in the late 1990s, and has written articles and his own book on the subject. Film maker Ken Klein visually shows the evidence in his DVD *Jerusalem and the Lost Temple of the Jews.* Toward the end of the video, Dr. Ward Sanford, United States Geological Survey Hydrologist, explains how the Gihon Spring, a karst spring, could propel 'living water' 40 stories up to the Temple, as Scripture and historical eyewitnesses describe. (No such biblical or historical claim is made for the Haram site of the Temple.)

Independent author Marilyn Sams has written a devastating book on the Haram site of the Temple titled *200 Ancient Descriptions Defy The Jerusalem Temple Mount Myth.* She cites Cornuke's work as useful. Cambridge scholar Dr. Margaret Barker has gone on video record since 2008 giving support with evidence developed through her own research. Prof. David Noel Friedman (editor-in-chief of the *Anchor Bible Dictionary*), before he died in 2008, gave welcome encouragement that the Gihon Temple concept was indeed radical but worthy of serious and rigorous study.

Chuck Missler, Dr. William Welty, and a team of researchers have examined the evidence and found it to be trustworthy. Several Messianic Christian scholars without institutional ties have checked Dr. Martin's evidence and found it to be reliable. Many were brought to the subject by Bob Cornuke's book on this subject.

Those who believe the alleged temple site is somewhere on the Haram esh-Sharif have more than a dozen differing theories where it was located on that platform. Contrary to what they would have you believe, they do ***not*** know where it was! They need to demonstrate how water came to the Haram. Antonia was larger and more massive than the Temple, and built upon a massive 50- cubit stone. Where was that rock? It is still there, below the Dome of the Rock, just as Josephus says, under Antonia. Why do the gates on the Haram not fit with the gates described by Josephus or the Mishna Middoth? Why don't the measures of the Temple by Josephus and the Mishnah fit the Haram? Many similar questions could be asked.[3]

If all this information is mysterious to you, then read Bob Cornuke's book, and for further information, read the original source book on this subject by Martin, *The Temples that Jerusalem Forgot,* and the supplementary material written after that book was published.

Tradition is ***not*** historical evidence, is rarely reliable, and often contradicts the Bible and actual history. The location of the Temple on the Haram has been challenged. I challenge those who claim the Haram location for the Temple to show us their evidence without hiding behind tradition."

1   Robert Cornuke, Temple: Amazing New Discoveries that Change Everything about the Location of Solomon's Temple (Charlotte, NC: LifeBridge Books, 2014).

2   Ernest L. Martin, *The Temples That Jerusalem Forgot* (Portland, OR: Associates for Scriptural Knowledge, 2000).

3   Marilyn Sams, The Jerusalem Temple Mount Myth: 200 Ancient Descriptions Defy It (2014).

CONCLUSION

As noted previously, Gordon Franz's longer article was "Cornuke's *Temple* Book: 'The Greatest Archaeological Blunder of All Time.'" Since Bob Cornuke's book confirms the theory of Dr. Martin, the inference might be drawn that Mr. Franz considers Dr. Martin's theory to be "the greatest archaeological blunder of all time." From Mr. Franz's Internet article comments and Mr. Sielaff's responses (rebuttals) as well as the other evidence presented in this book, do you agree with that statement?

CHAPTER 63

Puzzle Piece #9–Nancy L. Kuehl's "Temple"

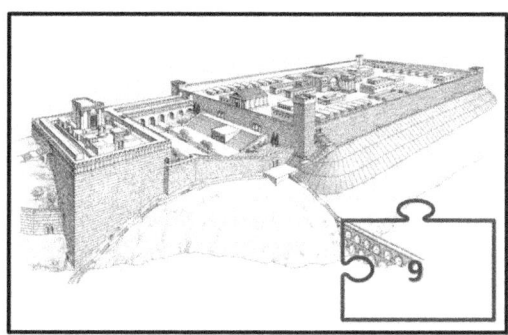

Kuehl's case for an alternative *"temple"* structure spoken of by Jesus in Matthew 24:1 is presented in this chapter as *Puzzle Piece #9*. Nancy L. Kuehl provides an alternative interpretation of Jesus' words:

*"Jesus left the **temple** and was walking away when his disciples came up to him to call his attention to **its buildings**. 'Do you see all these things?' he asked. 'I tell you the truth, **not one stone here will be left on another; every one will be thrown down**." (Matthew 24:1–2, NIV, emphasis added)*

Kuehl's case is that the temple was, indeed, located on the *traditional* "Temple Mount," but what Jesus was referring to were the administrative *"buildings" [oikos]* of the temple situated on the Mount of Olives, considered part of the Temple-Complex, which were, indeed, totally destroyed by the Romans.

Nancy L. Kuehl is the author of the landmark book, *A Book of Evidence–The Trials and Execution of Jesus* (2013),[420] which was extensively referenced in Part II, Section C: "*How* Did Jesus *Really* Die?" I highly recommend Kuehl's book.

In the Foreword of Kuehl's book is the following explanation about her research interests:

> "The author ... is among a growing number of people who are seeking to better know Jesus in the context of his Jewish roots. Ms. Kuehl has chosen to use the laws of both the Jews and Romans as the tool with which to diligently search and dig through to the light ... to glean for ourselves a more authentic look at Jesus." [421]

For your consideration, I am including this Chapter 63 with its material from Kuehl's book as it provides an alternative explanation related to the temple and Jesus' prophecy about its destruction. It provides a possible explanation for how the words of Jesus' prophecy (Luke 19:43–44 and Luke 21:5–6; see Chapter 56), related to the coming destruction of Jewish Jerusalem and the "Temple" down to its foundations, could have been satisfied and yet the *traditional* "Temple Mount" walls remain standing as we see today.

In Part III of this book, we are looking at the theory of Ernest L. Martin for a *different location of the temple*, being in the southern location of the City of David, over the Gihon Spring, as an interpretation for why the *traditional* "Temple Mount" walls are still standing despite Jesus' prophecy.

So, what is Kuehl's case, which includes the location of Herod's Temple on the *traditional* "Temple Mount" but with the temple's associated buildings (still considered an extension of the temple) on the Mount of Olives, as well as the Mount of Olives being the location of the crucifixion of Jesus? I am including a section from her Chapter 5, "Beth Pagi: The Place of the Crux," which includes an introduction to her case as well as providing you with a feel for her extensive research and writing. Interested readers will want to read her book, as it contains unique insights into many of the Jewish and Roman laws and conditions at the time of Jesus' death.

Here is a section quoted from Kuehl's book:

> "During the first century there was **an ecclesiastical district on the Mount of Olives called Beth Pagi**, *where Jesus was put to death*. It is the same site where Stephen and James the Just were later stoned. This important ecclesiastical district has been designated by many names in Scripture and in Jewish writings. The area included portions of the two central mountains in the Olivet chain. It has been called, as is customary in Hebrew practice, by a variety of appellations: Beth Pagi, Beth Hini, Beth Hanuyoth, the "Fountain", the Plaza, the Outer Court, the Spine, the Ridge, the Corner, the Wall, and most importantly, **Golgotha**. Sometimes, it is referred to in Jewish writings by the governmental departments located there; for example, *Beth HaKana* (the "Market") or

Beth HaSephar. It is also called the Footstool of *HaShem*. In the Talmud it is most often referred to as **Beth Pagi**, and in the Copper Scroll it is symbolically called Secacah and Beth Kerem (House of the spine).

This important site was, in fact, the most important ecclesiastical district for the City of Jerusalem. It is at this site that the armies of Israel had been mustered, where lepers had gathered, where merchants sold their wares, where the New Moon was determined, and where the judicial Sanhedrin met for *criminal* adjudication. It was important during the first century because it was the seat of the Temple Cult and the headquarters for the government of Israel.

When Jesus and his disciples sat "opposite the temple" (*hieron* – temple precincts), it was the buildings at this *governmental site* to which he referred (Matt. 24). This "branch" of the Temple extended from the Hill of Ophel on the west to the eastern extremity of the village of **Bethphage**. That village derived its name from the district of **Beth Pagi** (Place of Meeting) in which it sat. The region is sometimes referred to as the Beth Galeel (House of the Circle) or the **Beth Din (House of Judgment). It was also the place of public execution**. Note the wording of the New Covenant reference.

And Jesus went out, and departed from the temple [hieron]: and his disciples came to him to shew him the buildings [oikodome] of the temple [hieron] (Matt. 24:1).

Herod's Temple was a *singular* structure located upon the southern end of the present Temple platform. It was not the Herodian Temple sanctuary [*naos*] to which the disciples were referring but to the *"buildings (oikos) of the temple"* situated on the Mount of Olives. Mark 13:3 states that *"he [Jesus] sat upon the Mount of Olives over against [opposite] the temple";* but the word for temple here is *herion*. Strong's Concordance indicates that it was a "a sacred place; i.e., *the entire precincts* of the Temple" [whereas 3485 (*naos*) denotes the central sanctuary itself]. The word *naos* derives from the root *naio* and literally means "to dwell", so it was not the usual "dwelling place" of the *Shekinah,* that is sanctuary, to which Jesus referred but the place where the Shekinah rested when it left the Temple (Eze. 11:23).

It has already been established that the activities performed on the Mount of Olives were of a sacred nature, and that the Mount of Olives, itself, was considered a holy site (*b. Ber.* 9.5; *b. Yom.* 68b) primarily because the "glory" of YHWH had last rested there. These buildings, as we shall see, were located in the Plaza of Gulgoleth, perhaps extending as far as the village of Bethphage. The Bordeaux Pilgrim locates the village at one thousand paces (i.e., one thousand yards) southeast of the northern summit of Olivet. **Jesus had said that** *"one stone would not be left upon another,"* **yet there are many stones and structures left on and near the Temple Mount.** This has been adduced by modern archaeological experts.

He was, however, not speaking of the Herodian Temple Mount at all. Jesus was referring to these other *buildings* **(plural) attached to the Hill of Ophel in the form of a lateral appendage, or a** *wing* **that extended from the Woman's Court (at the Miphkad Gate) east of the Temple at Ophel, over a bridge that covered the Kidron Valley, and over the hill toward the Village of Bethphage** [this "wing" should not be confused with the "pinnacle" of the temple; to be sure there is also an ecclesiastical "wing" at the site of the pinnacle as well].

Part of the region of Beth Pagi was sometimes called the *topos* (as in the gospels), the "plaza". In the Old Covenant it had been referred to as the "Wall." **Since there are various archaeological ruins attached to the site of the Temple Mount, these could not have been the "buildings" to which Jesus referred**. An investigation into the extent of the Temple precincts (the *hieron*) will show that there is not a single whole stone to suggest that the "wing" or "outer court" (the ecclesiastical district) ever existed at all. It has been leveled to the ground. The Kidron Valley, which was at one time deep enough to accommodate a structure some six hundred feet in height, is now filled with centuries of debris. As a matter of fact, **Beth Pagi is today a cemetery! Even the once important priestly village of Bethphage has been destroyed.**

Yet historical, Scriptural, and archaeological sources prove that the village and the Plaza at Beth Pagi *did* exist during the first century, and that these sites were the meeting places for the government and the seat of the *criminal* courts [*beth din*] [there is a great difference between the criminal court and the court of the priests]. The Outer Court, traditionally

NEW INSIGHTS – WHERE WAS HEROD'S TEMPLE?

> depicted as being situated on the Herodian Temple Mount was actually on the Mount of Olives. It is here we find the meeting place for the rulers of the government of Israel. They were referred to as **"heads" of State**.
>
> … Naturally enough, one of the reasons the area became known as Gulgoleth (**Golgotha**) is because it was the site of meeting for the "Head" of the government yet there are other reasons as well. . ."[422]

Kuehl has many wonderful insights, one of which is that she supports the case for the site of the crucifixion of Jesus being on the Mount of Olives. She calls the area *Beth Pagi*, which is where she believes public executions under Jewish law were accomplished. I too support the conclusion that Jesus was executed on the Mount of Olives. However, I am not convinced by Kuehl's argument that the ancient Jewish Temples were located on the site of the *traditional* "Temple Mount." I leave it to each reader to decide whether Kuehl has offered evidence more compelling than that presented by Dr. Ernest Martin—as presented in this Part III.

CHAPTER 64

Final Movements of Jesus–With Martin's Temple Location

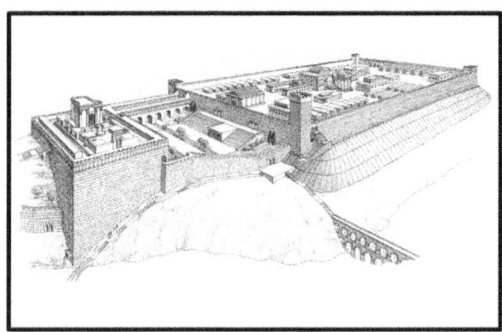

What would the final movements of Jesus look like if Herod's Temple was actually located in the ancient City of David over the Gihon Spring, as proposed by Dr. Ernest Martin? How would His movements from arrest at the Garden of Gethsemane to crucifixion and burial on the Mount of Olives be different than *tradition* would have us believe?

I am presenting Figure 64.1: "The Final Movements of Christ" and Figure 64.2: "Final Movements of Christ–Jerusalem Area." These two figures are from the ASK Timeline Project of Henry Dye and Tim Parrott (2015–2016) and the Associates for Scriptural Research (ASK) [*www.askelm.com/Timeline/Timeline.pdf*], and they are presented with their permission. Once again, I am showing these diagrams rotated 90 degrees and expanded, to make the text more readable. The figures represent what Dye and Parrott believe the final movements of Jesus would look like, based upon the details available from Dr. Martin's books and associated research materials. I am generally in agreement with these diagrams.

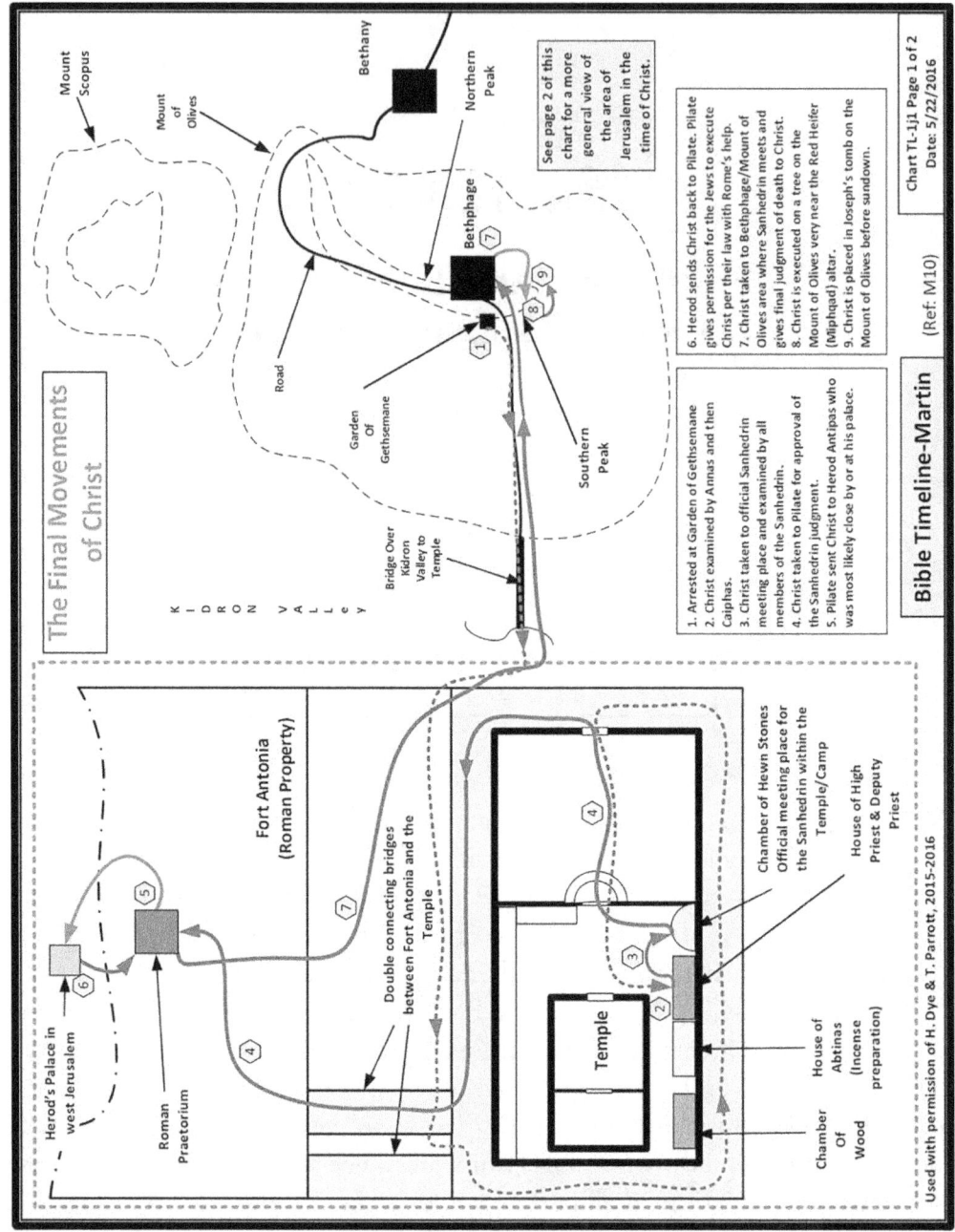

Figure 64.1. "The Final Movements of Christ" Used with permission of H. Dye and T. Parrott and ASK (see text)

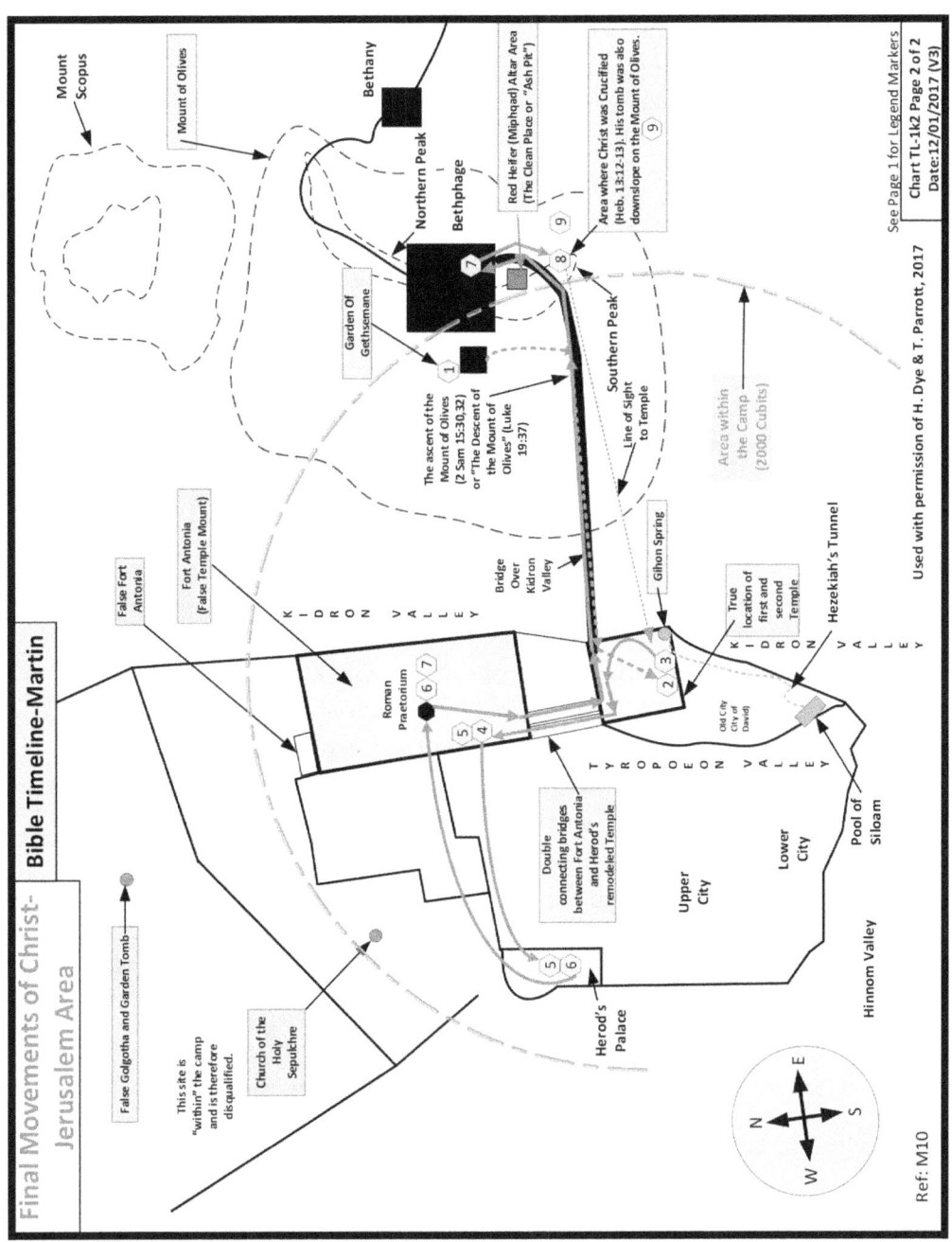

Figure 64.2. "Final Movements of Christ–Jerusalem Area" Used with permission of H. Dye and T. Parrott and ASK (see text)

As part of the ASK Timeline Project, Dye and Parrott also produced a remarkable detailed biblical chronology including various aspects of Jesus' birth and death, according to Dr. Martin's chronology. Much of this chronology from Dr. Martin is presented in this book. However, whereas Dye and Parrott assume a Thursday crucifixion in AD 30, the case presented in this book is for the crucifixion on Wednesday AD 30—for all the reasons laid out in Section A of Part II.

In Figures 64.1 and Figure 64.2, Dye and Parrott properly show the site of the crucifixion of Jesus being on the Mount of Olives, near the southern peak of the Olivet ridge, east of Herod's Temple, and outside of the "Camp of Israel." The "Camp of Israel" extended 2000 cubits from the threshold of the Holy of Holies in the temple. Dr. Martin provides further explanation of this "Camp of Israel" from his book, *The Temples That Jerusalem Forgot* (footnotes 681 and 682 on p. 459):

> The Jewish authorities in the first century chose the figure of 2000 cubits (3000 feet) because of the reference to the 2000 cubits mentioned in Joshua 3:4 that separated the Israelites from the Ark of the Covenant. The accounts in the earliest parts of the Talmuds known as the Mishnah show the use of these 2000 cubits in early Jewish interpretation (Rosh ha-Shanah 2:5, see also Sanhedrin 1:5 and Shebu'oth 2:2 for the authority of the Sanhedrin [the Supreme Court] of the Jews to set the limits of the three camps). As in the case of the Ark in the time of Joshua, the distance was determined "by measure" (Joshua 3:4). This was by walking the distance with a red or a line [a measuring rod] in the hand. The distance was determined by walking, not by measuring the distance of 2000 cubits from the Holy of Holies as a bird would fly.

> Whereas it was common for Jewish towns outside of Jerusalem to have their Sabbath day zones for walking at 2000 cubits from the walls of the various towns, in Jerusalem it was different because that is where the Temple (God's House) was situated. Since the Holy of Holies in the Temple was designed to contain the Ark of the Covenant and the 2000 cubits were originally reckoned from the Ark in the time of Joshua, the 2000 cubits for the limits of the Camp of Israel (the third camp) were measured in Jerusalem from the threshold of the Holy of Holies. This was considered to be the entrance to the abode of God on earth. This agreed with the 2000 cubits' distance between the Israelites and the Ark in the time of Joshua (Joshua 3:4).

Note that the 2000 cubits limit of the "Camp of Israel" was measured along the ground and not as a bird would fly. Due to the elevation changes from the temple to the Mount of Olives—both down and up in elevation—this 2000 distance would display on a *flat map* as less than 2000-cubits. Accordingly, I believe that the limit of the "Camp of Israel" would be displayed at a distance somewhat less than what is shown on Figure 64.2. As a result, the crucifixion site could have been closer to the temple than what is depicted.

Please note that the graphic of the crucifixion site previously illustrated on Figure 61.3 depicts the site being on the "*Southern Spur*" of the Olivet ridge, at less than a 2000-cubit distance from the threshold of the Holy of Holies. Therefore, there is a problem with that depiction of the crucifixion site shown on Figure 61.3. The crucifixion site shown in Figures 64.1 and 64.2, being on the southern part of the Olivet ridge (and not on the "*Southern Spur*") and being "outside the Camp of Israel" is a more accurate depiction.

We will next consider a burning question related to this new proposed temple location by Ernest Martin. It is, *"How in the world could the rabbis (and, really, all the world) over the centuries have forgotten the exact location of the temples in Jerusalem?"* The next chapter provides some insights into this intriguing question.

CHAPTER 65

How Could the Rabbis Forget?

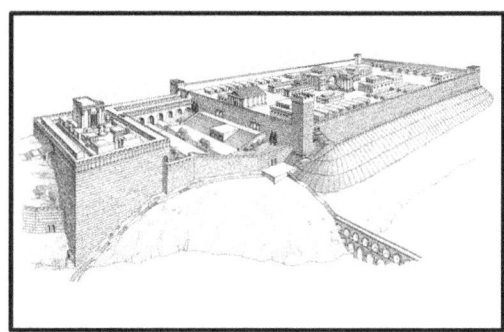

Indeed, how in the world could the true location of the temples of God that Solomon, Zerubbabel, Simon the Hasmonean, and Herod built in Jerusalem have been lost for so many hundreds of years, if the case I am presenting is true?

How could the *Rabbis* have forgotten their location? How could, actually, the *whole world* have forgotten, including all of the *Jewish people*? As Ernest L. Martin has stated,

> "Not only did all Israel *forget*, all the peoples of the surrounding nations also *forgot*. All the Arabs and even later, all the peoples of Islam *forgot*. And too, all Christians in the world *forgot*. In fact, everyone on earth (including me [Martin]) *forgot*."[423]

This has been a mystery, and it seems preposterous that Israelites would ever forget where the original Temples were built. However, there is a very strong case that the whole nation did, in fact, forget—extending even to today!

The answers to these questions about how everyone forgot about the true temple location are part of the extensive historical and biblical research by Martin and is reported in Chapter 35 of his book, *The Temples That Jerusalem Forgot* (2000), along with his article "How the Jews Started to Lose the Temples' Site"–Expanded

Internet Edition, June 1, 2000.[424] For those readers who have an interest in all the interesting historical details, I recommend reading the "Expanded Internet Edition" by Martin, which I have just cited. Chapter 64 of this book is a *summary* of Dr. Martin's research—just hitting some highlights—on how the Temples were forgotten.

Here is the bigger point to be made—this question goes beyond this case for how the Jews forgot the location of their temples. It is really an *object lesson* for how Christians, Muslims, and the Jews have forgotten so much about the truth of their heritage. In this book, we have been examining the mysteries of Jesus' life related to His birth, death, resurrection, and ascensions; they are mysteries because Christians have also forgotten much of the true history related to these events of Jesus' life.

Indeed, what happened to the Jewish people regarding their forgetting the location of their temples, has also been true for both Christians and Muslims. Here is "the rest of the story." It is not intended to cast stones at the Jewish people in any way. We are looking at it because of the insight it brings to all of us. This is Martin's statement related to these things:

> "The historical evidence helps to show how superficial and how temporary the memories of past religious beliefs can become in the estimation of people when certain contemporary events cause people to alter their former religious beliefs and customs. It can even lead to forgetting their most cherished of institutions. It has happened to all people. This has happened to Christians. It has happened to Muslims. And it has also happened to the Jewish authorities and people."[425]

A. How Many Temples Were There?

First, let's digress into another topic to illustrate how we can forget historical things. It has been easy to even "forget" how many temples there were. Ernest Martin has stated that there has been a total of *six* temples by his assessment. There is a usual tendency for Jewish scholars to call Herod's Temple the "Second Temple" and think of it as a mere adaptation of the same temple that was built by Zerubbabel after the Babylonian Captivity. However, it can be argued that Herod's Temple was actually the *"Sixth Temple"* from that of Solomon; indeed, Herod built an entirely *new temple* adjacent to the temple existing at the time of Herod's construction—and the temple activities continued within the existing temple during the construction of the new one. So, it was an entirely *new* temple which Herod built and not a renovation of the existing temple; the existing temple was then disassembled after Herod's new temple became functional. According to Martin's count, here is a complete listing of all the temples:[426]

1. *"First Temple"*: Solomon's Temple was, obviously, the first temple constructed around 960 BC. Nebuchadnezzar II later destroyed it around 586 BC.

2. *"Second Temple"*: In Jeremiah 41:4–5 we see that a *new* "House of God" (a temporary temple because it had the Altar of God) was raised up in Mizpah in approximately 585 BC, the year after the former Temple of Solomon was destroyed.

3. *"Third Temple"*: After the Babylonian Captivity, a further Altar was raised up in Jerusalem which was also called the "House of God" (compare Ezra 3:3 with 3:8). This Altar was also recognized as a Temple, raised up in approximately 534 BC. This *"Third Temple"* existed for about 18 years before the actual foundation of the structure of the "House of God" (the *"Fourth Temple"*) was built.

4. *"Fourth Temple"*: The foundation of the actual building called the "House of God" (the *"Fourth Temple"*) was begun in approximately 516 BC (compare Ezra 3:6 with all of Haggai). This *fourth* "House of God" lasted until the time of Simon the Hasmonian.

5. *"Fifth Temple"*: Simon the Hasmonian completely destroyed the temple which had been polluted both by Antiochus Epiphanes and the High Priest Alcimus (a Hellenist) in approximately 155 BC. Simon also cut down Ophel hill—on which the temple was located—also due to the perceived desecration. Simon's son, Hyrcanus, completed the construction of the new *"Fifth Temple"* in 124 B.C.[427]

6. *"Sixth Temple"*: King Herod started his *new* Temple in 37 BC, about 100 years after the completion of the Fifth Temple, which had been finished by Hyrcanus. After many years of construction, the Herodian Temple was completed—just a few years before Titus destroyed it in AD 70.

"Forgetting" the *number* of Jewish temples is nothing compared to the case for forgetting the *location* of the temples in Jerusalem. We can now look at that interesting history.

Seemingly, the Jews forgetting the location of their temples was due to incremental events happening over hundreds of years. It involved many instrumental individuals—Jewish, Christian, and Muslims. This chapter will introduce you to some of them. First, let's look at two Jewish attempts to rebuild the temple during the fourth century AD and notice where the site was for those two rebuilding attempts.

B. Fourth Century Attempts to Rebuild the Temple

One attempt to rebuild the temple occurred in the time of Constantine, after the Edict of Milan, allowing for more religious freedoms in the Roman empire. The other attempt occurred about 37 years later in the time of the Roman Emperor Julian the Apostate in AD 362, with the hope of completing the construction started earlier. These reconstruction attempts were not successful, and the second attempt ceased in AD 363 with the death of Julian. Remnant portions of these temple-rebuilding attempts existed and the *Bordeaux Pilgrim* reported sightings of these parts of this temple in AD 333.[428]

The location of this Jewish attempt to rebuild the temple, as reported by the eye-witness account of the *Bordeaux Pilgrim*, is telling—the site chosen was over and around the Gihon Spring.[429] This selection of the temple site was during the time when the Jews still retained a knowledge of the correct location of the temples. However, over time this knowledge was lost.

C. Testimony to a Unique Condition Concerning the Temple Site

Martin has uncovered a major "key" in locating the true temple site of God. It relates to a historical fact which stemmed from a reliable historical account of **Eutychius**, the first Christian-Arabic historian and church leader (*Said b. al-Bitrik*; Gk. Name *Eutychius*), in AD 876.

Eutychius had access to many earlier Arabic records, and he stated that the former temple site had never been built upon by either the Romans (from AD 70 to the time of Constantine in the AD 300's) or by the Byzantine Christians (from the fourth to the seventh centuries AD). Hence, **the Gentile Romans and the Byzantines left the site untouched by them**, in order for the prophecy of Jesus that *"not one stone would be found on top of another"* would remain fulfilled for the temple site in Jerusalem. The historical fact is that they left the southeast section of Jerusalem alone and never constructed any major churches or holy shrines in the area of the true Temple Mount.

Eutychius wrote of how **Omar**, the Second Caliph within Islam, and **Sophronius**, the Christian archbishop of Jerusalem, originally recognized the true site of the temples in Jerusalem—no Gentile construction had been accomplished at the temple site by the Romans or the Byzantines. This was not true for the Haram, on which an early Christian Church, the majestic *Church of the Holy Wisdom* had been constructed by Constantine over the "oblong rock" on the Haram; this church on the Haram was later destroyed by the Persians and Jews in AD 614, about 24 years before the discussions of Sophronius and Omar took place. **Note that this disqualifies the Haram (which later was the site of the Muslim *Dome of the Rock*, built towards the end of the ninth century AD) as being the site of the temples because Sophronius had told Omar that the former site of the temples had never been built on by the Romans or the Byzantines, whereas the Haram site had indeed been built on by the Romans with that church**. Here are the exact words of Eutychius, as given in F.E. Peters, "Jerusalem," pp. 189, 190:[430]

> "Then Omar [*Umar* in Arabic] said to him [to Sophronius]: 'You owe me a rightful debt. Give me a place in which I might build a sanctuary [*masjid* "a prayer shrine"].' The patriarch [Sophronius] said to him: 'I will give to the Commander of the Faithful a place to build a sanctuary **where the kings of *Rum* [the Romans] were unable to build**. It is a rock where God spoke to Jacob and which Jacob called the Gate of Heaven and the Israelites the Holy of Holies. It is the center of the world and was a Temple for the Israelites … [And], the Byzantines neglected it [they also left the site empty] and did not hold it in veneration, **nor did they build a church over it**" (capitalization and clarification by Martin; emphasis mine).[431]

Although Sophronius offered to Omar the site above the Gihon Spring to build his mosque, Omar selected a more northern site at the extreme south of the Haram to build what became the *Al Aqsa Mosque*; this was where he believed that Mohammad began his famous "Night Journey" on horseback from the "Farthest Mosque" into heaven. In addition, the true site of the temples in the former area of the City of David had become a garbage dump, and this did not suit Omar's desire for better ambiance for his planned Mosque; the Haram was lovely in comparison. However, from the true site of the Jewish temples, Omar retrieved many ruined stones from the same area that Sophronius finally said was the site of the Jewish Temple—in the *southeast* quadrant of Jerusalem over the Gihon Spring. He wanted to incorporate these stones which he imagined were from the original "Solomon's Temple" into his Muslim shrine, which he did. **Because of this, it became common for those in Jerusalem to refer to the new Mosque as the remains of "Solomon's Temple."**

This is also a key point in misdirecting the site of the Jewish temples from the area of the Gihon Spring to the Haram. Folklore started to change the location of the temples in the minds of the residents of Jerusalem.

In summary, the historical record argues against the Haram being the original site of the temples.

D. Muslim Principle of "Barakah" to Transfer Holiness to the Al Aqsa Mosque from the Temple Site

Omar took a single stone from the true temple site and re-positioned it within his new mosque. That stone became the *qibla,* the pillar stone that pointed Muslims to pray toward Mecca. With the stones taken by Omar from the original site of the temples, and the usage of the Muslim theological principle of **barakah**—which allowed the transference of holiness of one site to another site—Omar felt that he had transferred holiness to his mosque on the Haram.

Unfortunately, this use of **barakah** is the first error adopted by the people of Jerusalem that helped even the local people to lose sight of the former site of the temple. Even the Islamic people of Jerusalem began calling the Al Aqsa Mosque by the name "Solomon's Temple." **Later peoples forgot about the transference principle and accepted a more literal interpretation that the area at the southern area of the Haram was the exact spot where Solomon erected his Temple.**

As it was well known that Herod the Great expanded northward the size of the temple, doubling its previous dimensions; by further usage of *transference* (*barakah*), it was not difficult to call the Dome of the Rock a part of Herod's Temple. As Martin explains:

> "The **Dome of the Rock in Christian eyes finally became a part of the 'Temple' because Jesus' footprint was believed to be on the 'oblong stone'** and instead of the 'footprint' being placed there in the time of Pilate (as the original story stated), they changed the account into the event when Jesus was a baby and was placed in the arms of Simon the priest, One error of the story became superimposed on another error and contradictions galore began to occur in the various accounts."[432]

So, unfortunately, folklore became reality for Jews, Christians, and Muslims. Folklore accounts finally got the Dome of the Rock to be the site of the Temple. In the time of the Crusades, during the eleventh through thirteenth centuries AD, the Christians continued the myths by calling the Dome of the Rock "The Temple of God." It had come a long way from the meetings of Omar with Sophronius, as reported by Eutychius.

E. Jews Wanted to Live in the Southern Part of Jerusalem

The *Geniza documents* from Egypt provide some early and reliable Jewish historical records from the time of the discussions of Omar and Sophronius in Jerusalem. They report that Omar allowed **seventy families of Jews** to move from Tiberius, on the western side of the Sea of Galilee, to settle in Jerusalem. Where did these Jews want to settle in Jerusalem? Historical records show that they moved to the southern part of Jerusalem near the Siloam water source, the Gihon Spring, on the southeastern ridge. This was in the region of the real "Mount Zion" region.

Later, in the tenth century AD, some **Karaite Jews** settled in Jerusalem. They too wanted to live close to the true site of the ancient temples. They settled next to the Rabbinate Jews, establishing themselves on the eastern side of the Kedron Valley on the lower Olivet ridge.

The community of Jews of the original seventy families of Jews from Tiberius lived for over 400 years, from AD 638 to AD 1077 on this *southeastern* region—where the biblical records clearly indicate that the original Mount Zion of David was located. The Jews showed no interest in the *southwestern* hill of Jerusalem, where only Christian buildings were found during this period of Jewish settlement back in Jerusalem. This continued until some so-called tombs of David, Solomon and the kings of Israel were supposedly discovered below the ruins of an old Christian church in the mid-twelfth century AD. What was that all about?

Into the 1200's, other Jewish testimony from rabbis provide further descriptions of the desolation over the Gihon Spring area, being completely devoid of any Gentile buildings. This includes the testimony of **Rabbi David Kimchi**, otherwise known as RADAQ, being one of the great biblical commentators of the Jews; he lived from about AD 1160 to AD 1235. Rabbi Kimchi, in AD 1235, was the last Jewish authority who stated that the site of the former Temples in Jerusalem "were still in ruins" in his day and further stated that no Gentile buildings were then erected over the temple site. Note that this historical statement disqualifies the whole region of the Haram esh-Sharif (with its Dome of the Rock) from being the site of the temples, as the Muslim Al Aksa Mosque and the Dome were on the Haram.[433]

Even the famous **Maimonides**, who modernized Judaism with rationalistic doctrines in the twelfth century, wrote in the year AD 1180, during his travel to

Jerusalem, that even though there was utter desolation at the site of the temples, the site retained its sanctity.[434]

F. Jewish Belief that Dome of the Rock was the Temple Site Started with Benjamin of Tudela

Even with the testimonies of Rabbi Kimchi, Rabbi Samson, and Maimonides, there were some Jews who were beginning to think that the Dome of the Rock was, indeed, the temple location. Within another 100 years, *all Jews* accepted the changeover with the full sanction of the Jewish authorities. What happened? Who was responsible for this total misunderstanding? Can we even know this? The answer is "Yes," and his name is **Benjamin of Tudela**.

Benjamin of Tudela was the first Jew who unambiguously stated that the area of the Dome of the Rock on the Haram was the Temple site.[435] What prompted him to make that statement?

Benjamin was a traveler from the city of Tudela in northern Spain, traveling into Babylon, then to Egypt, and returning to Tudela. He made a short visit in Jerusalem about AD 1169. At the time, there were very few Jews living in Jerusalem, possibly only a handful; Benjamin found only four Jews living near the so-called Tower of David (near the Jaffa Gate in the upper/western city) This was the case because when the Christian Crusaders conquered Jerusalem in AD 1099, they forbad Jews or Muslims from entering the city, and this was strictly enforced for at least 52 or so years. Benjamin arrived in Jerusalem after the Crusaders had been there for 70 years.

An important thing to note is that for a period of 52 or so years (from AD 1099 to AD 1151), *no Jews* lived in Jerusalem. When they started to return, everything looked different—much tearing down of old buildings and new construction had been accomplished by the Crusaders, and old landmarks were no longer as they remember them. This is one reason for the Jews forgetting the location of their temples. As an analogy, think of the period from the founding of the nation of Israel in 1948 and the changes wrought in a 52-year period to 2000; the country became totally changed.

In AD 1152, however, one or two Jews were allowed to live near the Jaffa Gate in western Jerusalem. One of them was **Abraham al-Constantini**, who *Benjamin of Tudela* met in AD 1154, and it was this *Abraham al-Constantini* who told him of a remarkable discovery. **He told Benjamin that the Tombs of David, Solomon and the other Kings of Judah had been discovered underneath a church on the *southwest* hill of Jerusalem, then being called by the**

Christians "Mount Sion" (Christians used the term "Sion" rather than "Zion"). In his writings, Benjamin of Tudela tells us that it was this Abraham al-Constantini who informed the Christian bishop that the newly discovered tombs were those of David and the other kings.[436] Indeed, this could have been somewhat true, as Simon the Hasmonean in the second century BC moved David's "Tomb" (which he built as a *cenotaph*—a monument to honor King David, even though his body was elsewhere—and not an actual Tomb).

The effect of this "archeological discovery" was that this news traveled superfast throughout the Christian, Muslim, and Jewish worlds. Indeed, this new "Tomb area" was considered of great significance, and the interpretations based upon it began to change the way Christians, Muslims, and Jews viewed the early geography of Jerusalem. How so?

If these Tombs were reckoned to be real (and not a later *cenotaph*), then it meant that the *southwest* hill was indeed the real and proper "Mount Zion" and the *southeast* ridge was not the correct location, in spite of the thoughts of Sophronius, Omar, and Eutychius.

This "discovery" of the so-called "Tomb of David" caused some Jews to question the validity of the *southeast* hill. There is another factor which added credence to this interpretation. That was because this so-called "Tomb of David" was at a church that was believed to be built over the ruins of an old Jewish synagogue, having the same orientation as the church. Furthermore, it was thought that the holy niche in the building was oriented northward; Jewish tradition was that early synagogues in "Palestine" were normally oriented facing the temple, and this orientation was facing the Dome of the Rock. Hence, this appeared to be proof that the region of the Haram esh-Sharif must have been the true site of the Temple (and that the true site of the Temple was not situated on the *southeast* ridge as all biblical teaching and history demanded it to be located). As it turned out, there was NOT an ancient synagogue there—the ruins were merely those of a church which had been destroyed by the Persians in AD 614 or the Muslims in AD 965—so the whole analogy and conclusion was bogus. All this, however, was not known at the time of the "discovery."

The result of the misunderstanding about the "Tomb of David" and the "synagogue" resulted in the Jews at that time speaking with absolute conviction about the "Royal Tombs on Mount Zion." Dr. Martin provides the following commentary:[437]

> "(See the work *Sefer Qabbalath Sadiqei Eretz Israel* as cited by Prawer, *ibid.*, pp. 176–180). This is further confirmed by what is called *The Forged Itinerary of Rabbi Menahem of Hebron* in 1215 C.E. who spoke

of "the Tombs of the Kings on Mount Zion" (Prawer, *ibid.*, p. 223). And then in 1270 to 1291 there is *The Itinerary of the Anonymous Pupil of Nachmanides* who not only visited the site of the "Tomb of David" (and the other kings) but he described a building at the place which was then being called (hold on to your hats, folks), "the Temple of David" with the Hebrew name *Heikhal* describing it. This same Hebrew word was that which sometimes was used for the Holy of Holies in the actual Temples. And note this. This later Jewish traveler gave a further interpretation about this new site on the Christian "Mount Sion." He stated: "Some [Jews] say that the Ark of the Covenant which was brought by David [to Jerusalem] rested here [on the *southwest* hill] until he built the Temple." The author then added the further interpretation: "Not far away [from this "Temple"] is the Tower of David, built of huge stones." This was the Christian "Tower of David" located at the Jaffe Gate to the north and west. The author then stated that anyone can see that this *Tower of David* "is an ancient building" (J. Prawer, *ibid.*, pp. 239, 240)."

So, by the end of the thirteenth century AD, even the Jewish authorities worldwide had mistakenly gone over to believing that the *southwest* hill of Jerusalem was, indeed, the original "Mount Zion" of David's time. Also, with the "synagogue" at the site of the church (at the discovery site of the "Tomb of David") pointing toward the Dome of the Rock on the Haram, it was easy for the whole Jewish community (along with the Christians and Muslims) to identify the area of the Haram esh-Sharif as the former temple site of the Jews.[438]

All this background helps to explain *"How Could the Rabbis Forget?"*

But wait, there is more to the story. The Jews also began to believe that the so-called "Tower of David" at the Jaffe Gate in the *northwest* part of Jerusalem was the real "Tower" of David. That tower, however, was built no earlier than the sixth century AD and was, of course, located about three quarters of a mile northwest of the true Tower [Citadel] of David in the City of David on the *southeast* ridge.[439]

Martin summarized the situation at that time in history, as follows:

"From this time onward, the confusion (it should be called 'the *deception*') was now complete and **within two generations after the time of the Crusades, *all people* (including the Jews) now accepted the Dome of the Rock as the place near where the Holy of Holies once existed.** They forgot all about the proper place on the *southeast* ridge.

"This was the period when *all peoples* finally accepted the *southwest* hill of Jerusalem as the actual "Zion," and they forgot the real biblical "Zion" on the *southeast* hill. So certain did this false identification become in the eyes of all scholars, historians and theologians that even Robinson (one of the great explorers of Palestine in the early 19th century and after whom "Robinson's Arch" in the western wall of the Haram esh-Sharif is named) said the truth of the *southwest* hill as being the read "Mount Zion" was thoroughly unassailable. To him and his colleagues there was not the slightest doubt that the *southwest* hill was the correct biblical site. **Indeed, virtually everyone throughout the world (and at all official levels of academic and theological authorities of all religious persuasions) dogmatically accepted that the *southwest* hill was the true "Mount Zion."** The error brought chaos to the actual biblical geography of Jerusalem."[440]

This ends our summary of the historical account of **Benjamin of Tudela.** Basically, he was a sloppy and ignorant geographer, and he became a dangerous authority for later Jews because his accounts were accepted without questioning his conclusions. **Even the Jewish Rabbis accepted his erroneous conclusions, causing them to forget the true site of the Temples**. It is an interesting but sad story. That is how it seems to have unfolded.

G. Conclusion of "How Could the Rabbis Forget?"

Ernest Martin makes a strong historical case for how the Jewish Rabbis have forgotten where the temples were located, basing this on key events and key individuals in Jerusalem, following the destruction of Herod's Temple in AD 70.

Hopefully, soon, the Rabbis and, indeed, everyone will consider the case for the true location over the Gihon Spring on the southeast ridge of Jerusalem, as affirmed by *eye-witness* historical testimony, and not on the presently so-called "Temple Mount," the *traditional* site of the temples.

CHAPTER 66

Conclusion of *Where* Was Herod's Temple? – Martin's Proposed Location

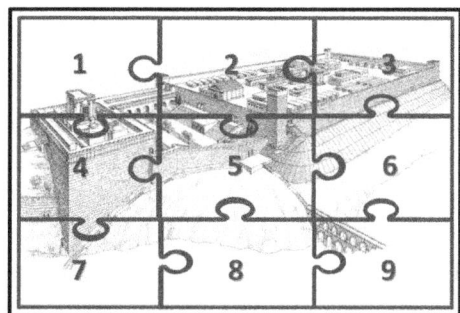

In summary, I believe the case for the temples being above the Gihon Spring in the southern location in the former City of David (and Fort Antonia being on the Haram esh Sharif to the north), as laid out by Ernest Martin, is credible and deserves serious consideration.

For me, the eye-witness testimony of Josephus and others mentioned in Chapter 56 is very compelling for the southern location. In addition, the literal reading of Jesus's prophecy of the complete destruction of the temple and [Jewish] Jerusalem as well as the eye-witness testimonies argues against the traditional "Temple Mount" being the location of the temples but argues for that being the location of Fort Antonia.

Undoubtedly, Martin's case is very controversial, and it must be said that the presently so-called "Temple Mount" site is supported by virtually all present-day historians, archaeologists, and tour guides.

Indeed, if the southern location is correct, then, for hundreds of years, the true location of the temples was "lost in history" and only very recently has been "found" again. It is almost like God has placed a veil over the eyes of almost everyone about these things—but that just recently the veil is being lifted.

One can easily argue that this is also the case for the true location of the crucifixion site being on the Mount of Olives. Wherever the location of Herod's Temple, the crucifixion site of Jesus was directly to the east, on the Mount of Olives, as has been laid out in Section B of Part II of this book.

After having read some of the evidence of the temples being above the Gihon Spring in the southern location of the City of David, what do you think?

If true, this has monumental repercussions to the Jewish people and the state of Israel as to where to rebuild the upcoming prophesized End-Times' Temple spoken of by the Prophet Daniel in Daniel 9:27–27; 11:31. This End-Times Temple relates to the period of the 70th Week of Daniel, the final seven-year period of the end of the Age, immediately before Jesus physically returns to earth with His raptured Church at the end of the 70th Week of Daniel.[441]

If the Jewish people decide to rebuild a temple at the historical site of all the temples, it seems that they may very well need to select the *southern* site above the Gihon Spring, to the south of the presently so-called "Temple Mount."

If they chose the southern location, they would not have to contend with the location of the present Muslim Dome of the Rock on the *traditional* "Temple Mount." They could build their temple over the Gihon Spring in the former City of David of Jerusalem, where there is good evidence for the locations of all the prior Jewish temples. However, before this could occur, the Jewish people would have to recognize and accept this as the true temple location. This would take a "God thing" for this to happen, which, of course, could be the case.

So, is this an "air-tight" case? Despite the mountain of evidence in support of Martin's case, there are still questions. However, the diagram which Martin has depicted for Herod's Temple and Fort Antonia is largely what Josephus "screams out" in his historical writings as to his eye-witness descriptions.

In final summary, I would have to say that there is still somewhat of a mystery about the location of Herod's Temple and the previous temples. Hopefully, additional evidence one way or the other will be uncovered to provide definitive proof for all to accept. We look for that day when this mystery will be totally solved for everyone—and, especially, the Jewish people.

Epilogue

You might well be wondering: **"What difference does all this make?" "Is any of this important?" "Why even present all of these cases!!??"**

I admit that the *mysteries* I have presented about the life of Jesus are—for the most part—not "salvation" issues. It is entirely possible for a believer to achieve salvation in Jesus while clinging to all sorts of pre-conceived notions and assumptions about His life. After all, the truth is sometimes very hard to come by. Scholars and theologians have argued for centuries about the interpretations of Scripture, about archaeological findings, about ancient writings, and about eyewitness testimony as they have sought to establish the truth about the life of Jesus. But even though truth is often elusive, I believe it is worth seeking—whenever and however we can.

If you have completed this book, then you have completed a rather lengthy journey through a total of 66 chapters, a journey which has taken you on an exploration of many unique—and sometimes controversial—mysteries in the life of Jesus. We have examined mysteries related to the *when and where* of His birth, the *when and where* of His death, and the *when and where* of His resurrection and ascensions (plural!). In addition, we have peeled back history, religious tradition, and Scripture to examine the mystery of *how* Jesus really died.

As a special bonus feature, we have also looked at the mystery regarding the actual location of the temples in Jerusalem. Aside from being an extremely interesting study, the true location of the temples is important because it directly affects the locations of the death and burial of Jesus as well as Jesus' prophecy about the destruction of the temple walls. As we discovered, both the death and burial occurred on the Mount of Olives, directly east of Herod's Temple. Our detailed study of the temple location also served as an illustration of how easily people can forget or be misled about the truth, and about how the truth can often be the first and greatest casualty of the passage of time and of the events that shape history.

There is one other thing that may have occurred to you: **"Why have I never heard about most of the information presented in this book?"**

Quite simply, most Christians—including most pastors and Bible scholars—have either not availed themselves of the evidence presented in this book or have chosen to ignore it when given the opportunity to investigate. Let's face it: people do not like to deal with ideas that run counter to established church *tradition*. Then there is the simple reality that much of this information has only recently been documented and made available for evaluation and discussion via books, articles, and online Posts—such are presented on my website (*www.truthinscripture.net*).

As you might suspect, if you bring up the subjects of the cases I have presented to most Christians, including your pastors, clergy, or lay leaders, you will probably get a "deer in the headlights" reaction—and a strained silence. Many will reject the topics outright. Others will offer canned arguments against what they perceive as a threat to the foundation of their beliefs. It's sort of a "reverse apologetic" effect. As I have discussed many times in our cases, *traditions* of the church are very difficult to overcome, even when the truth is there for the taking. Everyone *wants* to think that what they have been taught is correct.

Now, I am *not* saying that everything I have presented in these cases is true beyond the shadow of a doubt. Quite the opposite. Few of my proofs will meet the criteria of legal certainty, and many of these topics can be argued convincingly to the contrary by those who prefer to maintain the status quo.

However, bear in mind that reliable eyewitness accounts are considered the gold-standard evidence in legal inquiries, and I have included many accounts from Josephus and other eye witnesses in my case presentations. I believe that the evidence for the positions presented is strong and well worth considering. There is an awful lot of very solid information presented, and truth rings loud and clear in much of what I have presented. That is all I am saying.

Think back through some of the cases we have studied together. Think about the things which you have long-trusted as part of the *tradition* of your church up-bringing and of your regular worship experience. How often have you heard someone preach on something other than the "Good Friday" death of Jesus? Probably never! How about the birth of Jesus on some day other than December 25th? And what about the *traditional* crucifixion story, the one which involves a Roman cross instead of a living tree on the Mount of Olives? What about the added agony of stoning imposed by Jewish religious law? I doubt you have heard any of these things discussed in your place of worship or during your Bible study sessions.

Although Jesus died nearly 2000 years ago, we still do not have a firm grasp of many aspects of His life in first-century Israel. The truth is that Jesus was a real person, living in a real time, visiting real places, impacting real lives. It is important that we understand and appreciate His *real* history. It helps to build our faith in Him and our trust in the biblical account of his life and teachings. Remember that we must trust the Bible as the true, unerring word of God—every word of it. As always, the Bible must be the benchmark by which we establish truth and judge all things; and, whenever possible, we must let Scripture interpret Scripture to come to a true interpretation. Understanding and believing in the Bible also helps us in our witness to others, a witness which we must approach with humility, gentleness, and love.

During this journey, I have used Scripture as my guide in seeking to align the Word of God with reliable historical documents, archaeology, and the considerable work of other learned scholars and researchers. I want to be perfectly clear that this case material is NOT original to me. I claim virtually no original insights related to these things. The information from other researchers whom I greatly respect forms the foundation for most of what is presented. My role has been to validate, compile, and organize the information into what you have seen here. To a large degree, that compilation and organization is what is unique to this book.

The Apostle Paul entreated the people of Berea to check *even his teachings* to Scripture, to verify that what he was teaching was true. That is a lesson for each of us to heed. There is much deception in the world—some of it accidental, some not so much. Each of us needs to be vigilant in determining what is true. Remember that Satan can show himself as the "angel of light" when he is, in reality, the great deceiver and liar. Going forward, in all we do, we should be on guard against deception; and we should test everything against the Word of God. That includes the things which I have presented here, what you hear in the church you are attending, and all the way down to what your Jewish tour guide tells you about the location of the temple in Jerusalem. The Apostle Paul demanded as much of his own teaching.

With respect to my work, evaluate the evidence presented in each case and reach your own conclusions.

I need to emphasize that I am fallible. So, much of what I have presented is regularly argued by very learned people, and the absolute truth simply may not be known about many of these things. At least not now. There is, unfortunately, no way of knowing *with certainty* that everything I have presented is infallibly true.

Lastly, in the reading of the various cases in ***Mysteries of Jesus' Life Revealed***, you have reviewed a lot of Scripture. My prayer is that you will be blessed by the information presented and that your faith in Jesus will be increased as a result. I also hope that you will feel comfortable enough with what you have learned to share the information with others. The greatest possible blessing that could result from this work is that someone might come to know the Lord because of something learned from what is presented in this book.

In the **Afterword**, which follows this Epilogue, we look at the most important mystery of all: "Why Did Jesus Come to Die?" We look specifically at the reasons why this is so important to each of us.

Even after all of this, there remain many questions for which we simply have no answers. The Apostle Paul has told us:

> *"For now we see through a glass, darkly; but then face to face: now I know in part; but then shall I know even as also I am known."* (I Corinthians 13:12, KJV)

One day, we, as believers, will be able to ask Him all the questions we might have. Wow ... what a day that will be!

May God bless you in your walk ***with*** Him and in your witness ***for*** Him.

Afterword:
The Profound Mystery—*Why* Did Jesus Come to Die?

Indeed, why **did** Jesus come to die?

Popular theologian and author, John Piper, has answered that question in his book, *Fifty Reasons Why Jesus Came to Die* (2006).[442] He has stated the following:

> The most important questions anyone can ask are: Why was Jesus Christ crucified? Why did he suffer so much? What has this to do with me? Finally, who sent him to his death? The answer to the last question is that God did. Jesus was God's Son. The suffering was unsurpassed, but the whole message of the Bible leads to this answer.

> The central issue of Jesus' death is not the cause, but the *meaning*. What did God achieve for sinners like us in sending his Son to die?

Up to this point, we have examined the mysteries of *when* and *where* Jesus was born, died, resurrected, and ascended to the Father. We have even searched the mystery of what may have been involved in Jesus' death. These are mysteries not commonly understood or answered correctly by present church history or tradition. We have presented cases with credible evidence to help solve these mysteries of Jesus' life.

It is important for us to keep in mind that just to know *when* and *where* Jesus was born, died, resurrected, and ascended, as well as *how* He died will not matter one whit in eternity when you are standing before God. Knowing *about* Jesus is important for building our faith in Him and in Scripture, but it is not enough. However, **knowing Him** is everything!

By **knowing Him** I mean coming to faith in Him, trusting in Him for forgiveness of your sins, and worshiping Him as your Savior and Lord. He came and died so that you may have eternal life with Him, being at one with Him and He in you.

There is a lot going on "behind the scenes" related to this. Scripture providers a long list of reasons for Jesus coming to earth and dying, and they are all vitally important. In his book, John Piper lists 50 reasons. However, I am presenting only seven important reasons from the 2002 online article "Seven Reasons Why Jesus Was Born, by Donald Ward.[443]

A. Seven Reasons Why Jesus Was Born

1 Because of mankind's sin.

> From the book of Genesis, we know the story of the creation of the first man and woman by God. He placed them in an idyllic setting in the Garden of Eden and He supplied their every need. They had plentiful food, animals were tame, and God Himself accompanied them and was their loving teacher. Then they sinned by disobeying God and following Satan, and everything changed in an instant—there was a spiritual and physical separation from God.
>
> Jesus had to be born and die as a sacrifice to save mankind from its sins, which began with Adam and Eve in the Garden of Eden. Only He could be the perfect sacrifice.

AFTERWORD

2 Because God wanted to reveal His own character to humanity.

God wanted to reveal His righteous character to Adam and Eve and to all mankind so they could become like Him in mind and spirit. He created them in His own image (Genesis 1:26–27; 2:7) and gave them free will to choose good and evil. Unfortunately, they chose to follow Satan. Why did God's desire to reveal His character to mankind mean Jesus had to be born? Because Adam and Eve failed to carry out god's mandate to glorify Him in their lives, it was fulfilled in Jesus by ultimately coming and fulfilling the divine revelation of God's character and purpose for man.

3 To remove the sins of humankind through a perfect sacrifice.

Noah and the patriarchs (Abraham, Isaac, and Jacob) offered sacrifices to God. Hundreds of years before Jesus' birth, God revealed through Moses a religious system that included animal sacrifices and offerings. The problem with the model of the animal sacrifices was that these sacrifices were imperfect and, although they served to temporarily cover the peoples' sins, they could not take away the penalty of sin (Hebrews 10:4). That required a perfect sacrifice—a sinless, human sacrifice which was embodied in Jesus coming to die to pay the penalty of our sins.

4 For mankind to have a Mediator.

Jesus is the Mediator of the New Covenant. Under the New Covenant, God replaced the sacrifices of the Levitical priesthood with the ultimate sacrifice of Jesus Himself. In the New Covenant, God declared, *"I will put My laws in their mind and write them on their hearts; and I will be their God, and they shall be My people"* (Hebrews 8:10, quoting Jeremiah 31:31). Why does the need for a Mediator mean Jesus had to be born and die? It is because the priesthood, staffed by the Levites, as revealed in the Old Testament, was imperfect. It was only a forerunner. Jesus had to be born because the salvation of mankind requires something better.

5 To provide the promised Seed of Abraham.

God promised Abraham that through his (Abraham's) "seed," or descendants, all nations of the world would be blessed (Genesis 22:18; Galatians 3:14–16). If you are Christ's, then you are Abraham's seed, and heirs according to the promise (Galatians 3:28–29). Jesus had to be born to provide the promised spiritual fulfillment of the Seed of Israel. Jesus was a literal, physical descendant of Abraham. He was Abraham's Seed, through whom all nations of the world would be blessed.

6   For God to redeem mankind.

Jesus had to be born because He is our Redeemer. The salvation of mankind was dependent on Jesus coming to earth, living a perfect life, and dying as the perfect sacrifice for the sins of the whole world. Why does God require a Redeemer? The Bible states that *"the wages of sin is death, but the gift of God is eternal life through Christ Jesus our Lord"* (Romans 6:23), and *"all have sinned and fall short of the glory of God"* (Romans 3:23). Therefore, **all** have earned the death penalty by God for sin. However, thankfully, God has made provision for sinners to be redeemed, or bought back, from the death penalty by a Redeemer. The first man, Adam, brought sin into the world (Romans 5:12), and the second Adam—Jesus—brought redemption, reconciliation, and the hope of eternal life with God (Romans 5:6–10). Since the *"wages of sin is death,"* redemption requires the sacrificial death of the Redeemer, Jesus.

7   For God to make His Spirit available to all humankind.

Not only did Jesus have to be born, but He had to pay the penalty of our sins through His own death, then be resurrected to ascend to the Father as our High Priest. Only then could humanity receive the incredible gift of God's Holy Spirit. *"This Jesus God has raised up Jesus ... Therefore, being exalted to the right hand of God, and having received from the Father the promise of the Holy Spirit, He poured out this which you now see and hear"* (Acts 2:32–33). A few days after Jesus' resurrection, God poured out His Spirit on the assembled followers of Jesus at the Feast of Pentecost. Only through the receiving of God's Spirit can we receive eternal life. God made it possible for all mankind—every person—to come voluntarily into an intimate relationship with Him and receive His Holy Spirit. This could not have been possible, in God's great plan of redemption, without the birth and subsequent sacrificial death of His Son, Jesus Christ.

B.   The Profound Mystery: A Mystical Union with Christ

In addition to the seven reasons presented above for Jesus coming to earth and dying, there is an additional, all-important reason which does not get much coverage in commentaries. This relates to another mystery—a *profound mystery*—that, once understood, gives fuller meaning and perspective to all of the other mysteries about Jesus' life and death. It is also a mystery that is life changing!

The Apostle Paul explains it this way: *"**This mystery is profound**, and I am saying that **it** refers to Christ and the Church"* (Ephesians 5:32, RSV). The *"it"* refers to what comes before verse 32—a man and woman joined by the marriage union become *one* flesh. How this works is a *profound mystery*.

So is it with all who receive Christ by faith. Not only are sins forgiven, and everlasting inheritance assured, but **a profound mystical union** takes place, making believers one with Christ (one flesh); *"Christ in you, the hope of glory"* (Colossians 1:27). This *profound* mystical union conveys not just a piece of Christ in you, but Jesus Christ in His entirety; and with Him, the whole of the Father and the Holy Spirit. You are placed in God and God is in residence in you—completely, absolutely and forever. That is the *profound mystery*!

The disciple John provides further insight:

> *And this is the testimony, that God gave us eternal life, and this life is in his Son. He who has the Son has life; he who has not the Son of God has not life.* (1 John 5:11–12, RSV)

C. Your Decision Has Eternal Consequences

If you do not embrace eternal life in the Son, all that awaits you is an eternal separation from God. It's not what you know, but *who you know* that makes all the difference. To know Him is life. To deny Him is eternal death. But please understand that this "death" is not annihilation but rather eternal torment in a place called hell. This is what the Bible teaches (Matthew 25:31–46; Mark 9:43–48; Revelation 14:10; 20:10, 14–15). This is the punishment for sin against a holy and just God. However, there is a way of escape; we can be forever shielded from the wrath to come!

The choice is there for each of us. It is *your* choice! If you have not already done so, I would encourage you to make the choice today! But exactly what is this choice? It is the free-will choice to repent of your sins, trust in Him, and accept the personal salvation only He can offer (John 3:16–18, 36).

It is my hope that you—as a believer—now have the blessing of a deeper understanding of the life of Jesus and that you better understand how all things work together to achieve the purposes of God. Everything about Jesus' birth, death, resurrection and ascensions was precisely planned, arranged, and accomplished by God—*according to the Scriptures*—to bring redemption to mankind through Jesus, our Savior.

All this is why Jesus came to die. Now, what does it mean **to you**?

Appendix:
Longer Dedication Featuring *Handel's Messiah*

I began this book with a dedication of this book to Jesus. It is right to do that as this book is about the key events of the life of Jesus at His First Coming.

Hopefully, you now better understand how Scripture and reliable historical records weave together the dates and places of His birth, death, burial, resurrection, and ascensions. I have presented cases for what I believe are correct.

I want to end the book with another dedication to Jesus, forming bookends of dedication to Him. This is a "longer dedication," and I hope you find it edifying, as we reflect on what He means to each of us as our Savior, Lord, and soon returning King of kings and Lord of lords.

George Frederic Handel helps us do that.

Longer Dedication

As previously stated, this book is dedicated to Jesus. Praise God for Jesus. Praise God too for the testimony in musical form which George Frederic Handel has presented in his *oratorio (a large-scale musical composition for orchestra, choir, and soloists)* written to bring glory to Jesus Christ, which is also the intent of this book.

This tribute to the life of Jesus—His *birth, death, and resurrection*—of this longer dedication is made using the Movements of *Handel's Messiah*.

Peter Colon's article, "The Jewishness of Handel's *Messiah*,"[444] which appeared in *Israel My Glory*, provides the background for this longer dedication.

Handel's *Messiah* deals with the same themes as our book—Jesus' birth, death, and resurrection to glory. I am sharing some background of this applicable musical work as part of our longer Dedication to Jesus.

Background of Handel's Messiah: *Messiah* is the inspired *oratorio* penned by the Baroque composer George Frederic Handel in 1741, at age 56. Amazingly, he completed this work in 24 days, working nonstop from August 22 to September 14.

Many do not realize that the text, or libretto, was not written by Handel but was written by Charles Jennens, an English landowner, patron of the arts, and a devout Christian. Every word in the Messiah's libretto is taken directly from Scripture. Jennens collaborated with Handel on other works, and, as with "Messiah," his contributions were anonymous. Charles Jennens wrote the text and approached Handel to compose the musical score. We are blessed by this historical collaboration.

Handel used his *oratorio* to educate people in the Bible at a time when the Bible was not readily available to the average person. He set the truths of Scripture to music for people to hear, sing, and learn. It has been effective down through the ages and continues to be effective today.

The Messiah's Jewish connection is well known. Handel's *Messiah* is often associated with the traditional church celebrations of Christmas and Easter. However, Handel composed the work in the fall, near the three fall Jewish High Holy Days [Feast of Trumpets, Day of Atonement, and Feast of Tabernacles (Leviticus 23)] and used themes connected to them. As expected, the *oratorio* contains many passages from the Hebrew Scriptures.

Handel died in 1759, at age 74. He is buried in the south transept—the Poet's Corner—of Westminster Abbey in London. The monument containing his epitaph shows Handel holding a manuscript with the opening words of the *Third Movement* of Handel's *Messiah*, taken from the words of the Prophet Job, *"I know that my Redeemer liveth" (Job 19:25 KJV)*. Inscribed for posterity, these words testify to Handel's hope and the confident expectation of all who have trusted in Messiah Jesus for their personal salvation. Amen.

First Movement: The *First Movement* of Handel's dramatic *oratorio Messiah* features the **Messiah's *birth*.** Handel completed the *First Movement* on August 28, 1741, having composed it in seven days, near the onset of the three fall Jewish High Holy Days (Feast of Trumpets, Day of Atonement, and Feast of Tabernacles). The first of the fall Feasts, the Feast of Trumpets, features the blowing of the *shofar* (ram's horn) or trumpet to "raise a noise."

Peter Colon provides the following commentary related to the *First Movement* of Handel's *Messiah*:

> In this *First Movement*, Handel focused on the idea of making a 'joyful noise.' The oratorio opens with a male tenor solo singing the immortal words of Isaiah 40:1-3 (KJV):
>
> *Comfort ye, comfort ye my people, saith your God. Speak ye comfortably in Jerusalem, and cry unto her, that her warfare is accomplished, that her iniquity is pardoned: for she hath received of the Lord's hand double for all her sins. The voice of him that crieth in the wilderness, Prepare ye the way of the Lord, make straight in the desert a highway for our God.*
>
> Then a female alto voice sings the prophecy of the virgin birth: '*Behold* ***a virgin shall conceive and bear a son***, *and shall call His name Emmanuel, God with us*' (cf. Isa. 7:14; Mt. 1:23). The entire choir follows, singing the joyful noise of Christmas: '***For unto us a child is born***, *unto us a son is given: and the government shall be upon his shoulder: and his name shall be called Wonderful, Counsellor, The Mighty God, The Everlasting Father, The Prince of Peace*' (Isa. 9:6, KJV; emphasis mine).
>
> Other themes include the appearance of the angels to the shepherds (Lk. 2:8-15) and Christ's miracles on Earth, such as bringing sight to the blind (Isa. 35:5-6). The section closes with an adaptation of Matthew 11:28-29:
>
> *Come unto Him, all ye that labour, come unto Him that are heavy laden, and He will give you rest. Take his yoke upon you, and learn of Him, for He is meek and lowly of heart, and ye shall find rest unto your souls.*

Second Movement: The *Second Movement* of Handel's *Messiah* features the **Messiah's *suffering, burial, resurrection, and ascension*** and includes the majestic "Hallelujah Chorus."

The Day of Atonement, *Yom Kippur*, was the one day of the year when, in biblical times, the High Priest entered the Holy of Holies in the temple with the blood of the sacrifice and sprinkled it on the Mercy Seat, for atonement for the sins of the people of Israel (Lev. 16:17). This annual procedure of the High Priest foreshadowed the final acceptable sacrifice of Jesus, the Lamb of God, on the tree, atoning for mankind's sin and making eternal redemption possible for all who trust in Him (Hebrews 9:12).

Peter Colon presents insightful commentary related to the *Second Movement* of Handel's *Messiah*:

> The *[Second] Movement* opens with solemn alto voices singing, '*Behold the Lamb of God, that taketh away the sin of the world!*' (cf. Jn. 1:29, KJV). Selected portions from Isaiah 53 follow:
>
> *He was despised and rejected of men, a man of sorrows and acquainted with grief... Surely He hath borne our griefs, and carried our sorrows! He was wounded for our transgressions. He was bruised for our iniquities; the chastisement of our peace was upon Him. All we like sheep have gone astray* (cf. Isa. 53:3-6, KJV).
>
> The *Second Movement* then describes Jesus' death and resurrection. '*He was cut off out of the land of the living*' (Isa. 53:8, KJV). '*But Thou didst not leave His soul in hell; nor didst suffer Thy Holy One to see corruption*' (cf. Ps. 16:10).
>
> The closing involves four truths: the ascension (Ps. 24), the preaching of the gospel (Ps. 19:4; Isa. 52:7), the rejection of the gospel (Ps. 2:1-4), and God's power against His enemies (v. 9).
>
> At *Messiah's* London premier on March 23, 1743, it is said that King George II stood during the 'Hallelujah Chorus,' which compelled everyone to stand. Some viewed his action as an indication he recognized Christ as King of kings. Since then, audiences customarily stand during the chorus.[445]

Third Movement: This *Third Movement* of *Messiah* focuses on **Jesus' glorification in heaven** and the apostle Paul's teaching about the *future resurrection/rapture of believers*. The opening line is '*I know that my Redeemer liveth*' (Job 19:25, KJV).

APPENDIX

The *Third Movement* (final movement) was completed by Handel in less than one week, on September 14, 1741, midway between the Feast of Trumpets and the Day of Atonement (Yom Kippur). The third of the fall Feasts of the Lord, the Feast of Tabernacles, starts five days after Yom Kippur.

Peter Cohen offers the following commentary related to the *Third Movement* of *Messiah:*

> Other lines include, *'Behold, I tell you a mystery; … we shall all be changed in a moment'* (1 Cor. 15:51); *'Oh death, where is thy sting? … but thanks be to God'* (vv. 55, 57, KJV); and *'If God be for us, who can be against us?* (Rom. 8:31, KJV). Using Romans 8:31, 33-34, the movement also assures believers of their salvation through Jesus Christ.
>
> In contrast to the tempo of the 'Hallelujah Chorus,' the oratorio closes with a *largo*—a slow, solemn tempo. With full orchestra and choir, the magnificent work ends with a grand acknowledgment. *'Worthy is the Lamb that was slain and hath redeemed us to God by His blood, to receive power, and riches, and wisdom, and strength, and honour, and glory, and blessing'* (cf. Rev. 5:12, [KJV]).[446]

Praise God for the *oratorio Messiah* written by George Frederic Handel and for the glorification of Jesus which it has presented in musical form since it was written in 1741. **Indeed, to Jesus be all honor and glory.**

Endnotes

A Beginning Word

1   Avi Ben Mordechai, *Messiah Volume 2: Understanding the Life and Teachings in Hebraic Context* (Millennium 7000 Communications Int'l; 1997; 269 pages), p. 17.; clarifications in brackets mine.

Section A of Part I
Introduction to Section A

2   Sorcha Pollak, "Pope Benedict Disputes Jesus' Date of Birth (Internet article: *www.newsfeed.time.com/2012/11/22/pope-benedict-disputes-jesus-date-of-birth/*), 3 pages; (accessed 1/28/15).

3   Avi Ben Mordechai, *op. cit.*, p. 40.

4   Ernest L. Martin, The Star That Astonished the World—The Star of Bethlehem, Second Edition (ASK Publications, Portland, OR, 1996), 280 pages.

Chapter 1

5   Gerard and Patricia Del Re, *The Christmas Almanac* (1979), p. 17—as referenced in (29) *Holidays or Holy Days—Does It Matter Which Days We Observe?* (United Church of God, USA, 2008), p. 8.

6   *Ibid.*, pp. 5,7,8.

7   Darris McNeely, "When Was Jesus Born?" in the magazine *The Good News*, *www.Gnmagazine.org* (United Church of God, Cincinnati, OH: Volume 19, Number 6, November-December2014), p. 24.

8   Dr. Medeiros, "Christmas a Worldwide Celebration of the Incarnation" (Reformed Theological Seminary publication, Jackson, MS, December 2016).

9   *Ibid.*, p. 3.

10   *Ibid.*, pp. 3–4.

11   *Ibid.*, p. 4.

12   J. Finegan, *Handbook of Biblical Chronology, First Edition* (Princeton U. Press, 1964), p. 229; presented in Ernest L. Martin, *op. cit.*, p. 105.

13   Ernest L. Martin, *op. cit.*, pp. 103-104.

14   Ernest L. Martin, *op. cit.*, p. 35.

15   Jack Finegan, *Handbook of Biblical Chronology, First Edition* (Princeton U. Press, 1964), p. 291; presented in Jimmy Akin, "What Year Was Jesus Born? The Answer May Surprise You" (*www.ncregister.com/blog/jimmy-akin/what-year-was-jesus-born-the-answer-may-surprise-you#ixzz3Q8q2kBTE*), p. 3; accessed 1/28/15.

Chapter 3

16   Ernest L. Martin, *op. cit.*, pp. 67-80.

17   Bryan T. Huie, "Jesus' Real Birthday" (*http://www.herealittletherealittle.net/index.cfm?page_name=Jesus-Birthday* , December 16, 2000, revised April 6, 2014), pp. 1-2. Date accessed on internet: January 28, 2015.

18   Maranatha Church, Inc., "Birth of Christ Recalculated" (*http://www.versebyverse.org/coctrine/birthofchrist.html*), p. 12-13. Date accessed on internet: February 5, 2015.

19 Ibid., pp. 16-17.

20 William M. Ramsay, Was Christ Born at Bethlehem?—A Study on the Credibility of St. Luke (Hodder and Stroughton, London, 1898), p. 193.

Chapter 4

21 Tim Warner, *The Mystery of the Mazzaroth—Prophecy in the Constellations* (Answers in Revelation.org, Tampa, FL, 2013), p. 1.

22 F. Brown, S. Driver, and C. Briggs, *Brown-Driver-Briggs Hebrew Lexicon* (Hendrickson Publishers, 1996); as listed in Tim Warner, *op. cit.*, p. 1; clarification mine.

23 D. James Kennedy, *The Real Meaning of the Zodiac* (Coral Ridge Ministries, Ft. Lauderdale, FL, 1989), p. 6; clarification mine.

24 Ibid.

25 Joseph A. Seiss, *The Gospel in the Stars: Primeval Astronomy* (Kregel Publications, Grand Rapids, MI, reprinted in 1972 of the 1882 edition), 188 pages.

26 E. W. Bullinger, *The Witness of the Stars* (Kregel Publications, Grand Rapids, MI, reprinted in 1991 of the 1893 edition), 204 pages.

27 D. James Kennedy, *op. cit.*, p. 11.

28 Dale M. Sides, "Christological Astronomy: Reading Our Christological Profiles in the Heavens" (Liberating Ministries for Christ International, *http://www.lmci.org/articles.cfm?Articles=413*; 2007), p. 9. (Accessed February 2015).

29 Tim Warner, *op. cit.*, p. 8-9.

30 D. James Kennedy, *op. cit.*, pp. 14-15.

31 Image available from internet search for Revelation 12:1 images, accessed on 3/21/15; also available from article "Approximating the Birth of Christ" available on the internet, accessed on 3/21/15

32 Ernest L. Martin, *op. cit.*, p. 85; also available from article "Approximating the Birth of Christ" available on the internet; accessed 3/21/15.

33 Ernest L. Martin, *op. cit.*, p. 83; emphasis mine.

34 Victor Paul Wierwille, *Jesus Christ Our Promised Seed* (American Christian Press, The Way International, New Knoxville, Ohio, 1982), p. 85.

35 Nelson Walters, "Christmas and the End Times," Part 2 of 2 of the series, "The Gospel in the End Times" (*http://www.thegospelintheendtimes.com/pictures-of-end-times-in-the-bible/christmas-end-times/*) 12/11/14; pp. 1-6. (Accessed internet article 1/28/15.

36 *Ibid.*, p. 5.

37 Mark Davidson, *Daniel Revisited—Discovering the Four Mideast Signs Leading to the Antichrist* (West Bow Press, Bloomington, IN, 2014), 293 pages; pp. 90-92.

38 Ernest L. Martin, *op. cit.*, pp. 67-102.)

39 Joseph F. Dumond, Remembering the Sabbatical Years of 2016, 2023, 2030, 2037, and 2044 (Xlibris Corporation, 2013), p. 117.

Chapter 5

40 Sigmund Mowinckel, *Zondervan Pictorial Encyclopedia of the Bible*, II, p. 524. Referenced in Ernest L. Martin, *op. cit.*, p. 98.

41 M'Clintock and Strong, *Cyclopedia,* X. p. 568. Referenced in Ernest L. Martin, *op. cit.*, p. 95.

42 Edwin R. Thiele, *The Mysterious Numbers of the Hebrew Kings, Revised Edition* (Zonderan, 1984), pp. 28, 31, 161, and 163. Referenced in Ernest L. Martin, *op. cit.*, p. 95.

43 Ernest L. Martin, *op. cit.*, p. 97.

44 Ibid.; clarification and emphasis mine. Referenced in Ernest L. Martin, *op. cit.*, p. 101.

45 *The Complete Artscroll Machzor*, p. xvi. Referenced in Ernest L. Martin, *op. cit.*, p. 100; emphasis mine.

46 Ibid.

47 Avi Ben Mordechai, *Messiah–Volume 2: Understanding His Life and Teachings in Hebraic Context* (Millennium 7000 Communications International, 1997; 269 pages), pp. 25, 40.

48 Ernest L. Martin, *op. cit.*, pp. 79-80.

ENDNOTES

Chapter 6

49 Brent Landau, *Revelation of the Magi—The Lost Tale of the Wise Men's Journey to Bethlehem* (HarperCollins Publishers, New York, NY, 2010), 157 pages; p. 1. This is a translation of an ancient manuscript (pre-fifth century) that claimed to be the eyewitness account of the wise men; it was hidden for centuries in the vaults of the Vatican Library and discovered by Landau. It is fanciful and can be stated that it definitely was not written by the Magi.

50 Chuck Missler, "Who Were the Magi?" (*http://Idolphin.org/magi.html* internet article of Koinonia House Ministries, Coeur d'Alene, Idaho, November 1999) p. 2. Accessed 12/8/14.

51 Ibid., p. 2.

52 Victor Paul Wierwille, *op. cit.*, pp. 14-15; emphasis mine.

53 Ibid., pp. 15-16; emphasis mine.

54 Ibid, p. 16.

55 Henry M. Morris, "When They Saw the Star" (Institute for Creation Research; Dallas, TX, 2014), (*http://www.icr.org/home/resources/resources_tracts_whentheysawthestar/*), pp. 7-8. (Accessed January 2015).

56 Nelson Walters, "Did Daniel Provide the Gold, Frankincense and Myrrh for the Magi?" Part I of 2 of the series, "The Gospel in the End Times" (*http://www.thegospelintheendtimes.com/unsealing-of-the-book-of-daniel/daniel-provide-gold*); December 10, 2014), p. 5. Accessed on 1/28/15.

Chapter 7

57 Ernest L. Martin, *op. cit.*, p. 29; emphasis mine.

58 Author unstated—Maranatha Church, Inc., "Birth of Christ Recalculated" (*http://www.versebyverse.org/doctrine/birthofchrist.html*); Internet article, 1988), p. 7; emphasis mine. Accessed 2/5/15.

59 Ernest L. Martin, *op. cit.*, pp. 9–14.

60 Author unstated—Maranatha Church, *op. cit.*, pp. 6–7.

61 Victor Paul Wierwille, *op. cit.*, p. 85.

62 Victor Paul Wierwille, *op. cit.*, p. 86.

63 Joseph A. Seiss, *The Gospel in the Stars* (Kregel Publications, Grand Rapids, Michigan, 1882 and reprinted 1972), pp.161,166; clarification and emphasis mine.

64 Ernest L. Martin, *op. cit.*, p. 33; emphasis mine.

65 Ibid., p. 18; clarification and emphasis mine.

66 Colin R. Nicholl, *The Great Christ Comet---Revealing the True Star of Bethlehem* (Crossway, Wheaton, Illinois, 2015, 365 pages).

67 F. Steinmetzer (Irish Theological Quarterly, VII.61.

68 Ernest L. Martin, *op. cit.*, p. 57; emphasis mine.

69 Christopher Crockett, "What is Retrograde Motion?" (website: EarthSky (*http://earthsky.org/space/what-is-retrograde-motion/attachment/500px-retro-gradation-svg*, in Blogs/Space on 11/25/2012), p. 1. Accessed on 5/16/15. This is also illustrated by the diagram in: Ernest L. Martin, *op. cit.*, p. 58.

70 Walter Drum, Transcribed by John Szpytman, "Magi" (*The Catholic Encyclopedia, Volume IX*, Robert Appleton Company, 1910), p. 4; under "Additional Notes" connected to article by Chuck Missler, "Who Were the Magi?" (*http://ldolphin.org/magi.html* ; accessed on 12/4/14; Missler's article material is from *The Christmas Story: What Really Happened* (Koinonia House, November 12, 2014), 113 pages.

71 Ernest L. Martin, *op. cit.*, pp. 58-59; emphasis mine.

72 Ernest L. Martin, *op. cit.*, p. 64.

Chapter 8

73 Ernest L. Martin, *op. cit.*, p. 103.

74 Sir Ronald Syme, *The Crisis of 2 B.C.* (Sitzungsberichte der Bayerischen Akademie der Wissenschaften, Germany, 1974), p. 30; emphasis mine.

75 Ernest L. Martin, *op. cit.*, p. 114; emphasis mine.

76 Ernest L. Martin, *op. cit.*, p. 35.

77 E. J. Bickerman, *Chronology of the Ancient World* (Thames and Hudson, 1968), p. 77. As reported in Ernest L. Martin, *op. cit.*, p. 7.

78 Ernest L. Martin, *op. cit.*, p. 9.

79 William M. Ramsay, *op. cit.*, p. 193.

80 *The Encyclopaedia of Religion and Ethics*, XII (Bloomsbury T & T Clark, 2000), p. 49f. As reported in Ernest L. Martin, *op. cit.*, p. 11.

81 Ernest L. Martin, *op. cit.*, p. 181.

82 Ernest L. Martin, *op. cit.*, pp. 169, 180.

83 Josephus, *Antiquities*, XVII, p. 89. As cited in Ernest L. Martin, *op. cit.*, pp. 169-170.

84 Ernest L. Martin, *op. cit.*, p. 180.

85 Ernest L. Martin, *op. cit.*, p. 180.

86 Josephus, *Antiquities*, XVII, pp. 280,285,357,361. As cited in Ernest L. Martin, *op cit.*, p. 182.

87 Justin Martyr, *Apology*, I, p. 34. As cited in Ernest L. Martin, *op. cit.*, p. 183.

Chapter 9

88 Ernest L. Martin, *op. cit.*, p. 185; emphasis mine.

89 Ibid., p. 138.

90 Ibid., p. 121.

91 Ibid., pp. 122-135.

92 Ibid., p. 153.

93 The *Megillath Taanith* is a Jewish document called the "Scroll of Fasting" (although it also records festival days) which was composed, initially, shortly after the destruction of Jerusalem in AD 70. The scroll mentions two semi-festival days during which no mourning was permitted—Kislev 7 and Schebat 2 (corresponding to late January or early February). It is unstated why these two days of feasting are commemorated, but, obviously, they were joyful occasions ordained before the destruction of Jerusalem in AD 70. It very well might be that the death of Herod, who was hated by the Jews, on this date (Schebat 2: *January 28, 1 BC*) might be what this stated date is celebrating. This information is presented in Ernest L. Martin, *op. cit.*, p. 151–152.

94 Josephus, War I, p. 649. This is stated in: Ernest L. Martin, *op. cit.*, p. 153.

95 Ernest L. Martin, *op. cit.*, pp. 200–231.

96 Ibid., p. 147.

97 Ibid., pp. 147—150.

98 Ibid., pp. 120–122, 139–147.

99 Ibid., pp. 119–137, 150–155.

100 Ibid., p. 117.

101 Ibid., pp. 156-169.

102 Ibid., p. 159; referencing statement by Augustus in *Res Gestae,* 16.

103 Ibid., p. 157.

104 Ibid., p. 153.

105 Josephus, Antiquities, XVII, p. 218. As mentioned in: Ernest L. Martin, *op. cit.*, p. 154.

106 Josephus, *Contra Apion,* I, p. 34; mentioned in: Ernest L. Martin, *op. cit.*, p. 154.

107 Ibid.; mentioned in: Ernest L. Martin, *op. cit.*, p. 154.

Chapter 10

108 Ernest L. Martin, *op. cit.*, p. 243.

109 Ibid., pp. 241-248.

110 *Ibid*, pp. 252-253.

111 Jonathan Cahn, *The Mystery of the Shemitah* (FrontLine—Charisma Media/Charisma House Book Group, Lake Mary, FL, 2014), p. 29.

112 Kevin Howard and Marvin Rosenthal, *The Feasts of the Lord* (Thomas Nelson, Inc., Nashville, TN, 1997), pp. 197-198; clarification and emphasis mine.

113 Nathan Jones, "Jonathan Cahn on the Shemitah: Second Objection---Can the Year of Jonathan Cahn's Controversial Book, *The Mystery of the Shemitah,* be Pinpointed?" (Interview of David R. Reagan with Jonathan Cahn (February 4, 2015); *http://www.lamblion.us/2015/02/jonathan-cahn-on-shemitah-second.html*; p. 2 of 7; accessed on the Internet on 6/19/15; clarification and emphasis added.

ENDNOTES

114 Jonathan Cahn, *op. cit.*, p. 271.

115 Joseph F. Dumond, Remembering the Sabbatical Years of 2016, 2023, 2030, 2037, 2044 (Xlibris Corporation, 2013), p. 198.

116 Yves Peloquin, *Ezekiel 4–The Master Key to Unlock the Bible's Chronology* (see *http://www.EzekielMasterKey.com* for complete manuscript online, created Dec. 2004; continuous updates; referenced 2015), p. 157.

117 Ernest L. Martin, *The Star That Astonished the World* (ASK Publications, Portland, OR, 1996), p. 240.

118 Benedict Zuckermann, *Threatise on the Sabbatical Cycle and the Jubilee*, trans. A Lowy; (New York: Hermon, 1974); originally published as "Ueber Sabbatjahrcyclus and Jobelperiode," in *Jahresbericht des judisch-theologischen Seminars "Fraenckelscher Stiftung"* (Breslau, 1857).

119 Ben Zion Wacholder, "The Calendar of Sabbatical Cycles During the Second Temple and the Early Rabbinic Period," *HUCA* 44 (1973) 53-196; "Chronomessianism: The Timing of Messianic Movements and the Calendar of Sabbatical Cycles," *HUCA* 46 (1975) 201–218; "The Calendar of Sabbath Years during the Second Temple Era: A Response," *HUCA* 54 (1983) 123–133.

120 Wikipedia, "Historical Sabbatical Years" (*http://en.wikipedia.org/wiki/Historical_Sabbatical_Years*), p. 2 of 7; accessed on 5/19/2015.

121 Todd D. Bennett, Appointed Times–An Examination of the Scriptural Calendar and the Restoration of Creation (Shema Yisrael Publications, Herkimer, NY, 2012), p. 293.

122 Kevin Howard and Marvin Rosenthal, *The Feasts of the Lord* (Thomas Nelson, Inc., Nashville, TN, 1997), p. 196; emphasis mine.

123 Tim Warner, *op. cit.*, p. 227; emphasis mine.

124 Ernest L. Martin, *op. cit.*, p. 248.

125 Ibid., pp. 27-29. Also, Jonathan Cahn, *The Mystery of the Shemitah* (Front Line/Charisma Media/Charisma House Book Group, Lake Mary, FL, 2014), pp. 28-29.

126 *http://en*.wikipedia.org/wiki/Shmita ; accessed on April 15, 2015.

127 Joseph F. Dumond, *op. cit.*, p. 233, 235.

128 *www.JewishEncyclopedia.com*, 2002-2011 (*http://www.jewishencyclopedia.com/articles/12967-sabbatical-year-and-jubilee*), pp. 6–12; accessed 4/16/15.

129 Ernest L. Martin, *op. cit.*, pp. 239–259.

130 Ernest L. Martin, *The Star That Astonished the World, op. cit.*, pp. 248–249; clarification and emphasis added. Professor Wacholder's first study is in the *Hebrew Union College Annual*, 1973, titled "The Calendar of Sabbatical Cycles During the Second Temple and the Early Rabbinic Period" (pp. 183–196), and the same *Annual* for 1975, entitled "The Timing of Messianic Movements and the Calendar of Sabbatical Cycles" (pp. 201–218).

131 Ernest L. Martin, *op. cit.*, pp. 249–252.

132 Ibid., pp. 241-246, 293-310.

133 Josephus, *Antiquities*, Book XI, Chapter I; as mentioned in Tim Warner, *The Time of the End, op. cit.*, pp. 299-301.

134 Tim Warner, *op. cit.*, p. 237.

135 Yves Peloquin, *ibid.*, p. 149, 223.

136 Tim Warner, *Ibid.*, p. 309; clarification, editing, and emphasis added.

137 Yves Peloquin, *ibid.* p. 273.

138 Ibid., p. 158, 223, 273.

139 Ibid., p. 274.

Chapter 11

140 Victor Paul Wierwille, *op. cit.*, pp. xxi-xxiv.

141 Ernest L. Martin, *op. cit.*, pp. 228-231.

142 Avi Ben Mordechai, *Messiah Volume 2–Understanding His Life and Teaching* (Millennium 7000 Communications Int'l Publication, 1997), pp. 41–100.

Section B of Part I
Chapter 13

143 *http://www.BiblePlaces.com/bethlehem* (accessed 8/25/16).

Chapter 14

144 Cooper P. Abrams, III, "Where Was the Birth Place of the Lord Jesus?" (*http://www.bible-truth.org/BirthPlaceofJesus.html*), 12/26/04 pp. 1–6; accessed 8/12/16.

145 Ibid., p. 2 of 6; accessed on the Internet on 8/12/16; emphasis mine.

146 Ibid., p. 4 of 6.

147 Mishnah. The Mishnah was the first recording of the oral law of the Jews or its Rabbinic Judaism. The word in Hebrew means "repetition," which means it was memorized material. It is the major source of rabbinic teachings of Judaism. Next to the Scriptures, the Mishnah is the basic textbook of Jewish life and thought and is traditionally considered to be an integral part of the Torah revealed to Moses on Mount Sinai.

148 Targum. The Targum is an Aramaic translation of the Hebrew Bible (Tanak) which was written during Israel's seventy-year captivity in Babylon. Aramaic is one of the Semitic languages, and important group of languages known almost from the beginning of human history and including also Arabic, Hebrew, Ethiopic, and Akkadian (ancient Babylonian and Assyrian).

149 Alfred Edersheim, *The Life and Times of Jesus the Messiah–New Updated Edition, Complete and Unabridged in One Volume* (Hendrickson Publishers, Inc., USA; First Edition 1883; 1993, with Seventh Printing 2002; 1109 pages), p. 131. Bold emphasis mine.

Section A of Part II
Introduction to Section A

150 E. W. Bullinger, editor, *The Companion Bible, King James Version* (originally published 1922) (Kregel Publications, 1990, ISBN 08254-2288-4), 1914 pages + 227 pages of Appendices. The Authorized Version of 1611 with the structures and critical, explanatory and suggested notes with 198 Appendices. See specifically Appendix 153, "The Two Entries into Jerusalem" (p. 177), and Appendix 156, "Six Days Before the Passover (John 12:1)" (pp. 179–182).

151 Conner, Kevin J., *The Feasts of Israel* (Portland, OR: City Bible Publishing, 1980), 111 pages.

152 Kevin Howard and Marvin Rosenthal, *The Feasts of the Lord – God's Prophetic Calendar from Calvary to the Kingdom* (Orlando, FL: Zion's Hope, Inc., 1997), 224 pages.

153 James L. Boyer, Th.D. (Professor Emeritus of Grace Theological Seminary, Winona Lake, Indiana), *Study Graph: "Chronology of the Crucifixion and the Last Week"* (Winona Lake, IN: BMH BOOKS, 1976).

154 Internet article by Central Highlands Christian Publications, *"God's Calendar and the Sign of Jonah"* (Kingston, Vic. 3364 Australia: Central Highlands Christian Publications; *http://www.chcpublications.net/godcal.html* , 2003), pp. 15–21 of 25.

155 *http://www.gnmagazine.org/issues/gn51/goodfriday.html*

156 *http://www.biblestudymanuals.net/crucifixion_chronology.html*

157 *http://www.centuryone.com/crucifixion.html*

158 Avi Ben Mordechai, *Messiah: Volume 2–Understanding His Life and Teaching in Hebraic Context* (Millennium 7000 Communications, formerly of Colorado Springs, Colorado, 1997), 269 pages.

159 Nancy L. Kuehl, *A Book of Evidence–The Trials and Execution of Jesus* (RESOURCE Publications, Eugene, OR, 2013), 233 pages.

160 Avi Ben Mordechai, *Messiah–Volume 2: Understanding His Life and Teachings in Hebraic Context* (Millennium 7000 Communications Int'l Publication, 269 pages), pp. 41–42; clarification and emphasis mine.

Chapter 17

161 David L. Brown, PhD pastor, "'Good Friday' Was Not Celebrated in the Early Church–Did Jesus Die on 'Good Friday' or Wednesday?" (Logos Communication Consortium: *http://www.firstbaptistchurchoc.org/Sermons_01/Friday.htm* (Copyright 2012-2015); accessed 12/3/16.

162 Ibid.

163 *http://www.etymonline.com/index.php?allowed_in_frame=0&search=good.html* ; accessed on 12/3/16.

164 *http://www.christianitytoday.com/history/2008/august/goodness-of-good-Friday.html* ; accessed on 12/3/16.

165 *http://www.encyclopedia2.thefreedictionary.com/Good+Friday.html*; accessed on 12/3/16.

Chapter 19

166 Avi Ben Mordechai, *op. cit.*, p. 45.

167 Ibid., p. 69.

168 Ibid., p. 70.

169 Ibid., p. 70.

170 Ibid., p. 71.

171 Ibid., p. 71.

172 Ibid., p. 79.

173 Ibid., p. 79.

174 Ibid., p. 54; footnotes: (1) Hillcot Melachim 11:4, (2) Soncino rabbinic footnote: "Propound (sic) new meanings and interpretations of the Torah," (3) Soncino rabbinic footnote: "He will point out where they have misunderstood the Torah. v. infra. XCIX, 8 (Midrash Rabbah 99:8) on this verse."

Chapter 20

175 Ibid., pp. 43–44.

176 Avi Ben Mordechai, *op. cit.*, p. 44; clarification and emphasis mine; with footnote 1: "The normal daily evening sacrifice (*Shemot* 29:38–39) was done between 2:30 p.m. and 3:30 p.m. **However, if Pesach fell on the eve of a regular weekly Shabbat (*i.e.,* Friday) then two extra hours were added so as to not infringe upon the Shabbat, hence *Pesach* offerings were done between 12:30–1:30 p.m.** For a reference to Y'shua's [Jesus'] death in the middle afternoon, see Mark 15:34, Luke 23:44."

177 Avi ben Mordechai, *op. cit.*, p. 44; clarification and emphasis added; footnote 2: Talmud *Pesachim* 58a.

178 Avi Ben Mordechai, *op. cit.*, p. 44; emphasis added.

179 Avi Ben Mordechai, *op. cit.*, p. 44; clarification and emphasis added.

Chapter 21

180 Complete Artscroll Machzor, *Pesach*, *siddar* liturgy section, *"Conclusion of Yom Tov;"* as stated in footnote 2 of Avi Ben Mordechai, *op. cit.*, p. 46.

181 Avi Ben Mordechai, *op. cit.*, p. 53.

182 Talmud tractate Berechot 3b; Berechot 4a; Shabbat 88a, as stated by Avi Ben Mordechai, *op. cit.*, p. 47.

183 Avi Ben Mordechai, *op. cit.*, p. 47.

184 Flavius Josephus, *Antiquities of the Jews* (3.10.5)–New Updated Edition, translated by William Whiston (Peabody, MA: Hendrickson Publishers, Inc., 1987), 926 pages. As also listed in Joseph Lenard and Donald Zoller, *The Last Shofar! ibid.*, Appendix III, p. 285.

185 Kevin Howard and Marvin Rosenthal, *The Feasts of the Lord* (Orlando, FL: Zion's Hope, Inc., 1997), p. 76.

186 Lehman Strauss, *God's Prophetic Calendar* (Neptune, NJ: Loizeaux Brothers, 1987), p. 57.

187 E. F. Bullinger, editor, *The Companion Bible, King James Version* (originally published 1922) (Kregel Publications, 1990, ISBN 08254-2288-4), 1914 pages + 227 pages of Appendices; Appendix 156, p. 182 of Appendix.

Chapter 22

188 Avi Ben Mordechai, *op. cit.*, p. 56.

189 Ibid., p. 58; E.W. Faulstitch, new moon and date conversion software.

190 Ibid., p. 58.

191 Ibid., p. 65.

192 Ibid., p. 71; modified title.

193 Ibid., p. 69; modified title.

194 His Holiness Benedict XVI, Homily of His Holiness Benedict XVI (Basilica of St. John Lateran, Holy Thursday, April 5, 2007). Benedict XVI makes mention of the *Essene Passover*: " … Jesus truly shed his blood on the eve of Easter at the time of the immolation of the lambs. In all likelihood, however, he celebrated the Passover with his disciples in accordance with the **Qumran**

calendar, hence, at least one day earlier; **he celebrated it without a lamb** [Essene Passover seder], like the Qumran community that did not recognize Herod's temple and was waiting for the new temple. (emphasis added)."

195 Additional information on the Essene Passover is found in a book by Hershel Shanks, Editor, *Understanding the Dead Sea Scrolls: A Reader From the Biblical Archaeology Review* (see hhttp://www.amazon.com/Understanding-Dead-Sea-Scrolls-Archeology/dp/0679744452/ref=sr_1_6?ie=UTF8&s=-books&qid=1210349332&sr=1-6). This book has a chapter related to the issue of early Christianity and the Essenes, and explains well the calendar issue discrepancy between the Synoptic Gospels and John's Gospel. The idea that John was using the *Essenes calendar* is supported (and that an *Essene Passover* is described by John). This is also cited in Joseph Lenard and Donald Zoller, *The Last Shofar!, op. cit.,* p. 300.

196 E. F. Bullinger, *op. cit.,* Appendix 156, p. 181.

Chapter 24

197 Jonathan Sarfati, Ph.D., *Refuting Compromise* (Master Books, Green Forest, AR, 2004, 411 pages), pp. 73–74.

198 Avi Ben Mordechai, *Messiah: Volume 2, op. cit.,* p. 41.

Chapter 25

199 Rev. Jack Barr, "Jewish burial." Last updated: 10/29/2012. *http://www.barr-family.com/godsword/burial.htm*

200 Ralph R. Gower, *The Manners and Customs of Bible Times* (Chicago, IL, The Moody Bible Institute of Chicago, 2005, pp. 72–74.

201 Avi Ben Mordechai, *op. cit.,* p. 72.

Chapter 26

202 Trent C. Butler, Editor, "Ointment," Holman Bible Dictionary.

203 Avi Ben Mordechai, *op. cit.,* p. 82.

204 Ketubot 37a, 50a; Shabbat 15a; Nedarim 76b, an exact period of 24-hours. Avi Ben Mordechai, *op. cit.,* p. 82.

205 Avi Ben Mordechai, *op. cit.*, p. 82; clarification added.

206 Ibid., p. 82; modified title and added "Women come to anoint the body of Jesus."

207 Talmud tractate Beitzah 6a; Avi Ben Mordechai, *op., cit.*, p. 98; emphasis added.

208 Talmud tractate Eruvin 42a; Avi Ben Mordechai, *op. cit.*, p. 98; clarification and emphasis added.

209 Avi Ben Mordechai, *op. cit.*, p. 98; clarification added.

210 Ibid., p. 98.

211 Englishmen's Greek New Testament, "Matthew 28:1" (London, England: Samuel Bagster and Sons, 1877), p. 86; emphasis mine.

212 John N. Darby, *New Testament, The Holy Bible* (London, England: G. Moorrish, 1920) Matthew 28:1; emphasis mine.

213 Berean Literal Translation, "Matthew 28:1." Bible Hub; 1st edition; emphasis mine. *http://biblehub.com/bib/matthew/28.htm. 2016.*

214 John Gill, "Exposition of the Whole." Matthew 28:1. *https://www.studylight.org/dictionaries/hbd/o/ointment.* 1991.

215 Wikipedia, Matthew 28:1. Modified: 05/15/2016. *https://en.wikipedia.org/wiki/Matthew_28:1*

Chapter 28

216 E. W. Faulstitch, new moon and date conversion software (referenced in Avi Ben Mordechai, *Messiah Volume 2–Understanding His Life and Teachings in Hebraic Context* (Millennium 7000 Communications International), p. 58. From this computer-calculated astronomy in the year 30 CE (AD 30), the new moon for the seventh month of Nisan— which determines the first of the month (Nisan 1)—is on the sixth day of the week, on *Friday*. Therefore, Nisan 13 for that year would fall on *Wednesday* and Nisan 14 would fall on *Thursday*. This is in alignment with our case for the crucifixion of Jesus being on Wednesday afternoon in AD 30.

217 Kevin Howard and Marvin Rosenthal, *The Feasts of the Lord* (Orlando, FL: Zion's Hope, Inc., 1997), p. 7.

ENDNOTES

218 Ibid., p. 76.

Chapter 31

219 *http://www.gnmagazine.org/issues/gn51/goodfriday_thirdday.htm* , p. 1–2; emphasis mine.

220 E. F. Bullinger, *op. cit.,* Appendix 156, pp. 179–182.

Chapter 33

221 Richard Booker, *Celebrating Jesus in the Biblical Feasts* (Shippensburg, PA: Destiny Image Publishers, Inc., 2009), p. 85.]

222 Kevin Howard & Marvin Rosenthal, *Feasts of the Lord–God's Prophetic Calendar from Calvary to the Kingdom* (Nashville, TN: Thomas Nelson, 1997), pp. 77–79.

223 Richard Booker, *op. cit.,* p. 86; emphasis added.

224 Jay P. Green, Sr., General Editor and Translator, *The Interlinear Bible, Volume IV, GreekEnglish New Testament, Revised Third Edition* (Lafayette, TN: Sovereign Grace Publishers, 2005), p. 359; emphasis added.

225 Richard Booker, *op. cit.,* p. 85; emphasis added.

Chapter 34

226 Ernest L. Martin, The Star of Bethlehem–The Star That Astonished the World, op. cit., pp. 228–231.

227 Ibid., pp. 153–155, 228–231.

228 Papyrus codex Bodmer V of the *Proto-Evangelium of James* written in Egypt in the fourth century; it states that the Magi were able to see Jesus "*standing by the side of his mother Mary*" (21:3).

229 Ernest L. Martin, *Secrets of Golgotha–The Lost History of Jesus' Crucifixion, Second Edition* (Associates for Scriptural Knowledge, Portland, OR, 1996), pp. 361–362.

230 Ibid.*,* p. 361.

231 Ibid., p. 362.

232 Ibid., pp. 366–368.

233 Ibid., pp. 364–365.

234 Ibid., pp. 368–369.

235 Ibid., p. 362.

236 Ibid., p. 361; emphasis added.

237 Ibid., p. 363; emphasis added.

238 Avi Ben Mordechai, *Messiah Vol. II, op. cit.*, pp. 41–100, 62; and Avi Ben Mordechai, *Signs in the Heavens–A Jewish Messianic Perspective of the Last Days & Coming Millennium* (Millennium 7000 Communications International Publication, 1996), p. 231.

239 Nancy L. Kuehl, *A Book of Evidence–The Trials and Execution of Jesus* (Resource Publications, Eugene, OR, 2013), pp. 170-171.

240 Avi Ben Mordechai, *op. cit.*, p. 100; clarifications mine.

241 This Figure is similar to Diagram III.2 in *The Last Shofar!* but with some changes due to additional insights acquired after writing *The Last Shofar!*, as to AD 30 and Jewish law and customs.

Section B of Part II
Introduction to Section B

242 W. J. Hutchinson, *Palestine Exploration Quarterly*, 1870, pp. 379-381.

243 W. J. Hutchinson, *Palestine Exploration Quarterly*, 1873, p. 115. Cited in website article by James Tabor, cited below (2008).

244 Nikos Kokkinos, *The Enigma of Jesus the Galilean* (Athens: *Chryse Tome*, 1980) [Out of Print; replaced by *The Enigma of Jesus the Galilean – Greek New Paperback Edition* (Athens: *Ekdoseis Alolos*, 2007), 400 pages. Cited in James Tabor's website article cited below (2008).

245 Ernest L. Martin, *The Place of Christ's Crucifixion: Its Discovery and Significance* (Charlestown, NH: Foundation for Biblical Research, 1984).

246 Ernest L. Martin, *Secrets of Golgotha: The Forgotten History of Christ's Crucifixion – Second Edition* (Portland, OR: Associates for Scriptural Knowledge, 1996),

455 pages. This book and has much good information on the Temple rituals foreshadowing the Crucifixion of Jesus (Chapter 26), the spiritual significance of Golgotha (Chapter 27), as well as the case for the best credentials for the site of Jesus' burial and resurrection being the cave/tomb under the ruins of the Eleona Church of which the Carmelite Convent at the *Pater Noster* Church on the top of the Mount of Olives is the custodian (Chapter 28, pp. 402-403). This book also contains interesting historical information as to why the Jewish people worship at the "Wailing Wall" of the Temple Mount and the biblical significance tied to the Song of Songs (verse 2:9 *"He standeth behind our wall,"* referring to the Messiah) (Addendum 2, "Jesus and Modern Judaism," pp. 438-447).

247 Ernest L. Martin, *The Temples that Jerusalem Forgot* (ASK: Associates for Scriptural Knowledge, Portland, OR, 2000), 485 pages.

248 Ernest L. Martin, "Updated Information on the Crucifixion of Jesus" (Website article: *http://www.askelm.com/doctrine/d920401.htm*, 1992).

249 Doug Jacoby, "The Red Heifer and the Crucifixion" (Website article: *http://www.greatcommission.com/TheRedHeiferandtheCrucifixion.html*, 1997).

250 James Tabor, "The Place of Jesus' Crucifixion" (Website article: *http://www.jesusdynasty.com/blog/2008/08/24/the-place-of-jesus-crucifixion/*, 2008).

251 Nancy L. Kuehl, *A book of Evidence–The Trials and Execution of Jesus* (Resource Publications, Eugene, OR, 2013), 233 pages.

252 Ibid.

Chapter 36

253 Gabriel Barkay, "The Garden Tomb – Was Jesus Buried Here?" (*Biblical Archeology Review* 12/2:40-57, 1986), pp. 40-57.

254 Doug Jacoby, "The Red Heifer and the Crucifixion" (Website article: *http://www.greatcommission.com/TheRedHeiferandtheCrucifixion.html*, 1997), p. 7.

255 Joan Taylor, "Golgotha: A Reconstruction of the Evidence for the Sites of Jesus' Crucifixion and Burial" (*Bible and Spade* 15/2:39-50, 2002), pp. 39-50.

256 Doug Jacoby, *op. cit.*, p. 7.

257 Ibid., pp. 7, 12. Jacoby is citing Eusebius, *The Life of Constantine* 3:28.

258 Randall Price, *The Stones Cry Out* (Harvest House Publishers, Eugene, OR, 1997), p. 312.

Chapter 39

259 Leen Ritmeyer, *The Quest – Revealing the Temple Mount in Jerusalem* (Carta, Jerusalem: Ahva, Jerusalem; The LAMB Foundation, 2006), p. 390.

260 Leen Ritmeyer, *Secrets of Jerusalem's Temple Mount – Updated & Enlarged Edition* (Washington, DC: Biblical Archeology Society, 2006), pp. 110-111.

261 Leen Ritmeyer, *Secrets of Jerusalem's Temple Mount – Updated & Enlarged Edition* (Washington, DC: Biblical Archeology Society, 2006), pp. 110-111; emphasis mine.

262 Jacob Neusner, *The Mishnah: A New Translation* (New Haven and London: Yale University Press, 1988), p. 876; emphasis mine.

263 Randall Price, *Rose Guide to The Temple* (Torrance, CA: Rose Publishing, Inc., 2012), p. 86.

264 Leen and Kathleen Ritmeyer, *Secrets of Jerusalem's Temple Mount – Updated & Enlarged Edition* (Washington, DC: Biblical Archaeology Society, 2006), p. 150.

265 Leen and Kathleen Ritmeyer, *Ibid.*, p. 150.

266 David Ulansey, "The Heavenly Veil Torn: Mark's Cosmic '*Inclusio*'" (*Journal of Biblical Literature* 110/1(Spring):123-125, 1991), pp. 2-3.

267 Flavius Josephus, *The Works of Josephus – Complete and Unabridged; New Updated Edition*; translated by William Whiston; Book 5/Chapter 5 (Peabody, MA: Hendrickson Publishers, Inc., 1987), pp. 207-212.

268 Alfred Edersheim, *The Life and Times of Jesus the Messiah* (Peabody, MA: Hendrickson Publishers, Inc., 1993 [republished date]; also available at *Google Books*), pp. 611-612.

269 Leen Ritmeyer, *The Quest – op. cit.*, p. 112.

270 Jacob Neuser, *op. cit.*, p. 1016.

271 Leen Ritmeyer, *The Quest – op. cit.*, p. 113.

Chapter 40

272 Chaim Richman, *The Holy Temple of Jerusalem* (Carta, Jerusalem: The Temple Institute, 1997), p. 31.

273 Chaim Richman, *Ibid.*, p. 31.

274 Chaim Richman, *Ibid.*, p. 31.

275 Doug Jacoby, *op. cit.*, pp. 4, 11.

276 Kevin Howard and Marvin Rosenthal, "The Feasts of the Lord – God's Prophetic Calendar from Calvary to the Kingdom (Orlando, FL: Zion's Fire, 1997), p. 121.

277 Chaim Richman, *op. cit.*, p. 31.

278 Ernest L. Martin, "Updated Information on the Crucifixion of Jesus," *op. cit.*, pp. 43-44.

279 Leen Ritmeyer, *The Quest – op. cit.*, p. 108.

280 Ernest L. Martin, Secrets of Golgotha: The Forgotten History of Christ's Crucifixion – Second Edition, op. cit., pp. 43-44.

281 Doug Jacoby, *op. cit.*, p. 5.

282 James Tabor, *op. cit.*, p. 2.

283 Chaim Richman, *op. cit.*, p. 31, 61, 92-93.

284 Leen Ritmeyer, *The Quest – op. cit.*, pp. 198-199.

285 Doug Jacoby, *op. cit.*, p. 4.

286 Doug Jacoby, *op. cit.*, p. 4.

287 Doug Jacoby, *op. cit.*, p. 4.

288 Chaim Richman, *op. cit.*, p. 50, 52, 61.

289 Doug Jacoby, *op. cit.*, p. 5.

290 Doug Jacoby, *op. cit.*, p. 6.

Chapter 41

291 James Tabor, *op. cit.*, p. 2.

292 Ernest L. Martin, "Updated Information on the Crucifixion of Jesus," *op. cit.*, p. 4.

Chapter 42

293 Abraham Cohen, *Everyman's Talmud – The Major Teachings of the Rabbinic Sages* (Lexington, KY: BN Publishing: *www.bnpublishing.net*, 2008), p. 317.

294 Ernest L. Martin, "Updated Information on the Crucifixion of Jesus," *op. cit.*, p. 4.

295 Ibid.

296 Ibid.

297 Jacob Neuser, *op. cit.*, p. 301-302, 584, 623.

298 Ernest L. Martin, "Updated Information on the Crucifixion of Jesus," *op. cit.*, p. 4.

299 James Tabor, *op. cit.*, p. 2.

Chapter 43

300 Kevin Conner, *The Feasts of Israel* (Portland, OR: City Christian Publishing, 1980), p. 31.

301 Kevin Howard and Marvin Rosenthal, *op. cit.*

302 Barney Kasdan, *God's Appointed Times – A Practical Guide for Understanding and Celebrating the Biblical Holidays* (Baltimore, Maryland: Messianic Jewish Publishers, Div. of Lederer/Messianic Jewish Communications, 1993), 135 pages.

303 Kevin Conner, *op. cit.*

304 Joseph Lenard and Donald Zoller, *The Last Shofar!–What the Fall Feasts Are Telling the Church* (Xulon Press, USA, 2014), Chapters 6 and 7.

305 Kevin Howard and Marvin Rosenthal, *op. cit.*, pp. 77-78.

306 Kevin Howard and Marvin Rosenthal, *op. cit.*, p. 79.

Chapter 44

307 James Tabor, ***op. cit.,*** p. 1.

Chapter 46

308 Nancy L. Kuehl, A Book of Evidence–The Trials and Execution of Jesus, op. cit., 233 pages.

309 Ernest L. Martin, The Temples That Jerusalem Forgot, op. cit., 485 pages.

310 Text of the Ethiopic "Book of Enoch" as rendered by Matthew Black, *Studia in Vetreris Testamenti Pseudepigrapha*, pp. 3940; as quoted in Martin, *The Temples That Jerusalem Forgot, op. cit.,* quotation on pp. 278–279 and footnote 368 on p. 279.

311 II Kings 23:13, quoted by Martin, *The Temple That Jerusalem Forgot, op. cit.,* p. 281; clarifications and italics by Martin; bold fonts added.

312 Ernest L. Martin, *Secrets of Golgotha (Second Edition)–The Lost History of Jesus' Crucifixion* (Associates for Scriptural Knowledge, Portland, OR, 1996), 455 pages.

313 Ibid., p. 475.

314 Ernest L. Martin, The Temple That Jerusalem Forgot, op. cit., p. 266.

Section C of Part II
Chapter 50

315 Aiyar, S. Srinivasa, *The Legality of the Trial of Jesus* (New Orleans, LA; Chas. E. George, 1914); pp. 6–7; in Kuehl, *op. cit.,* p. 77.

316 Nancy L. Kuehl, *op. cit.,* p. 74.

317 *The Jewish Encyclopedia (J.E.).* "Accusatory and Inquisitorial Procedure." "Sanhedrin." (Funk and Wagnalls Company, New York, NY; 1901); as referenced in Kuehl, *op. cit.,* p. 73.

318 The Jewish Encyclopedia, "Caiaphas, Joseph–Caiaphas," p. 493; as referenced in Kuehl, *op. cit.,* pp. 73–74.

319 Nancy L. Kuehl, *op. cit.,* p. 50.

320 Mishnah, *Sanhedrin*, 11:4a–c; as referenced in Kuehl, *op. cit.,* p. 45.

321 Nancy L. Kuehl, *op. cit.,* p. 45.

322 Josephus, *Antiquities* XVIII.29; Mishnah *Yoma* 1:8; as stated in Martin, *Secrets of Golgotha, op. cit.,* p. 125.

323 Encyclopedia Judaica, vol.III,.991; as stated in Martin, Secrets of Golgotha, op. cit., p. 114.

324 Ernest L. Martin, Secrets of Golgotha, op. cit., p. 142.

325 Ibid., pp. 121–122.

326 Nancy L. Kuehl, *op. cit.*, pp. 51–52.

327 Talmud, Sanhedrin 4:1; as mentioned in Martin, Secrets of Golgotha, op. cit., p. 113.

328 Ernest L. Martin, Secrets of Golgotha, op. cit., p. 126.

329 Ernest L. Martin, Secrets of Golgotha, op. cit., p. 118.

330 Nancy L. Kuehl, *op. cit.*, p. 161; emphasis mine.

331 Sabbath 15a; and Rosh ha-Shanah 31a,b; as stated in Martin, Secrets of Golgotha, op. cit., pp. 116–121.

332 Nancy L. Kuehl, *op. cit.*, p. 200.

333 Ibid., p. 199.

334 Ibid., p. 200; emphasis mine.

335 Ibid., p. 201; emphasis mine.

336 Ibid., p. 194; emphasis and [explanation] mine.

337 Ernest L. Martin, *Secrets of Golgotha*, p. 318; emphasis mine.

338 Nancy L. Kuehl, *op. cit.*, pp. 126–132.

339 Clarifications by Nancy L. Kuehl, *op. cit.*, p. 150; and emphasis mine.

Chapter 51

340 Ernest L. Martin, *Secrets of Golgotha, op. cit.*, p. 307; emphasis mine.

341 Ibid., pp. 307–308.

342 Ibid., p. 309; emphasis mine.

343 Ibid., p. 312–313.

ENDNOTES

Chapter 52

344 Ibid., p. 325.

345 Ibid., p. 324–325; emphasis mine.

346 Ibid., pp. 52–53.

347 John Wilkinson, *Egeria's Travels, Third Edition* (1999), p. 185, note 1; as stated in Ernest L. Martin, *Secrets of Golgotha, op. cit.*, p. 325–326; emphasis mine.

Part III
Introduction to Part III

348 Ernest L. Martin, *The Temples That Jerusalem Forgot* (ASK Publications, Portland, OR, 2000), p. 6; clarification and emphasis added.

349 Randall Price, *The Stones Cry Out* (Harvest House Publishers, Eugene, OR, 1997), Chapters 10 and 11, pp. 175–220.

350 Ibid., p. 332.

351 Ernest L. Martin, The Temples That Jerusalem Forgot, op. cit., 485 pages.

352 Robert Corneke, Temple–Amazing New Discoveries That Change Everything About the Location of Solomon's Temple (LifeBridge Books, Charlotte, NC, 2014), 207 pages.

353 George Wesley Buchanan, "In Search of King Solomon's Temple" (June 2009; available on *www.askelm.com*, search 3/10/17; p. 5.

354 Ibid., p. 5.

355 Ernest L. Martin, short introductory article: "The Temple That Jerusalem Forgot" (2000) (available on *www.askelm.com*, search on 3/10/17; p. 1.

356 Ibid., pp. 2–3.

357 Nancy L. Kuehl, *A Book of Evidence–The Trials and Execution of Jesus* (Resource Publications, Eugene, OR), 233 pages.

358 Ernest L. Martin, *op. cit.*, p. 2.

Chapter 55

359 Josephus, *War* VII.1,1 Whiston translation; clarification and emphasis added. Listed in Ernest L. Martin, *op. cit.*, pp. 14–15.

360 Ernest L. Martin, The Temples That Jerusalem Forgot, op. cit., p. 21.

361 Ibid., p. 22; emphasis added.

362 Ibid., p. 22; clarification and emphasis added.

Chapter 56

363 Eleazer's account recorded by Josephus, *War* VII.8,7; recorded in Martin, *op. cit.*, p. 29; clarification and emphasis added.

364 Eleazer's account recorded by Josephus, *War* VII.8,6 Loeb; recorded in Martin, *op. cit.*, p. 29.

365 *War* VII.8,7; recorded in Martin, *op. cit.*, p. 30; emphasis added.

366 Ernest L. Martin, The Temples That Jerusalem Forgot, op. cit., p. 30–31.

367 Ibid., p. 32.

368 Ibid., p. 48.

Chapter 57

369 Josephus, *War* V.4.1.

370 Ernest L. Martin, The Temples That Jerusalem Forgot, op. cit., p. 262.

371 Ibid., p. 262–263.

372 *War* V.4.1.; Martin, *op. cit.*, p. 263.

373 Ernest L. Martin, *op. cit.*, p. 263.

374 Internet image of ancient Jerusalem and Mount of Olives, accessed on 5/17/17.

375 Karbel Multimedia, copyright 2009 LOGOS BIBLE SOFTWARE; from internet, accessed on 5/17/17.]

376 R. H. Charles, *Pseudepigrapha*, Vol. II, p. 105, lines 105-6; brackets and italics are by Martin; listed in Ernest L. Martin, *op. cit.*, p. 267.

377 Ibid., p. 105, lines 83–84; brackets and italics by Martin; bold is mine; shown in Ernest L. Martin, *op. cit.,* p. 269.

378 Revelation 21:2,6; 22:1,17; clarification and emphasis added by Martin; Martin, *The Temples That Jerusalem Forgot, op. cit.,* p. 293.

379 Ibid., p. 293.

380 I Kings 1:38–39; Martin, *op. cit.,* p. 295.

381 Kerithoth 5b; Martin, *op. cit.,* p. 295.

382 Ernest L. Martin, *op. cit,.,* p. 295; emphasis added.

383 Aristeas; Prof. Gifford of England translated an English version of this early writer, from Eusebius' recording of Aristeas, Ch. 38; as stated in Martin, *op. cit.,* pp. 283–284; emphasis added. Note: Eusebius, the Greek historian of Christianity who became the bishop of Caesarea Maritima about AD 314, has passed down the account given by Aristeas.

384 Tacitus, *History,* Bk. 5, para. 12; in Martin, *op. cit.,* p. 284.

Chapter 58

385 Ernest L. Martin, The Temples That Jerusalem Forgot, op. cit., p. 294.

386 Ibid., p. 294.

Chapter 59

387 Ernest L. Martin, *op. cit.,* p. 12.

388 Ibid., p. 13.

389 *War* VI.9,4; Martin, *op. cit.,* p. 19; clarifications added by Martin; emphasis mine.

390 Ernest L. Martin, The Temples That Jerusalem Forgot, op. cit., p. 31; emphasis added.

391 Ibid., pp. 31–32; emphasis added.

392 Benjamin Mazar, *The Mountain of the Lord* (Doubleday, 1975), p. 36; Martin, *op. cit.,* p. 51.

393 Randall Price, The Stones Cry Out–What Archaeology Reveals About the Truth of the Bible (Harvest House Publishers, Eugene, OR, 1997), p. 189.

394 *War* III.5,2.; Martin, *op. cit.*, p. 52.

395 Ernest L. Martin, *op. cit.*, p. 65.

396 Ibid., p. 42.

397 *War* V.5,8; Loeb translation; Martin, *op. cit.*, p. 57.

398 Ernest L. Martin, *op. cit.*, p. 57.

Chapter 60

399 Ernest L. Martin, The Temples that Jerusalem Forgot, op. cit., pp. 79-81, 95.

400 *Jewish War*, V.v.8 para. 238; Martin, *op. cit.*, p. 96; emphasis added.

401 Wilkerson, *Jerusalem Pilgrims Before the Crusades*, p. 204; Martin, *op. cit.*, p. 97; clarifications and emphasis added.

402 Ernest L. Martin, *op. cit.*, p. 97.

403 Ibid., pp. 80–81; clarification mine.

Chapter 61

404 Ernest L. Martin, "A Critique by Dr. Leen Ritmeyer Rebuttal by Dr. Martin–Expanded Internet Edition," May 1, 2001 (*http://www.askelm.com/temple/t010513.htm*); p. 2 of 16; accessed on 2/3/17.

405 *War* VI.2,6. Referenced in Ernest L. Martin, *the Temples That Jerusalem Forgot, op. cit.*, p. 413, 468.

406 Model of Herod's Temple on *traditional* "Temple Mount" and Fort Antonia in upper right (NW) corner. From internet search of "Temple Mount graphics."

407 Ernest L. Martin, The Temples That Jerusalem Forgot, op. cit.

408 Ibid., p. 466 and footnote 698 on p. 466.

409 Ibid., p. 466.

410 Leen Ritmeyer, *The Quest–Revealing the Temple Mount in Jerusalem* (CARTA, Jerusalem, 2006), 440 pages.

ENDNOTES

411 Ibid., p. 11; emphasis mine.

412 Ernest L. Martin, *op. cit.*, p. 464.

Chapter 62

413 Ernest L. Martin, "A Critique by Dr. Leen Ritmeyer, Rebuttal by Dr. Martin– Expanded Internet Edition, May 1, 2001 (*http://www.askelm.com/temple/ t010513.htm* ; accessed from internet on 2/3/17), p. 1; emphasis mine.

414 Ibid., p. 2; emphasis mine.

415 Ibid., pp. 2–4; emphasis mine.

416 Ibid., p. 5; emphasis mine.

417 Ibid., p. 16; emphasis mine.

418 Ibid., p. 16.

419 Ibid., p. 16; emphasis mine.

Chapter 63

420 Nancy L. Kuehl, A Book of Evidence–The Trials and Execution of Jesus (op. cit., 2013).

421 Ibid., p. ix.

422 Ibid., pp. 151–153; emphasis (bold) and Scripture in italics mine.

Chapter 64

423 Ernest L. Martin, The Temples That Jerusalem Forgot, op. cit., p. 473.

424 Ernest L. Martin, "How the Jews Started to Lose the Temples' Site" Expanded Internet Edition–June 2000 (*http://www.askelm.com/temple/t000601.htm*; accessed 3/9/1017; 17 pages.

425 Ibid., p. 2.

426 Ernest L. Martin, The Temples That Jerusalem Forgot, op. cit., pp. 473–474.

427 Ibid., pp. 341, 402.

428 Ibid., p. 219.

429 Ibid, p. 219.

430 Citing from D. Baldi, *Enchiridion Locorum Sanctorum*, pp. 447–448; as referenced in Martin, *ibid.*, pp. 122–126.

431 Ernest L. Martin, *ibid.*, pp. 122–126, and Martin, article: "How the Jews Started to Lose the Temples' Site–Expanded Internet Edition-June 1, 2000" (*http://www.askelm.com/temple/t000601.htm*), p. 3.

432 Ernest L. Martin, The temples That Jerusalem Forgot, op. cit., p. 5; emphasis mine.

433 Ibid., p. 9.

434 Maimonides, *Misneh Torah, eighth section,* written in the year AD 1180; cited by Martin, "How the Jews Started to Lose the Temples' Site, Expanded Internet Edition–June 1, 2000, pp. 8–9.

435 Ernest L. Martin, The Temples That Jerusalem Forgot, ibid., p. 10.

436 Ibid., p. 11.

437 Ernest L. Martin, "How the Jews Started to Lose the Temples' Site," Expanded Internet Edition, June 1, 2000, on Associates for Scriptural Knowledge website (*http://www.askelm.com/temple/t000601.htm*), p. 12 of 17; accessed 3/31/17.

438 Ibid., p. 12

439 Ibid., p. 12.

440 Ibid., p. 13; emphasis added.

Chapter 65

441 Joseph Lenard and Donald Zoller, ***The Last Shofar!, op. cit.,*** Chapter 7, "Making Our Case," pp. 129–157.]

Afterword

442 John Piper, *Fifty Reasons Why Jesus Came to Die* (Crossway, First Edition, 2006), 128 pages.

443 Donald Ward, "Seven reasons Why Jesus Was Born" (*https://www.ucg.org/the-good-news/seven-reasons-why-jesus-was-born* ; accessed 4/27/17; 9 pages.

Appendix
Longer Dedication

444 Peter Colon, "The Jewishness of Handel's Messiah—A Look at the Interesting Link Between Israel's Holiest Holidays and this World-Renowned *Oratorio*" [*Israel My Glory* (magazine of The Friends of Israel Gospel Ministry, Inc.), Volume 74, Number 6, November/December 2016, pp. 28–31.

445 Ibid., pp. 28–31.

446 Ibid., pp. 28–31.

Other Information

Section Images and Attributions

Part I, Section A:

Attribution not needed.

Part I, Section B:

Photo courtesy of Abir Sultan/EPA, UKmedia.org.

Part II, Section A:

Attribution not needed.

Part II, Section B:

Image from painting by Frederic Edwin Church, 1870

Part II, Section C:

Attribution not needed.

Part III:

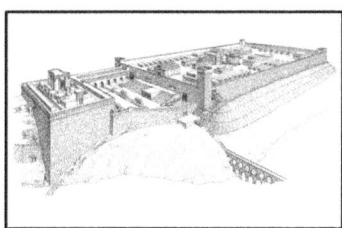

Image from Dr. Ernest L. Martin and available on the website that supports his work at *http://www.askelm.com/index.asp*. Permission received from David Sielaff, Director of Associates for Scriptural Knowledge, for using information and graphics from all of Dr. Martin's books, materials, and website.

Epilogue and Front Cover:

Usage rights purchased from Dreamstime.com. Image copyright Denis Kelly, ID 21974393 (Life of Jesus Christ in Stained Glass). Labels added.

Afterword:

Stained glass from the Pullman Memorial Universalist Church in Albion, New York, created by the Tiffany Glass and Decorating Company.

Appendix:

Stained glass at St. John the Baptist's Anglican Church, Ashfield, New South Wales, from Wikimedia Commons. Photo: Toby Hudson.

Endnotes:

Public Domain image from Pixaby:
https://pixabay.com/en/church-dom-window-stained-glass-578535/.

Other Information:

Stained glass window from St. Paul's Episcopal Church in Milwaukee, Wisconsin.

Website:

Photo of Jerusalem skyline.

NOTE: Puzzle-piece images have been overlaid by the author on some of the Section images.

About the Author

Joseph A. Lenard

Joseph was born in Philadelphia, Pennsylvania and grew up in the Orlando, Florida area, with Godly parents. From humble beginnings, he felt God's hand leading him and protecting him.

Joseph graduated from the Georgia Institute of Technology (BCE), Florida State University (MBA), University of North Carolina at Chapel Hill [doctorate in dental surgery (DDS)], and University of Connecticut [orthodontics specialty residency (Certificate in Orthodontics)]. He is currently retired from his orthodontic practice in Pinehurst, North Carolina.

As a serious student of the Bible for over 30 years, Joseph has made five trips to Israel for "on-site" biblical study and research. His research interests focus on study of the Hebrew roots of our Christian faith and biblical topics—including biblical prophecy, archeology, history, as well as Christian apologetics (creation-science and general apologetics). He is co-author with Donald Zoller of *The Last Shofar–What the Fall Feasts of the Lord Are Telling the Church* (2014).

Joseph and his wife, Judy, live in Southern Pines, North Carolina and are founding members of Trinity Christian Fellowship in Pinehurst, North Carolina and founding members of the Sandhills Apologetics Society.

Website for *Mysteries of Jesus' Life Revealed* and *The Last Shofar!*

For additional information related to *Mysteries of Jesus' Life Revealed–His Birth, Death, Resurrection, and Ascensions* (2017) as well as for information on the book co-authored with Donald Zoller, *The Last Shofar!* (2014), please visit our website:

www.truthinscripture.net

Discover:

- Information on this book and website Postings of edited versions of chapters.
- Information on *The Last Shofar!* and electronic copy of that book.
- Further insights into the last days.
- Additional research related to Hebrew roots of our Christian faith.
- Valuable links to study resources and pertinent current events.
- Opportunity to leave feedback under "**Contact**."

Acknowledgement:

Our website is designed and maintained by Bob Brown, and he is the author of the website Postings of edited versions of the chapters of this book; these are available on the website for access by anyone in the world. He is also the website administrator for our church, *Trinity Christian Fellowship* in Pinehurst, NC (*www.trinitycf.net*).

I am grateful for all that Bob has done and continues to do to help with this book and the promotion on the website.